The World of the American Indian

The World of the American Indian

NATIONAL GEOGRAPHIC SOCIETY

Staff for this Book

JULES B. BILLARD
Editor

CHARLES O. HYMAN
Art Director

ANNE DIRKES KOBOR
Illustrations Editor

MARY H. DICKINSON
Chief Researcher

THOMAS B. ALLEN
ROSS BENNETT
SEYMOUR L. FISHBEIN
MARY S. HOOVER
EDWARD LANOUETTE
DAVID F. ROBINSON
VERLA LEE SMITH
Editor-Writers

PAMELA MUCCI
SHIRLEY L. SCOTT
ANNE E. WITHERS
Editorial Research

WILHELM R. SAAKE
Production Manager

CONSTANCE BROWN BOLTZ
Design

KAREN F. EDWARDS
Production

BARBARA G. STEWART
Illustrations Research

JAMES R. WHITNEY
Engraving and Printing

WERNER JANNEY, *Style*

GEORGE I. BURNESTON, III
BRIT AABAKKEN PETERSON
Index

SARAH L. ROBINSON, *Assistant*

With contributions by
JOHN D. GARST, JOHN J. PUTMAN,
GEORGE E. STUART, TIBOR G. TOTH,
National Geographic Staff, and NATHANIEL
T. KENNEY, DIANE S. MARTON

448 Illustrations, 362 in full color

First printing 550,000 copies, second 370,000
Library of Congress CIP data page 398

THE WORLD OF THE AMERICAN INDIAN
A VOLUME IN THE STORY OF MAN LIBRARY

PUBLISHED BY THE NATIONAL GEOGRAPHIC SOCIETY
MELVIN M. PAYNE, *Chairman of the Board*
ROBERT E. DOYLE, *President*
OWEN R. ANDERSON, *Secretary*
MELVILLE BELL GROSVENOR, *Editor Emeritus*
GILBERT M. GROSVENOR, *Editor*

PREPARED BY
NATIONAL GEOGRAPHIC BOOK SERVICE

VINE DELORIA, Jr., WILLIAM C. STURTEVANT
Consultants

Chapters by

WALLACE L. CHAFE

Professor of Linguistics, University of California at Berkeley; former linguist with the Bureau of American Ethnology, Smithsonian Institution; author of Meaning and the Structure of Language, Seneca Morphology and Dictionary, *and other works.*

DAVID DAMAS

Professor of Anthropology, McMaster University, Hamilton, Ontario; former Arctic Ethnologist for the National Museum of Canada, Ottawa; field research among Copper, Iglulik, and Netsilik Eskimos; author of Igluligmiut Kinship and Local Groupings *and other works on Arctic cultures.*

VINE DELORIA, Jr.

Founder, Institute for the Development of Indian Law; former executive director, National Congress of American Indians; professor of political science, University of Arizona; author of God Is Red, Custer Died for Your Sins, We Talk, You Listen, *and numerous other books and articles.*

JOHN C. EWERS

Senior Ethnologist Emeritus, Department of Anthropology, Smithsonian Institution; former curator of the Museum of the Plains Indian, Browning, Montana; member editorial board, The American West; *author of* Indian Life on the Upper Missouri, Artists of the Old West, The Blackfeet, *and other books.*

Shrubbery hair sprouting from its rotted crown, the remnant pillar of a Kwakiutl dwelling returns to the forest from which the carver claimed it; Adelaide de Menil. Pages 2-3: Costumes blend a patchwork of color and cultures at an Apache celebration, Mescalero, New Mexico; David Hiser. Pages 6-7: Where once coastal Indians came to fish and hunt, a canoeist paddles below sun-flecked rapids—foreshortened by a telephoto lens—on Maine's Allagash River; Farrell Grehan.

ROBERT F. HEIZER

Professor Emeritus of Anthropology, University of California at Berkeley; editor of California volume of the Smithsonian's Handbook of North American Indians; co-author of The California Indians, Almost Ancestors, Field Methods in Archaeology; *author of numerous articles.*

JESSE D. JENNINGS

Professor of Anthropology, University of Utah; curator Utah Museum of Natural History; former editor American Antiquity; co-editor of The Native Americans; *editor of* Ancient Native Americans; *author of* Prehistory of North America *and of numerous articles, papers, and reports.*

D'ARCY McNICKLE

Former Program Director, Center for the History of the American Indian, Newberry Library, Chicago; former Professor of Anthropology, University of Saskatchewan; former Director of Tribal Relations, Bureau of Indian Affairs; author of many histories, biographies, novels, and articles.

N. SCOTT MOMADAY

Professor of English and Comparative Literature, Stanford University; exchange lecturer to the Soviet Union (1974); author of House Made of Dawn *(Pulitzer Prize 1969),* The Way to Rainy Mountain, *and other books and poems.*

ALFONSO ORTIZ

Professor of Anthropology, University of New Mexico; former president of the Association on American Indian Affairs; member of the National Humanities Faculty; editor of New Perspectives on the Pueblos; *author of* The Tewa World *and other publications.*

WILLIAM C. STURTEVANT

Curator of North American Ethnology, Department of Anthropology, Smithsonian Institution; former general anthropologist with the Bureau of American Ethnology; general editor of the Smithsonian's 20-volume Handbook of North American Indians; author of many articles in books and journals.

Contents

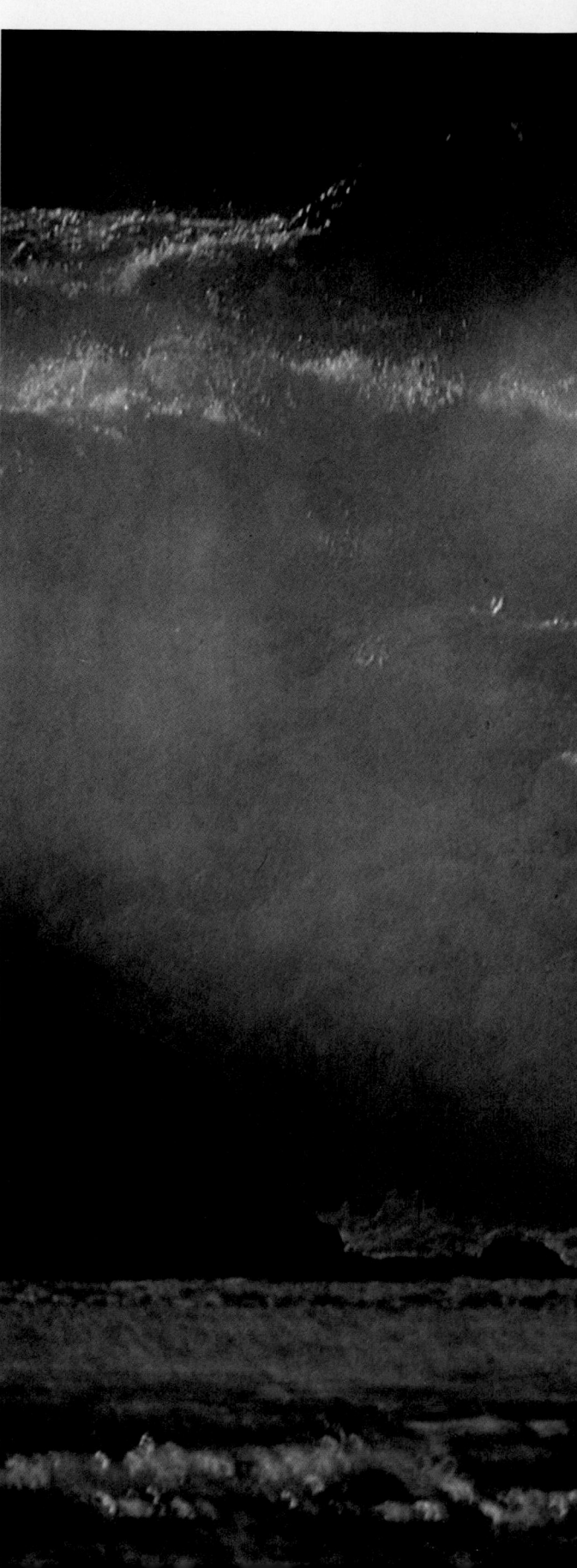

8

DOMED OVEN AND WATER DIPPED FROM A STREAM TIE SUNSET-TOUCHED TAOS TO CENTURIES-OLD WAYS; MARTIN ROGERS

Foreword

All too often the image of the aboriginal Indian that comes to mind today is of some painted apparition who lived in a far distant past. Yet the past is only yesterday. I think of 'Ik'yahámpik, a venerable hereditary chief of the Shasta tribe. As a young warrior he saw his first white man, in a westering covered wagon; at his death something more than a decade ago space capsules streaked the skies. His lifetime spanned from bow and arrow to guided missile, from smoke signal to color television–"Those cowboy and Indian stories aren't very accurate," he once said with a twinkle in his eye.

The old chief's life and words sum up a paradox. Though our link to the red man's past may be close, our picture of him may be far from the facts. Variously the Indian has been type-cast as a primitive barbarian impeding civilization's march or as a romanticized "noble savage" more in tune with natural ideals than European man in his complex society. Not too often emerges a realization of the Indian as an ordinary human being with strengths and intelligence to make constant adjustments to the environment.

Therein lies a purpose of this book: to show the Indian as he was—his beliefs, his customs, his appearance—and to provide an understanding of what he is today.

When the National Geographic's Book Service staff first showed me page layouts of *The World of the American Indian,* I was struck by the rich array of cultural detail presented. This book goes far beyond the Society's popular and long out-of-print predecessor volume, *Indians of the Americas.* Intensive hours of searching in museums, private collections, and photographic sources were required to assemble the remarkable illustrations, many never before published in a popular book on North American Indians. Authoritative text by distinguished authors describes man's arrival on this continent and traces his spread across the land, developing cultures as varied as the regions he settled. It tells too the story of cultures clashing as the white tide came. Such stories —often-tragic sagas of aggressive peoples overcoming the less powerful—have been repeated countless times in the pageant of man. But perhaps never before has the clash been on such a scale.

I recall the poignant words of Seattle, the Duwamish chief from whom the city took its name: "When the last red man shall have perished, and the memory of my tribe shall have become a myth among the white men, these shores will swarm with the invisible dead of my tribe . . . they will throng with the returning hosts that once filled and still love this beautiful land. The white man will never be alone. Let him be just and deal kindly with my people, for the dead are not powerless. Dead, did I say? There is no death, only a change of worlds."

Seattle's prediction was wrong in one respect. The red man did not disappear. Though tribes were shattered and remnants were squeezed onto reservations, the Indian endured—never as subdued in spirit as in body. Now his numbers are increasing at a rate greater than that of the rest of the nation's population. And, as it has been expressed by the late D'Arcy McNickle, a Flathead and one of the four authors of Indian descent who contributed to this book, "while Indians have changed their dress, their economies, their housing, their speech, even somewhat their ritual life, still they are Indians."

To unfold for you the fascinating life-styles of these remarkably diverse people, the Society proudly offers *The World of the American Indian.*

Gilbert M. Grosvenor

I Am Alive...

N. Scott Momaday

Sacred pipestem a symbolic bridge to the sky, a Sioux offers a sunset prayer. Self-reliance instilled by harmony with the land made the North American Indian an individualist within the framework of a tribal group. Physical types and cultures varied region by region; today's Indian is the product of many heritages, a new man with old ways still in him.

RICHARD ERDOES

My grandfather Mammedaty was given a horse; he was given a fine black horse in Oklahoma. This was some years ago, before I was born. And yet it is an important event in my mind, important to me and to my understanding of an Indian heritage. I remember it, as it were, in the way that we human beings seem at times to remember Genesis—across evolutionary distances. It is a memory that persists in the blood, and there only.

Here and there near Rainy Mountain, especially in the summer, the Kiowa gather themselves in groups and dance in order to celebrate their collective lives, to express their spirit as a people. They do so now, and they have done so for as long as anyone knows.

For Mammedaty, then, this expression was simply a matter of necessity; it was spontaneous, appropriate, and sacred, and it was therefore made without pretension, easily, with dignity and good will. He was delighted and restored in it.

The horse was given to Mammedaty about 1920 on the occasion of a meeting of the Taimpe, or Gourd Dance Society, of which he was a member. The gourd dancers represented an old warrior element; in their keeping were some of the oldest and most sacred songs of the tribe.

There was a great crowd, not only of members of the society, but of onlookers as well, including visitors from neighboring tribes—Comanches, Osages, Arapahos, Creeks—and there was a certain electric atmosphere, a festival excitement, upon the whole scene, an intensity of color and motion centered in a deep, green hollow of the land. The dark foliage along the Washita River shimmered in the currents of heat; the sun was high, and it set a hard, thin glaze upon the sky and the grasses and the leaves of the trees. Far away in the north was a black smudge at the edge of the

"Prancing, they come! Neighing, they come! A horse nation...." That refrain from a Plains chant echoes the intimate role of animals in Indian song, legend, and daily life. From animal spirits—which often took human form—came wisdom and power. Clans often had animal totems—the Ojibwa word *totem* means "my fellow clansman." In return for the favor of meat or skin, slain game was accorded deep respect.

earth, and in it all that day there were flashes of lightning, and from it there emanated across the whole expanse of the southern plains the most delicate, delicious scent of rain.

Mammedaty sat in the circle of dancers near the drums, waiting for the songs to begin. The gourd dancers were good-looking in their bright regalia; they wore shoulder blankets, half red and half blue, velvet sashes of various colors, and mescal bean bandoliers. Each of them carried a shaker, or gourd rattle, in his right hand and a fan made of feathers in his left.

Mammedaty's shaker shone like polished bone and his fan was made of eagle feathers; the hands that held them were small and rather long. He wore his hair drawn close to his scalp in braids, which were wrapped with rich, dark otter fur. His leggings were made of buckskin, and their fringes reached to the ground; his moccasins were decorated with fine beadwork.

Directly a song was begun, and Mammedaty let the motion of the music flow over him, and after a time he stood, swaying, flexing his knees and fitting the shaker precisely to the beat of the drums. The singers came to the center of the song; there were three hard beats, and Mammedaty made a slight bow and took small, mincing steps toward the center of the dance ground. And in time, with the others, he raised the shaker high and brought the song to an end in a sound that was like rushing water.

There was a giveaway ceremony, a rite of sharing that occurred in varying ways in tribal cultures across the land. A prominent family of eight or ten members entered the circle. They carried baskets of rich things to give away, beautiful blankets and shawls, German silver and beadwork, money and yard goods. They called out the names of well known and highly respected people, those who were most worthy of honors and renown.

Mammedaty's name was called out, and he arose and stepped forward. At the same moment a boy came running into the circle, leading a big, black horse. There was suddenly a murmur on the crowd, a wave of sheer excitement and delight. The horse shone like shale; it was dancing, blowing, its flesh rippling; it was perfectly beautiful and full of life. There was white at its eyes; there were bright ribbons and eagle feathers in its mane, and there was a beautiful new red blanket spread upon its back.

The horse was presented to Mammedaty, and he graciously returned his thanks, shaking hands with each member of the family. There were nods of approval all around the crowd, and some of the women emitted the shrill, tremolo cries of delight which are peculiar to them. But for all of its color and commotion, it was a moment of great meaning and propriety. All was well with the Kiowa; everything in the world was intact and in place, as it ought to be.

This blood recollection, which is an intricate image indeed, composed of innumerable details, is especially vivid and immediate to me, a whole and irrevocable act of the imagination. I have the sense always that the event, the dramatic action, is just now, in a moment, taking place in the real world. I have held on to this vision for many years, keeping it within my reach, bringing it into focus in moments of peace and quiet. I have walked about in this vision, taken it into account from many different angles, across many distances, in many different lights. And I have thought about it; I have tried to understand it in its own terms; I have tried to perceive myself in it.

In this experience which I have related concerning Mammedaty and the horse, which experience is of a very particular kind, there is a synthesis of other, more general experiences, I believe. In such things there is an evocation of the tribal intelligence, an exposition of racial memory.

The American Indian is distinguished by certain things, certain perceptions of himself in relation to the world around him. This is to say that the American Indian—or indeed any man—is someone who thinks of himself in a certain way; he is precisely equal to his own idea of himself. In the case of the American Indian the idea of the self is based upon a number of equations. They constitute a philosophy, a world view that is peculiarly native, indeed definitive:

You see, I am alive.
You see, I stand in good relation to the earth.
You see, I stand in good relation to the gods.
*You see, I stand in good relation to all that is
    beautiful.*
You see, I stand in good relation to you.
You see, I am alive, I am alive.

The first of these relationships is a perception of the landscape. From the time the Indian first set foot upon this continent, he has centered his life in the natural world. He is deeply invested in the earth, committed to it both in his consciousness and in his instinct. In him the sense of place is paramount. Only in reference to the earth can he persist in his true identity.

There is on the part of most people in our society a tacit assumption that the land is a commodity, an object of trade and utility. But for the Indian this is a false view, a failure to imagine the landscape truly, in its own terms. The landscape cannot be appropriated to individual ownership. Rather it is (continued on page 23)

You see, I am alive.

You see,
I stand
in good relation
to the earth.

"Mother Earth, Father Sky." Thus speaks the Navajo of his kinship with the stark Arizona homeland encompassing monolith and dune in Monument Valley. In the contrast between red man and white, perhaps no concepts so differed as those concerning ownership of land. Westering settlers felt little guilt about taking the soil from "savages who never worked it." But to the Indian the earth was for the use of all and belonged to none. He could no more sell the land, said the Shawnee chief Tecumseh, than he could the sea or the air he breathed. But in the clash of cultures of a changing world, not always was the Indian able to sustain old concepts and honored traditions.

BRUCE DALE, NATIONAL GEOGRAPHIC PHOTOGRAPHER

You see,
I stand
in good relation
to the gods.

Menacing in mien but devised to teach
Hopi children the tribal pantheon,
kachina dolls march against a desert
sky. Religion was a unifying force
in Indian cultures, and though forms
varied, each wrought a deep faith,
a personal commitment. Many tribes
paid heed to spirits in every aspect
of nature. Some united the people's
spiritual powers into an overall force—
the Algonquian *manitou*, Sioux *wakan*,
Iroquois *orenda*. A few recognized
a supreme creator, one whites labeled
the "Great Spirit." Most had a mythical
hero who had given the tribe its way
of life, and a jokester whose pranks
and mishaps taught men moral lessons.

RICHARD NOBLE

You see,

> *I stand*

in good relation

> *to all that is*

> *beautiful.*

Nature is good, believes the Indian, and so is man because
he is part of her. From low, fog-wreathed ocean shores
where the Duwamish lived to high, aspen-filled valleys where
once the Paiute roamed, beauty blesses man and land.
Indian eloquence on this and other topics surprised whites.
Thomas Jefferson wished that Congressmen could orate half
so well; William Penn knew no European tongue that
"hath more words of sweetness and greatness . . . than theirs."

SAM ABELL (ABOVE) AND ENTHEOS

You see, I stand in good relation to you.

DETAIL OF "FROM THE EARTH WE CAME" BY PATRICK SWAZO HINDS, TESUQUE PUEBLO ARTIST, 1968; COURTESY BUREAU OF INDIAN AFFAIRS

Twin strengths of clan and tribe influenced Indian character. The clan gave close kinship ties and guides on specific problems; the tribe handled general affairs, shaped customs, formed a group within which individuals could express themselves truly as people. Most of the tribal names that Indians gave themselves translate into such English terms as "The People," "First Men," and "Original People."

there for all men alike, as a dimension in which they have existence with other creatures.

For the Indian conceives of himself in terms of the land. His imagination of himself is also and at once an imagination of the physical world from which he proceeds and to which he returns in the journey of his life. The landscape is his natural element; it is the only dimension in which his life is possible. The notion that he is independent of the earth, that he can be severed from it and remain whole, does not occur to him; such a notion is false and would therefore be unworthy of him.

In his view the earth is sacred, then, inasmuch as it is pervasive in its influence upon him and because it is informed with life. It is a living entity, in which living entities have origin and destiny. The Indian does not lose sight of it, ever; he is bound to the earth forever in his spirit. To the non-Indian this may seem an extraordinary perception, but to the Indian it is altogether ordinary, appropriate, natural in the best sense; that is, it is in keeping with humane conduct, worthy of man in the full expression of his humanity. By means of his involvement in the natural world does the Indian insure his own well being:

You see, I stand in good relation to the earth.

The second perception of himself which serves to define the Indian is religious in kind; it is essentially a sense of the sacred, and it is everywhere in his tradition.

The Indian is profoundly religious in his character. The formalities of his life are religious formalities; so much is evident in the construction of his ceremonies and rituals. Less obvious, but just as real, is the comparable extent to which religion permeates even his most casual and personal attitudes. His most deliberate words and deeds revolve upon religious considerations. I

have never known an Indian who had not a highly developed sense of the sacred and who did not understand clearly that his view of himself and the world was preeminently a religious view.

I have had some close and personal experience of American Indian religion. When I lived at Jemez Pueblo in New Mexico as a boy, I entered into the current of life there and perceived the great spiritual tides that move upon that world and determine virtually everything within it. I have seen the ancient races which are run at dawn, the descent from the hills at first light of men who are buffalo and deer, and the harvest dances, in which all the sound and motion of the universe is the one dimension of the music and the dance.

Once I went with the people of Jemez to plant the cacique's fields—those fields which are reserved for the chief of the village, and which are planted ceremonially by the townspeople in his honor. And I felt that I had entered into some primordial migration of man through time. I felt the seeds in the earth and ate of their yield, and all of this culminated in the profound reality of spiritual affirmation and fellowship.

And some years later, when I was grown, I visited my grandmother for the last time. Together we went to the place where Tai-me is preserved. Tai-me is the Sun Dance fetish of the Kiowa, a doll, as I have heard, that is the representation of the sun. It is kept as a medicine bundle—kept from view except on ceremonial occasions, wrapped in blankets according to ancient Plains Indian tradition.

Tai-me is considered an extremely potent medicine, or talisman, and must therefore be regarded with appropriate respect. It was acquired by the Kiowa almost three hundred years ago, in the course of their migration from the headwaters of the Yellowstone River to the southern plains.

Pleasant it looked,
This newly created world.
Along the entire length and breadth
Of the earth, our grandmother,
Extended the green reflection
Of her covering
And the escaping odors
Were pleasant to inhale.

                Winnebago

I shall vanish and be no more,
But the land over which I now roam
Shall remain
And change not.

            Omaha

Do you see me! . . .
Do you all help me!
My words are tied in one
With the great mountains,
With the great rocks,
With the great trees,
In one with my body
And my heart.
Do you all help me
With supernatural power,
And you, day,
And you, night!
All of you see me
One with this world!

             Yokuts

I had known of this medicine bundle from the time that I was a child, but I had not understood that it was extant, that it continued to be a vital element in the Kiowa culture long after the Kiowa Sun Dance, of which it was the central figure, had passed from existence.

After a long and preliminary instruction, a preparation of my mind and spirit, as it were, my grandmother, my father, and I were ushered into Tai-me's presence. The bundle was suspended, even as in Sun Dance times, from the fork of a sacred tree. As I had been instructed to do, I made an offering to Tai-me, a gift of red cloth, a kind of material that is prized among Kiowa women and is used to make the traditional women's dress—a full garment with flowing half sleeves and an apronlike sash. When I draped the material over the bundle, my grandmother prayed aloud in the Kiowa language. She prayed for a long time, while I stood before Tai-me. During those moments, which seemed somehow apart from time, I felt that I had come to the full religious meaning of my life.

You see, I stand in good relation to the gods.

And again, a few years later, I was taken into the membership of the Taimpe Society. And now, at each annual celebration of that society in July, I dance with my kinsmen to the drums and the ancient songs, even as Mammedaty did before I was born. There have been times when I have wondered what the dance is and what it means, and what I am inside of it. And there have been times when I have known. Always there comes a moment when the dance takes hold of me, becomes itself the most meaningful and appropriate expression of my being. And always, afterwards, there is rejoicing among us. We have made our prayer, and we have made good our humanity in the process. There are lively feelings. There is

much good talk and laughter — and much that goes without saying.

The Indian exerts his spirit upon the world by means of religious activity, and he transcends himself in a sense; he expands his awareness to include all of creation. And in this he is restored as a man and as a race. Nothing in his universe is exclusive of him, but he is part of all that is and forever was and will be.

There is a remarkable esthetic perception which marks the Indian world, a sense of beauty, of proportion and design. Perhaps this quality is most obvious in children, where it seems especially precocious.

An Indian child, by virtue of his whole experience, hereditary as well as environmental, sees the world according to this esthetic sense, I believe. His view is sure to be incisive and composed; he perceives an order in the objects of his sight, an arrangement that his native intelligence superimposes upon the world — as in astronomy we superimpose line drawings upon the stars. He sees with both his physical eye and the eye of his mind; he sees what is really there to be seen, including the effect of his own observation upon the scene. It is the kind of vision that is developed in poets and painters and photographers, often over a span of many years.

The practical result of this vision one finds in the extraordinary variety and achievement of Indian art, an artistic expression wonderfully native and distinct. It includes such diverse elements as painting, weaving, sculpture, ceramics, featherwork, beadwork, basketry, silversmithy, costume design and manufacture, to name only a few. In the area of religious ritual, many Indian ceremonies incorporate all the elements of drama, music, and dance that characterize the performing

The lands around my dwelling
Are more beautiful
From the day
When it is given me to see
Faces I have never seen before.
All is more beautiful,
All is more beautiful,
And life is thankfulness.
These guests of mine
Make my house grand.

Eskimo

In the house of long life,
*   there I wander.*
In the house of happiness,
*   there I wander.*
Beauty before me,
*   with it I wander.*
Beauty behind me,
*   with it I wander.*
Beauty below me,
*   with it I wander.*
Beauty above me,
*   with it I wander.*
Beauty all around me,
*   with it I wander.*
In old age traveling,
*   with it I wander.*
On the beautiful trail I am,
*   with it I wander.*

Navajo

Loosing mighty peal and lightning flash, a thunderbird swoops from the sky's blue dome; swallows sound the rumble that trails a bolt's loud crack. Thus a Pawnee ceremonial drum depicts the mythical source of violent plains storms. One of man's oldest musical instruments, drums have fired Indian zeal in war, timed his step in ritual; now they boom as Indians seek new strengths from trusted ways of the past.

FIELD MUSEUM OF NATURAL HISTORY, CHICAGO

arts of the non-Indian world. In my experience Indian art, in its highest expression, is at once universal and unique. It is the essence of abstraction, and the abstraction of essences.

Perhaps this quality of abstraction, this understanding of order and spatial relationships, proportion and design, is most fully realized in language. The oral tradition of the Indian, even more than his plastic arts, is vast and various. His stories and songs, his legends and lore and prayers, are exceptionally rich and imaginative. They reflect an understanding of, and belief in, the power and beauty of language that is very nearly lost upon us who have, by and large, only the experience of a written tradition. So great is this oral tradition of the native American that in the increasing light of it we must begin to revise our understanding of our American heritage, I believe. And in this respect, too, the Indian affirms his commitment to an esthetic ideal.

You see, I stand in good relation to all that is beautiful.

Finally, the Indian's perception is humane. It is centered upon an ideal understanding of man in the whole context of his humanity; it is therefore an ethical perception, a moral regard for the beings, animate and inanimate, among which man must live his life.

In his view of the world, the Indian sees deep into the nature and potential of his human being. His best idea of himself is, after all, an idea of all men, an idea of humanity. And this ideal he holds always before him, in all that he thinks and does and is. Perhaps this is the most pervasive and intangible of the equations that I have enumerated, for it is indivisible with and indistinguishable from them in large measure. Notwithstanding, it is a cardinal principle of life in the Indian world, and a sacred trust.

You see, I stand in good relation to you.
You see, I am alive, I am alive.

I believe that the American Indian is possessed of a vision that is unique, a perception of the human condition that distinguishes him as a man and as a race. I have tried to suggest some aspects of this perception which seem to me definitive. In terms of these considerations—the sense of place, of the sacred, of the beautiful, of humanity—the Indian has had and continues to have a singular and vital role in the story of man on this planet. There, at the center, he stands in good relation to all points in the wide circle of the world.

Mammedaty was a man who believed in things. The quality of his belief was very rich and rare.

The light is flat and white on the hard ground, which reverberates with the music and motion of the dance. Suddenly there is a breaking apart of the whole scene, a splintering of colors and planes. The black horse enters into the circle and wheels, its great body bunched, tense and taut as the head of a drum. It is a vision, a vision of great moment and beauty; it has certainly to be believed in order to be seen.

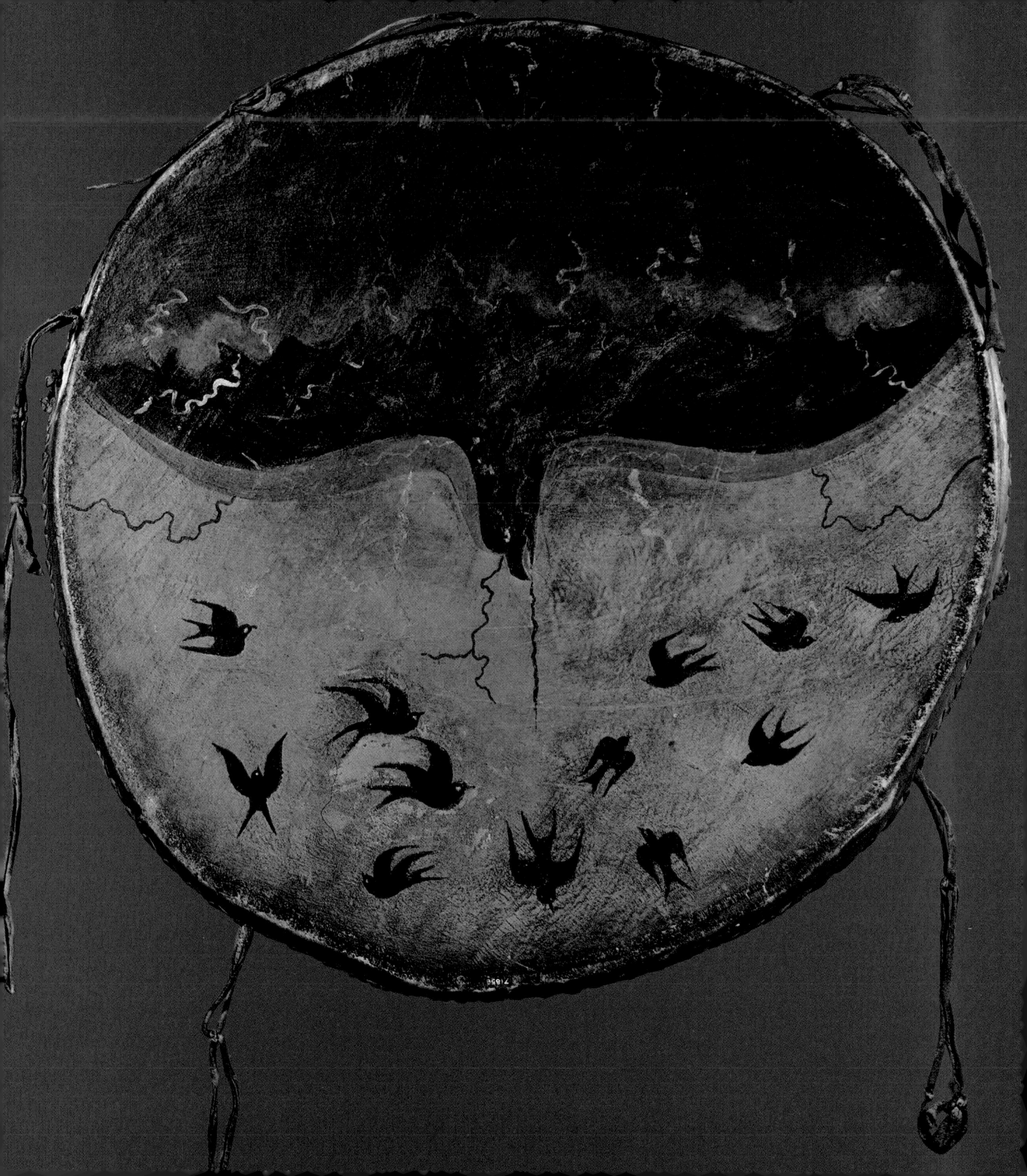

Across an Arctic Bridge

Jesse D. Jennings

Man discovers America—not with pomp and proclamation but with the tramp of wandering feet on tundra that once was sea floor. No pioneering zeal spurred these ancestral Indians; a quest for game probably lured hunting families from Siberia onto a land link with Alaska millenniums ago. Today the seas roil again over the place where the Indian's saga began.

PAINTING BY ARTHUR LIDOV

The story I tell is of the American Indian before the writing of his history began. It is a story no scribe ever carved in stone, no wise old chieftain ever told to a circle of eager young faces. Archeologists have had to tease it from the stubborn earth at a thousand places where its paragraphs and chapters lay hidden beneath the sediment of ages.

With sensitive instruments and such techniques as measuring the "age" of carbon 14, a radioactive isotope all living things contain, we have dated our finds. In ancient beams, and even in chunks of charcoal, we have read growth patterns in tree rings that can tell us, sometimes to the very year, when the tree lived and died. Pottery and weapon styles have told their stories too, as fashions came and went. Through many sciences we have peered into the past at a fascinating human adventure, now clear in outline but still distressingly obscure in some of the major details.

A learned Jesuit, Father José de Acosta, read the scanty evidence available 400 years ago and announced that the American Indian must be of Asiatic origin. Scholars have agreed with him ever since. But the good padre did not know how the immigrants came; "by shipwracke and tempest of wether," he guessed. Now we know better: They merely walked across the Bering Strait.

Today the strait is a 50-mile-wide stretch of shallow sea, some 200 feet deep at the most, separating Alaska and Siberia. But in the Pleistocene ice age, as massive glaciers grew and waned, sea levels fell and rose to the same rhythm. As ice sheets locked up more and more of the world's water, the oceans shrank away from their ancient shores, and shallows became dry land.

Thus it was that, at several times during a two-million-year period, the floor of the Bering Strait stood high and dry, linking Siberia and Alaska in

Usually, though, a corridor would have been open.

Such were the mechanical problems of a human invasion of the Americas. But whether the ice formed a corridor or a barrier, men could have come into the refuge at least as early as 25,000 B.C.—but did they? And if so, what were these first Americans like?

E vidence of early arrivals has cropped up in a dozen places throughout the refuge, but one location stands out: Old Crow Flats at the north end of Canada's Yukon Territory. Here, in a layer of animal bones, scientists dug up a toothed scraper ten inches long, made from a caribou leg bone. It is the careful work of human hands, and the bones found with it are cracked and broken as ancient man's food bones often are.

A bit of the scraper was radiocarbon dated to about 25,000 B.C.—a time when both land bridge and corridor probably stood open. And so we can be certain of man in the refuge, and indeed at its farthest eastern edge, by then. Old Crow Flats lies at the northern end of where the corridor would have been. Was the man who made the scraper heading south? Had others already trekked down the ice-free valleys to live and die beyond the glaciers' southern reach?

The answer is a definite "yes." In half a dozen scattered locations—Oregon, Idaho, Missouri, Pennsylvania, even Venezuela—there are deposits older than 10,000 B.C. Oldest is Meadowcroft Shelter near Pittsburgh, securely radiocarbon dated at 17,000 B.C. We can no longer doubt that the pioneer founder population had begun the New World conquest well ahead of the 9500 B.C. date long thought to mark the first incursion into the midcontinent plains.

What other kinds of tools did these people have? Usually nondescript, shapeless flakes used

a broad stretch of tundra now called Beringia. Most recently the land bridge was open intermittently between about 25,000 and 8000 B.C.

But there was a complication. When the bridge was broadest—over a thousand miles wide and teeming with big game—so were the glaciers. One ice mass spread out of the Canadian Rockies, another radiated from central Canada; as the two crept toward each other they pinched access southward out of Beringia to a narrow corridor. For short periods the glaciers may have overlapped, thus closing the corridor entirely with an ice sheet, perhaps a mile thick in places, that stretched from ocean to ocean and from the Arctic to the northern tier of states. At those times Alaska, much of which has not been recently glaciated, would have been a dead end, the so-called Alaskan or Beringian Refuge, full of mammoth and caribou but with no avenue south.

Musk ox,
Bootherium nivicolens

**Great North American
short-faced bear,**
Arctodus simus

Woolly mammoth,
Mammuthus primigenius

Stag-moose,
Cervalces alaskensis

Lionlike cat,
Panthera atrox

Beasts now fallen by time's wayside shared Alaskan tundra when man arrived. In this artist's bestiary, all are extinct. Similar species survive, but the only close relative is a modern Alaskan musk ox. Remains link the early Indian with the mammoth, though he may have known them all. This beast must have been a dangerous diehard; its thick hide and crushing weight would make any kill a triumph. Musk ox and stag-moose would fall more easily. But if the short-faced bear were cornered or the lionlike cat attacked, man the predator might become the prey, defending himself with stone knives or bone-tipped spears. Little could he know that his descendants would prosper while the big cat and lanky bear, ground sloth, saber-toothed cat, camel, and mastodon slowly died out.

DRAWINGS BY JAY H. MATTERNES

as knives—in whatever form happened to split from the flint block. Just as we would expect, they are the crude kinds of assorted flakes for cutting and scraping that we associate with the same Paleolithic time period in Central Asia. Obviously the stone technology brought into the refuge would be no more advanced than in the lands the wanderers left behind.

A s for the people themselves, again nothing is known, for no human bones proven to be as old as the scraper have been found. Our knowledge of the earliest Americans is based on evidence of their handiwork alone. The two oldest skeletal remains whose dates I can accept are less than 12,000 years old—and yet they offer a basis for reconstructing the physical appearance of the hunters who first trod Beringia.

From a ranch near Midland, Texas, came the fragmentary skull of a small, delicately boned female—dubbed Midland Man, of course! And on the Marmes ranch in southeastern Washington scientists found fragments of not one skull but three. All four skulls are of fully *Homo sapiens* type, yet they show neither significant Asiatic nor specifically American Indian attributes.

From such evidence experts reconstruct the first Americans—a long-headed, slender, graceful people who don't easily fit into any of today's major population groups. This is no surprise; most authorities agree that the differences between the modern world's racial groups developed during the past 20,000 years. And with the bridge and the corridor occasionally closed during that time, only sporadic inputs of new racial stock were possible. This left the early Indian on his own to evolve into a population unlike any other.

Typically, the modern Indian's skin is red-bronze, and it tans readily. The hair on his head is

jet black; there is little or none on his face and body. His incisors are shovel-shaped, with lateral ridges on the back side; his cheekbones are broad, his stature short. There is, of course, much variation between groups and areas; the rangy Plains Indian whose craggy profile looks out from the once-familiar nickel would tower over the short, stocky pueblo dweller of the southwest. But the American Indian cannot be mistaken for other ethnic or racial groups.

What an enormous diversity of terrain and climate awaited these first hardy wanderers and their descendants! North America was relatively free of barriers to travel; climate ranged from arctic to subtropical. The Sierra Nevada and Rocky Mountains offered low passes where travelers could cross; the Appalachian Mountains posed even less of a problem. And food was almost everywhere.

North America fell rather neatly into five major environments—and because the Indian lived by exploiting local resources, his culture types fell into the same five physiographic areas. The plains were rich in big game; east of the Mississippi River both game and a variety of vegetable foods characterized the woodlands. In the arid southwest and Great Basin there were animals and edible plants, but in far shorter supply. The cultures of the west coast looked to the rivers or the sea for food. And the arctic cultures have always depended on mammals of both land and sea.

Nature's bulldozer, the glacier, does a thorough job of obliterating the kind of sites we archeologists seek. And so our data on early cultures grow more solid in areas never glaciated, such as the Great Plains south of Canada, the Great Basin of the west, and much of the Atlantic coast. Ideally, remains and artifacts occur within a geological

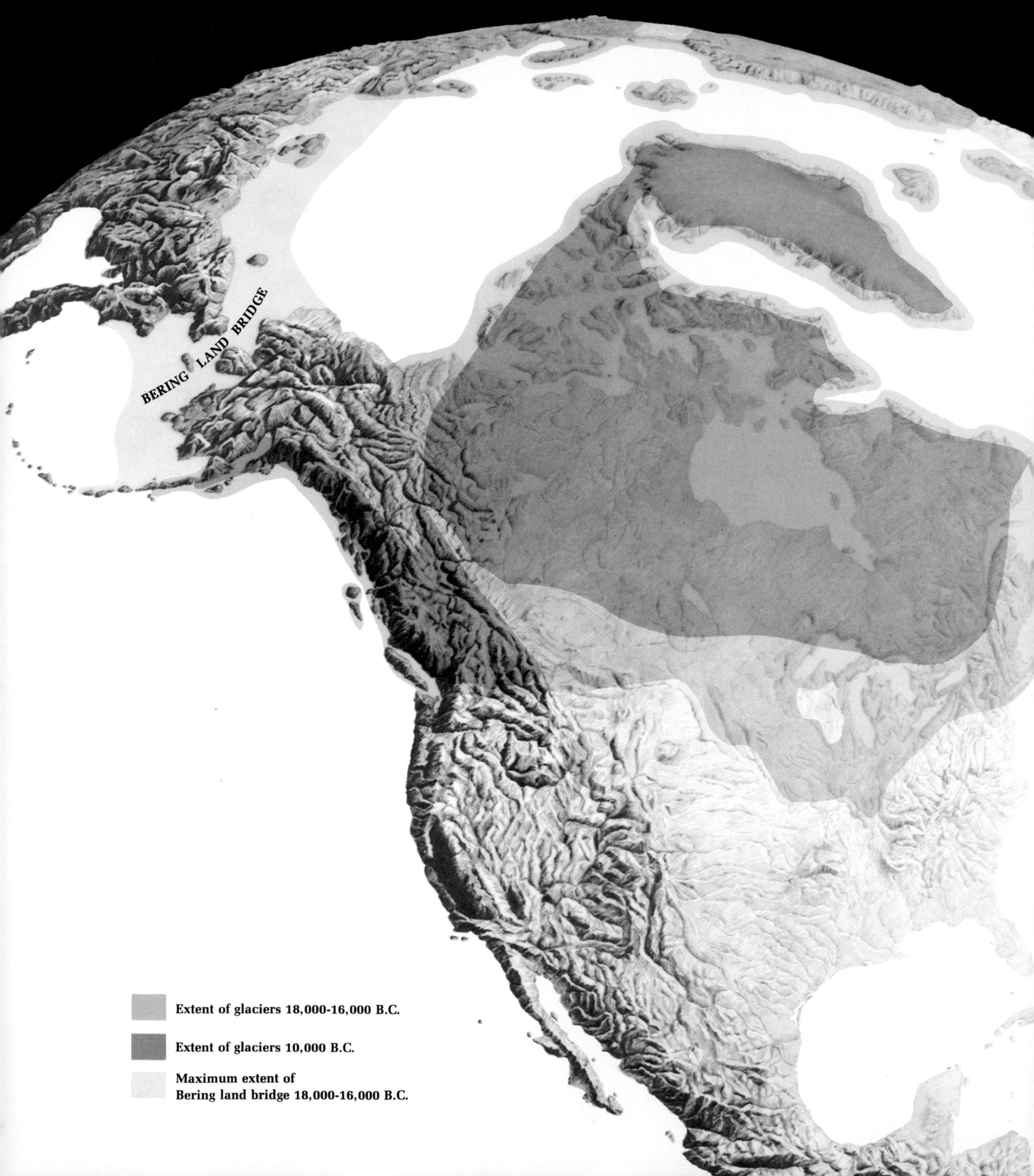

BERING LAND BRIDGE

Extent of glaciers 18,000-16,000 B.C.

Extent of glaciers 10,000 B.C.

Maximum extent of
Bering land bridge 18,000-16,000 B.C.

As astronauts might have seen it, the Bering land bridge beckons Siberian herds to Alaska, where mountains catch the snow and keep lowlands glacier-free. Science cannot say why earth chills into ice ages. But archeology has shown that, during recent glaciations, ancestors of the Indian migrated across the bridge, often finding a narrow route southward between ice sheets that grew or shrank.

DRAWING BY TIBOR TOTH; RESEARCH BY VIRGINIA L. BAZA

stratum of known antiquity, and the deposit is sealed by later natural strata. Add two or three consistent radiocarbon dates, and we have a believable Paleo-Indian site.

All such sites found thus far have been firmly dated no earlier than 10,000 or 11,000 B.C. But evidence that man knew and hunted animals now extinct in North America — beasts like the mammoth, camel, long-horned bison, and tapir — is secure.

In 1952 an Arizona rancher named E. F. Lehner was riding along a newly cut arroyo when he noticed a band of black mucky soil near the bottom of the opposite bank. Embedded in it he could see huge teeth and large bones. He invited Dr. Emil Haury and other University of Arizona scholars to examine the find. They did — and shortly began to unearth the best record of mammoth hunts yet found in the Americas.

On what had been the banks of an ancient stream lay the dismembered skeletons of nine immature mammoths. With the remains were the lance points used in the kills, a distinctive type called Clovis Fluted, found thus far only at mammoth kills and as isolated surface finds. (Among the drawings of prehistoric Indian artifacts on the map in the back pocket of this book is one of a typical Clovis Fluted point, skillfully chipped out of chert or chalcedony, with a long flake scar, or flute, running from the base partway to the tip.)

The animals had been butchered about 9500 B.C. and the remains covered with sediment as the stream valley slowly filled in. Though there were no human remains, it was a complete record of kill and feast — not the slaughter of a herd, Dr. Haury thinks, but rather a series of hunts involving a single animal each time.

One of the most famous of ancient sites lies near Folsom, New Mexico. Again a cowman, again a chance exposure of bones in a gully — but these were the remains not of mammoth but of huge, long-horned bison, 23 of them, cornered and killed in a box canyon, then sealed under layers of sediment. With the bones were several beautiful, slender points, each with a long flake scar from base to tip. These were quite different from the Clovis style, and have come to be known as Folsom Fluted. Several such bison kills have been unearthed, and all date between 9000 and 7000 B.C.

The Folsom site has been sacred ground to American prehistorians since 1926, when it established, once and for all, that man had lived in America early enough to have preyed upon huge animals now extinct. Indeed, some scholars believe that, in the warming centuries when the ice was retreating, the herds were already in a precarious balance with the changing environment; man, the most skillful predator of all, tipped the balance against the great beasts.

The people who fashioned the Clovis points seem to have felled their prey one by one, perhaps surrounding a beast trapped in the mud, then jabbing and stoning until its bellowing ceased. But by the time of the Folsom people a major invention had been introduced: the jump or fall, a simple, totally effective hunting method that persisted for 10,000 years until the late 19th century. This technique was an important social invention, too, because it called for a group of hunters — and after the kill a group of butchers — acting cooperatively, probably under one leader, in tasks no small family band could handle.

Imagine a herd of several bison, or even hundreds of them, grazing on an ancient plain. Suddenly a wall of yelling, waving hunters rises up on three sides. The animals stampede out the open side, thundering blindly over a cliff, into a deep arroyo, or down a dead end such as the Folsom

In the mind's eye of a scientist an extinct "superbison" of 31,000 years ago lives again. Gold miners hosing away silt in Alaska found the frozen mummy in a trove of animal remains. No one knows whether the Paleo-Indian hunted these grazers or their larger relatives whose horns spanned up to 7 feet. But at a canyon near Folsom, New Mexico, a blade lying among bones of the extinct *Bison antiquus* (below) linked man firmly to Ice Age prey.

A caribou-bone scraper (opposite) proved man was in the Yukon by 25,000 B.C. Only its serrated tip remains; after making casts, experts sacrificed the rest for dating tests. Reconstructing the world of America's prehistoric Indians has intrigued scholars since Thomas Jefferson dug a trench through an Indian mound. His sectioning technique is used today.

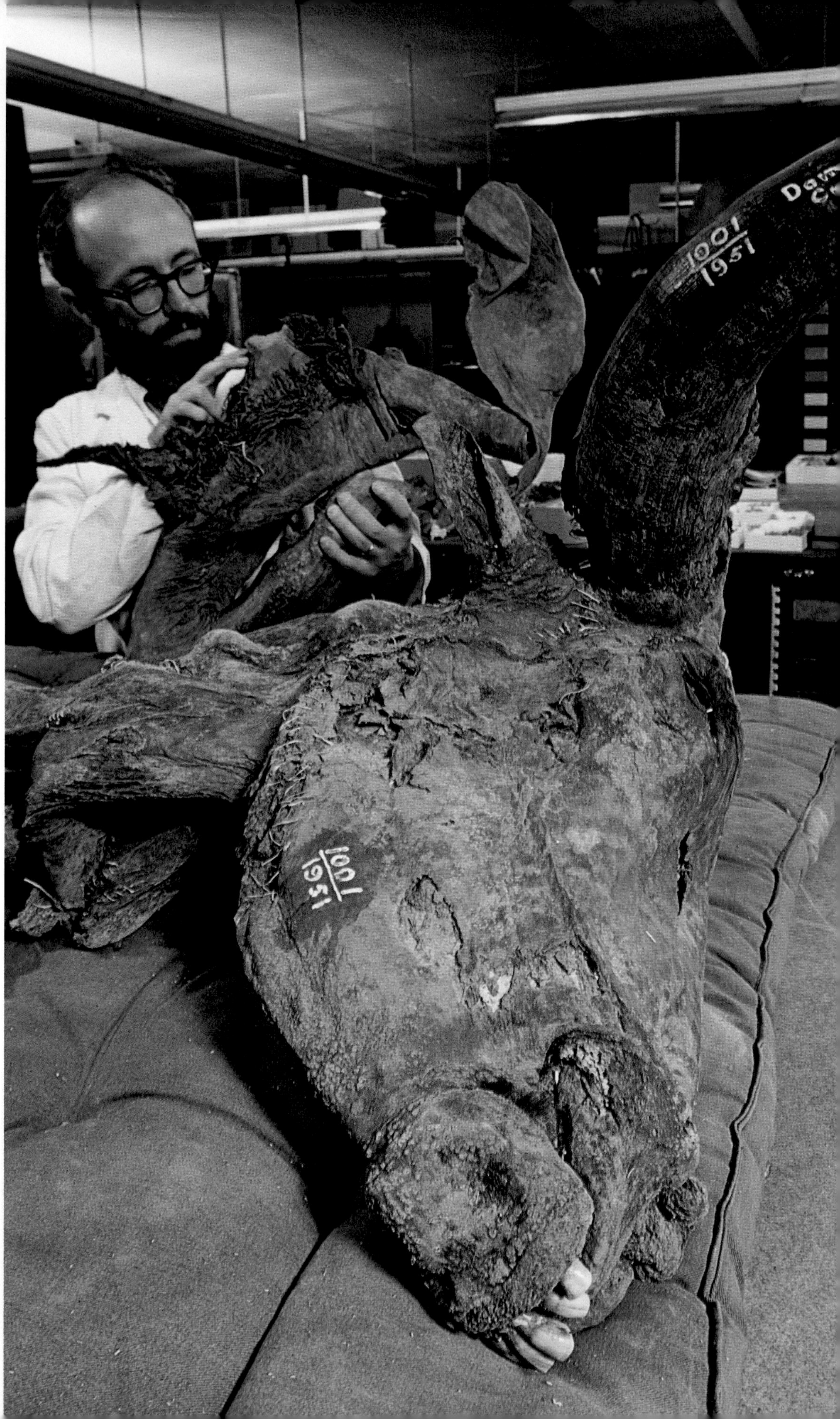

DENVER MUSEUM OF NATURAL HISTORY. RIGHT: JAMES E. RUSSELL. OPPOSITE: NATIONAL MUSEUMS OF CANADA

canyon. Amid the drovers' shouts, the clouds of dust, and the bellows of the maddened beasts, the herd's own momentum does the job; in a cascade of shaggy bodies the animals pile up, killed by the fall or by the crush of others upon them.

Imagine too the anticipation and relish as the butchering begins. A bite of rich, raw liver, still warm, or a tender slice of tongue—and then a methodical disjointing and fleshing of the animals, indicated by the way the bones seem to lie in piles at kill sites, and supported by observations of Plains Indians in historic times. The beast is balanced on its belly; the forelegs and shoulders are cut free and stripped of meat, the bones cast aside in a heap. The hump meat is removed. Ribs and hindquarters follow, stacked in turn when stripped. The hides are cleaned and tanned. Perhaps skulls are broken so the brains can be eaten or used to tan the hides. Surplus meat is dried, yielding a supply of jerky.

If only a few animals are killed, the hunters—and probably their women and children as well—work swiftly and waste little. But if the kill is larger than their needs, the group will have to move on with tons of meat left unharvested. Imagine, then, the final act in the drama, as the stench of decay hovers over the kill and the ravens and eagles fight over their inheritance.

The greatest of all the Paleo-Indian sites was discovered six years after the Folsom find, at Blackwater Draw, south of Clovis, New Mexico, whence Clovis points got their name. Since its breakthrough discovery in 1932, more than 20 scientific expeditions had worked the Clovis site—yet not one had fully reported its findings. Finally Dr. James J. Hester of Southern Methodist University rescued far-flung notes, records, and artifacts and in 1972 put together a complete picture of the sequence of Paleo-Indian cultures.

The site, he found, had once been a huge oval pond. Dozens of mammoths were hunted down, one at a time, by Clovis spearmen in a boggy swamp along the west bank. Later, Folsom hunters felled and butchered large numbers of long-horned bison. Still later, modern species such as the short-horned bison were ambushed by people of a culture period called Plano. All these kills and the articles lost or broken in the excitement of the hunt were sealed in sediment and in perfect stratigraphic sequence: Clovis at the bottom, Folsom next, then Plano. In later times the pond dried up, and in the upper strata we can read the story of thirsty people digging deep wells, with steps cut in the sides, to reach the lowering water table where the center of the pond once had been.

Besides being the chronological yardstick for the entire plains area and parts of the southwest, Blackwater Draw offers many subtle hints about life among the Paleo-Indians. For example, nearly all of the 223 Clovis points found here were made of stone quarried 100 miles to the northeast; most of the 534 Folsom points came from 150 miles to the southeast. So to these peoples the pond was probably just one campsite and hunting ground on a far-ranging seasonal itinerary. In the game they slew we can see the disappearance of Ice Age giants and the dwindling of later species. And we can see man's growing dependence on plants for food as the big herds thinned out: among Plano peoples, here and at many other important digs throughout the west, we find the first seed-grinding mills. A stone slab called a metate held the grain, and a round hand-held stone called a mano was used to grind it.

Because our first and best finds have come from the western plains, it might seem that the Paleo-Indian lived only there. In fact, more fluted points

Thunder from the ground echoes across the plains as hunters of perhaps a hundred centuries ago stampede bison over a cliff. The author guided the artist in re-creating the stirring scene. Modern man knows only the smaller relative of huge bison that long ago roamed the grasslands; bulls stood seven or eight feet tall at the hump and weighed more than a ton. Even a small herd of such large animals might yield more meat than the hunters could carry away. At some kill sites, archeologists find remains of animals that were never butchered; at others they find skeletons with only tail bones missing, suggesting that the hunters' main object was to harvest hides for robes and shelter.

Some experts say such overkills upset the ancient balance maintained when men killed only what they needed, and hastened extinction for species already imperiled by climatic change. Others disagree. Plains Indians used the "jump" or "fall" technique up to the 1870's, yet buffalo by the millions still grazed in seemingly endless herds. Only when the white man arrived with firearms and a market for hides was the mainstay of plains tribes gunned to the brink of oblivion.

PAINTING BY ARTHUR LIDOV

Canvasback drake decoy from Lovelock Cave, Nevada

Winnowing basket made of twined willow strips

points have been discovered at Flint Run near Front Royal, Virginia, and at Shawnee-Minisink in Pennsylvania. They still are being studied, but they offer evidence supporting my belief that a sparse population spread rapidly from sea to sea, with little time for culture and technology to change. In the virgin continent there was no human competition, and game that had never learned to fear man was relatively easy to take. Social units at first would have been family bands of two or three generations, probably with the venerated sire of the group as leader. Then the big kills began, and for them the small family bands had to unite, choosing a skilled hunter as leader and giving him at least temporary command over several dozen people.

This was the legacy of the earliest Americans. The saga of the Paleo-Indian quickens the pulse because it is really the fascinating but incomplete story of Stone Age pioneers.

have been found in the midwest and east than in the plains. Although they do resemble the classic Clovis and Folsom types, they are not identical. And being surface finds, they cannot be dated; they have not been found in undisturbed strata or in company with bones of extinct animals.

Happily there are four exceptions. One, the intensely interesting Debert site in Nova Scotia, was less than 50 miles from a glacier's edge in a spot overlooking a vast plain where caribou ranged. Concentrations of artifacts, chipping debris, and fire pits dot a wide area. These appear to be campsites, suggesting that the place was visited often, probably in summer, and probably for hunting caribou.

Another, Bull Brook near Ipswich, Massachusetts, was also a campsite. It too yielded a large collection of knives, scrapers, and fluted points very close to the Clovis style. Both Debert and Bull Brook also show many Folsom traits, though Debert's dates average around 8600 B.C. and Bull Brook's around 7000 B.C.

Campsites of hunters using more typical Clovis

By about 8000 B.C., the world of the Folsom hunters had begun to change. As the last glacial ice retreated, the climate became more arid, particularly west of the Rockies. Deserts took over much of the west. The great beasts of the Pleistocene era died out. The old life-styles no longer worked; unless the Paleo-Indian could adapt, he too might disappear.

The almost endless variety of his adaptations makes up the second era in Indian prehistory, a period we call the Archaic. Despite a more demanding environment, these life-styles were comparatively rich and easy, based on the hunting of game and the collecting of vegetable foods in whatever combination each environment allowed. Foraging involves wandering from one ecozone to another as foods become seasonally available, but does not require the social organization needed

Artist and ethologist, a Western
Archaic Indian fashions a bogus
duck to feast on a real one. In his
foragings at lakeside—for eggs,
seeds, fish, muskrats, anything
the fertile shallows might yield—
he has watched wary waterfowl
splash down among their kind.
And from his insights came
the duck decoy, a brainstorm that
lures fowl to the gun today.

Studies of historic western
Indians and the artifacts of their
distant ancestors suggest the steps
in a duck hunt of about 2500 B.C.;
the artist blends them in this
painting. Around a framework of tule
the hunter binds strands of cattail
leaves or yucca strips, finishing
his lifelike fake with feathers
and paint. Where open water begins
he sets his decoy afloat, then
hides himself in the rushes close by,
his black hair camouflaged with
yellow cattail pollen, his fingers
dabbling the water to mimic sounds
of feeding ducks. A patient wait
and a sudden lunge will put tasty
duck on this day's cooking fire.

PAINTING BY ARTHUR LIDOV

for the bison stampede. Thus we can envision family bands making the rounds with the seasons, using a wide variety of tools for the varied tasks of harvesting, yet keeping them light and portable.

Eventually the foraging way of life covered the continent. In the western deserts, game was sparser than in the plains, so vegetable foods — seeds of grasses and desert shrubs, edible bulbs, fruits, nuts, and tender spring shoots — were the staples. The choice of meat ranged from kangaroo rats and rabbits to waterfowl, with an occasional antelope or bighorn sheep when luck was with the hunters.

In the woodlands of the east the resources were richer; game included succulent deer, beaver, opossums, squirrels, rabbits, fish, turtles, shellfish, turkeys, and waterfowl. Plant foods were also abundant. According to recent calculations, a ten-square-mile patch of the lower Illinois Valley would yield in a year at least 180,000 bushels of walnuts and hickory nuts, 50,000 bushels of acorns, 100 deer, 10,000 squirrels, 200 turkeys, and even five black bear! Add to this all the fruits in season and thousands of rabbits, raccoons, and woodchucks, and it is easy to see why "high living" is the hallmark of Eastern Archaic.

But in addition to the bounties of nature's wild gardens, nut groves, and game preserves, the Archaic peoples had developed at least the *concept* of horticulture. Unusual seeds of such plants as amaranth, sunflower, goosefoot, and marsh elder have turned up. The seeds are much larger than normal. They lead us to think that these species were being cultivated as "grains" — not domesticated, merely tended or protected. Possibly they were even planted in ideal locations where yields would be bigger or better.

In the humid, well-watered eastern woodlands, many of the Archaic sites are in the open, so

Spiny fingers bright with sun-gold, cholla cacti sink thirsty toes into southwestern sands, vying with frazzle-topped yucca for the desert's precious treasure: water. Few would call this farmland. Yet the Hohokam two millenniums ago coaxed corn, beans, and squash from such arid ground, leading water from rivers to fragile crops in elaborate networks of canals.

For four decades Dr. Emil Haury has studied these migrants from the south, tracing ancient waterways with aerial photographs, digging with trowel and giant earthmover, poring over some 1,500,000 shards from the 300-acre settlement at Snaketown near Phoenix, Arizona. Among finds are the western world's first etchings— made by daubing shells with pitch and bathing them in acid, probably fermented cactus juice—and the southwest's finest canals, the oldest of them a broad watercourse some three miles long and 2,300 years old. Later branches (above) went deep and narrow to slow evaporation. Pima Indians who helped Dr. Haury may descend from the Hohokam; in the Pima tongue the name means "perished ones."

ENTHEOS. ABOVE: HELGA TEIWES, ARIZONA STATE MUSEUM, TUCSON

Civil engineering of a thousand years ago: With pointed sticks and flat, rectangular stones Hohokam men carve a channel, probably "reading" the terrain and choosing a route by eye. Occasionally they misjudge and must re-dig when water won't flow. Women in skirts of shredded fiber haul the dirt away in baskets. Later they may fashion pottery and tend children as the men wield these same stick and stone tools to cultivate fields where corn grows in random hills perhaps a dozen feet apart.

Diversion dams on the Salt and Gila Rivers supplied more than 500 miles of canals; one early artery measured two feet deep and twenty feet wide. At intervals a "fence" of poles crossed a channel; mats laid against it became dams for regulating the flow.

When Snaketown died eight centuries ago, other Hohokam villages lived on, still irrigating from the old canals. Mormon farmers used portions of the network in the 19th century. Pima Indians water crops with ditches today, often along routes where the lifeblood of their probable forebears flowed.

PAINTING BY ARTHUR LIDOV

50

Awestruck cowboy Richard Wetherill discovered in 1888 what no white man had ever seen: this silent stone city sheltered by the overhanging brow of a Colorado mesa. Today visitors to Mesa Verde National Park wonder, as men did then, what emptied Cliff Palace and the thousands of sites in the park that were home to the Anasazi for 700 years. First in pit houses, then in stone pueblos with up to 75 rooms, these hunter-farmers inhabited the flat mesa-top, digging pools and ditches to gather rainwater for their corn, beans, and squash. They kept dogs and turkeys, probably using the birds less for food than for the feathers their men worked into warm leggings and blankets. About A.D. 1150 they began to abandon mesa-top homes, crowding into cliff-hung citadels whence they clambered by toeholds cut in rock to tend fields, fetch water, hunt bighorn sheep and deer. About 100 years later they left even these. Aided by National Geographic Society grants, studies here and at other sites recaptured the lost life-style.

Zigzags on a typical pitcher from Pueblo Bonito in Chaco Canyon may suggest lightning, harbinger of rain to ease the drought that perhaps drove these farmers from their homes. Its artistry bespeaks too the leisure of folk attuned to their environment.

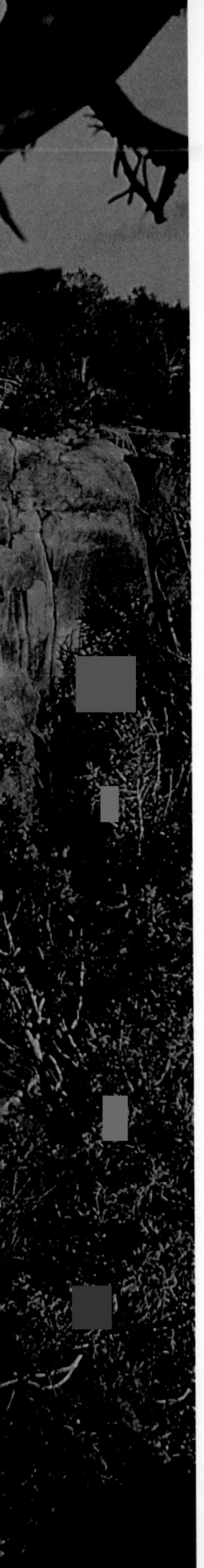

preservation of materials that decay (such as seeds) is rare. But in the west, beneath dry overhangs and in dusty caves, everything has been preserved —everything, from grass stems to cactus pads, from worn-out moccasins to human excrement.

Two of the many western caves stand out: Danger and Hogup Caves on opposite sides of Utah's Great Salt Desert. On Danger's floor the debris lay 13 feet deep, dating from 8500 or 9000 B.C. to nearly historic times. Hogup was occupied from about 6400 B.C. into the 19th century.

The contents of the two were quite similar. Flat coiled baskets made of willow withes sewn with grass fibers were used to parch seeds. On metates—nearly a thousand were found whole or in pieces in Danger alone—the seeds were ground for mush or gruel, the local staff of life. But all was not toil; ancient bone dice, perhaps for games or rites, rattled again in the excavator's sieve.

Though animal bones were numerous, the scrap in both caves was largely vegetable material; investigators identified more than 60 kinds of plants in the Hogup fill. In the list we can see a selective harvesting of foods in season—and in old photographs and eyewitness accounts we can see tribes of the west pursuing exactly the same lifeway, almost within living memory.

There is little glamour in analyzing ancient human feces, but there is much to be learned thereby. A variety of seeds, small bones of rodents and fish, the horny skin of cactus fruit with the spines singed off, and animal hair help to tell us what foods the residents favored. Even clues to their ailments are found, as eggs of pinworm, roundworm, and fluke come to light. Americans,

it seems, have supported these unwelcome guests, as well as lice and other external pests, for at least 10,000 years. But not without a fight; plant remains suggest the use of natural remedies. Diarrhea, bronchial trouble, sore eyes, fevers, and even allergies may well have been treated with herbs strong in the specific chemical required.

The flexibility of the Archaic lifeway stands out when we compare these caves to Lovelock Cave in Nevada. Nearby spread the vast shallow Humboldt Lake, teeming with fish and edged with acres of marsh where waterfowl and shorebirds fed and nested. And in the cave excavators found lifelike duck decoys of buoyant rushes, and long trotlines with barbed hooks of bone still dangling.

There was a great stability about the Archaic cultures, east and west. They were fully efficient, exploiting a thousand local environments in the same general way. And they were fully flexible, adjusting diets and harvesting schedules in tune with nature's changes. In fact, I believe some Archaic peoples may even have improved upon their own natural environment, as tribes have done in historic times—for example, by burning over a meadow where deer browse and berries grow, in order to keep it from reverting to woodland.

If the Paleo-Indian hunter and the Archaic forager lived in close harmony with their environment, there would seem little reason for the rise of a new life-style. But gradually the first indications of change appeared. By about 2500 B.C., foragers in present-day Mexico had succeeded in domesticating a cluster of high-yield plants native to the Americas, among them corn, beans, chili peppers, squash, and avocados. And the cultural

As life depended on corn, and corn on rain, so the Anasazi depended on the gods to bestow summer's rains on the thirsty lands they farmed. Modern man can only guess at the rites that unfolded in scores of kivas. Accounts from historic times and the evidence of archeology guided the artist's hand in shaping this glimpse into a ritual for rain and fertility seven centuries ago.

Much in the rite focuses on rain. Gourd rattles imitate its pattering sound; fringed sashes around the dancers' waists suggest the look of falling torrents. Sprigs of spruce symbolize rain's green blessing on the land.

A fire casts warmth and light, shielded by a stone slab from an air shaft behind. A roof hole lets smoke out, participants and invited guests in. No women share the secret solemnity of this rite. But at other times they may enter to bring food, witness special rituals, and even join in.

Between ceremonies the men may sit on the hard clay floor to spin, weave, and gossip — or stretch out for a night's sleep — in this workshop, club, ritual center, and occasional bachelor dormitory.

PAINTING BY ARTHUR LIDOV

Casa Rinconada spans 64 feet of Chaco Canyon's floor, its mud-and-log roof lost to time. Mystery veils this Great Kiva of the 11th century. Were oblong wells "foot-drums," planked over to resonate dancers' steps? Was its trench a tunnel enabling performers to pop up from its floor? No one knows.
DAVID HISER

effects were enormous. Reliance on wild foods dwindled, though use of wild plants for raw materials, medicines, and edibles was never abandoned. Man turned more and more to tending basic crop plants—so-called cultigens—thus reducing time available for hunting and gathering.

Did increasing population force the invention of gardening as a way of improving the natural food supply, or did the surpluses of gardening lead to greater population? We cannot say, but there is no doubt that hamlets, villages, and even small towns with permanent houses dotted most of Mexico by 1500 B.C. Some of the farming villages began building ceremonial centers with pyramidal mounds, and the seeds of the splendid Mexican civilizations were sown.

In the southwest—roughly, present-day Arizona, Utah, Colorado, New Mexico, and parts of northern Mexico—agriculture finally appeared. The first signs of serious dependence on farming occur at a place called Snaketown near Phoenix. Evidence suggests to Dr. Emil Haury, Snaketown's principal excavator, that migrants from the northwest Mexican lowlands arrived around 300 or 400 B.C. These settlers were fully equipped to survive; they had the cultigens, they knew how to irrigate, and they brought along both esthetic arts and practical skills. The culture they launched is known as the Hohokam.

Out of the sands of Snaketown, excavators in the 1930's and 1960's brought well-formed pottery, sculpted stone bowls, carved shells, turquoise mosaics. These, along with sophisticated concepts of water management—all without precedent in the southwest—appeared together in the lowest levels of Snaketown. Even the raucous macaw, otherwise unknown here for a thousand years, had preened his brilliant plumes as the

Potters of Acoma Pueblo in New Mexico display products of their skill at one of the oldest of Indian arts. Today's pueblo peoples descend from the Anasazi, who left impressive ruins in cliffs and canyons nearby. Motifs the ancient ones might recognize emblazon pots made in the old way.

RICHARD NOBLE

settlers sank their roots; perhaps these pet parrots yielded feathers for rituals.

Finds from later levels bore out the theory of Mexican colonization, and indicated continuing contact. There were platform mounds, arenas similar to Mexican ball courts, and tiny copper bells like those made in western Mexico. Certainly Mexican influence here was strong—and in turn the Hohokam farmers' influence radiated over the southwest throughout Snaketown's existence, an unbroken span of around 1,500 years.

In few places on earth would a life geared to gardening seem less likely than on the arid steppes and plateaus of the southwest. But the cultigens and the concept of water management changed foragers to farmers all over the area. Western Archaic peoples rapidly accepted the new ideas, modified to fit their varied environments.

Archaic peoples living some 200 miles east of Snaketown knew the rudiments of farming long before the Hohokam arrived. In New Mexico's Bat Cave and Tularosa Cave we have found cobs of a primitive type of corn. But agriculture had no serious impact in that region until after the time of Christ. By 300 B.C. the Tularosa people were making a characteristic brown pottery and living in pit-house villages. From these beginnings a culture called the Mogollon evolved—and probably spread northward to trigger what many call the zenith of southwestern traditions, the Anasazi.

Visitors today stroll about the empty shells of Anasazi communities in and around the Four Corners area—the spot where the four Southwestern states intersect—and wonder what emptied them long ago. When the first white men came, not even the Indians they met could remember who had built such cities. In the elaborate

Seeds of farming bore magnificent fruit in central Mexico, where cave dwellers began taming wild plants some 7,000 years ago. About A.D. 100, unknown architects engineered the mighty Pyramid of the Sun in grain-rich Teotihuacán. Aztecs later thought this ruined city the home of deities like Tlaloc (opposite), their rain god, whose hand here clutches the precious gift of corn. Perhaps from Mexico came the idea that set eastern Indians to making mounds by the thousands.

apartment houses nestled in the cliffs of Mesa Verde and the imposing stone complexes of Chaco Canyon we see the full range of Anasazi architecture. Yet their grandeur obscures the fact that these vacant citadels grew out of a culture called Basketmaker, whose people made no pottery until A.D. 400—when they seem to have learned how from the Mogollon—and lived in pit houses until the end of the seventh century.

As the Anasazi tradition developed, the pit house—a low log-and-mud superstructure over a shallow pit—evolved in two directions. By A.D. 700 or 800, dwellings became surface affairs of stone, often joined one to another in sprawling pueblos with populations in the hundreds. And the concept of a house partly underground also led to the development of the round, fully subterranean chamber called the kiva, an exclusive preserve where the men carried on their sedentary chores, spinning yarn of cotton fibers, weaving warm blankets of feathers plucked from domesticated turkeys. Here too they performed a variety of religious ceremonies, dancing on a hard clay floor that in some kivas was buffed with rubbing stones to a surface resembling cement. Many kivas had a small round hole in the floor, occasionally

lined with the neck of a broken pot; this was the sipapu, gateway to and from the spirit world.

In the remains of Anasazi burials, some of them under the floors of dwelling rooms, we encounter ancient woes. Poor teeth throbbed, worn down by the grit from sandstone metates, and joints ached with arthritis and rheumatism.

The bones also show close kinship to present-day Indians; this was no lost superrace, as once believed, but rather the ancestors of Indians now living in pueblos of Arizona and New Mexico. Some of the tools and pottery in use there today can hardly be distinguished from those found in the cliff dwellings. And sometimes, from their own experience, modern Indians can answer riddles an archeologist cannot: Ancient pieces of canelike grass charred at one end were recognized as cigarette butts, like grass stems stuffed with tobacco and smoked in the kivas today.

In the multistory pueblos of Chaco Canyon we can study the high-water mark of Anasazi achievement. Here we find the huge Great Kivas in the plazas—and small kivas tucked among the dwellings, apparently for private use of families or clans.

The early architects of Chaco Canyon seem to have developed their own local style. But in later features we begin to see indications of Mexican influence—features like colonnades and round towers, or the distinctive technique of building a wall like a vertical sandwich, with a core of rubble between two layers of cut stone. There is even a suggestion of a cult of Quetzalcoatl, the feathered serpent worshiped in Middle America.

There was no long decline in the Anasazi tradition. It simply disappeared, and with a suddenness that left no firm clues as to why. A prolonged drought? Attack by invaders? An overloading of the environment by peaceful immigrants? Any of these is possible, but the best guess is that drought and soil loss forced the Anasazi southward to better land, where their descendants live in pueblos today. Thus the farmer's frustration: When he takes up gardening, both his roaming days and his adaptability may be lost.

In the east the living was good and the Archaic sites are many. They have yielded dozens of radiocarbon dates, ranging all the way from 8000 to 1000 B.C. or a little later. And they tell the same story of seasonal harvest from an abundance of choices, and of a gradual shift from wandering to a more settled life. All the sites were along rivers or large creeks, or on quiet coastal waters where mussels, fish, turtles, and fowl provided an inexhaustible larder. Wooded bottomlands added a wealth of plant and animal fare.

In a few eastern caves and cliff shelters we have found basketry, woven sandals, fur robes, mats, and other perishables. But usually the caves were damp and preservation was no better than in the open. Even so, we know a great deal about Eastern Archaic life and its seasonal rhythms.

The Riverton community of eastern Illinois and western Indiana, for example, centered around a winter settlement, where diggers found evidence of permanent houses, domestic chores, and food storage. Up and down the Wabash River, summer base camps, spring and autumn transient camps, and short-term, special-use camps were discovered; tools and food scrap told the story of each. At their winter home the Riverton people hunted deer and turkeys; at spring camp they concentrated on turtles; at the summer site they dined on turtles and venison; and at autumn camp they brought down waterfowl.

From Indian Knoll, a two-acre site on an old channel of the Green River in Kentucky, came the greatest bonanza of Eastern Archaic artifacts—

55,000 items from a single dig by Dr. William S. Webb of the University of Kentucky. His crews found flint tools by the thousand, river pearls and ornaments of shell, awls of bone for basketmaking, delicate bone fishhooks, rattles of tortoise shells filled with pebbles, stone slabs with dimples for cracking nuts, even bone pins for the hair or for holding skin cloaks together—the varied possessions of a people with roots sunk in the land, and a generous land that left them with time for leisure, arts, and ceremony.

Perhaps, with time to think, these peoples of 3000 B.C. began to ponder death. For here, flexed in round, well-like grave shafts or stretched out under shallow surface mounds, Webb found nearly 900 skeletons, many with offerings and ornaments, and most with a residue of red ocher that had been smeared on the body. Even 21 small dogs were found in graves like those of humans.

Only in graves were the rattles found, and we must guess at the rituals that saw them placed there. But of the celebrants, there can be no doubt: They were a wiry people of medium height with fine bones, long high-vaulted heads, and broad cheeks, altogether a handsome group, yet lacking some of the physical attributes of the modern Indian. Though a few men, with good luck, might live past 70 years, their women usually died at about 30, after a life of chores and childbearing.

Ever since white men arrived they have wondered about the thousands of mounds—some small, others man-made hills—that dot the east, relics of peoples once lumped together in popular lore and called simply the Mound Builders. We know now that widely different cultures built the mounds at different times, and for different purposes. In the period around 1000 B.C. to A.D. 700 the mounds contained tombs. Later they were built as flat-topped bases for temples. Some even depict

World's largest serpent effigy, a coiled quarter-mile of heaped earth in Ohio, is seen best from aloft—a vantage its creators never attained. Scholars believe Indians of the Adena culture built this mound for ritual use 13 to 30 centuries ago. The oval may be an egg or the snake's own open mouth.
GEORG GERSTER

birds, beasts, and men in sprawling effigies too large to be "read" from the ground; only from an aerial vantage point do the great images take shape. And so far, archeology offers no vantage point from which to discern their purpose.

North America's oldest Indian mounds are the large rings of piled shells that dot coastal and river sites from South Carolina to Florida. One of the largest of these, on Sapelo Island, Georgia, measures more than 300 feet across, a mysterious, seven-foot-high palisade of saltwater shells constructed some 4,000 years ago. And within these mounds archeologists have found examples of the first pottery to appear on the continent. It was made of clay tempered with plant fibers; some pieces bore geometric designs around the rims.

Pots and shell rings like these have been found together in only one other place: the Caribbean coast of Colombia. It may be only a remarkable coincidence, but to some this suggests an intriguing possibility: Around 2400 B.C. American Indians may have made long coastal voyages from South America to Georgia and South Carolina, bringing with them elements to enrich the Archaic cultures of the North American east.

Other hints of outside influence come from an Archaic earth-mound site at Poverty Point, Louisiana. Clay figurines of about 1500 B.C. strongly resemble jade ones made by the Olmec, pioneer architects of Mexico's ceremonial centers.

As we excavate the earliest sites of the Burial Mound period—those of the Adena culture in Ohio and Kentucky dating back to about 1000 B.C.— we are struck with what seems a new society, although showing so far no evidence of agriculture. Well-made pottery, ornate art objects, jewelry, and tubular smoking pipes of stone come to light. The mysterious monumental enclosures of earth

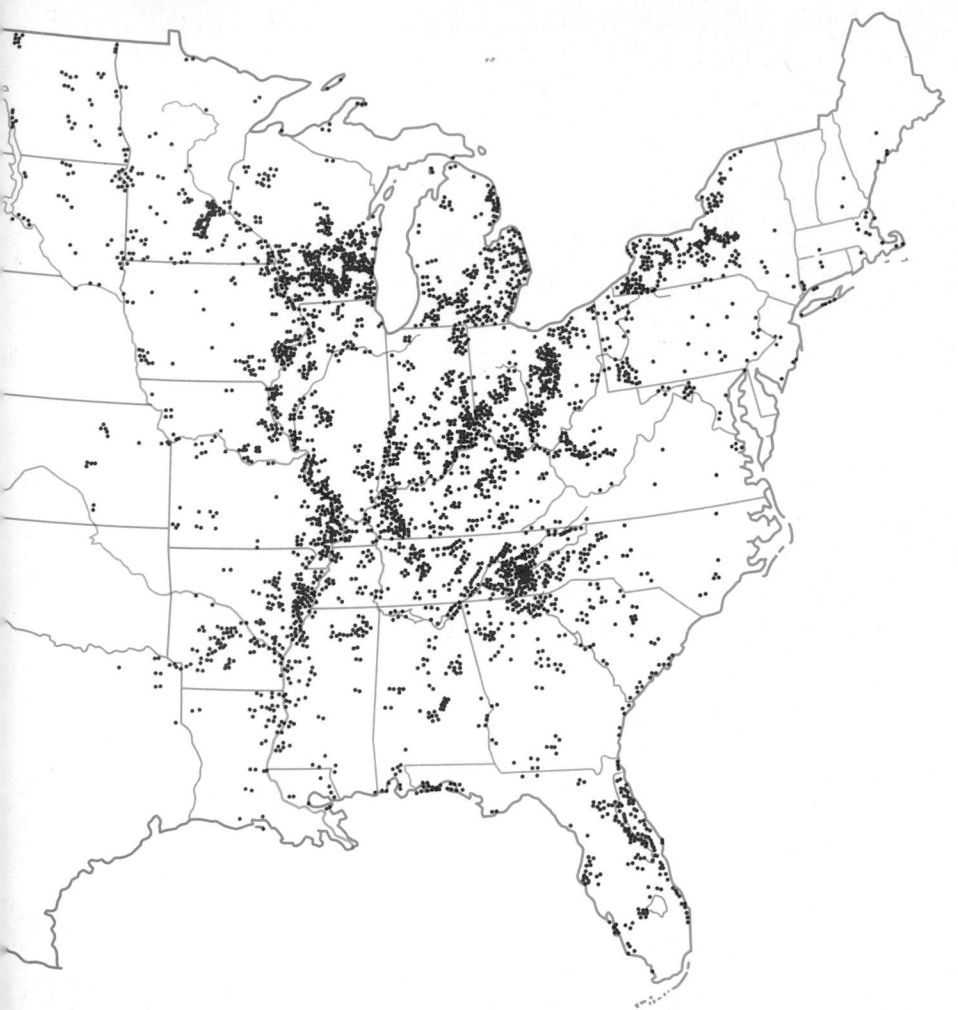

imported from the Gulf of Mexico. Embossed breastplates, ear ornaments, and ritual weapons were hammered from copper picked up as nuggets or mined around the northern Great Lakes.

Pearls by the thousand were plucked from river mussels, drilled, and sewed on garments or strung about throat, wrist, and ankle. Today we cannot help admiring such treasures as we contemplate them across the gulf of time and culture.

Like ripples on a pond, Hopewell influence spread southward, then languished through quiet centuries peopled by what one scholar calls "the good gray cultures." But by about A.D. 700 a vibrant, well-organized way of life called the Mississippian culture arose, geared to farming and with a strongly Mexican flavor to its arts. This culture transformed the east during the 1,000-year Temple Mound period.

Unlike the Hopewell, the Mississippian peoples raised huge pyramidal hills, usually around a central plaza, with temples on the flat summits—strong evidence of a powerful class of ruler-priests. Supporting each center and its priests, nobles, and craftsmen were the surrounding villages where farmers, hunters, and traders toiled to provide the necessities of life for both themselves and their betters at the temple complex.

From its apparent beginnings in the fertile lands of the lower Mississippi Valley, the new culture spawned famous centers hundreds of miles away. Dozens of these temple mounds still rear their great hulks, many preserved in state or national parklands. Most are situated in the rich, broad bottomlands along southern rivers, but the largest of all rises at Cahokia in western Illinois. Its central mound looms 100 feet high with a base covering some 16 acres, while satellite mound-clusters dot the fertile plain for miles around.

suggest an upper class able to command large labor forces for public works. All these products are seemingly based on an obsessive preoccupation with honoring the dead, whose graves and burial offerings fill most Adena mounds.

Gradually the cultigens began to appear. Within a few centuries of the Adena culture the Hopewell arose in Illinois with an intensified expression of the death-ritual cult and hints of agriculture. Large burial mounds containing elaborate log tombs full of rich offerings were built in Illinois, Ohio, and New York. Specialists in art appeared: potters, stone carvers, coppersmiths, workers in shell and mica. Their raw material flowed in as trade or tribute from sources far distant. Fine obsidian came from what is now Yellowstone Park, more than a thousand miles away. Huge conch shells for ceremonial vessels and ornaments were

Incised shell gorget
unearthed in Texas

Six-inch wood
panther from Key Marco

Wood head, preserved
in salty mud of Key
Marco, Florida

Birdlike head made of
conch shell, found near
Spiro, Oklahoma

Stone bird pipe
found in Georgia

An Indian Metropolis

Across the Mississippi from St. Louis, motorists pass Monks Mound (above), tilled by Trappists in the early 1800's. Few envision the city that surrounded it in the 12th century, an urban center with clustered housing, rigid social strata, and specialists in the arts.

Cahokia, crown jewel of the Mississippian culture, sprawled along Cahokia Creek for miles and boasted 30,000 residents in its heyday. Some built clay-and-pole homes inside a 15-foot-high stockade, rebuilding on the ashes of the old home if sparks from cooking fires ignited its thatched roof. On fertile lands outside, farmers with flint hoes pampered corn, beans, and squash. Hunters bagged deer, ducks, geese, swans; fishermen worked lakes and streams. Canoes brought in raw materials and bore the artisans' wares afar.

Life focused on the great mound, its 16-acre base surpassing that of Egypt's Great Pyramid. From its 100-foot summit chiefs gazed across a plaza to a truncated pyramid where nobles were prepared for burial in a conical knoll nearby. The great mound, some 700 by 1,000 feet, is not even partly a natural hill; thousands of laborers without wheels or draft animals built it by the basketful in at least 14 stages between A.D. 900 and 1100.

Mounds by the score held temples, burials, homes of the elite. One yielded a noble and six slain retainers; nearby lay 53 women in a mass grave, apparently sent with their master to the afterlife. Diggers also found remains of "Woodhenges"—circles hundreds of feet across, once ringed with massive posts whose alignment with the sun may have told farmers when to sow.

Cahokia reached its peak about A.D. 1200, then faded as nearby centers grew. Eventually it was abandoned.

Throughout the Mississippian culture we find strong echoes of the Hopewell people's concern with death. But by about A.D. 1300, rulers were going to their graves amid the temple mounds with an array of offerings ascribed to a new Southern Cult. Motifs reminiscent of Mexico appeared—the plumed rattlesnake, for example, on pottery at Moundville, Alabama. In a stone pipe from Spiro, Oklahoma, a glowering executioner cleaves his groveling victim's skull; the resemblance to Mexican sacrificial rites is intriguing.

What processions climbed to temples on the great Southern Cult mounds? What strange rites unfolded inside? A wealth of sacred artifacts invites the imagination to wander. Ritual must have pervaded life; in tombs we find even children in sacred feather capes with ritual weapons in miniature, probably heirs to a family role in ceremony.

The Mississippian splendor was already fading when the first Europeans arrived. In short order they destroyed this rich and fascinating culture, both by conquest and by introducing diseases for which the Indians had no immunity.

Early explorers give us only tantalizing glimpses of Mississippian grandeur. Garcilaso de la Vega, chronicler of de Soto's expedition of 1539-1542, wrote of a Savannah River temple whose "ceiling ...from the walls upward, was adorned like the roof outside with designs of shells interspersed with strands of pearls.... Among those decorations were great headdresses of different colors of feathers...it was an agreeable sight to behold."

North to southern Wisconsin the Mississippian culture had spread, and into the Ohio and Tennessee Valleys; many of its elements had reached Georgia, Alabama, and North Carolina. Symbols like the scalloped sun disk and cross occur repeatedly in shell, stone, and copper down into Florida. We can detect the last echoes of this cul-

ture among historic southern tribes like the Creek and Natchez, but only until about 1750.

While burial and temple mounds were rising in the farmlands, the Archaic life had continued in the north and the Great Basin of the west, unchanged in population strength, social structure, or adaptation. But change had begun in the eastern plains; by A.D. 800 or 900 some tribes were dividing their efforts between hunting bison and cultivating corn, beans, and squash. By 1700 the Europeans had introduced the horse, and some plains tribes rode off in new directions.

And here the saga of the American Indian becomes not only the archeologist's story but also the historian's. From the men in glistening armor or in coarse robes hung with crosses, the Indian learned to become an outsider in a land his forebears had tamed, and into which his lifestyles had so wonderfully fit.

Vigorous remnants of the southwestern peoples still survive and practice their old crafts and faiths. The scattered pueblo dwellers of the west descend from Mogollon and Anasazi roots. The Pima-Papago may be the last remnants of the Hohokam. Navajo sites have been traced back to the 16th century.

Towns and ceremonial centers of the Natchez and Creek have been excavated and dated back to the 17th century. Prehistoric Mandan, Pawnee, and Arikara cultures are known in detail, and so are Iroquois, Eskimo, and a host of others.

For more than four decades I have studied and taught the saga of peoples whose individual adventures can never be told. But what can be known of their cultures excites my deep admiration for their achievements and their close harmony with nature. Now the Indian's adaptability is being challenged anew. And another chapter in his story has already begun.

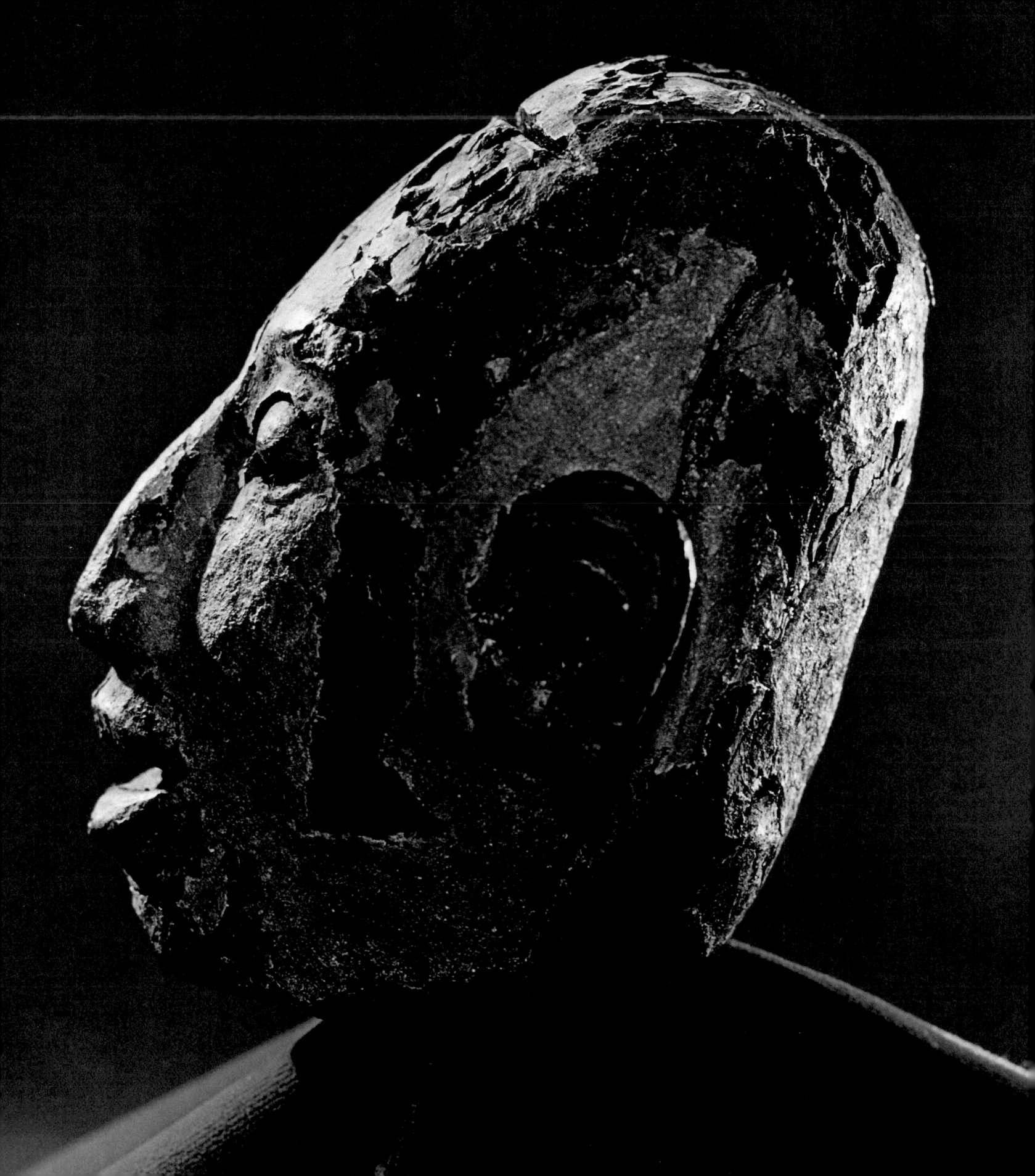

Nomads of the North

David Damas

The day was as cold as any I had known—probably below minus 50° F. Vapor clouds trailed above the panting dogs as they hauled our sledge over a thin cover of snow made gritty by the intense cold. My Eskimo companion and I rode or, when our feet grew too numb, ran alongside the sled until circulation returned. Our track had pointed dead into the wind for the last few days and my cheeks and nose, despite the protection of a parka hood trimmed with wolverine fur, bore painful scabs of frostbite. I was eager to reach our destination: a trio of snowhouses huddled on the sea ice off the eastern tip of Crown Prince Frederik Island, a place known to my Eskimo friends simply as Qiqiktaq, The Island.

My guide and I had been on the trail ten days, traveling through the haze and bright sunlight of a Canadian Arctic winter. From Igloolik, an isolated settlement in northern Foxe Basin, we had set a northwesterly course for Agu Bay in the Gulf of Boothia. Our journey had taken us over the unbroken ice of the narrow strait that divides the mainland from Baffin Island, and we had logged better than 30 miles a day when not pinned down by raging winds and drifting snow.

Now the loom of land in the misty half-light told us the day's journey was nearing its end. Our eyes scanned the gray-white world around us, searching for some signs of snowhouses amid the frost haze and blend of snow on snow.

Then, ahead of us, we saw a few dark objects . . . dogs! Moments later the dome-shaped dwellings materialized from the mist and, simultaneously, a tumultuous chorus of howls shattered the vast and empty stillness. Our dogs and those of the village were sounding the greeting that has welcomed the Arctic traveler for countless years.

I had come to this remote camp inhabited by some 20 Iglulik Eskimos to conduct a genealogical

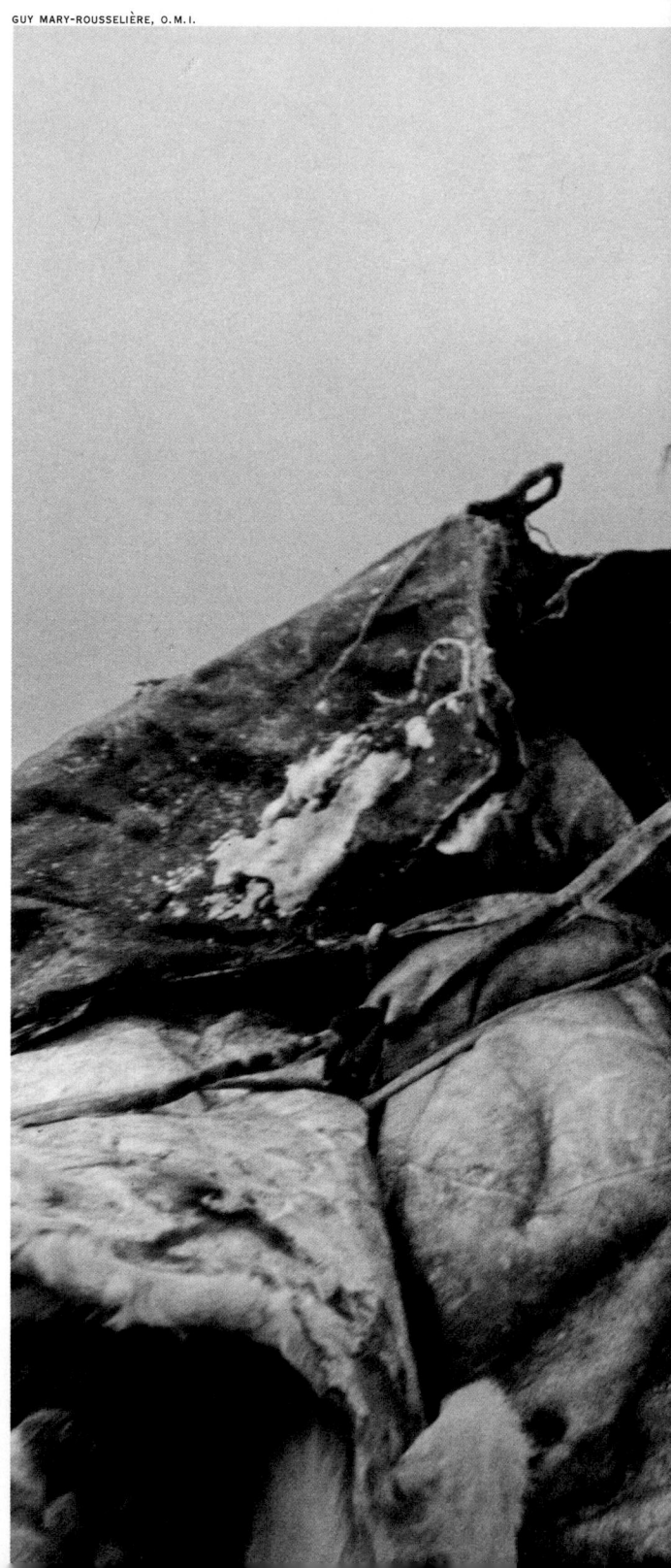

Reliving migrations of a bygone era, a Netsilik Eskimo family treks across the tundra to its autumn fishing camp on Canada's Kellett River. Father carries a three-pronged fishing spear called a leister, while mother (below) checks their sleepy daughter who rides piggyback atop caribou-skin bedding. Dogs, too, earned their keep on these seasonal

GUY MARY-ROUSSELIÈRE, O.M.I.

census—one of several I would undertake during the winter of 1961—and to study a way of life that even then was rapidly disappearing. For me, the next few days and nights were a romantic excursion into the past, a way to recapture something of the customs and traditions of a people still largely untouched by civilization. Here I lived in a snowhouse heated with blubber-fueled lamps. At night I shared with my host family the crowded warmth of a snow sleeping platform. I watched the villagers harpoon seals through breathing holes in the same manner their ancestors had, heard the dogs snarl and yelp over their evening meals, and enjoyed the earthy humor and gentle hospitality of these dwellers of the Far North. It was an experience I shared with early explorers— one that can no longer be enjoyed.

The land of the Eskimo is truly vast, stretching 4,000 miles from eastern Siberia to Greenland. It is forbidding country, treeless, clouded with insects in summer, and beset by gales and sunless gloom in the depths of winter. Although snowfall is generally light (there is less precipitation in many Arctic areas than in the Sahara), much of what snow does fall stays on the ground until well into the next summer. Summers are brief and cool—a time when the green of the tundra plains

journeys over the barrens, packing 40- to 50-pound loads
on their backs in summer or hauling sledges in winter.
Even pups and children carried bundles scaled to their
strength. The scene, reenacted for a filmed documentary,
is a fading memory among today's northland people. Most now
live in permanent settlements — in prefabricated houses.

ago, they moved to Alaska and to the eastern extremity of Asia. These people eventually developed the culture known as the Arctic Small Tool Tradition, distinguished chiefly by tiny, exquisitely fashioned stone implements.

They spread northeastward across the uninhabited top of the continent — perhaps because unlike ancestral Indians they already were adept at hunting sea animals — and reached Greenland by about 2,000 B.C. In the eastern Arctic their tradition developed into the Dorset culture, hunters of seal and caribou who worked with stone tools and lived in skin tents raised on low stone walls. They probably invented the snowhouse and, as evidence of their passing, left an archeological legacy of superbly crafted objects such as projectile points, amulets, toys, and figurines.

Meanwhile, in the western Arctic, along the coast of the Beaufort Sea, a culture known as Thule emerged. Although skilled at hunting creatures of both land and sea, the Thule people were especially noted as whale hunters. They ranged the open waters in skin-covered boats — kayaks and the larger umiaks — in search of sea mammals. They had sleds drawn by dogs and probably wore caribou-skin clothing. Their domed, semisubterranean dwellings had walls and roofs of sod laid over slabs of limestone and rafters of whale rib.

About A.D. 800, the Thule people began a rapid sweep eastward. In less than 300 years they overran the entire Arctic, reaching Greenland by way of Ellesmere Island and absorbing the Dorset people. They settled the ice-free shores of Greenland and roamed as far south as Labrador.

Then, beginning about 1200, the climate began to change. Summers grew shorter, winters colder and longer. Sea ice gradually choked off the straits, basins, bays, and inlets of the Canadian archipelago even in summer, severely restricting the

contrasts sharply with the brownish gravels of low glacial ridges and the blue of numberless lakes. Not all the Arctic is flat and featureless. In parts of Alaska and eastern Canada, glacier-wreathed mountains rise from the sea, and in Greenland, deep, green, fingerlike fjords probe the great ice cap that covers most of the land.

The Arctic can also be a place of great beauty — brilliant auroral displays, vivid polychrome skies, exuberant bursts of summer growth. Its waters, and at times the tundra itself, teem with animal life. A harsh land, yes, but the Eskimos learned early to cope with its rigors.

No one knows exactly when or how the ancestors of today's Eskimos arrived in North America, only that they were the last aboriginal people to populate the continent. Some archeologists believe the original home of these ancestral Eskimos was the surface of the Bering land bridge, and that as the seas rose to inundate it about 10,000 years

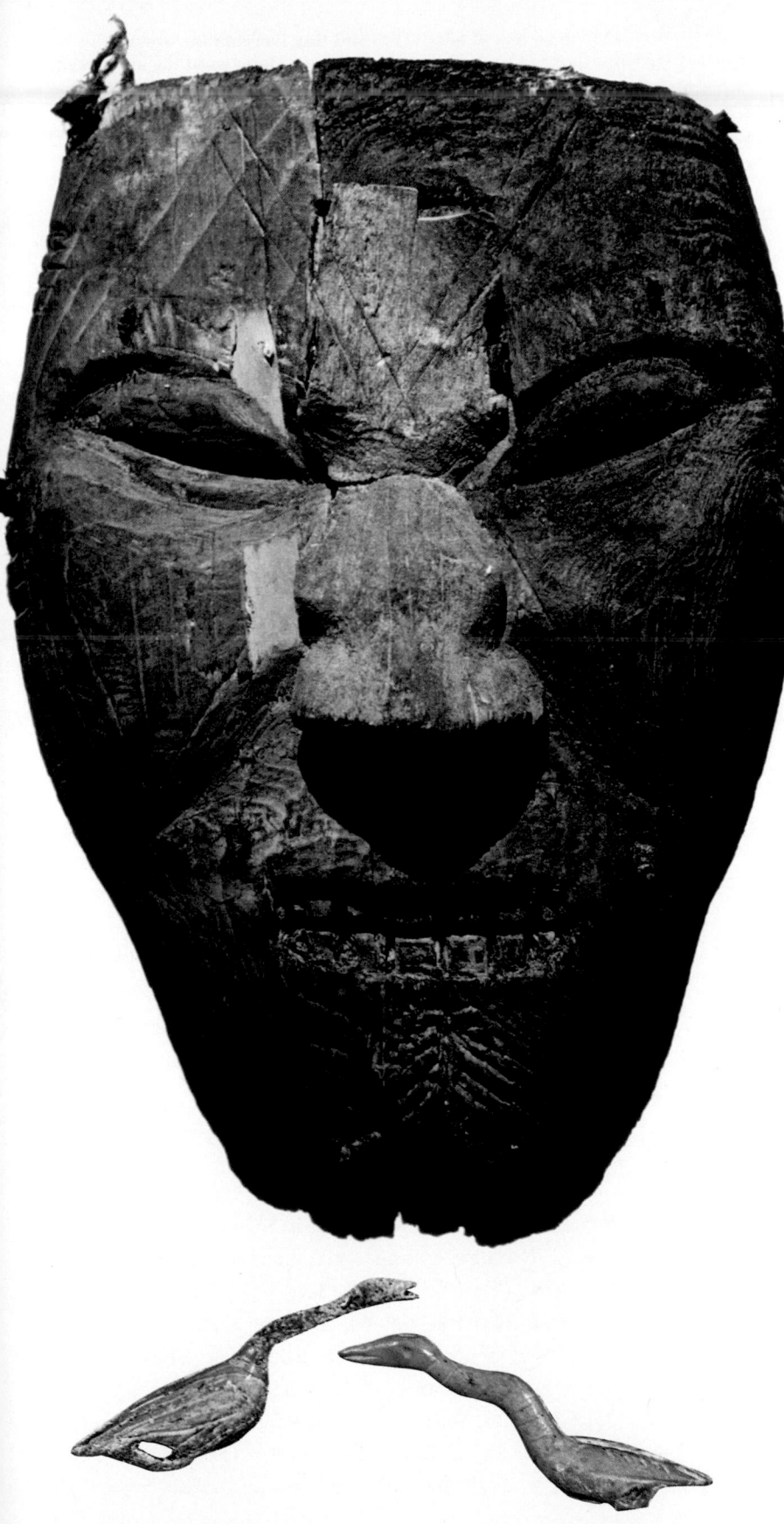

movement of whales. As whaling declined, the Thule people abandoned many of their northernmost islands. They moved south in small groups and took up a nomadic existence in their search for alternate sources of game.

Little is known about the Thule people, although their tools resemble those used by Eskimos in historic times. Bone deposits suggest that both hunted the same animals, and in similar fashion. Bone needles found at old sites indicate that the Thule people, too, wore tailored skin clothing. While predators have scattered most human remains, those that have been found suggest that today's Eskimo descended directly from forebears of Thule and earlier times. Linguists, too, comparing various modern Eskimo and Aleutian languages and dialects, have shown that all of them stem from a single language spoken by the Far North's earliest proto-Eskimo inhabitants.

Eskimo lore recalls the Dorset people as dwarfs, while the Thule people are remembered as giants, mighty hunters who could haul home a 2,000-pound walrus as though it were a mere seal. Relative sizes of Thule and Dorset house ruins probably gave rise to these myths.

The Eskimo of the past was a hunter without peer. He had to be. His powers of observation often were so acute he could retrace a trail traveled once—in his youth. Explorer Knud Rasmussen's guide, Alorneq, readily identified individuals by their footprints and by the way they built their snow huts. Once the two men set out for a distant village in a blizzard so thick "we could scarcely see more than a yard or two ahead....Now and then we could find the trail by lying flat down and scraping the snow away. And when Alorneq ran ahead with his nose right down on the trail it took all my strength to keep dogs and sledge back. At precisely five o'clock the whole team suddenly

Arctic solitaire: Homeward bound after a fruitless day in the field, an Alaskan hunter pauses along the trail through Anaktuvuk Pass. Here, amid the awesome vastness of the central Brooks Range, caribou antlers wedged in a rock cleft mark the course—and assure the traveler that others, too, have passed this way. An Eskimo venturing into unfamiliar country casts frequent glances over his shoulder, committing to memory terrain features that will guide his return trip.

ENTHEOS

disappeared from the surface of the ice and, when we took a closer look, we found that they had rushed into a house passage, and we were in the middle of the . . . settlement. . . ."

I, too, have marveled at the navigational abilities of Eskimos, particularly among the people of eastern Canada who often travel hundreds of miles to visit relatives. But at other times and other places I have been less impressed. Once, near the Bathurst Inlet area of central Canada, my guide and I wandered 27 days on a trip that should have taken no more than a week or two.

Much has been written about Eskimo resourcefulness and mechanical ability. Father Guy Mary-Rousselière, an Oblate missionary in northeastern Canada most of his adult life, tells of two Iglulik Eskimos who sledged 100 miles to recover a tractor abandoned near a radar site. When they found it, its glass fuel-settling bowl was broken, so the men promptly carved a new one from a piece of wood and drove triumphantly back to their village.

But it is my impression that such men are rare. Only one man in a village where I spent nearly a year regularly repaired engines, clocks, rifles, and other equipment. His skill was special, and recognized as such. Far more impressive to me than an individual's skill is the adaptability of all Eskimos to their environment through the ages.

In a land with so few natural resources, Eskimos of former times had to make do with whatever was at hand—bone, hide, sinew, rock, and occasional pieces of driftwood. Around Queen Maud Gulf and other parts of the central Arctic, even driftwood was so rare that Eskimos who lived there believed that forests, like seaweed, grew on the bottom of the sea. I have seen scrapers made of wood and copper, wood and iron, bone, and sandstone,

Winter coats in tatters, caribou thunder across the greening tundra of Alaska's North Slope. "The whole earth seems to be moving . . . one can see neither the beginning of them nor the end," said an old Eskimo, remembering the great herds of his youth. To sustain family and dogs, an inland hunter had to kill 150 or more of these animals a year. Their importance in his life was reflected in his art—here as a motif incised on the handle of an Alaskan bow drill (opposite).

depending on what was available. All were made in the same shape, all used for the same purpose.

Spears, harpoons, sleds, kayaks—even bows—had to be pieced together from lengths of antler or brittle driftwood. To give a bow suppleness, it was backed with strips of sealskin and braided caribou sinew. And if there was no wood for a sled, a serviceable one could be made with runners of frozen hide and crosspieces of antler or even frozen fish lashed together. Salt from dog urine might serve as bait for caribou pitfall traps, and tightly coiled whalebone strips embedded in frozen blubber balls sometimes made "death pills" for unsuspecting wolves. Swallowed whole, the fist-size lumps thawed and the baleen coil sprang open, splitting the animal's stomach.

But perhaps the Eskimo's greatest triumphs were his clothing, his kayak, and his *igluvigaq*—snowhouse. (The term "igloo" simply means "house," anything from a sod hut to a modern, two-story frame dwelling.)

A winter outfit of caribou skins—a pair of boots and boot linings, two suits of trousers and hooded jackets, and a pair of mittens—weighs about ten pounds and can keep its wearer warm in the coldest weather. An Eskimo wore the inner suit with the fur next to the body, the outer one with the fur facing out. Air warmed by the body remained trapped among the hollow hairs of the inner garments as well as between the two suits. In warm weather only the inner layer was worn; and where caribou were scarce or nonexistent, Eskimos improvised with sealskin (heavier and less pliant than caribou), polar bear fur (much heavier than caribou), fox, eider down—even dog. An adult's caribou wardrobe required seven or eight hides, preferably from animals killed in summer when the hair was less than half an inch long.

Hunched over a seal's breathing hole, a Pelly Bay Eskimo watches for signs of his prey. Its approach creates a rush of air that stirs a swan's down indicator suspended in the cavity. The hunter then harpoons his quarry sight unseen and chops the hole large enough to land it. In late spring Eskimos stalked seals basking on the ice by mimicking them: slithering through puddles of meltwater and pretending to doze or scratch for lice until close enough to hurl a harpoon.

GUY MARY-ROUSSELIÈRE, O.M.I. OPPOSITE: FRED BRUEMMER

The kayak, sleek, swift, and silent, is one of the most beautiful and efficient hunting boats ever devised. Fashioned of skins of seal or caribou stretched tightly over a driftwood frame lashed together with thongs, it is light enough to be carried by one man and is extremely maneuverable — an ideal craft for chasing seals or for hunting caribou as they swim across lakes and rivers.

The umiak, an open, hide-covered boat up to 30 feet long, originally was used to hunt whales and walruses. Its tough, supple covering made it nearly impervious to damage by chunks of drifting ice and, as explorer Vilhjalmur Stefansson noted, it could carry a cargo much larger than a 28-foot wooden whaleboat which was three or four times heavier than the one made of hide. Because the umiak stowed more than a ton, it was also used to transport families over open water when shifting from one summer camp to another. "It is a gay sight to see one of these vessels," writes Danish anthropologist Kaj Birket-Smith. "It is packed to the gunwale with skin tents, boxes, cooking pots, skin bags full of clothing or blubber, big pieces of bloody seal meat, children, and puppies. The women row with short, quick strokes. . . . In the stern sits the head of the family with the steering oar, and a number of men follow in their kayaks like torpedo boats escorting a dreadnought."

The snowhouse, an unsupported dome erected by placing blocks of wind-packed snow in an inward-leaning spiral, served as a winter home throughout the central Arctic region. Working with a long-bladed snow knife of antler or bone, a man could build a snug shelter for his family in an hour or so, slicing most of the blocks from a circle that would become the sunken floor and the rest from a trench that formed the low, tunnel-like entry. The snowhouse, like the Eskimo's hooded coat, took advantage of the principle that warm air rises. Body heat and the warmth of a stone lamp

Caribou lances within easy reach,
a young hunter maneuvers his graceful
kayak along the shores of Ennadai
Lake, 200 miles west of Hudson Bay.
Craft like these once cruised for game
on inland waters or Arctic seas.
Sixteenth-century explorer Martin
Frobisher, searching for the Northwest
Passage to Cathay, described fur-clad
men paddling among the floes of
Davis Strait "in small boates made
of leather." Now only a few are left,
used mostly by Greenland's Eskimos.

Atop a boulder bench near Pelly Bay
a Netsilik Eskimo kayak takes shape.
Such boats ranged from 15 to 25 feet in
length and weighed 25 to 100 pounds.
Their driftwood frames, lashed together
with sinew, were sheathed in skins
of the bearded seal. Animal oil rubbed
into the covering kept it watertight.

A hooded jacket bound tightly around
face, wrists, and cockpit coaming
kept a hunter dry even in a heavy sea.
To escape the brunt of a wave, a skilled
paddler, according to an early
missionary, "overturns himself quite
so that his head hangs perpendicular
underwater; in this dreadful posture
he gives himself a swing with a stroke
of his paddle, and raises himself
aloft again on which side he will."

FRITZ GORO, TIME-LIFE PICTURE AGENCY.
OPPOSITE: GUY MARY-ROUSSELIÈRE, O.M.I.

near the entry made the abode relatively comfortable even in a gale. Fresh air entered from the tunnel while stale air escaped from a small hole cut in the roof. The snowhouse probably was invented in north-central Canada, and although knowledge of it spread through much of the Arctic, other Eskimos used it only as a temporary shelter while hunting or traveling. Eskimos of Alaska, western Canada, and Greenland normally lived in sod-and-stone huts during the winter. All Eskimos switched to skin tents for the summer.

Eskimos of former times, like other aboriginal people, lived in harmony with the seasons. In the spring, as the sun's rays gathered strength, they hunted seals that came up on the ice to bask. When the ice broke up, the people of Alaska, Greenland, and the eastern Canadian Arctic stayed near the coast to hunt for seals, whales, and walruses. Other groups, such as the Copper and Netsilik Eskimos of north-central Canada, turned inland instead, splitting into small bands to search for caribou. They fished or hunted through summer and well into autumn, when the wandering herds returned to the sparse forests of the south.

Scattered throughout Arctic America are traces of these traditional caribou hunts: long rows of stones set on edge or piled on top of one another. In some places a single row runs along a ridgetop; at other places two rows converge, forming a huge V. The upturned stones, vaguely resembling human forms, acted as "scarecrows" to frighten caribou, and were known as *inukhuit*, "likenesses of men." Near the Perry River one spring I met an old hunter who described hunts of his youth that had made use of these cairns. Whenever caribou were sighted, he said, women and children crept behind the animals and drove them into the open end of the V, funneling them toward hunters concealed in shallow pits where the rows came together. Or, if the drive ended at a lake or stream, kayakers ambushed the animals as they swam. In this way, the old hunter said, it was possible to kill several animals at a time.

As autumn waned, hunters who had gone inland returned to the coast. Women sewed new clothing; men fished or retrieved food caches; and by January groups of 100 or more people gathered on the sea ice to build their snowhouse villages. Here they would spend the winter, hunting seals at breathing holes or walruses along floe edges.

Until recently Eskimos lived almost entirely on meat and fat, much of it eaten raw. Hence their name, Eskimo, which derives from an Algonquian word meaning "eaters of raw meat." But at least once a day they ate cooked meat, boiled in a rich broth. Many Eskimos today prefer to be called *Inuit,* the word for "people" in dialects of Greenland, Canada, and northern Alaska.

In the beginning, according to one myth, there was nothing...no light...no animals...no Inuit. "There was once a world before this," an Iglulik woman told Rasmussen. "But the pillars of the earth collapsed, and all was destroyed. And the world was emptiness.

"Then two men grew up from a hummock of earth. They were born and fully grown all at once. And they wished to have children. A magic song changed one of them into a woman, and they had children. These were our earliest forefathers."

Great Raven, believed the people of Alaska, created light by throwing dazzling pieces of mica into the sky. The creatures of the ocean are the gift of the Great Woman who lives on the bottom of the sea. Although her name differs from tribe to tribe, her tale remains essentially the same: Sedna, as she was known in the central Arctic, was a maiden tricked into marriage (continued on page 90)

GUY MARY-ROUSSELIÈRE, O.M.I.

To Catch a Fish

In the blustery cold of a late autumn day the fisherman waits. Hour after hour he sits or kneels, back to the wind, by the side of a small hole he has chopped in the river's fresh ice. Every second or so he twitches a short baton from which dangles his hookless lure — a strip of belly skin from a salmon or a small piece of ivory carved to resemble a fish. Patiently he peers into the depths, from time to time using a scoop made from musk ox horn to clear away congealing ice. It is lonely, wearying, bone-chilling work and to help ease the hours he sings:

> *Oft do I return*
> *To my little song.*
> *And patiently I hum it*
> *Above the fishing hole*
> *In the ice.*
>
> *This simple little song*
> *I can keep on humming,*
> *I, who else too quickly*
> *Tire when fishing*
> *Up the stream. . . .*

Suddenly, he catches the silvery glint of his prey — a salmon nosing slowly toward the lure. The fisherman moves swiftly, surely, drawing the bait to the surface with one hand while with the other he thrusts the triple-tined fishing spear through the hole. If his aim is

true — like that of the Pelly Bay Eskimo above — the flailing prize is his. To release the impaled fish, the man pries apart the spear's flexible outer prongs of caribou horn and his catch drops free on the ice.

Thus, until recent years, did the caribou hunters of northern Canada occupy the weeks between freeze-up and their trek to the coast to set up winter sealing camps. If the summer hunt had been good, they might not ice-fish at all; otherwise, their daily catch was all that stood between them and hunger.

A good fishing spot was held in almost sacred awe. Pregnant or menstruating women could not approach it, no fish could be eaten near it. To ensure continued luck, a fisherman placed his catch about him in a large circle, heads pointed toward the hole in the ice. Doing so, he believed, enabled the fish's spirit to return to the water and speak favorably of the man who had dealt honorably with him. A fish's head and dorsal fin must never be eaten, water must not be spilled the day a man goes fishing, and his wife must never cook a fish over a lamp that had been used to boil meat.

In a Harsh Land
Every Morsel Counts

"Now we'll all go down!" At the lookout's signal, joyful whoops ring from the tents of the fishing camp on the Kugarjuk near its outlet to Pelly Bay. Men, women, and children spill into the river, heedless of the icy water and the nip of autumn in the air. For the char are running now, shoaling in from the sea to spawn in ancestral lakes and streams. They have entered the dam-like weir that blocks the river and now mill about inside, trapped. The slaughter is on!

"The fish dashed wildly about, in between the legs of the Eskimos, who stabbed away with their leisters," wrote explorer Knud Rasmussen of a scene like the one above. "It was always a riddle to me that in this scuffle . . . the people preserved their toes unscathed."

Soon the excitement is over. Exultant fishermen drag their catches ashore on long thong lines, strewing the tundra with hundreds of chrome-colored fish. Children like the little girl with the wedge-shaped *ulu*, or woman's knife (opposite), soon will feast happily on fish eyes—like candy to an Arctic child—while their

mothers fillet the char and hang them on racks to dry in the sun. Cached beyond reach of prowling carnivores, dried fish provided a midwinter delicacy to palates jaded by a nonstop diet of seal. Eskimos also preserved meat and fish by freezing. Smoke curing, common among Indians, was unknown in a land where every driftwood scrap was precious.

Although in former times the Inuit of north-central Canada mainly hunted seal and caribou, fish were an important dietary supplement, especially in spring and fall when meat supplies ran low. And the land yielded other game—from musk ox and an occasional polar bear to burrowing voles and lemmings.

Birds were snared with seal-thong nets or felled by darts, sticks, and stones. Baleen nooses strung just below the surface of shallow lakes entangled ducks and other waterfowl. Molting geese were herded into large, stone-walled enclosures and killed with sticks. To catch gulls, Eskimos baited hooks of sharpened bone with lumps of meat. In winter they might bait the roof of a small snowhouse, catching the birds through a hole when they landed to take the meat.

Box traps made of rock, pitfalls dug in snow, and deadfall traps caught larger animals such as foxes, wolves—even a few caribou. To catch a wolf, Eskimos occasionally used what one explorer called "the most fiendish trap ever devised"—sharpened splinters of caribou bone set into ice and smeared with blood and fat. When a wolf licked the bait, it slashed its tongue and, goaded by the taste of its own fresh blood, kept lapping until it bled to death. Dogs helped hunt bear and musk ox, holding the quarry at bay until men with bows and arrows or spears rallied for the kill.

Until modern times Eskimos lived on a diet virtually free of vegetable matter. But they ate almost every part of any creature killed, at times including the contents of stomachs. The bulk of their food, lean meat and fat from animals, fish, and birds, provided them with an array of vitamins and minerals, as well as with all the protein and energy needed for an active life under Arctic conditions. Delicacies, too, supplied nutrients: *muktuk*, the raw skin of a white whale or narwhal, was rich in vitamin C. Raw seal liver contained vitamins A and D, and the partly digested shrimp in a seal's stomach made a paste especially rich in minerals.

FRED BRUEMMER

Coaxing hollow, mysterious sounds from a disk-shaped drum, a Netsilik Eskimo sings and dances during Christmas festivities at Pelly Bay; villagers act as a chorus, chanting a mesmeric refrain, often for hours at a time. To play his instrument, the dancer twirls it so that one side of the rim and then the other strikes the nearly motionless drumstick, vibrating the caribou-skin membrane.
GUY MARY-ROUSSELIÈRE, O.M.I.

with a stormy petrel in the guise of a man. She went to live with him, and was miserable. One day her father found her. He tried to take her home in his kayak, but the petrel discovered his wife's escape and stirred a great tempest. The father, in mortal fear, threw his daughter into the water. When the girl tried to cling to his boat, he severed her fingers with a knife. Sedna sank. Now she lives on the bottom of the sea and her missing fingers are her children—whales and seals and walruses.

The spirit world of the Inuit swarmed with supernatural beings. They might not all be wicked, but all had to be placated with taboos, amulets, and magic words or through the ministrations of a shaman—a person empowered to deal with the unknown. Care had to be taken not to offend the spirits of animals that provided sustenance. A seal or walrus killed in a hunt must be offered a drink of fresh water, no bone could be broken while butchering a caribou, creatures of land and sea could not be cooked in the same pot.

Eskimo tribes had various views of the afterlife. Among the Netsiliks, for example, heaven was an indeterminate place reserved for the skillful hunter and the woman with beautiful tattoos. It was a land of plenty, where spirits of the departed played kickball with the laughing skull of a walrus. Hell did not exist, but there was a kind of limbo, "The Land of the Crestfallen," where lazy men and untattooed women sat through eternity with bowed heads—eating only butterflies.

Eskimos have always been fond of songs, dances, games, and contests of strength or skill. When stormbound in the old days an entire village might assemble in a large snowhouse to take part in a drum dance, watch wrestling matches, or witness a shaman's attempt to quell the storm. Often regarded as fatalists, most Eskimos actually are su-

premely practical people who avoid undue risks and seek realistic solutions to problems.

Although some villages had a chief or headman —usually an older hunter with many close relatives—others did not. But even in leaderless communities an exceptionally wise or gifted man might be asked to lead a hunt from time to time. A man was judged by his skill with bow and spear, his courage and indifference to hardship, his respect for parents and kin, and his humility. And if he was willing to share his possessions or the bounty of a hunt, he was highly regarded by all.

A woman was gauged by many of the same traits, as well as by her ability to bear children, and her domestic skills. She cooked and sewed, raised the children, and prepared the skins her husband brought home. "A man is the hunter his wife makes him," Greenlanders say, for without proper clothing no man can long endure the bitter cold. The wife also shared the heavier work: making and breaking camp, hauling a sledge, or backpacking to a new encampment.

Children brought pride and joy to their parents, although groups such as the Copper and Netsilik Eskimos sometimes practiced female infanticide. Cruel environment forced such measures, for food often was scarce and a girl was likely to marry and move away just as she had mastered the household arts. But a boy might be expected to become a hunter, and as such would provide for his parents in their old age. Eskimo children were raised with patience and understanding. "The parents," writes Birket-Smith, "surround them with the deepest affection, give them the best pieces of food to eat, make toys for them and, in their games, teach them their coming work."

An Inuit community had no courts or councils. Taboos and the esteem of his fellows guided a person's conduct. A man's greatest reward was

To pass the time during winter's long and dreary hours, Eskimos take delight in visits—sharing the warm glow of a seal-oil lamp or the camaraderie of songs, dances, and rough-and-tumble games. The women below play *nugluktaq*, trying to poke sharpened sticks through a twirling spindle strung from the ceiling of a large communal snowhouse.

GUY MARY-ROUSSELIÈRE, O.M.I., FOR EDUCATION DEVELOPMENT CENTER, INC.

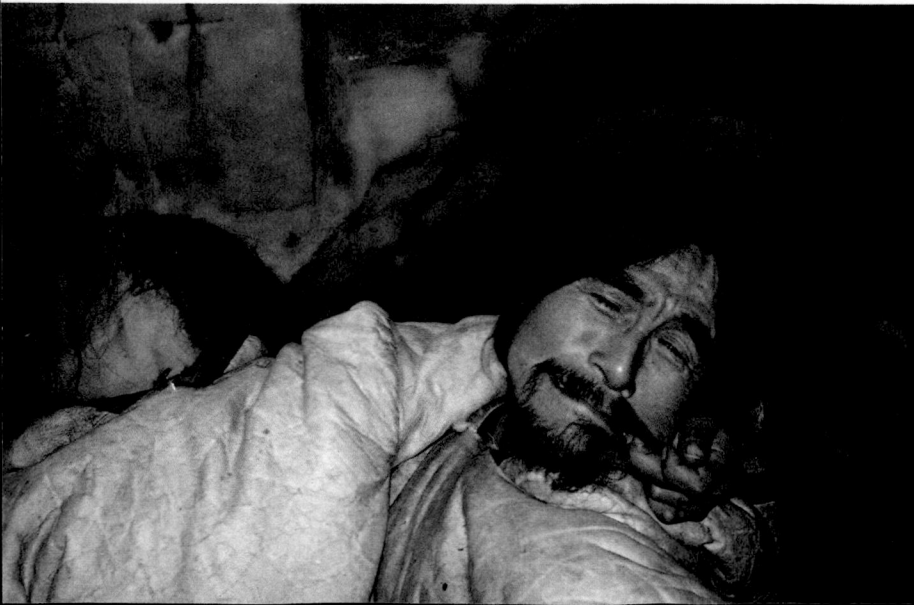

Grimacing men (opposite lower) undergo a painful test of strength and endurance in a round of *iqiruutijuk*. Each tugs at his opponent's mouth until one gives up. Tattoos on arms and legs, achieved by stitching the skin with sooty thread, once were considered marks of feminine beauty. Men of some Alaskan tribes adorned their lower lips with ivory plugs.

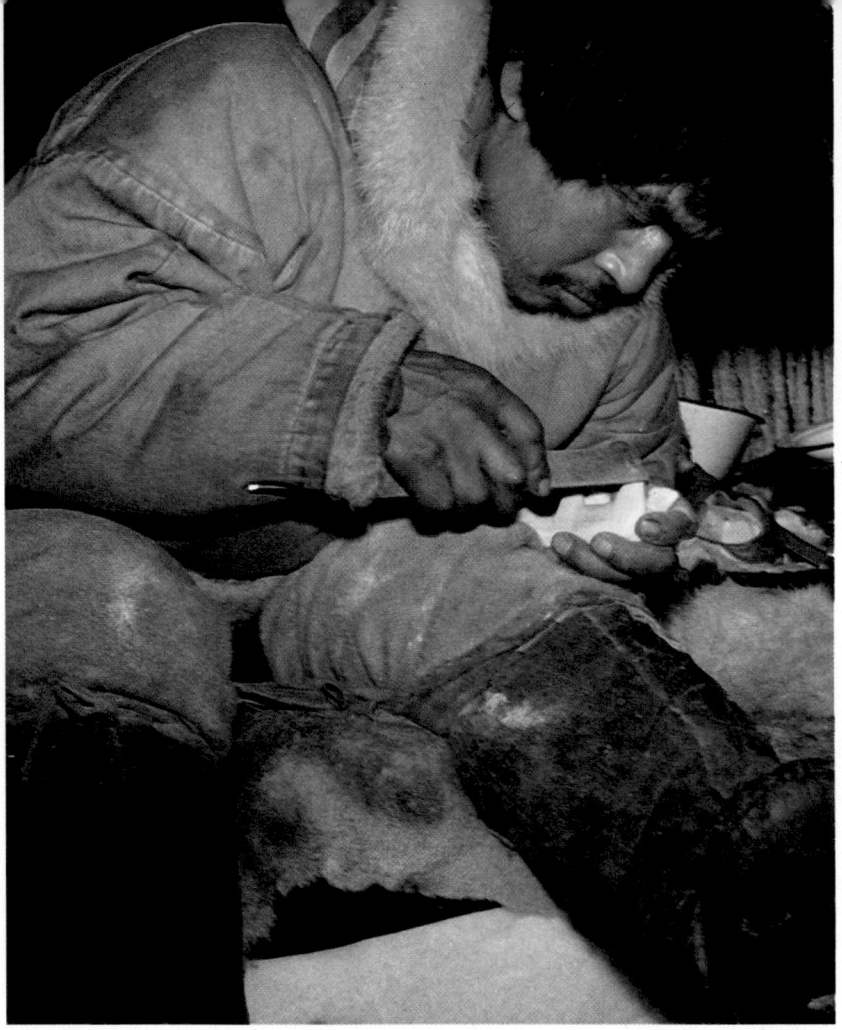

"There is only one great thing," runs an old Eskimo song, "to live, to see ... the great day that dawns, and the light that fills the world." Sunrise—at noon in mid-February—brings a Baffin Island family from its home of snow and turf to celebrate the sun's return after weeks of winter darkness. Pallid rays linger but a few minutes atop the mountains that flank Navy Board Inlet, signaling a time of joy, hope, and renewal across the Arctic's frozen wastes.

In the gloom of winter modern Eskimos carve in stone or ivory. A bear emerges from a piece of walrus tusk in the skilled hands of a Pelly Bay craftsman. His Thule ancestors, using cruder tools, hundreds of years ago fashioned the ivory goggles to ward off snow blindness.

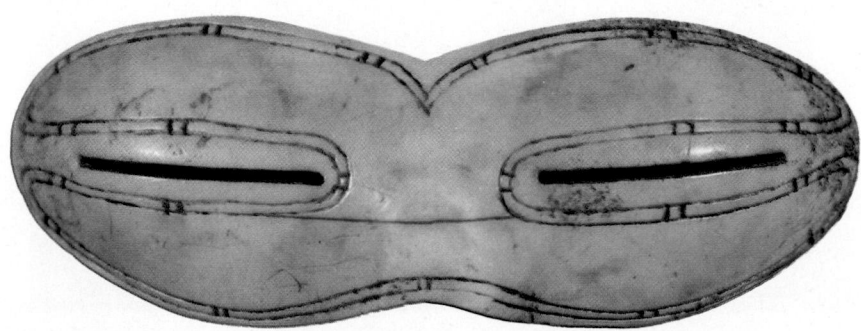

approval by his group; his greatest punishment, ridicule or ostracism. Quarrels usually were settled with insult-singing contests in which the disputants publicly lampooned one another's shortcomings; or, if the quarrel was serious, the two might take turns punching one another, each delivering a blow while the other stood defenseless. Occasionally, murderers, wife stealers, and chronic troublemakers were put to death by common agreement. To avoid a feud between families, a close relative of the condemned carried out the sentence—usually with knife or harpoon.

While much has been written about Eskimo wife swapping, such arrangements seldom were undertaken lightly or promiscuously. Spouse exchange required the consent of all partners involved and almost always served to help forge bonds of kinship between otherwise unrelated families.

Eskimos frequently remained active into their 60's, especially in Alaska and Greenland where life was less strenuous. But in the harsher regions of the central Canadian Arctic, where famine and the rigors of life on the march sapped their energies, older people often asked to be left behind when the group broke camp.

A thousand miles south of the Arctic Circle, on a chain of storm-swept islands marking the southern limit of the Bering Sea, lived the Aleut, hardy seafarers culturally and genetically linked to the Eskimo. Like their neighbors to the north, they wore tailored fur clothing in winter and hunted sea mammals in hide-covered boats. They lived in large semisubterranean houses; their tools resembled those of the Eskimo.

Unlike Eskimos, the Aleut had a structured society that consisted of chiefs, honorables, commoners, and slaves—the latter usually captives taken in raids on neighboring islands. All villages

Soapstone seal hunter
hefts an ivory harpoon

Bulbous walrus
brandishes his tusks

Poised for the thrust, a hunter cocks his weapon arm;
a walrus warily surveys his domain; man and bear lock
in mortal combat—such is the stuff of modern Eskimo art,
glimpses of life fixed in stone and executed with power and
grace. The Eskimo of old knew no word for art or artist.
To him the carving of a soapstone cooking pot, the shaping
of a harpoon head, the creation of a talisman simply
was part of his everyday experience. His work was eminently
practical. By the time he reached adulthood, a male had
to be able to work with wood, bone, ivory, and stone to make
tools and weapons needed for survival. Lifelike animal
figurines—probably made to propitiate spirits—show a keen
understanding of anatomy gained by practice in butchering.
Contact with the outside world in recent years has lent new
impetus to his practicality—now he carves for money too.

THE WINNIPEG ART GALLERY, TOM PRESCOTT.
OPPOSITE AND LEFT: VICTOR R. BOSWELL, JR., NATIONAL GEOGRAPHIC PHOTOGRAPHER

**Hunter stabs
an ivory-toothed bear**

Man's Arctic companion, chained to a whale-rib post, gives voice to a soulful howl beneath the midnight sun. Dogs like these once were indispensable to life in the Far North. A team of six or eight could haul a sledge 20 or 30 miles a day; they helped hunt musk ox and bear, and sniffed out seals' breathing holes. But as the old ways vanish, dogs, too, are disappearing—replaced by snowmobiles.

THOMAS J. ABERCROMBIE, NATIONAL GEOGRAPHIC STAFF

on an island were united under an over-all ruler and each village was governed by a chief. He and his relatives formed a class of honorables who amassed wealth—furs, shells, and slaves. Slaves worked at menial tasks such as paddling or carrying water, and although generally well treated, their lives hung on the whim of their masters.

Russian explorers discovered the Aleutian Islands in 1741. Waters teeming with fur seals, sea otters, and other mammals soon drew traders and trappers who left a bloody record of murder, rape, pillage, and slavery. What the sealers didn't destroy, famine and disease did. From a population of about 20,000, only a few hundred remained when the United States acquired Alaska in 1867. In the years since, their numbers have increased slowly to about 6,000 people.

In the "land of little sticks"—the taiga forests of northern Canada—lived the nearest Indian neighbors of the Inuit. These were tribes divided into two major language groups: Algonquian and Athapaskan. Algonquians inhabited the eastern subarctic from below Hudson Bay to Labrador and lived somewhat like woodland Indians farther south. Athapaskans roamed from Lake Athabasca in central Canada to Alaska's Yukon River.

Like their neighbors of the tundra, northern Indians led nomadic lives, fishing the streams and hunting moose, caribou, and bear with little regard for boundaries. Unlike Eskimos, they ate only cooked meat—boiled in bark or hide containers. In summer they preserved meat by smoking it.

Athapaskans and northern Algonquians paddled the waterways in birch-bark canoes, wore caribou-hide clothing, and lived in conical tents made of skin or bark. In the deep, soft snows of the forest, they traveled on snowshoes, and pulled their belongings on spruce-plank toboggans.

Hunting groups of three or four families and their kin frequently trekked and camped together for months at a time. Several groups might hunt or fish cooperatively during a fish run or when a large caribou herd entered an area. Such gatherings provided occasions for marriages to be arranged, and for games and ceremonies.

Contact with the white man profoundly affected the lives of these Indians. The growth of fur trapping as a livelihood curtailed seasonal migrations; diets changed as flour, tea, and sugar supplemented meat, fish, birds, and berries. By the end of the 19th century, most subarctic Indians wore cloth instead of skin garments in the summer, and their skin tents and birch-bark canoes gave way to products made of wood and canvas. Today most live in settlements built around trading posts, schools, missions, and government facilities.

As it was with the Indian, so it was with the Eskimo. White men's diseases brought death and depopulation; in areas of heaviest contact, nine tenths of some Inuit groups fell to smallpox, measles, influenza. World War II, and establishment in the 1950's of radar stations across the Arctic, hastened the end of traditional ways. By 1970 Inuit hunting camps had virtually disappeared.

Today Eskimo populations are increasing, but the Eskimo lives between two cultures, belonging entirely to neither. He may read and write in Eskimo, English, Danish, or Russian, and only a few elders remember the old tales and traditions. He lives in a large community—in an oil-heated, prefabricated house—with a school, a public health center, and a cannery or handicraft industry. But his income does not always sustain him, so he must often depend on welfare. And the howling of his dogs—that ancient Arctic chorus that greeted my arrival at Qiqiktaq—succumbs to the insistent roar of charter plane or motorized sled.

Woodsmen and Villagers of the East

William C. Sturtevant

Their elaborate tribal structure had a nobility topped by an exalted royal family called Suns—and a class of lowly commoners called Stinkards. They lived in a fertile land of creeks and canebrakes—cane whose stalks soared 15 feet or more and grew for mile on mile. Waterfowl darkened the skies in such numbers that "the Thunder of their Wings, with their united squaling Tongues exhibits a scene of confusion . . . as if the desolution of Nature was at hand." The French explorer La Salle, traveling down the Mississippi in 1682, found the tribe the "largest, strongest and proudest" on the lower reaches of the river. They were the Natchez Indians.

Their palisaded villages clustered a few miles from the Mississippi near the present-day city of Natchez. An early French account put the tribe's population at perhaps 5,000, but added that their numbers had decreased by a third in the six years after the explorers first came down the river. "It appears," related the chronicler, ". . . that God wishes that they yield their place to new peoples." By 1731 the conjecture became fact; the Natchez had been all but wiped out, the remnants scattered.

Time after time that pattern—a native people decimated by the arrival of Europeans—repeated itself among the tribes of hunters and farmers in the eastern woodlands. Their cultures varied as subtly as the change in agriculture from south to north. Their political organizations differed strikingly, shaped even by influences from distant Mexico. Sometimes we know tantalizingly little of their aboriginal ways, for change racing ahead of the white man's advance altered life-styles before observers could record them. But the story of the woodland Indians—their societies, their adaptations to the environment, the colossal clash of cultures that changed their world—is an absorbing one. Consider the Natchez.

Apparition in the snow, an Onondaga wearer of a False Face Society mask glowers with wooden visage. Iroquois belief populated forests with grimacing beings that caused sickness; such medicine societies as the False Faces appeased them. Curing rites threaded lifeways where hunting rivaled farming in importance among cultures of the eastern woodlands.

NATHAN BENN

Colonists of Sir Walter Raleigh's first expedition, sailing toward the Carolina coast (below) "smelt so sweet and so strong a smel, as if we had bene in the midst of some delicate garden." That forest fragrance wafting miles offshore had impressed explorers since Giovanni da Verrazano's voyage in 1524. But this was no pristine wilderness the Europeans came

Atop the Natchez' complex social structure sat the Great Sun, an absolute ruler who traced his lineage to the divine sun. When he spoke, reported a French visitor, commoners were obliged "to salute him with three *hous* as soon as he has finished." When he ate, only his wife could join him; if he deigned to leave food for his courtiers, "he pushes the dishes to them with his feet." He rode in a litter or walked on mats lest the ground profane him. And when he died, his wife and all his Stinkard servants were strangled with bowstrings at a great funeral—the "victims deeming themselves... honored to accompany their chief."

Other Suns in the royal family enjoyed deference on a lesser scale; they held the chieftainships of the satellite villages, or key tribal posts there and in the central village where the Great Sun resided. Secondary positions were filled from the ranks of Nobles who made up the rest of the tribe's upper class. Linked to the Stinkards was a

to settle. Indian farmers for centuries had cleared, planted, and moved on, with new growth reclaiming what they abandoned. Though Raleigh's attempts to colonize failed—one group vanishing with only a cryptic "Croatoan" carved on a post as a clue— they opened the first English window into the ways of these native woodsmen-villagers (pink and green areas, cultural map).

higher ranking called Honored Men; male commoners could gain that title through notable exploits in war or through the sacrifice of a close relative at the funeral of a Sun.

Rigid rules about hereditary status and marriage bound Natchez society. Members of the nobility —both men and women—had to choose their spouses from among the Stinkards. Even the Great Sun himself had to marry a commoner.

Offspring of a noble mother took her rank, but those of a noble father were born into the next lower one. Thus children of a Sun father and Stinkard mother would be Nobles, those of a Noble would be Honored Men, and of an Honored Man, Stinkards. Progeny of a female Sun and a Stinkard father, however, would remain Suns. As a result, the eldest male born of the Great Sun's sister, not the ruler's own son, inherited the throne.

Reckoning heritage on the mother's side, as did the Natchez and other matrilineal societies, made at least half the parentage sure—"a fact . . . most certain," tribesmen explained to a contemporary Frenchman, "since the womb can not lie." And giving Stinkards a way of rising into Honored ranking provided an incentive for daring in battle —plus exemption from having to marry a Sun, with its attendant complication of ritual strangulation on the death of a spouse.

Natchez tribesmen tattooed their bodies. Men plucked beards with mussel-shell tweezers, women blackened their teeth by chewing ashes. In summer they wore merely "a piece of cloth or skin with which they conceal what ought to be concealed," and in winter donned skin robes or cloaks made from turkey feathers.

Men hunted deer, bear, and other game. Women carried the kill home. But bounteous crops of maize, beans, and squash made the Natchez a nation of farmers, working fields with mattocks made from hickory or shoulder blades of bison.

Natchez houses had thatched roofs and walls made of poles plastered with mud. Their villages had a broad square, with the chief's house and a temple facing each other across the expanse. Both structures stood atop large mounds, built by tribesmen carrying basketloads of earth. At daybreak the Great Sun went to the temple, blew tobacco smoke to greet "the rising of his elder brother," then, with a wave of his hand, showed "the direction . . . he must take in his course."

Disease, tribal wars, and clashes with the French thinned the Natchez ranks. Finally, in retaliation for an attack on a white settlement, the French in 1731 destroyed the Natchez villages, sold even the Great Sun and his family into Caribbean slavery. The sprinkling of survivors melded with nearby tribes. Thus disappeared a notable remnant of the ancient Temple Mound culture, a tribe whose towns and ceremonies and social hierarchy hint strongly of influences from Mexico.

Similar small states once existed all along the Gulf coast. Normally a flourishing agriculture makes possible the leisure time and the marshaling of manpower needed to create such realms; nomadic hunters pressed constantly to search for food seldom develop elaborate societies. But on the western tip of the Florida peninsula, Spanish explorers met a highly organized people who knew no agriculture except perhaps the raising of a few gourds. These were the Calusa Indians.

For them, the sea offered the bounty that permitted their advanced religious and political activities. Observers wrote that they lived "only on fish and roots." When Pedro Menéndez de Avilés, founder of St. Augustine, visited the Calusa in 1566, he and his men were entertained with a ceremonial meal of "many (continued on page 110)

"The Manner of Their Fishing"

In a score of paintings John White, who as governor of the Raleigh colony went back to England for supplies in 1587 and escaped his countrymen's fate, carefully recorded tidewater Indians of North Carolina. His scenes portray ways typical of Algonquian tribes over much of the northeast. Often his paintings are composites, cataloging activities rather than specific events. Here he shows Algonquian fishermen using paddles to propel dugout canoes, boating their catch with multi-pronged spear and dip net, attracting fish at night with a fire blazing on a clay hearth amidships. In the shallows Indians set weirs and spear fish with "longe Rodds" pointed with "prickles of . . . fishes." Coastal peoples also gathered clams, mussels, and other shellfish, and took shad in "great store . . . for sweetness and fatnes a reasonable good fish."

Their rype corne ti

Their greene corne

Corne newly sprong.

Their sittmg at meate.

"Sitting at Meate" in the Village of Secotan

John White's illustrations supply keys to the past that the enduring bones and artifacts of archeological digs cannot: the appearance of things made from perishable skins or feathers or wood, and the way people looked, dressed, acted. Little is known about White, yet no other early artist has left so full a record from which to read the aboriginal culture of a group of Indians.

His watercolor of the village of Secotan, probably located on the banks of the Pamlico River near the present Bonnerton, North Carolina—limns an entire agricultural season, from corn "newly sprong" in individual hills to fully grown stalks. In a shelter erected among the "rype corne" sat a watchman who made "continual cryes & noyse" to shoo away "fowles, and beasts." Sixteenth-century engravings based on White's drawings, with notes by a scientist accompanying the Raleigh colonists, elaborate on the scenes. They show plots of pumpkins and tobacco. Coastal Algonquians also grew sunflowers, making bread and soup from the seeds, and collected such plants as amaranth, whose leaves made a vegetable and whose ashes yielded salt.

Houses tidewater Indians built along village streets had pole frameworks covered by bark or by mats made of rushes—usually the stalks of cattail. The mats could be rolled up to give light and air. In his painting White omitted some of the matting to reveal hard-packed dirt floors and platforms used for lounging and sleeping. He shows people hunting, walking a path to the river "from whence they fetch their water," eating. "They

solemnise their feasts in the nigt, and therfore they keepe verye great fyres to auoyde darkness." The couple squatting on a mat illustrates his reliability. Artists of this early period often gave Indians a European look; White's bent-legged diners have a decidedly non-European posture, though one common among other peoples. The wood platter probably holds hominy—corn treated with lye to remove hulls, then puffed by boiling. Ground corn also was made into mush, into a soup to which meat might be added, and into bread cooked on hot stones. Game and fish of many kinds abounded, to be grilled or smoked on racks.

Men wore hair shorn to a roach, or cut short on one side "that it might not hinder them by flappinge about ther bow stringe when they draw it to shoott." Women used two shells to "grate away the haire of any fashion they please." Clothes, of deerskin, might be a loose mantle, or breechclout and leggings. The latter, which left hip and thigh bare, were adopted two centuries later by young white blades on the Pennsylvania frontier. This nudity "in places of public worship," commented an elderly observer recalling his youth, "did not add much to the devotion of the young ladies."

PAINTINGS BY JOHN WHITE, C. 1585; BRITISH MUSEUM, LONDON

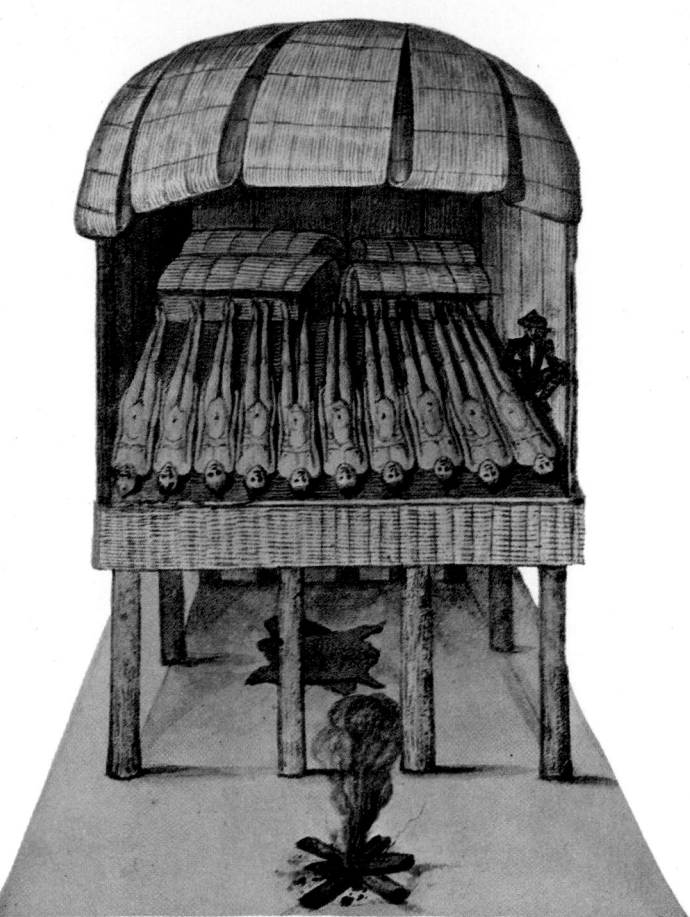

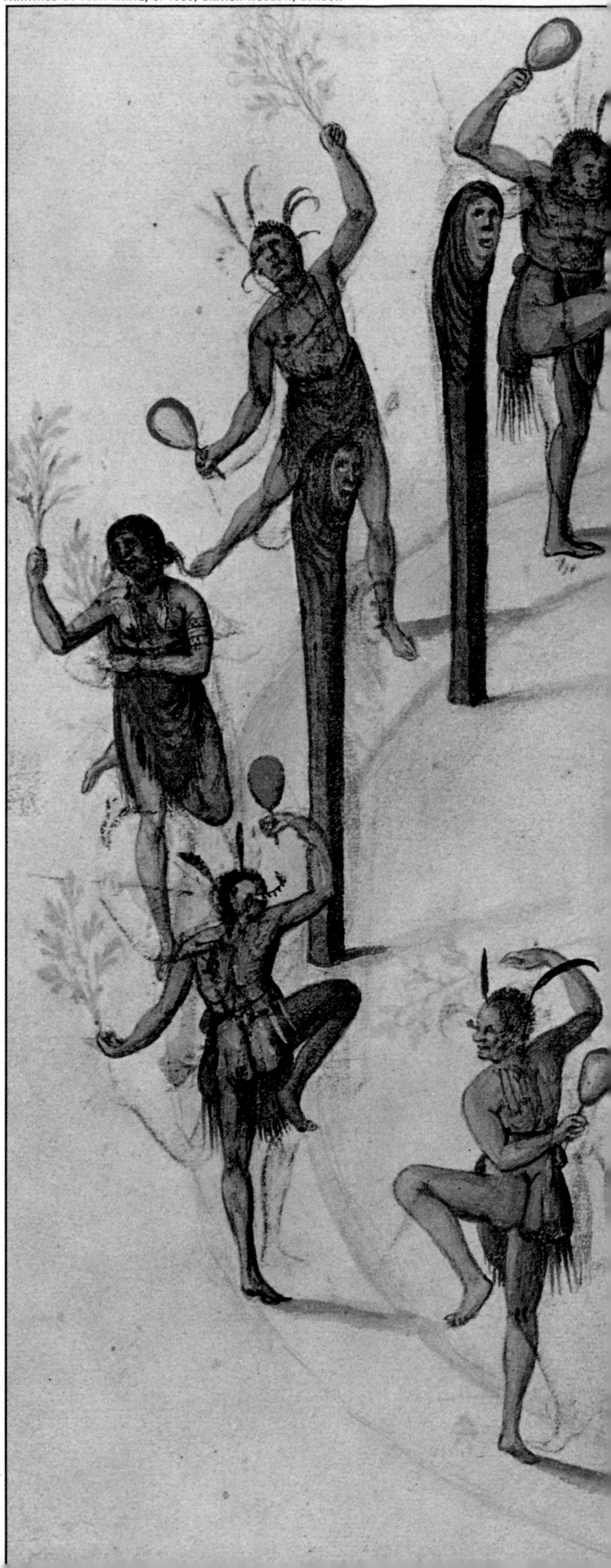

"Strange Jesturs and Songs Dansing Abowt Posts"

For tidewater Algonquians, ceremonial dances seemed a "sport . . . almost as frequent and necessary as their meat and drynck." John White painted one such affair with Indians circling stakes topped by carved faces. Similar chiseled posts were built into temples by the Delaware tribe; the countenances suggest masks of the Iroquois False Face Society. Both men and women danced, stepping "with all the antick postures they can invent." Bodies were painted—Algonquians used plant and mineral pigments mixed with animal fats—and tattooing was practiced, legs, hands, breasts, and faces "cunningly imbroidered with diverse workes."

White also depicted burial customs in a watercolor of the tomb of their "cheefe lordes." Ordinary persons were interred, but bodies of chieftains were preserved in a temple guarded by a carved idol. Retainers removed the skin, which they cured by drying and oiling; they picked the flesh from the bones, wrapped the skeleton in leather, then replaced the skin. A guardian priest bedded on hides under the temple.

kinds of very good fish, boiled and roasted, and . . . oysters, without anything else."

This tribe of "great fishermen and divers" had a chief the Spaniards called Carlos, "most powerful of all that coast," who held sway over "more than seventy towns of his own, without counting another . . . great number which pay him tribute."

Carlos's capital is thought to have stood on an island in Estero Bay. There a symmetrical, 30-foot-high mound built of shells, sand, and debris dominates the mangrove-matted landscape. Down such a mound a parade of masked Indians filed from their temple to meet the Spaniards. In the showy procession marched the "nobles and captains" and the "principal men" who had religious and political roles in the stratified society.

How copious the sea was in providing the food base for this advanced culture can be surmised from the tremendous shell middens that dot the region. One heap covered more than 70 acres to a depth of as much as 15 feet; from one small section mined for construction work in recent decades came 150,000 cubic yards of material.

Halfway up the Florida peninsula, where agriculture again became dominant in tribal economies, lay the territory of the Timucua. French colonists who settled briefly among the Timucua found them "very gentle, courteous, and good natured." They had clans and a caste system, the commoners paying "great obedience to their kings, elders, and superiors." The French likewise accorded respect to Timucua chiefs. One contemporary sketch showed Indian and French commanders with arms about each other; to depict the chief's importance, the artist drew him half a head taller than the rest.

Similar regard appears in accounts of Spanish expeditions that came to establish missions

Misty, watery woodlands that Henry David Thoreau one day would characterize as "all mossy and moosey" provided a homeland for Algonquian tribes of New England. Their small villages and ways of life resembled those of the tidewater Algonquians portrayed by John White. But a shorter growing-season made farming less important than hunting, fishing, and gathering wild fruits and berries. And touches of the shamanism and hunting magic of nomadic tribes to the north appeared in their culture.

Bark that grows in sheetlike layers gave the paper birch its name—and Indians of the cool, moist woodlands a versatile resource. Outer layers of the bark were thick and white, inner ones were thin and brownish. The size of the tree and the time of year it was cut influenced use. Bark peeled in spring when it was heaviest went into canoes, shaped

"INDIAN ENCAMPMENT ON LAKE HURON," BY PAUL KANE, C. 1845; ART GALLERY OF ONTARIO, TORONTO, LEFT: CHARLES STEINHACKER

and colonies. Not only did the Spaniards refer to the "Kings" and "Queens" and "Nobles" of the tribes, but they treated them as such. And the same was true of the English at Jamestown.

Powhatan, the powerful chief in whose territory the James River colonists settled, received a crown and mantle on orders from England's King James I. In turn he had regally greeted the redoubtable Capt. John Smith while ensconced "upon a seat like a bedstead . . . covered with a great robe, made of rarowcun [raccoon] skins, and all the tayles hanging by." Powhatan's actual name was Wahunsonacock, but the English called him and his realm by the name of his favorite village.

When Jamestown was founded in 1607, Powhatan ruled more than 200 towns, whose inhabitants paid him "eight parts of ten tribute of all commodities which their country yieldth, as of wheat, pease, beanes . . . skyns, and furrs." Curiously, his fiefdom stood unique in the great sweep of tribal groups along the Atlantic seaboard. His was a conquest state. Evidence suggests that he had six towns under him when he became chief

dark-side out on a cedar frame, sewed with spruce roots, and caulked with pine gum. Big trees were felled to obtain coverings for canoes and wigwams, either dome-shaped or conical. Small pieces cut from standing trees made torches, scrolls, buckets, boxes, pots. From cradle decoration to winding sheet, *wigwass*—birch bark—spanned Indian life.

and that he vanquished the rest in the decades
before Jamestown's founding.

The structure of his state looks surprisingly
European. Years earlier — in 1561 — a Spanish ship
had touched in the region and taken a captive
back to Spain. That Indian, baptized Don Luis de
Velasco, returned in 1570 with a party of Jesuit
missionaries. But he promptly decamped, and a
few months later led an Indian raid which killed
all the priests. Don Luis had acquired an education in European ways through stays in Mexico
and the West Indies as well as Spain; he apparently came from a politically powerful Indian family
— perhaps Powhatan's own. It is intriguing to
speculate whether Don Luis's influence might
have been involved in the disappearance of Raleigh's Roanoke colony — and perhaps affected the
structure of Powhatan's state.

Villagers under Powhatan's sway spoke related
languages of a great language family known as the
Algonquian. One of the most widespread on the
continent, it extended from the Carolinas to Newfoundland and west to the Great Lakes region and
beyond. A wedge of Iroquoian-speaking peoples
divided the Algonquian into an upside-down V,

undergrowth was burned to lure deer partial to tender
shoots of regrowth. More often drives were held; explorer
Samuel de Champlain told how Indians howling like wolves
and beating on shoulder-blade bones chased quarry into
a stockade. Spring snares also took game; William Bradford
of Plymouth once got caught in one such "very pretty device."

one leg skirting the Atlantic coast. Most of these woodland tribesmen—Iroquois and Algonquian—combined hunting and agriculture as a way of life.

From Virginia into New England existed a series of small, more or less independent communities with a gradual shifting in dialects and types of social and political structures. Usually towns stood beside garden plots strung along streams that cut the Atlantic coastal plain, which tapers from broad in the south to narrow in the north. In spring the people planted their crops, then moved to camps along river or seashore for a summer of fishing and collecting shellfish. In autumn they returned to their villages for the harvest and to gather wild fruits and hunt game—including turkey "of an incridible Bigness" and animals "very fatt in the Fall of the Leaf," an early observer reported. There were also wild onions that "eate well . . . in sallet or in bakt meats."

Tribal populations tended to be denser in the north—nearly three times more people per square mile in coastal New York and Connecticut than in Virginia and North Carolina. Perhaps, one authority suggests, the narrow plain brought shore and upland close together and so provided an easier, more varied subsistence. Denser populations thus could be supported.

The land impressed European explorers with the "mildnesse of the ayre, the fertilitie of the soyle, and situation of the rivers." They noted particularly that it was "thick sett with woodes of divers sort"—forests that perfumed the air for miles out to sea. The Indians who farmed this region cleared their plots by girdling trees with stone axes, then burning the killed timber and underbrush. The ashes helped fertilize the soil.

Dead trees and stumps remained. Among them tribal farmers poked holes in the ground with a

Turtle

Wolf

Bear

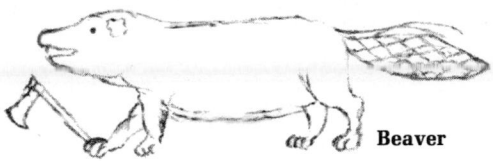

Beaver

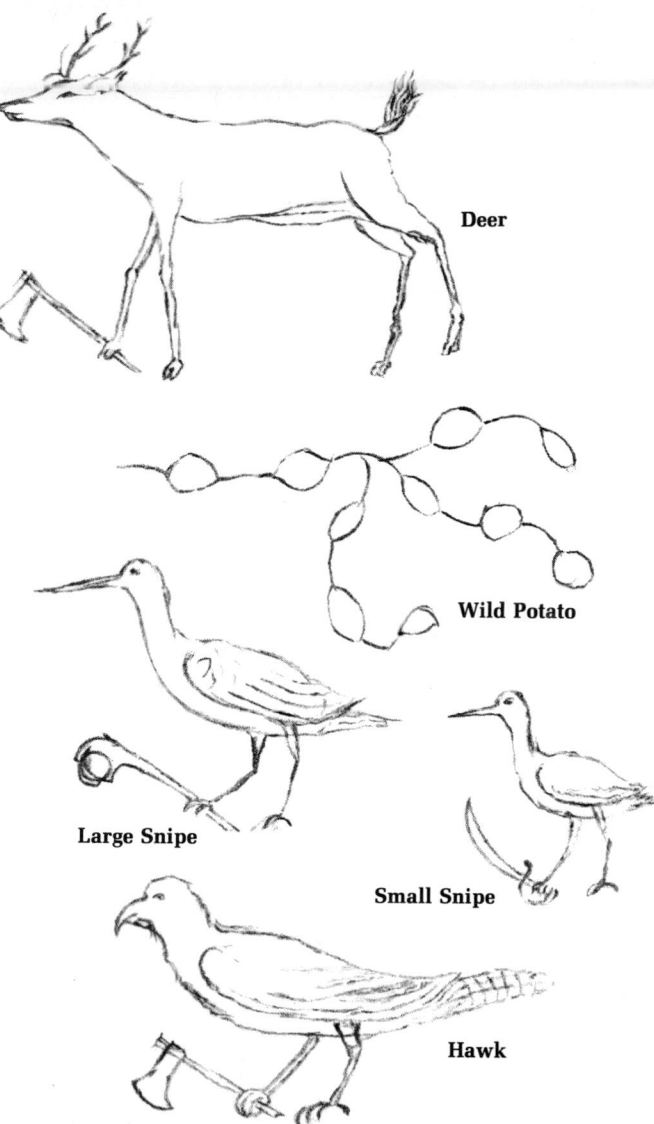

Deer

Wild Potato

Large Snipe

Small Snipe

Hawk

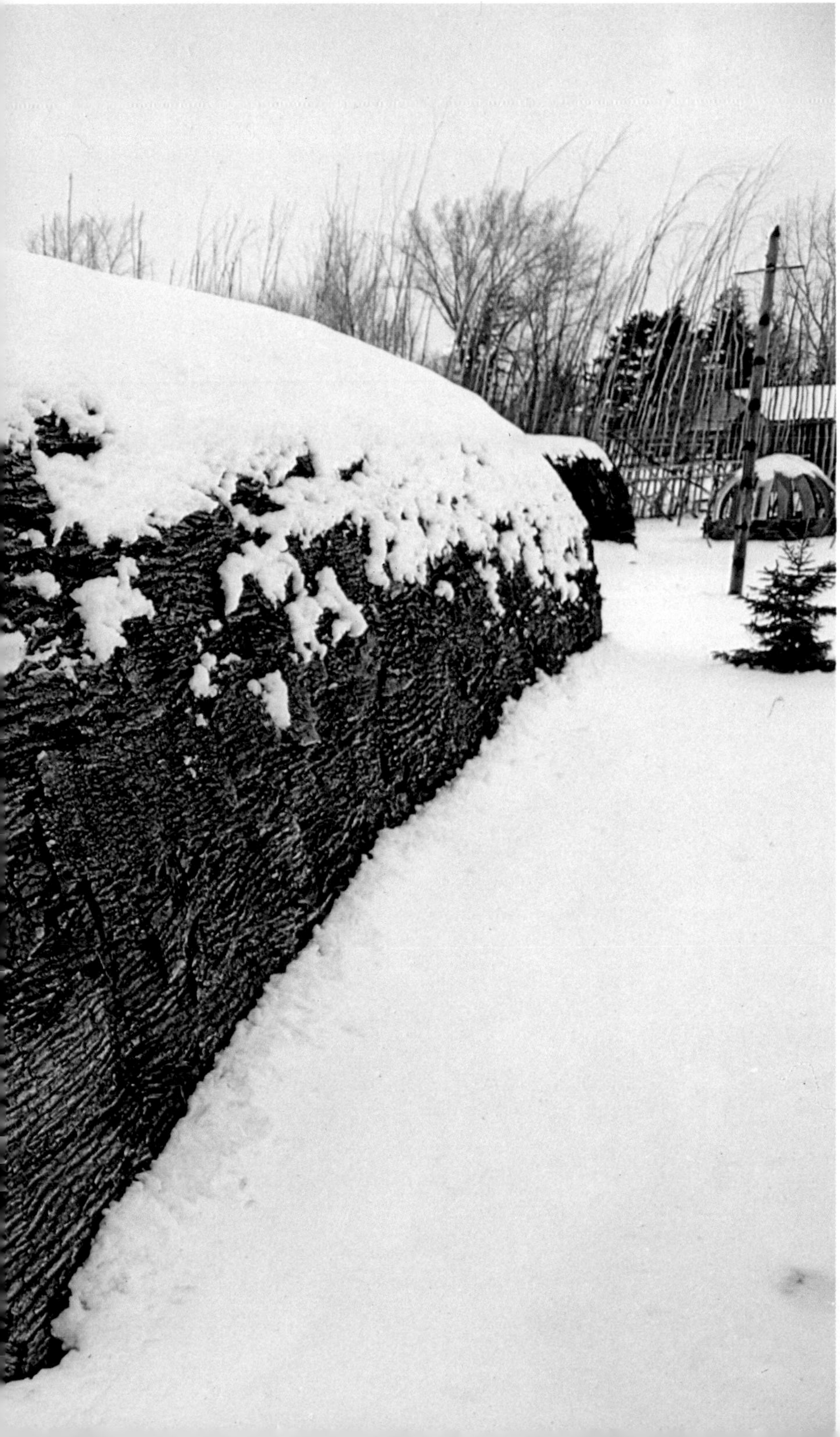

Hodínonhsonih **– housebuilders – they called themselves in Seneca. They were Iroquois, and they built great houses of poles covered with slabs of bark. Lacking birch, they used elm for home and canoe; their rough bark warcraft – upended against a foe's palisade – doubled as scaling ladder. Iroquois longhouses in historic times stood some 20 feet wide and 150 long, though older ones of as much as 400 feet have been dug up. They sheltered families in compartments facing each other across shared hearths along the aisle.**

Ties by blood and marriage on the female side bound longhouse residents. Children were born into the mother's clan, and each longhouse had a clan totem. A French priest in 1666 recorded clan crests (above) used by the Seneca. In common with other Iroquois tribes, they marked houses with such symbols, painted them on trees to tell what war or hunting party had passed. Clans aligned into moieties, or halves – four clans in an "animal" half, five in a "bird." Moieties drew spouses from each other, had ceremonial duties.

RECONSTRUCTED LONGHOUSE, OWASCO INDIAN VILLAGE; NATHAN BENN.
DRAWINGS AFTER FRENCH DOCUMENT, 1666; ARCHIVES NATIONALES, PARIS

stick to plant their maize and beans and pumpkins, often mixing seeds in the same hill. Bean plants thus might climb a supporting cornstalk. And a legume fixed nitrogen in the soil for another plant which could benefit from it; Europeans accomplished the same end by rotating crops.

Indian agriculture followed the swidden—slash and burn—technique. When farm plots around a village became exhausted, or firewood within easy distance used up, the Indians moved. Another village was built, other plots cleared. And in 10 or 15 or 20 years the same thing happened again. Each time new timbered growth reclaimed the land. The process had gone on for century upon century. Thus when Europeans arrived, the wooded valleys and lowlands where Indians lived had been cycled and recycled by swidden farming; they weren't the "forest primeval" the "discoverers" eulogized.

In European eyes the red man's mixed crops, irregular plots, and scrabbling in the ground didn't count as proper farming. And a peculiar contradiction resulted that persists today. Indians got tagged as wandering hunters from whom whites had a right to claim land for better use. Yet at the same time Europeans recognized that such crops as corn and squash, and dishes like succotash, hominy, and corn pone, had been adopted from Indian farmers. And that their friendship helped save the early English colonies.

Schoolbook readers learn about the Pilgrims and Squanto and Samoset, who "came bouldly amongst them, and spoke to them in broken English, which they . . . marvelled at." Fishermen, fur traders, and adventurers had been touching along the Atlantic coast since at least the early 1500's, and Squanto and Samoset learned English after being picked up by adventurers some years before Plymouth's founding. Familiar is the story of how

Squanto taught the colonists to put a fish in each corn hill for fertilizer. Not so familiar is the realization that corncribs and husking pins and perhaps even clambakes and husking bees as social institutions trace to Indian sources. So do dozens upon dozens of everyday words and place names—most of which got into English from the tribal languages of Virginia and New England.

Indians, of course, picked up words and tools and traits from the whites. Occasionally time may dim the origin of such exchanges; what one thinks of today as an Indian characteristic may actually be an old-fashioned European one which Indians preserved. For example, splint basketry enjoys a reputation as an Indian craft. Yet evidence argues that Swedish settlers in the Delaware Valley introduced the technique, and that it spread rapidly, replacing containers of fiber once used in this region that lay between the cane basketry of the south and the birch bark of the north.

The light bronze of Indians' skins prompted such early chroniclers as Rhode Island's Roger Williams to believe they were born white but became darkened by "the Sunne and their annoyntings." New England tribesmen often painted and tattooed their bodies, and coated them with fish oil or animal fat—for protection against insects or to help keep warm in winter.

Like their Virginia relatives they lived in wigwams made of poles bent into an arch and covered with bark or mats—sometimes "very little and homely" for temporary camps, or as much as a hundred feet long for winter dwellings. Decorated mats might line the interior. Skins on raised platforms served as bedding. Clay pots and wooden spoons and bowls made up the few utensils.

To the men fell tasks of clearing the land, shaping articles from wood and stone, performing

The Tree That Sheltered the Longhouse

"Brothers, with this belt I open your ears that you may hear ... I clean the seats of the council-house that you may sit at ease." Thus ceremonial wampum and elaborate protocol opened grand councils of the League of the Iroquois. Fancifully depicted with European pose and classical drapery in a 1724 engraving, its members governed a remarkable union of tribes that for a century held two European powers at bay.

The league likened itself to the longhouse that knit Iroquois family life. Tribes held adjacent lands south of Lake Ontario. At the eastern end of the region the Mohawk, whose name meant "people of the flint," held the league title "Keepers of the Eastern Door." In the west the Seneca, "great hill" people, were "Keepers of the Western Door." In mid-region the Onondaga, "on the mountain," became "Keepers of the Central Fire"; most powerful of the tribes, they filled the major posts. The Cayuga, "at the landing," and the Oneida, "of the standing rock," had intermediate positions, geographically and in the council.

Fifty sachems—tribal chiefs—held council seats. The Onondaga, with 14, had the most; seats and titles were inherited by tribe and clan, though women leaders chose the individual sachems. Each of the five tribes had a single vote. Decisions had to be unanimous, and came after a process that put a premium on oratory and diplomacy. The system spread power and responsibility. Repeated at tribe and clan levels, it gave everyone a say; chiefs had to lead, not command. Whites often failed to understand that among many Indian tribes chiefs had less control than the title might indicate.

League members were "brothers," elder or younger depending upon position in the symbolic longhouse. To such tribes as the Delaware the Iroquois were "uncles"—owning that seniority in a military and economic sense as well as in mythical older origin. Other terms—"grandfather," "nephew"—occurred. White coinage of "Great White Father" for the U. S. Government reflected adaptation to this "forest diplomacy."

In his dream of a great peace the legendary founder of the league envisioned a mighty tree sheltering nations in a world of order, law, and justice. Iroquois power was shattered in the American Revolution. But the tribes and the league and the dream live on.

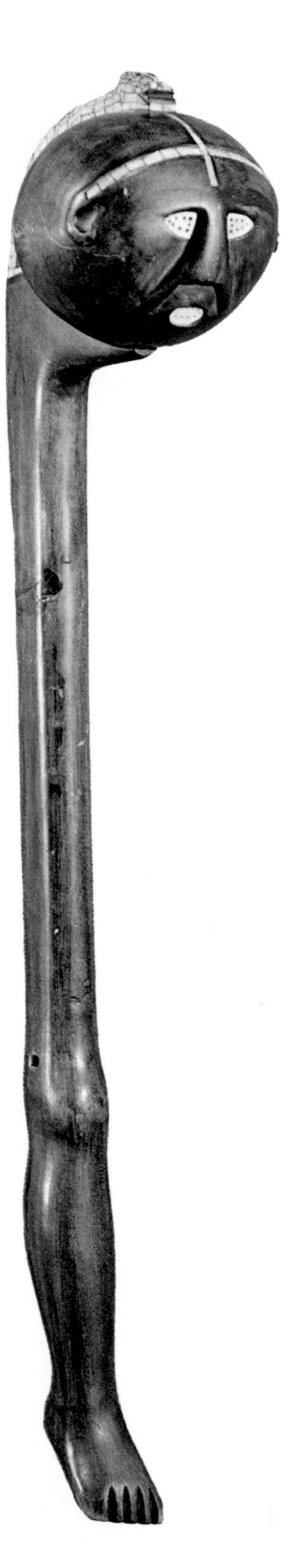

"IROQUOIS ALLANT À LA DÉCOUVERTE" BY J. GRASSET DE ST. SAUVEUR, 1787; NEW YORK HISTORICAL SOCIETY. DRAWINGS AFTER FRENCH DOCUMENT, 1666; ARCHIVES NATIONALES, PARIS. LEFT: DANISH NATIONAL MUSEUM, COPENHAGEN

With manner befitting name, an Iroquois—"terrifying man" in Algonquian—scowls from a 1787 engraving. Fringe on breechclout, undersize snowshoes, overdecorated club, long tailpiece, and other errors suggest the artist never saw a real Indian. Such drawings helped spread tales of Iroquois ferocity. Even into the 20th century Labrador Indians used the word "Iroquois" to scare children. Trained tacticians, the warriors gloried in combat, displayed scalps on poles, shackled prisoners with special "slave straps." Weapons included "tomahawks...two foote and a halfe long," with a knob "as round and bigge as a football." A fine 17th century example (opposite), thought to be Delaware, has bone inlays.

religious duties, hunting, going to war. At leisure, they sat and smoked, played games, or gambled. Such pursuits—heightened when white dominance of the land deprived the male of his traditional place as hunter and warrior—created the stereotype of the "lazy Indian."

Until the white man's weapons changed the character of woodland Indian warfare, that combat was "more for pastime, than to...subdue enemies," one Puritan captain reported. Pitched battles between massed tribesmen were rare, casualties relatively few. A display of courage could do as much to end a conflict as wholesale slaughter—and made strategic sense, since tribes generally were small in population and couldn't afford heavy losses of manpower.

To the women fell the everyday labor of life. The "Indesses" might be "very comely...and generally plumt of their Bodies," but they spent their days in a constant round of caring for the children, cooking, minding the houses—and moving them when the time came—gathering shellfish, tanning skins. And, of course, tending the fields.

Agriculture had spread over the continent from an origin in Mexico. The farther north it reached, the less importance it held and the more important hunting became. In the south, where two or three crops a year could be grown, farming provided the major part of the sustenance. In New England, tribes were less dependent on maize, and hunting equaled gardening in meeting food needs.

Cultural gradations went along with the gradual shift in agriculture's significance. A maize economy in Mississippi could support populous settlements with complex social hierarchies; religions could be elaborate, usually woven around ceremonies tied to the cultivation cycle. Populations in Virginia and New England might have harvest festivals and planting rites, but also paid more attention to other aspects of ritual than did their southern neighbors.

Algonquian tribes believed in a pantheon of guiding spirits, a creator who had peopled the world and bestowed its bounty, and an afterlife similar to life on earth. Religious leaders—often called medicine men because their activities included curing the sick—wielded great influence through their communication with the spirits.

Farther north, such tribes as the Algonquin—whose name now labels the vast language family—and the Ojibwa lived mainly above the climate line marking the limit where corn varieties known to aboriginal populations could grow. For them, shamanism, curing, and hunting magic dominated ritual. Beliefs centered on keeping in harmony with the beings that gave shape and essence to each plant or animal, stone or hill, storm or star that touched their lives.

The Ojibwa, or Chippewa—both names are corruptions of an Indian word whose meaning is uncertain—peopled a vast, watery, timbered region around the upper Great Lakes. A hunter and fisher folk, they lived in scattered bands of 100 to 150 people related by blood. They gathered wild rice along waterways, or traded for grain with such farming tribes as the Huron to the south and east. Dome-shaped wigwams of bark housed them, tanned skins clothed them. Their secret *Midéwiwin*—Grand Medicine Society—powerfully influenced tribal customs and healed the sick.

Ojibwa lifeways repeat among peoples along the northern edge of the wooded east— tribes such as the Menominee, the "wild rice people"; the Ottawa, shrewd traders of the Georgian Bay region; and the Abenaki, "people of the dawn land," who inhabited the easternmost part of New England when the Pilgrims arrived.

Those God-fearing pioneers came on the heels of a deadly epidemic that had swept along the coast. Its cause was unknown—perhaps measles, perhaps plague, perhaps a combination of maladies to which Indians lacked immunity; contemporary writers threw up their hands and called it a "pestilential sickness." Undoubtedly white traders or fishermen plying the coast had introduced it. Tribes were decimated, power balances upset. In some places not enough survivors remained to bury the dead. One Massachusetts Bay colonist came across "such a spectacle" of skulls and bones "that . . . it seemed to mee a new found Golgotha." The Pilgrims had been primed to meet unfriendly savages; at the spot where they happened to land, the natives had been all but wiped out. The colonists counted the epidemic God's will, a sign that "divine providence made way for the quiet and peaceable settlement" of His elect.

"A clumsy vizard of wood . . . grinning mouth set awry"— so a colonial traveler described a mask used by the Iroquois in the curing rites of the False Face Society. After 300 years of Indian-white contact, these portraits of supernatural beings still are carved to standards set in origin legends. One, "Crooked Mouth," had his visage skewed

LEE FRIEDLANDER; COURTESY NEW YORK STATE HISTORICAL ASSOCIATION.
ONONDAGA MASK, 1937; CRANBROOK INSTITUTE OF SCIENCE, BLOOMFIELD HILLS, MICHIGAN

by an onrushing mountain when he dared test the creator's might. Each image shares the power of the False Face being; worn for prayers and offerings, it constrains the being to cure ills the False Faces cause. Carving it from a living tree reinforces the life in the mask. Hair from horses' tails makes tresses; metal eye plates gleam in ceremonial firelight.

Forest trails and river roads long had laced the continent; trade and contact—and inevitably pestilence—flowed along them. Shells from the Gulf of Mexico could find their way to tribes far up the Mississippi. Iroquois raiding parties could follow paths into Cherokee country in the south. And an English seaman named David Ingram, set ashore somewhere in Mexico in 1568, could leave a tale of walking along travel routes to reach the Atlantic coast—an incredible trip of "about eleaven monethes in the whole"—before he was picked up by a French fishing boat.

Pestilence spreading ahead of a wave of settlers is only one example of how the influence of a frontier travels in advance of that frontier. Also, tribal alliances are reoriented, trade patterns reshaped, whole tribal economies changed.

The Ojibwa, for example, could acquire—and become dependent on—the white man's metal knives and pots and vermilion before ever having contact with a white trader. Tribes that once defended hunting grounds to protect their source of food might now zealously guard them for the furs they contained. More aggressive nations might go to war to gain a richer territory or to wipe out a rival tribe. Thus did the Iroquois vault to power.

Tribes speaking Iroquoian languages ranged from the Cherokee in the south through the Erie and Susquehanna in Ohio and Pennsylvania to the Huron around Georgian Bay in the north. But the five tribes grouped as the Iroquois —the Mohawk, Oneida, Onondaga, Cayuga, and Seneca—held a land across central New York State "full of chestnutts and oakes" and passenger pigeons so abundant "that in a nett 15 or 1600 att once might be taken."

The Iroquois lived in bark-covered longhouses flanking the central street of villages ringed by log stockades as tall as 20 feet. A dozen or more families had allotted spaces in each longhouse, a structure likened by an early writer to a noisy "prison [with] four other great discomforts—cold, heat, smoke, and dogs." Outside the palisades lay fields "of all sides of Indian corne" tended by the women, whose child-bearing abilities, the Iroquois believed, were magically associated with the productivity of Mother Earth.

As woodland farmers, the Iroquois had agricultural rites tied to such events as the maturing of the corn or the ripening of wild strawberries. As northern hunters, the Iroquois also had shamans with supernatural powers to deal with the spirits.

Religion wove itself into every aspect of daily life. Dreams had significance and offered guidance, and often were recounted in a ceremony at the beginning of the year. Through everything ran a force Mohawks called *orenda*, the mystic essence that bound all things including man. Individuals could accumulate orenda for inner strength. A shaman had especially powerful orenda, and members of one tribal society gained orenda to intercede with the False Faces—grotesque bodiless beings that roamed the dark forests and bewitched people into illness.

The Iroquois woman had a freer, more influential place in the world she lived in than her European counterpart did in hers. Like many tribes, the Iroquois traced descent on the mother's side. A matriarch ruled each longhouse, and within it all the women were related; when a girl married, the husband moved, not the wife. Women named the children and raised them. Women owned the houses and belongings and fields—to the extent, at least, that anyone could be considered as owning land. Indians all over the continent generally held that tribal terrain was a trust to be used, and no more saleable than the air.

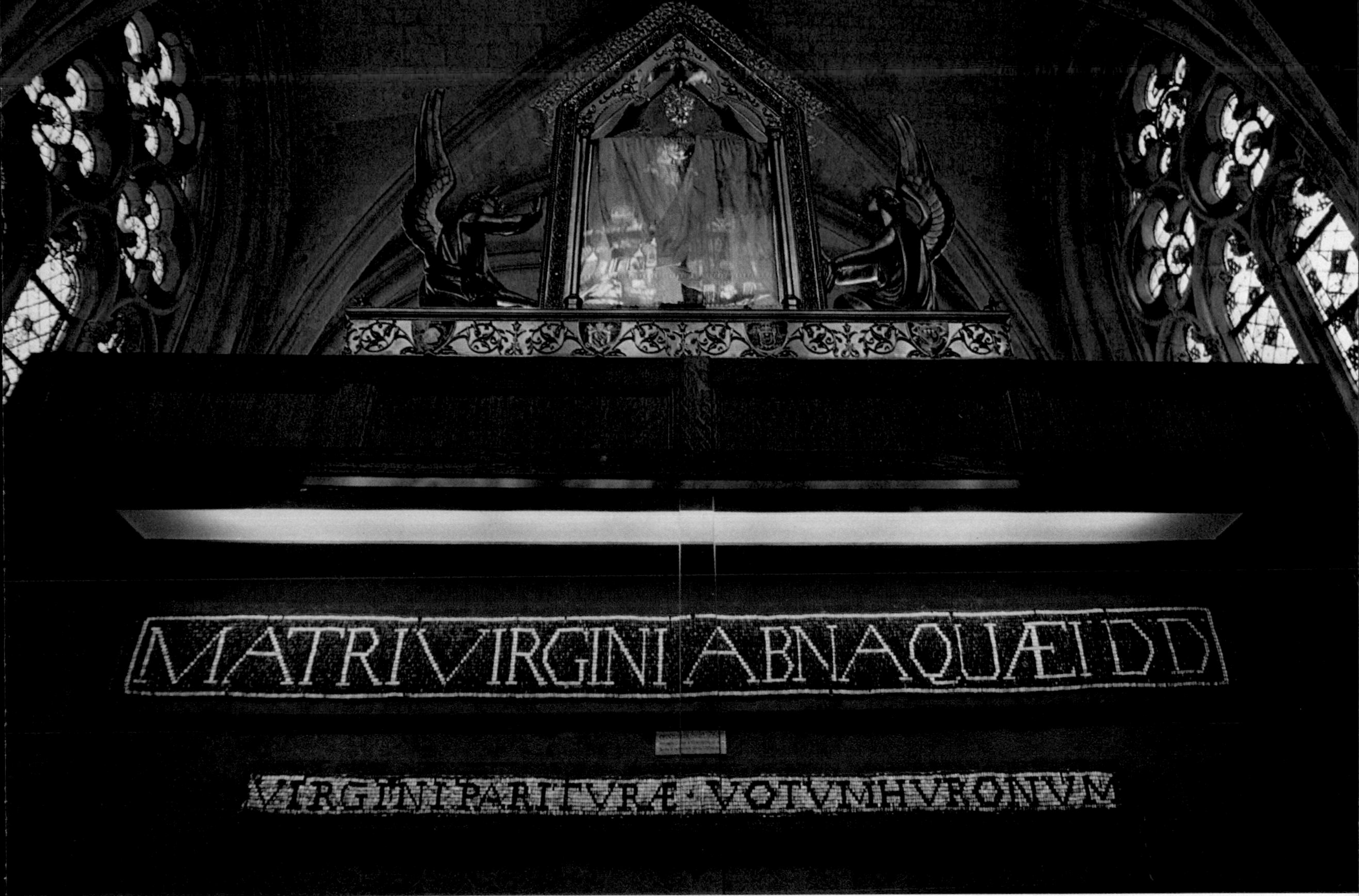

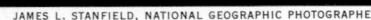

MATRI VIRGINI ABNAQUÆI DD
VIRGINI PARITVRÆ · VOTVM HVRONVM

JAMES L. STANFIELD, NATIONAL GEOGRAPHIC PHOTOGRAPHER

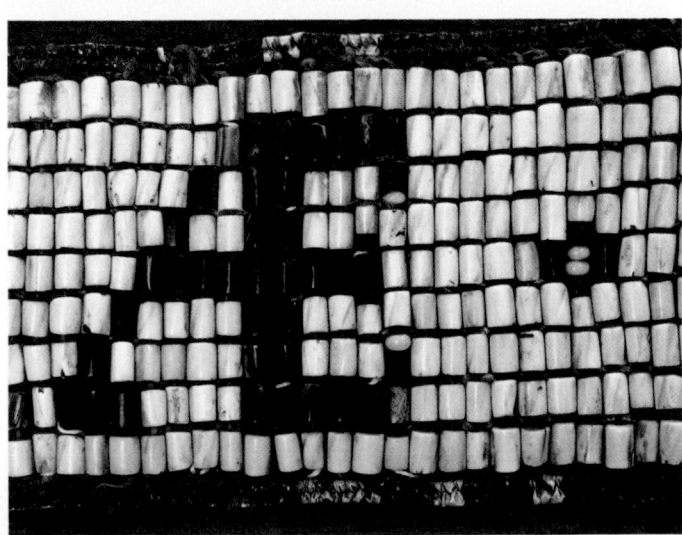

A *petit présent*—worked in wampum by Abenaki and Huron converts at Jesuit missions along the St. Lawrence River—reposes in France's Chartres Cathedral. Each "little gift" inscribed to the Virgin Mother is an elaborate wampum belt, traditional symbol of diplomatic and ceremonial relationships among northeastern Indians. Both are edged with dyed porcupine quills. The larger, about six inches wide and seven feet long, was presented in 1699, the other in 1678.

Wampum came from shell—white usually from the central column of whelks; purple, twice as valuable, from quahog clams. The word itself stems from the Algonquian *wampumpeag*—cylindrical shell beads. Beds along Narragansett Bay and Long Island Sound were major shell sources. A person could round and drill from 100 to 200 of the quarter-inch beads a day. About 2,000 went into a two-foot belt; as many as 20 belts might be needed for one ceremony. As the fur trade boomed its use, wampum served more for money and less for ritual. With white mass production, value—and usage—fell.

Ho Nee Yeath Taw No Row   **Tee Yee Neen Ho Ga Row**   **Etow Oh Koam**

COURTESY LORD PETRE OF INGATESTONE

"Four INDIAN KINGS lately arriv'd . . ."

London's *Daily Courant* in 1710 capitalized news that set the city agog. A century earlier William Shakespeare had noted Europe's curiosity about Indians; his jester in *The Tempest* jibed at people who "when they will not give a doit to relieve a lame beggar . . . will lay out ten to see a dead Indian." Now here were four live ones, lauded as rulers of their realms, come for a diplomatically vital audience with Queen Anne.

The delegation "made a great bruit thro' the whole kingdom." Hawkers peddled handbills extolling their "exquisite Sense, and a quick Apprehension." Ballads were written about them. They attended opera, saw *Hamlet*, heard concerts, enjoyed marionettes, visited hospitals, had portraits "Done from ye Life" by Dutch artist John Verelst on commission from the queen.

Three were Mohawks, one a Mahican. Various spellings mark their Indian names. But they also were known by English ones: John of Canajoharie, whom Verelst painted with bow in hand and wolf totem in the background. Hendrick, also a wolf and the ranking

sachem of the group in ability and influence, depicted in black court dress. Nicholas, a Mahican of the turtle clan. Brant, a bear, whose elaborate tattoos won "not . . . so much Terror as Regard."

The visit was a ploy by colonial leaders to generate crown enthusiasm for the border struggle against the French and to impress the chiefs with English might. Both aims succeeded. Redcoats did conquer Canada. And a long alliance saw Brant's grandson Joseph lead Iroquois warriors on Britain's side in the Revolution.

The four kings went home loaded with gifts that ranged from scarlet cloaks to a "Magick Lanthorn with Pictures." In turn they presented to the queen "Neck-Laces . . . and other Curiosities," including belts of wampum. The latter served to seal their words, as was the Indian custom. Northeastern tribes—especially the Iroquois—prized wampum strings as sacred symbols of agreement and as mnemonic devices whose designs recorded events, conveyed messages, or set out the correct recitation of a ritual.

128

Gem-cut by ancient glaciers, the watery labyrinth of the Great Lakes region silvers
a wild land where loons call and bears roam. Menominee Indians still bag
bear, which in old days had great ritual as well as economic importance. Its fur
gave warm coverings, its flesh "very toothsome sweet venison," its fat—saved
in bags made from the animal's stomach—provided such items as cooking oil, salves,
and insect repellents. Even paws had worth: as food and for making claw ornaments.

The Iroquois differed from other matrilineal societies in the amount of power women held. Matriarchs chose the chiefs and could depose them. Men held tribal offices and did the speaking, but women exerted real influence behind the scenes. And when a captive was brought home from a raid, women had final say in whether he would be adopted or be put to death by torture.

Indian warfare, before white contact, was as much a ceremony as a deadly business. Through war a young man could prove valor and win status. Swift commando raids by small war parties was the usual pattern. Wrote a French Jesuit: "They come like Foxes through the woods. They attack like lions. They take flight like birds. . . ."

A prisoner taken in a raid faced punishment along the trail to the Iroquois village. Once there, he had to run a gauntlet of women and children wielding sticks, thongs, and branches. If he survived all this bravely, he might be adopted into the tribe by a family that had lost a warrior in battle; the Seneca at one time reportedly counted more aliens than natives in the male population. If marked for death, he faced hours of agony at the hands of enemies who "delight to tormente men in the most bloodie manner that may be; fleaing some alive . . . cutting of[f] the members, and joynts of others by peese-meale and broiling on the coles, eate the collops of their flesh in their sight while they live."

Though brutal, the torture had overtones of religious sacrifice. Victims might be feasted before their ordeal, treated with deference through it. Eating a bit of the body was a way to get some of the fortitude of an especially courageous sufferer. For he had a role, and played it—defiantly singing his death song, taunting his captors.

Savagery did not rest exclusively with "wild Salvages," however. The times saw a Europe inured to public executions, drawings and quarterings, severed heads paraded on pikestaffs. In the colonies, governments offered bounties for

Song of thanksgiving for winter's first snowfall gives cadence to the snowshoe dance of the Ojibwa. Hunters exult; now game floundering in drifts becomes easier prey for men buoyed on webbed frames. Ojibwa bands roamed northern fringes of the Great Lakes. Their wigwams had coverings of birch bark, rush mats, and—as cultures interlaced—white man's canvas.

Indian scalps. A Revolutionary Army lieutenant could nonchalantly skin two Indians to make leather leggings for himself and his major.

People today tend to dwell on horrors of Indian warfare, and to forget it was a kind of ritual occupation, with accepted rules and less killing and economic loss than European war of the day.

White contact changed that character. And the Iroquois exemplified the profound consequences. Their lands overlooked trading routes down the Hudson and St. Lawrence Rivers; when the beaver dwindled in their hunting grounds, they reached out for the territories of others. In the 1640's they fell on their relatives the Huron. These were no commando raids, but warriors by the thousand waging a determined war of destruction. With the Huron broken, the Attiwendaronk—better known as the Neutral Nation—came next in liquidation. Then the Erie. Others followed. Thus the Iroquois leaped to dominance over a territory that at its height reached from New England to Illinois.

MICHAEL KOPP

Menomin, Ojibwas called it. It grew wild, reported an early traveler, "in the water in 3 or 4 foote deepe" over regions too far north for Indian corn to thrive. It was a "a kinde of rice, much like oats"; a handful "putt in the pott . . . swells so much that it can suffice a man." To such tribes as the Ojibwa, the grain—like rice an aquatic grass, though not a true rice—had such import it figured in rituals and offerings. For control of rice lands Ojibwas drove onto the plains woodland Sioux who once had possessed them.

Indigenous to North America, *Zizania aquatica* thrives in the muck of shallow lake and torpid stream. Varieties can be found from the Rockies to the Atlantic, from the Gulf to Lake Winnipeg. But in the Great Lakes country, it turns watery flats into green meadows, and Indians still harvest in age-old ways. Two to a canoe, they course waterways, then pole through the growth. One, seated, bends down stalks with a stick, and with another knocks loose the grains nestled in their sheaths. Parching, hulling by treading underfoot, and winnowing follow. Harvest time sees joyous social gatherings.

Fierce fighters though they were, the Iroquois also had an edge in tactical training and organization. That organization was reflected in the novel political system—perhaps the most complicated north of Mexico—that linked the five tribes. We know it as the League of the Iroquois.

Tradition puts its beginnings at some time in the 1500's. Before then, the accounts say, the Mohawk, Oneida, Onondaga, Cayuga, and Seneca were feuding kin. They constantly raided each other and—because of their division —suffered at the hands of Algonquian neighbors.

But a visionary Huron named Deganawidah dreamed of a mighty tree of "Great Peace" anchored by roots among the Five Nations. He and his disciple Hiawatha—an Onondaga, not the imaginary Ojibwa hero of Longfellow's poem— traveled among the tribes to forge that unity. The league that resulted formed a primitive democracy with what amounted to an oral constitution and governing council. That body dealt only with affairs affecting the whole league, left purely tribal matters to the individual nations. (The five became six when the Tuscarora, pushed out of Carolina by white settlement, were admitted about 1722.)

Our own nation's founding fathers knew about the Iroquois confederacy and admired its effectiveness. Wrote Benjamin Franklin: "It would be a very strange Thing, if six Nations of ignorant Savages should be capable of forming a Scheme for such a Union . . . and yet that a like Union should be impracticable for ten or a Dozen English Colonies, to whom it is more necessary."

The confederacy cemented a lasting peace between Iroquois tribes—and freed them to war on others. The time of its founding, and the ends to which it was put, suggest that the league's formation was a native invention to meet both the promise and the threat of European contact. Promise because of the goods and guns and power that control of trade routes would bring. Threat because of the disruption brought about by what was happening to Indian peoples along the seaboard.

That the league may have been a reaction to influences reaching in advance of the frontier does not, of course, make the results any less interesting or admirable. Nor does it mean that the league found a mold in European patterns. What occurred was a purely Indian adjustment to the turmoil seething along the coast. And the dream of a mighty tree of peace brought the reality of a remarkably effective political institution.

Kaskaskia bowl represents a beaver, to some tribes a symbol of plenty. Effigy bowls once were common, but only a few examples survive.

Iroquois strength helped the British against the French in the wars that won Canada for the English crown. But the Six Nations divided in the Revolutionary War, and George Washington sent Gen. John Sullivan against tribes that sided with the British. His orders read that the Indian territory was "not to be merely overrun, but destroyed." Sullivan obeyed. He razed 40 villages, demolished 160,000 bushels of corn, leveled orchard after orchard and field upon field of corn. Indians gave him the name "Corn-cutter."

Iroquois power never recovered. But out of the demoralization came a hope for the future advanced by a prophet whose English name was Handsome Lake. He had a vision of a new religion, a "Good Message" that the Indians "might observe . . . for statutes and Ordinances . . . from Generation to Generation." The doctrine advocated adopting some white ways and mingling them with old traditions "as the only way . . . of worshiping the great Spirit." That message still has adherents among Iroquois today.

While the Iroquois could organize against the advancing frontier—thanks partly to the buffer

LEFT AND LOWER LEFT: W. E. GARRETT, NATIONAL GEOGRAPHIC STAFF. BOWL, C. 1795; UNIVERSITY MUSEUM, PHILADELPHIA. BOX, C. 1912; DENVER ART MUSEUM. BAG, 1850-1900; MUSEUM OF THE AMERICAN INDIAN, HEYE FOUNDATION, NEW YORK

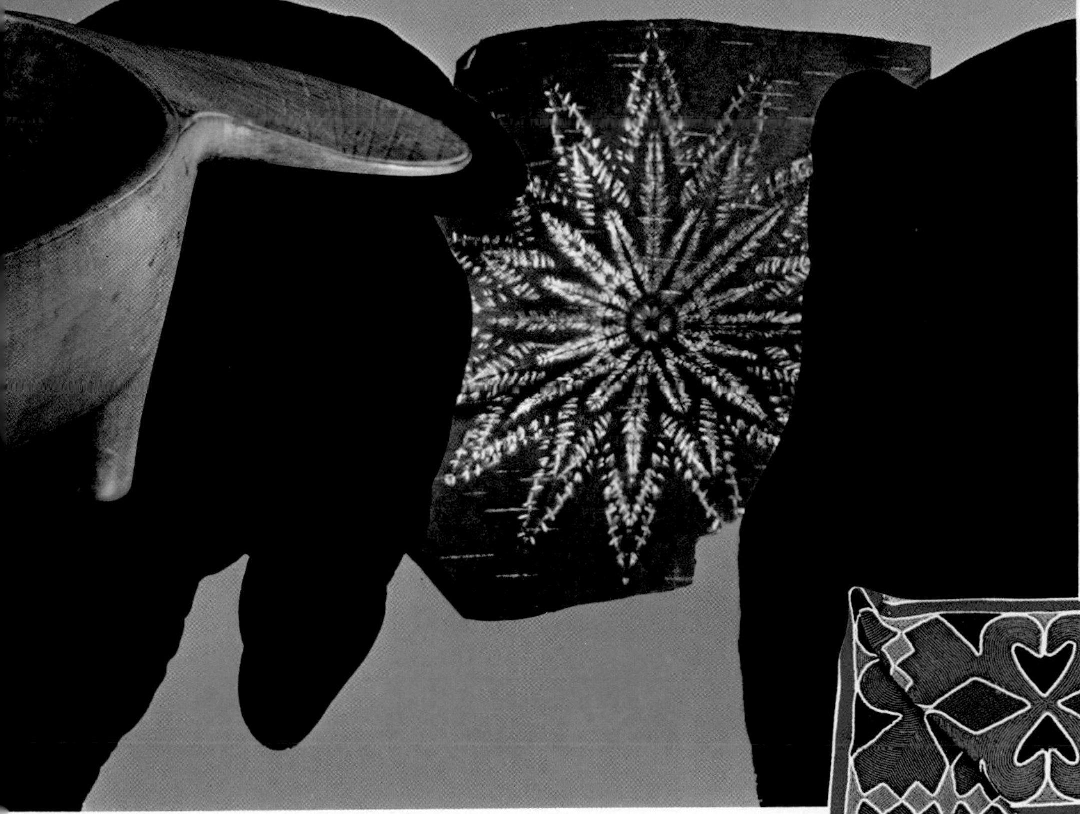

Bark, bone, a hank of hair—from materials at hand the woodland artisan imparted both beauty and utility to everyday items. White contact brought new resources, new needs, new designs. Old crafts disappeared. But some linger on: A Cree matron nibbles thin birch bark folded so patterns repeat. Opened, a snowflake appears. Bark biting once may have created guides for beadwork.

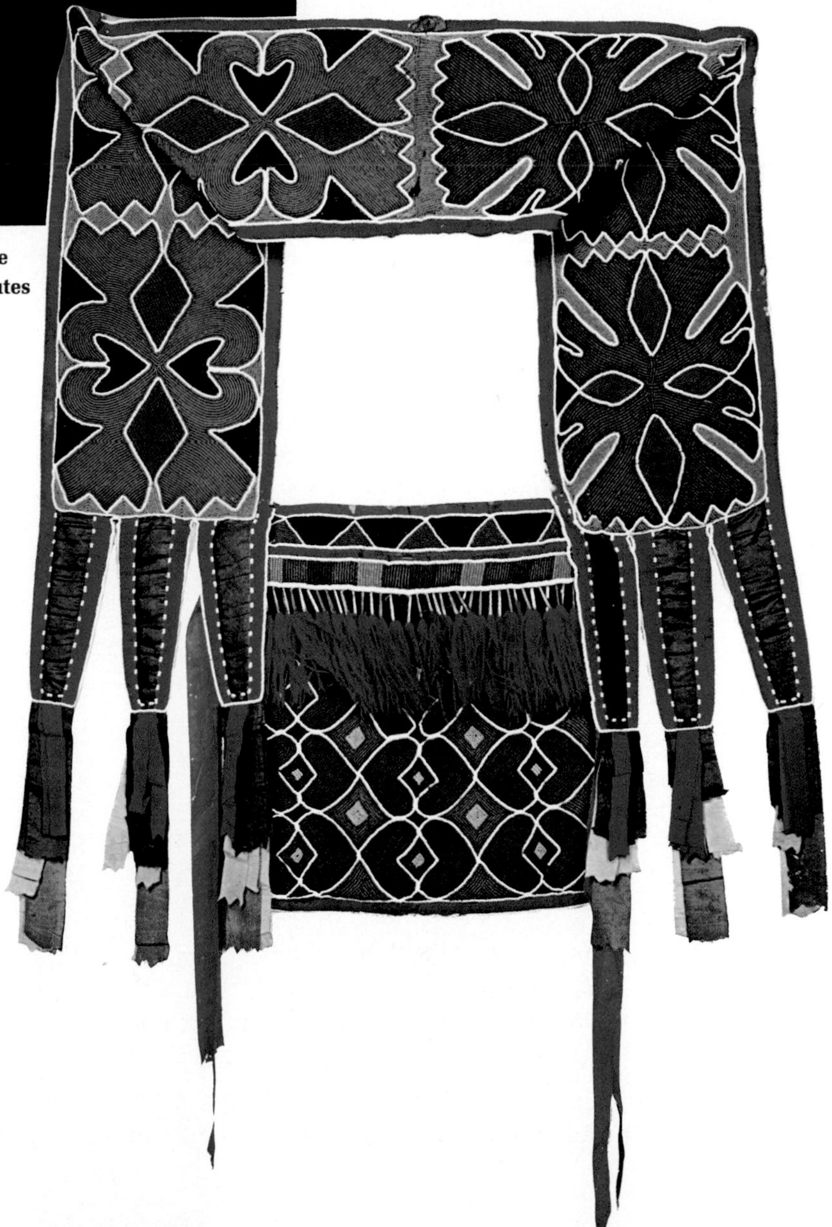

On a Delaware shoulder bag, strap and purse glow with ribbonwork and beading—substitutes for dyed moose hair and quills of aboriginal embroidery; yarn replaces deer-hair fringe.

Penobscot box of birch bark has spruce-root lacing; double-curve motif antedates floral embellishment adapted from European patterns.

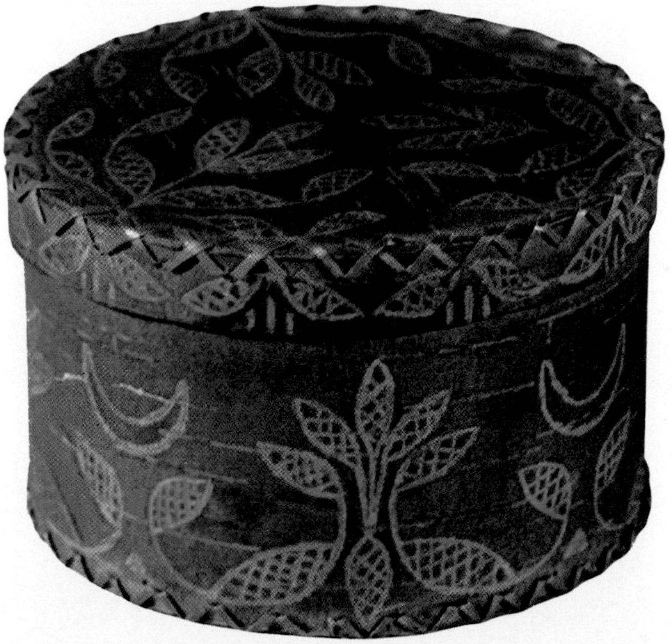

ELIOT PORTER. LEFT: "SEQUOYAH," LITHOGRAPH FROM A PAINTING BY CHARLES BIRD KING, 1828; LIBRARY OF CONGRESS

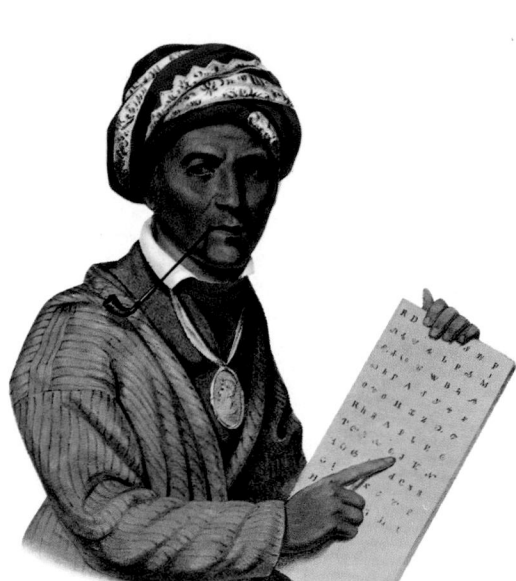

Hills round-shouldered by age nuzzle an Appalachian skyline with cloud-napped blankets of green. Here myriad leaves exude a haze of water vapor and oil that gives the Great Smoky Mountains their name. And here lies the home of the Cherokee. Legend puts their origin in the north—they are related linguistically to the Iroquois—but modern archeology suggests their culture developed on Appalachian slopes, where de Soto met them on his 1540's march.

Largest tribe in the southeast, the Cherokee wrested productive farms from wooded highlands—woods that were to shelter a moody dreamer, Sequoyah (above). His dreams gave the Cherokee writing (page 151). Born about 1760, he died on a trip to Mexico in 1843.

Siding with the British in 1776 hastened Cherokee loss of their realm. Land-hungry settlers pressed in, then discovery of gold triggered a forced removal of the tribe to territory in the west. Several hundred managed to elude the herding troops and hide in the hills. Their descendants live on amid the mist-wreathed ridges today.

provided by Algonquian tribes along the northeastern coast—a different pattern arose in the southeast. Hernando de Soto on his march through that region in the 1540's encountered "valiant and spirited inhabitants" who apparently lived in little states somewhat like those of the Calusa or the Natchez. But when whites next penetrated in numbers more than a century later, those states had disappeared. In their places stood simpler, less structured confederacies of dispersed villages not too dissimilar from those in the north.

Most likely, epidemics and disruption of populations lay at the root of the change. De Soto found no people at one locality "because the previous pestilence had been more rigorous and devastating in this town than in any other of the whole province." But whereas the influence of the frontier in the northeast brought increasing cultural complexity to the interior, in the southeast the opposite occurred.

You see evidence of this in metaphors woodland Indians used for political relationships between tribes. Both the Iroquois league in the north and the Creek confederacy in the south had intertribal councils with representatives from local units. In theirs, the Iroquois spoke of dealings among "brothers" or "uncles" or "cousins," and the kinship term implied the relative standing of the groups. By contrast the Creeks spoke of delegates from "red" towns or "white" ones, of "war" towns or "peace" towns. Applying simple family terms to more elaborate associations marks an advance from small-scale societies. But the more sophisticated terms of the south suggest an even higher level—in this case a lingering echo of the statehoods hinted at in de Soto's time.

Iroquoian tribes—particularly the Cherokee and Tuscarora—and such Muskogean-speaking groups as the Choctaw, Chickasaw, and Creek dominated the southeast when European colonization brought intensive white contact. The Cherokee were the most numerous. The Chickasaw earned a reputation as warlike troublemakers. The Choctaw, generally peaceful farmers, got the name "long hairs" because, unlike many eastern tribesmen, males left their locks unshorn. The aggressive Creek in Georgia and Alabama comprised a multilingual grouping of townsmen—speakers of Muskogee, Hitchiti, Yuchi, Shawnee, and others. English traders encountered a group living along a Georgia creek and called them "Creek Indians"—a name that came to be applied to all the townsmen, as well as to the Muskogee language spoken by one of the tribes.

Early visitors found the men of the region "tall, erect, and moderately robust." But one apparent misogynist reported that the women "being condemned . . . to . . . perform all the hard labor [were] without one soft blandishment to render them desirable." Accounts often mention the duties of Indian wives, but their lot may not have been more onerous than that of frontier white women; on occasion the latter refused chances to return home after having lived among the Indians.

All the southeastern tribes had similar cultures. They were farmers, growing beans and multicolored corn—"some white, some red, some yellow, and some blew"—as well as pumpkins, squash, and gourds. Farms stood around a village with a central plaza—a "stomp ground" for dances and ceremonies linked to the agricultural cycle.

Houses had thatched roofs and walls of poles which the villagers "weave . . . with their split saplings, and daub them all over about six or seven inches thick with tough clay, well mixt with withered grass." A fire burning inside in winter prompted English (continued on page 147)

MISSISSIPPI CHOCTAW HERBALIST; DICK DURRANCE II, NATIONAL GEOGRAPHIC PHOTOGRAPHER

Red Man's Materia Medica

Snakeroot to cure snakebites. Willow for fever. Tobacco for "fleame & other grosse humors." So reads the pharmacopoeia of Indian medicine. From bark of root to leaf of shrub tribal healers drew on a rich array of botanicals about them. Tribal lore and trial-and-error yielded the medicines; modern science accords validity to many. Nearly 200 "yarbs and roots" have gone into official compendiums; willow bark, for example, contains the salicin now produced synthetically as the effective ingredient in aspirin. Indians recognized both natural and supernatural sources of ailments. Treatment was by individual practitioners — herbalists who handled symptoms and medicine men who dealt with origins — and by the "social" approach of medicine societies. Pioneering whites had such faith in Indian healing that 19th-century charlatans could reap success peddling "Modoc Oil," "Old Sachem Bitters," or "Kickapoo Cough Syrup"—the latter a concoction of rum and molasses.

Cane to Double,
Fire to Burn and Corn to Bubble

Indians of the southeast—"particularly the *Choctaughs* and *Chigasaws*," wrote an observer in the 1730's— made "masterpieces in mechanicks" from the versatile material. He was speaking of river cane *(Arundinaria tecta)* which grew in great profusion along stream banks. It served aboriginal tribesmen in multiple ways—torches, building material, mats, knives, blowguns, arrows, shields, drills, tubes to tuck up hair, seeds for food. And, of course, "diverce faire . . . baskets."

Choctaw artisans in Mississippi still practice basketry typical of old skills of woodland Indians. The cane is split into narrow splints, trimmed, scraped, dyed, then woven. Once colors came from such sources as bloodroot, butternut, and black walnut. Designs stemmed from memory or tribal lore, with patterns worked by varying the colors or the over-and-under crossing of warp and weft. Basic techniques included twilling (below) and the simpler checkerwork whose splints

could be butted tightly or spaced to create meshes of different sizes. A sifter fashioned this way (left) drops corn into a scooplike winnowing basket.

Eastern agriculturists ground their corn in a log mortar hollowed by charring and scraping. The shape of the cavity kept the grains churning beneath the log pestle (above). To remove hulls, kernels were soaked in lye water obtained by leaching wood ashes, or were broken in a mortar and the chaff winnowed out. Sufficient pounding produced a meal for bread, cooked in husk wrappers or baked on hot stones. But larger pieces "they lett boyle . . . three or four howres, and thereof make a straung thick pottage"—hominy grits. Choctaw cooks (top) wear tribal dress that reflects an adaptation of 19th-century white styles.

DICK DURRANCE II, NATIONAL GEOGRAPHIC PHOTOGRAPHER. PAGES 144-145: LITHOGRAPH OF "BALL PLAY" BY GEORGE CATLIN, C. 1834; RARE BOOK DIVISION, NEW YORK PUBLIC LIBRARY

Mayhem in the "Younger Brother of War"

Woodland tribes enjoyed a wide variety of games based on dexterity or on chance—shooting arrows, playing a kind of soccer, tossing lances at a rolling disk, guessing which moccasin held a stone or marker, gambling by tossing split lengths of cane for scores determined by the number of convex or concave surfaces turned up, cat's cradle, and others. But the wildest of woodland sports was stickball, named lacrosse by the French because rackets used resembled a bishop's crosier (la crosse). The modern sport developed from the Iroquois game with its single stick. Southern tribes used two.

Choctaws (opposite) keep stickball alive, holding championship matches in an annual fair at Philadelphia, Mississippi. There men also compete at target shooting with blowguns, in aboriginal days a boy's weapon for hunting small game using darts feathered with thistledown.

Modern rules eliminate much of the violence that marked the old stickball, frequently considered a substitute for war. Then almost anything went—pushing, pulling, butting, biting—in what painter George Catlin labeled "almost superhuman struggles for the ball." Bloodshed and broken bones were common. The game's object was to pass or carry a ball to a goal—sometimes a broad post, sometimes two poles set at varying distances apart. Length of the field and number of players on a team also varied. The ball was made of deer hair wrapped with deer hide, occasionally with a flea or inchworm inside as "medicine." Teams might play from mid-morning to late afternoon without a break.

Betting was heavy. Spectators even staked services of wives and selves; tribes wagered hunting grounds. In Oklahoma, Catlin pictured a Choctaw game (pages 144-145), peopling it with more than the usual number of players, but showing body paint and horsetail decorations often worn—plus, as commonly happened, a woman spectator encouraging a laggard contestant with a whip.

Palmetto-thatched and open-sided, chickees give a Miccosukee family a storehouse and sleeping quarters around a central kitchen. Like their neighbor-kin the Seminole, the Miccosukee held to old ways in compounds tucked amid saw grass and swamp of the Everglades. Hair pinned over a cardboard frame and bright flowing dress of a Seminole matron reflect tribal elaboration of 19th-century white fashions. Patchwork patterns grew in complexity with arrival of the sewing machine.

OTIS IMBODEN, NATIONAL GEOGRAPHIC PHOTOGRAPHER

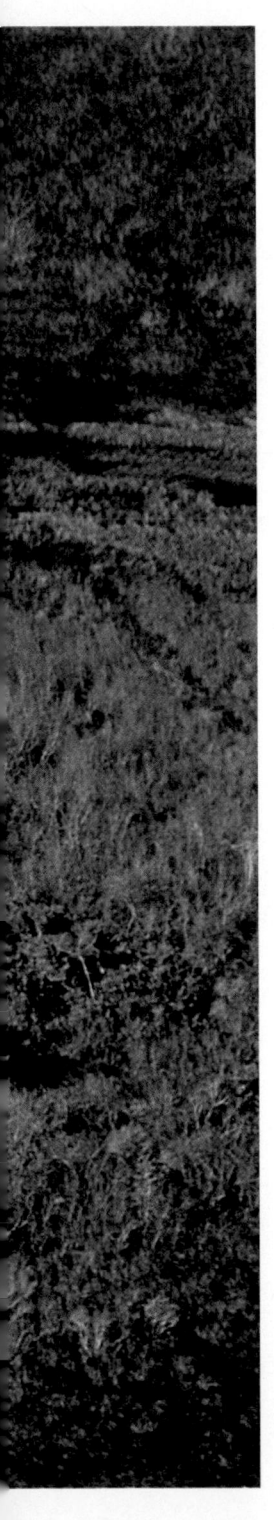

observers to call them "hot houses." Summer residences were more open. Around house interiors, shelflike platforms served as beds.

Skins provided bedding. Deerskin—"always softened like velvet-cloth"—also made breechclouts, shirts, women's skirts, and cloaks. Heavy trade in deerskins marked early contact with whites. Colonial records tabulate thousands upon thousands of pounds of skins flowing from the interior—to use for military uniforms, cannon wadding, gloves, and countless other items. In return went diplomatic gifts and trade goods.

Cherokee and Creek tribes sat between the English, French, and Spanish in the early struggle for dominance, and played one power against the other. In the Revolutionary War the Cherokee allied with the English, only to suffer retaliation. Then—with a man named Sequoyah among the warriors—they fought beside Andrew Jackson at Horseshoe Bend in the Creek War of 1813-14.

By then European influences had steered the southeastern red man toward adoption of white ways. An 18th-century observer had said "it is very wrong to call men savages who know how to ... think justly, who have prudence, good faith, and generosity much more than certain civilized nations." Now those "savages" took to white practices with plantations, ownership of slaves, sending children off to school. Sequoyah invented a writing system for the Cherokee in 1821; the Creek at about the same time established a written code of laws, an educational system, a legislature. Yet even by becoming "civilized" they couldn't save their homelands. A gold rush and white greed for land triggered events that led to their removal—along with the Choctaw, Chickasaw, and Seminole—to lands across the Mississippi in the 1830's.

The Seminole were an offshoot group that had arisen in Florida. Their name derived from a Muskogee word—itself an adaptation of the Spanish *cimarrón*, describing something once domesticated but that has turned feral, gone wild. In its Muskogee usage it had a connotation of "emigrant" or "frontiersman" rather than "runaway."

Spain's settlement at St. Augustine had existed mainly to carry Christianity to the Indians of

northern Florida. It had few soldiers, followed a policy of not allowing arms for the natives. Then the founding of Charleston in 1670 brought an aggressive English colony that funneled guns to Creek tribes and encouraged raids into Spanish territory. Disease had already halved Indian populations there; warring and slave raids fragmented the rest. By 1710 Carolinian Thomas Nairne could report that slavery depredations had "brought in and sold many Hundreds . . . and Dayly now continue . . . so that in some few years thay'le Reduce these Barbarians to a farr less number."

Nairne predicted better than he knew. When the Spanish left Florida in 1763, they took with them the 83 Christianized survivors of a Timucua population that once had numbered 15,000.

Lands left vacant by elimination of native peoples drew Seminole pioneers from northern Creek towns. At first they lived as hunters and traders, then gradually established settlements that in time acted independently of the Creek confederacy of which they had once been a part.

Seminole lifeways in the Florida peninsula followed traditional Creek patterns. To their settlements came runaway slaves from southern plantations. Though the Negroes found haven and lived in association with the Seminole, most evidence indicates there was little mingling and intermarriage. But removal to Oklahoma and wars against U. S. forces reduced the Seminole to scattered refuges amid the saw grass and sloughs of the Everglades and Big Cypress Swamp. There, too few and too weak to pose a threat, they hid for decades —the last practitioners of swidden agriculture in the eastern woodlands. Their descendants have tribal havens there today, part of some 100 communities of native Americans that survive in the East—much changed, but still Indians.

Their ritual rooted in the mound builder cultures of the distant past, Creek Indians dance at a tribal stomp ground in Oklahoma. They participate in the Busk, or Green Corn ceremony, a four-day observance common among woodland farmers since prehistoric times and held when the corn is mature enough to be eaten. Through this most important of all rites tied to the agricultural cycle, Indians gave thanks for past growth, prayed for continued fertility, sought prevention of sickness, saw past transgressions forgiven, cemented social bonds.

Each tribe has its own variation of the Busk. Among the Creek, bough arbors flank the dance ground and the fire whose sacred rekindling marks a new year's beginning. A name-giving ceremony installing youths into full tribal stature intersperses the rounds of dances. Of the latter, two hold special import. Women and girls parade in a ribbon dance with touches harking to scalp displays of long ago. Men bob plume-tipped poles and sing in a feather dance which climaxes the Green Corn ceremony. Before taking part they purify themselves with draughts of "the black drink"—an emetic that in early days was made from leaves of a kind of holly *(Ilex vomitoria)*. Once warriors held a similar cleansing before taking the warpath.

ROBERT W. MADDEN, NATIONAL GEOGRAPHIC PHOTOGRAPHER

About Language:
A Richness of Words, A Babel of Tongues

Wallace L. Chafe

Exploring a Canadian headland in 1534, one of Jacques Cartier's longboats encountered a large band of Indians. Outnumbered, the Frenchmen rowed off. Seven canoes paddled after them, the chronicle relates, the Indians "showing many signs of joy and of their desire to be friends, saying to us in their language: *Napou tou daman asurtat,* and other words we did not understand."

Those were the first Indian words recorded by Europeans north of the Rio Grande, and they evidently were spoken in friendship. But the shape of things to come was foreshadowed in the explorers' reaction: "... we shot off two fire-lances which ... frightened them so much that they began to paddle off in very great haste...."

No one knows the language recorded; likely it was Micmac, of the Algonquian family and one of 500 to 600 spoken in North America at that time. Scholars have sought to link them with Asian languages; the results remain inconclusive. Thousands of years of separation have obscured any clear linguistic connections between the continents. And there is no special reason to think that all Indian tongues had a common origin; probably separate migrations at different times introduced linguistic variety from the very beginning.

A reasonable consensus today distinguishes 18 language families, each containing from one to more than 20 languages. Those in a family are believed to have a common ancestor. For all we know, the families themselves may be as independent in ancestry as, say, English and Japanese.

Language and culture are sometimes closely related; Eskimos from Alaska to Greenland share an Arctic culture and a single language. On the other hand, tribes in the same language family may be quite distant in culture and geography. The Penobscot of Maine, the Ojibwa of the Great Lakes, and the Blackfoot of the Great Plains all speak Algonquian languages. The 20 members of the Athapaskan language family include the Kutchin of Alaska, the Hupa of northern California, the Navajo and Apache of the southwest. Of the southeastern people who came to be known as the Five Civilized Tribes, the Chickasaw, Choctaw, Creek, and Seminole speak Muskogean languages; the Cherokee speak an Iroquoian language.

Europeans often mistakenly concluded that Indian languages were somehow more "primitive" than those of "civilized" Europe. Indians, it was alleged, could not express general concepts, and therefore used several specific terms where Europeans might employ one generic word.

As an example, one eminent linguist claimed that Cherokee had no single word for "washing," but instead used different words according to

"Talking leaves" bear eloquent witness
to a unique achievement—the invention,
by one man, of a writing system.
Sequoyah, a mixed-blood Cherokee of
Tennessee, knew no English; but he saw
men look at scrawled paper—and the
pages spoke to them! To preserve men's
thoughts in this way, he felt, was like
"catching a wild animal and taming it."
In the New World before Columbus only
the Maya and a few other Middle
American groups had written languages.

Sequoyah tried representing Cherokee
words with animal figures and symbols;
the list grew hopelessly long. Then he
broke words into syllables and sought
symbols for them. For 12 years he
labored with pin on stone, with knife
or charred stick on bark, with pen on
paper. In 1821 he put his syllabary
to a test that stilled skeptics.
Men spoke to one of his children out
of Sequoyah's hearing. The child wrote;
the father read. Soon thousands could
read and write; the 86 characters were
easily learned. Some Sequoyah made up;
others he borrowed from our alphabet.
Thus the symbols G W Y spell *tsa-la-gi*,
a Cherokee form of the tribe's name.

At New Echota, Georgia, the tribe's
last eastern capital, the restored
print shop displays type, the tribal
constitution and an Old Testament
in Cherokee, the bilingual newspaper
begun in 1828, and a portrait
of the genius who made them possible.

JOHN LOPINOT

Sign Language: The Poetry of Motion

Roaming the plains, buffalo hunters of many tribes could trade, make treaties, tell hunting tales and legends—without uttering a word. Sign language, derived from pantomime, gave them a medium of fluency and grace—"the very poetry of motion," as one admiring ethnologist put it. But theirs was a flexible art, and they could experiment—as charade players do today—until mutually intelligible gestures evolved. Plains Indians, visiting in the East in historic times, loved to discourse with the deaf. In no time they chatted easily, without an interpreter cramping their style.

Forefingers placed like horns signify the second name of the Dakota chief Eagle Bull.

A Hidatsa says "log house" with fingers set like logs.

An Apache says "cold" or "winter." With querying signs it becomes "How many winters?" or "How old are you?"

"Head of tribe," gestures a Paiute.

Drooping digits betoken rainfall in Shoshone; placed near the eyes, they signal weeping.

what is washed: "*Gadawo'a*—I am washing myself"; "*Gagun'sgwo'a*—I am washing my face."

Actually, the verb stem—*(a)wo*—is the same in each instance. The confusion arises from the fact that in Cherokee, as in other Indian languages, a single word may incorporate all the elements of a sentence. And the word can vary to indicate the tense and grammatical mood of the verb, as well as the person, gender, and number of the subject and object nouns. Far from primitive, such languages show a grammatical complexity which can take a lifetime of scholarship to unravel.

Some Indian languages also express subtleties which English glosses over. When I say "He is chopping wood," the words give no hint about how I came to know this. In the Wintu language of northern California, I would say "*pi k'upabe*" if I had seen the woodsman at work. If I had heard but not seen him, I would say "*pi k'upanthe.*" If someone told me about it, the form would be "*pi k'upake*—I understand he is chopping wood." Or if I guess the act is going on because that is what the person usually does at this time, I would make it "*pi k'upa'el*—I assume he is chopping wood." Distinctions like these are hard to reconcile with the notion that Wintu is "primitive."

The richness of vocabulary on a given topic varies, depending upon its importance to the community. Woodland Indians have many more words dealing with wood and trees than do Plains Indians. In the southwest elaborate religious ceremonials gave rise to rich ceremonial vocabularies.

Sometimes such evidence helps us reconstruct prehistory. The Iroquois, for instance, have two kinds of traditional religious practices, one associated with the agricultural cycle and the other with the curing and prevention of disease—with the so-called medicine societies. Linguistic studies show that the vocabulary of the healing rites

SKETCHES FROM "SIGN LANGUAGE AMONG NORTH AMERICAN INDIANS" BY GARRICK MALLERY, 1881

is much older. Since medicine societies are characteristic of northeastern cultures, the evidence suggests that the Iroquois have lived in the northeast a long time. Apparently they are not, as was once thought, recent immigrants from the south who brought agriculture with them. Thus language can serve the culture historian in the way that rock strata help the geologist read the past.

But unlike solid rock, languages are remarkably adaptable, easily borrowing or coining new words as circumstances change. The horse, unknown when the Spanish landed, soon took on a central role among many tribes, and words for the horse and its many uses were introduced. One device was to borrow some form of the Spanish word *caballo*. Another was to invent a descriptive term. Indians of eastern New York State used a word meaning "one rides its back"; in the western part the word for horse means "it hauls out logs." Presumably these were the first uses of horses seen in the two areas. Among the Kwakiutl of British Columbia a steamboat was "fire on its back moving on the water." To the Tsimshian of the same area the word for rice was "looking like maggots."

Borrowing worked both ways. English acquired Indian words for many plants and animals and for aspects of culture first found in North America—such words as raccoon, skunk, moose, squash, pecan, persimmon, moccasin, tipi, wampum, toboggan, totem, succotash, and hominy.

Translation at times mangled the meaning of Indian words. A chief's title which meant "recklessly brave" was recorded in English as "crazy." "Bear bearing down [an opponent]" was rendered "Stumbling Bear." A Kiowa title lauded its holder as a fighter always on the warpath, too busy to remove his horse's saddle blanket; in English the name became "Stinking Saddle Blanket."

Indian languages show a great variety of sounds,

What's in a Name?

"Leaving natural breaths, sounds of rain and winds... they depart, charging the water and the land with names." So Walt Whitman heard the music of Indian names that dot the land by the tens of thousands. Half our states take their names from Indian words. The following derivations, with meanings where known, are based on contemporary scholarship:

Alabama — from the Muskogee tribe name *alipama*; the state motto, "Here we rest," is a legendary interpretation. **Alaska** — from alakhskhakh, Aleut name for the Alaska Peninsula. **Arizona** — a Spanish mining camp, from the Papago for "little spring." **Arkansas** — from *akansea*, the Illinois name for the Quapaw. **Connecticut** — from the Mohegan for "long river." **Illinois** — French tribal name from Algonquian *iliniwak* — men. **Iowa** — tribal name, via French, from the Fox *aayahooweewa*, perhaps ultimately Dakota *ayuhba*, interpreted as "sleepy." **Kansas** — from the Kaw name for themselves, via Illinois and French. **Kentucky** — first recorded as a river name, but perhaps from an Iroquois word for "planted field." **Massachusetts** — adaptation of a tribal name derived from the name for Blue Hill south of Boston; literally "big hill." **Michigan** — perhaps Ottawa for "big lake." **Minnesota** — from *mnisota* — "cloudy water," a Dakota river name. **Mississippi** — Illinois for "big river." **Missouri** — French adaptation of an Illinois name meaning "those with dugout canoes."

Nebraska — from *nibdhathka* — "flat river," the Omaha name for the Platte. **New Mexico** — from the Aztec name of Mexico City, believed by some scholars to mean "place of the god Mexitli." **North and South Dakota** — from *dakhota* — "friendly ones," the Dakota name for themselves. **Ohio** — French form of the Seneca name for the Allegheny-Ohio; means "beautiful river." **Oklahoma** — Choctaw for "red men"; the name "Oklahoma Territory" was coined by a Choctaw leader as a translation of "Indian Territory." **Tennessee** — from *tanasi*, a Cherokee name for the Little Tennessee River. **Texas** — see page 154. **Utah** — from *yuuttaa*, the Ute name for themselves. **Wisconsin** — an Algonquian river name. **Wyoming** — Delaware for "big river-flats," the name of a Pennsylvania valley widely popularized in a romantic tale of the 19th century.

Indian tongues, no longer scorned, keep a tenuous hold among the old and the proud; English advances—but often now to join the old languages, not replace them. Worshipers in Mississippi hear Bible verses in Choctaw; nearby, a high school girl polishes her English in a language lab. Sequoyah's symbols invite Oklahoma Cherokees into the First National Bank of Tahlequah, the old capital of the Cherokee Nation.

but this is not really surprising. We find such variety even among the related languages of Europe; witness the nasal vowels of French, the trilled r of Spanish, the "guttural" ch of German. Many Indian languages make use of the so-called glottal stop, or catch in the throat (we do the same thing in the middle of the exclamation "oh oh!"). Indian speech treats the stop as a consonant as common as p or t. And though tone languages of the Chinese variety are lacking, some Indian languages do have a "pitch accent," whereby different syllables of a word are given either high, low, or falling pitch, or some other distinctive pitch pattern.

Attempts by explorers and settlers to spell Indian words could lead to surprising results. The Caddo term tayša (pronounced roughly "tie Shah") meant "friend" or "ally"; it often referred to people of the Caddo Confederacy of what is now Louisiana and Texas. The Spanish at the time spelled the sh sound as x; adding the plural yielded Texas. We have reinterpreted the x by English conventions and produced a word that sounds quite remote from its origin. Finally, the Caddo borrowed back the word as a place name; in Caddo the Lone Star State is called tihsis.

Though Sequoyah's syllabary was the most famous, several Indian writing systems were devised by missionaries to provide religious materials in native languages. The most workable of these was the Cree syllabary invented by James Evans around 1840. A unique feature of Evans's creation is that the orientation of the character indicates the vowel; thus triangles pointed in different directions, △, ▽, ▷, ◁, represent the syllables hee, hay, ho, and hah respectively. The Cree system has been adapted for the Eskimo language and is still in use for both.

Language provides the most elaborate form of human communication, but Indians, like people everywhere, have developed other forms to serve limited functions. Sign language was one of these. Smoke signaling was another; across the open country of the plains and the southwest, Indians apparently employed combinations of long and short puffs to represent such messages as the presence of buffalo or the approach of enemies.

In view of the treatment accorded Indian speakers by Cartier's men and the Europeans who came after, it is remarkable that more than half of the native languages survived into the late 20th century. But the number of Indian languages in active use continues to decline. Probably the greatest single factor in their disappearance is the increasing importance of mass media in the lives of all of us, including Indians. Radio, the movies, and television have revolutionized the kind of contact people have with the world beyond their immediate surroundings. And almost all of this contact takes place in the English language.

Most Indian communities are aware of the great loss in the disappearance of their languages, and many have established programs to teach their native tongues to the children. It is too early to tell whether such programs will succeed. It may be that only a few of the most widely spoken languages, such as Cree, Ojibwa, Dakota, Cherokee, Navajo, and Eskimo, will survive indefinitely.

The white man has destroyed many fine and beautiful things on this continent, not the least of them the rich cultures that had evolved here for unknown millenniums. Language is the lifeblood of a culture. When the last speaker of a language dies, a wonderful tradition of thought and expressive power, extending from the infinite depths of man's history, dies too. Sadly, such a passing goes almost totally unnoticed, even now, as if an entire world were lost without anyone caring.

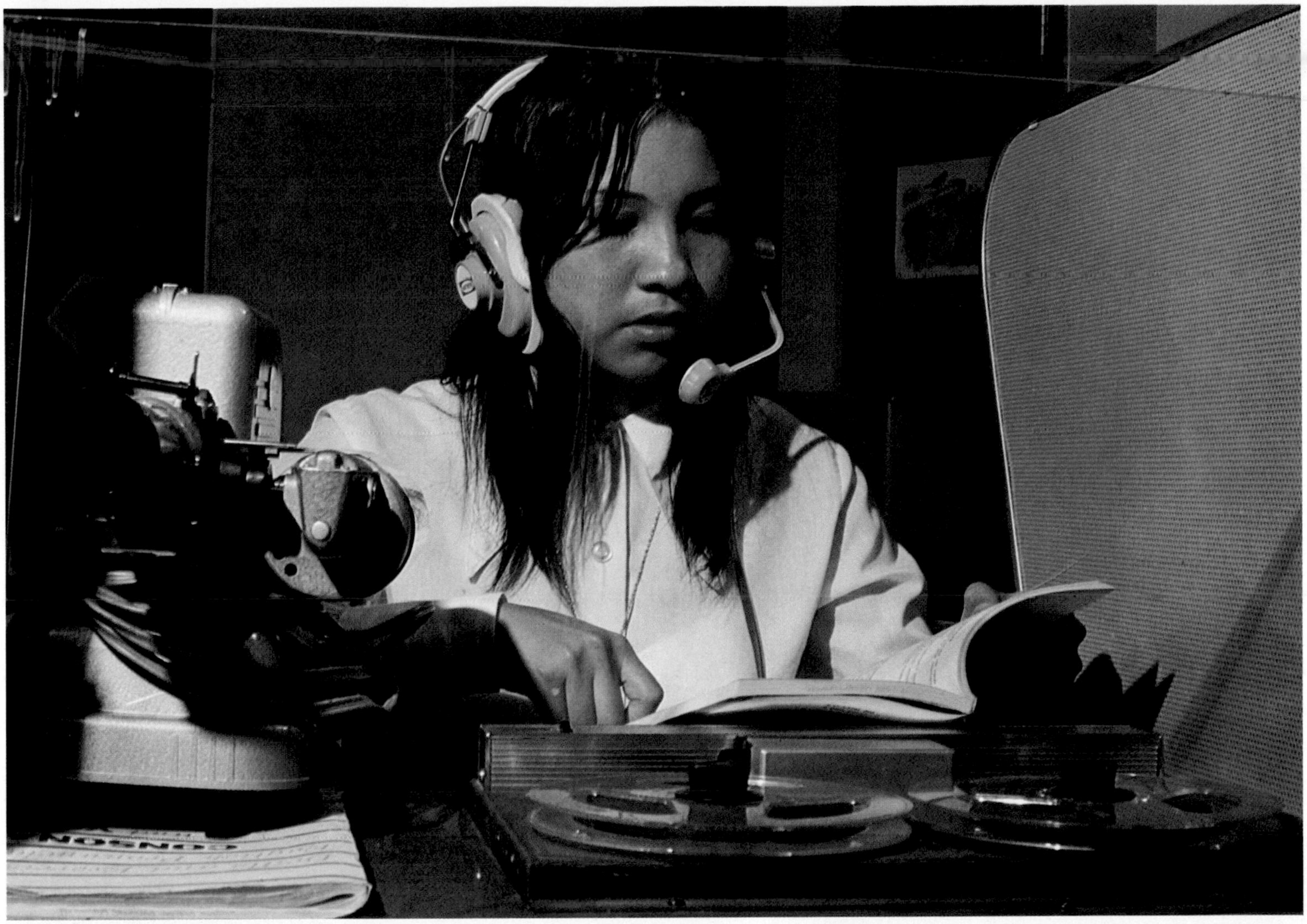

Farmers and Raiders of the Southwest

Alfonso Ortiz

Legacy of an ageless art, a basket woven of wild grasses reflects the southwest Indian's sun-drenched landscape. Where life and religion were one, basketry served a priestly Hopi society in symbol and substance—as cradle, food vessel, or divine offering. At shrines or in rituals, trays emblazoned with sacred images bore aloft the people's prayers.

One summer a few years ago I undertook a very special kind of journey, a pilgrimage, to the ancient homeland of the Tewa Indians in southwestern Colorado. My companion, an old man, had never been in that part of the state before. He was, like me, a Tewa.

A massive outcropping called Chimney Rock loomed larger and larger ahead of us. His recognition grew. Pointing, he said, "There is Fire Mountain! It is just as the old people spoke of it." He gazed at distinct features of the place and proceeded to unfold tale after tale of the early life of our people around Fire Mountain. Ghostly pueblo ruins a thousand years old stand in mute testimony to the Tewa's presence here long ago.

Every feature along the road came to life for us, and as my friend spoke of that remembered place, we realized that we were retracing part of the ancient journey of our people, a journey which began beneath a lake somewhere in this corner of Colorado, who knows how many thousands of years before. It is a journey which, as long as there are Tewa to tell of it, shall always end again at this lake of emergence, for in Tewa belief each one of us will return there after death.

By the time we neared the town of Pagosa Springs, it was no longer the 20th century, but another time, a time in and out of time. This place is called Warm Sands in Tewa, for here lie sands kept warm by the hot springs that gave birth to the town —sands which are able to melt snow and moderate the winter cold, sands which in other times our religious men had made pilgrimages to obtain.

He wanted to stop, as did I, to gather some of the sands near the springs. He knelt and ran the grains through his fingers. And then he wept. He remembered his grandfather and other ancestors who had preceded him. He had never journeyed here before, but now it was as if he had come home.

Arizona's rock-walled Canyon de Chelly
drops a violet curtain on the ruined
dwellings of prehistoric Pueblo
Indians. They and their forebears
found shelter here and in neighboring
sites for a thousand years. Then,
harassed by drought and roving tribes,
they moved southeast to farm and
build villages in the desert and
along the Rio Grande. Legend tells
of a colony trapped by a storm atop
misty Enchanted Mesa (top right).

Settlers in a stark Arizona moonscape
scratched permanent records in the
stratified rock. The southwest, a land
of "rocks and eagles, sand and snakes,"
nurtured a multitude of peoples on a
vast stage extending from southern
Utah and Colorado to northern Mexico.

By Coronado's time, nomadic hunters—
the Apache and Navajo—roamed northern
New Mexico, "threading the labyrinthine
canyons with their eyes on the stars."
The Navajo stayed in the canyons, soon
to mingle with the Pueblos and learn
farming, weaving, and ceremony, while
the Apache moved up to the mountains.
Around them the shadowy presence
of Ute, Comanche, and Kiowa formed a
link with the tribes of the Great Plains.

TERRY EILER. OPPOSITE: MARTIN ROGERS (UPPER) AND BRUCE DALE, NATIONAL GEOGRAPHIC PHOTOGRAPHER

In the southwest, as nowhere else in Indian America, all that is vital in life remains as it was, timeless. By the middle of the 16th century, most of the tribes were living where they are now, or nearby. Some were settled in permanent villages; strong tribal organization and a rich ceremonial life gave them unity and purpose. Because much of the land was in desert or mountain country unwanted for white settlement, the southwestern Indians were not hustled off to far-away reservations. The many tribes who live on this rugged and beautiful land share a vision of life, a felt sense of continuity with a tradition that has survived years of foreign domination.

Here we have the oldest continuous record of human habitation on the continent outside Mexico. The evidence is everywhere, in potsherds and pit houses that go back hundreds of years, in petroglyphs and chipped stone tools fashioned millenniums ago. Pottery making and the cultivation of corn, beans, and squash had come up to the southwest from Mexico centuries before the dawn of Christianity. In Bat Cave, New Mexico, a primitive corn some five thousand years old has been found, along with the tools of the Indians who used it. By the beginning of the Christian era, three cultures were forming in the southwest: the Hohokam, the Mogollon, and the Pueblo.

The Hohokam had grown up along the Salt and Gila Rivers in southern Arizona, a land which can be most inhospitable; but the Hohokam adapted well to their seared landscape, constructing a system of irrigation canals that remains their most impressive legacy. These ancient people were succeeded on the land by the Pima and Papago, who may even be their direct descendants. The Pima farmed and hunted; the desert-dwelling Papago — the bean people — were named for the only crop that would grow in dry summers. The games and

Indian corn struggles in the desert below a Hopi mesa, watered as in ages past by flash floods. Winnowed in a basket, ground in a mealing bin, corn gave the Hopi some 30 dishes. One mythical Corn Mother planted bits of her heart to yield the first grain; perfect ears are reserved for ceremonies.

TERRY EILER. BELOW: MARCIA KEEGAN

ceremonies of the Pima and Papago whisper of ties with Mexico; their language is related to Aztec.

North of the Gila River, up close to timberline, roamed the hunters, gatherers, and raiders—the Upland Yuman. They and their relatives the River Yuman, close neighbors of the Hohokam, believed that the spirit of the dead could be released by cremation. The ceremony was held in the open: As the flames rose higher and higher around the funeral pyre, mourners gathered to throw in offerings to their dead relatives. Sometimes women, wailing and moaning, ripped off their own clothes and threw them in the flames.

The Mogollon culture centered in the rugged mountains of western New Mexico and eastern Arizona. The Mimbres people, who represent the culture's highest development, created the finest pottery designs of any Indians north of Mexico. But Mimbres architecture and other cultural artifacts are not as impressive. By the present millennium—before the passing of the Hohokam—the Mimbres had been absorbed by another culture to the north, one that survives today after hundreds of years in the same ancient homeland.

This heritage of the past groups many tribes speaking different languages and dialects. They live in villages of multistoried houses that are responsible for the name they now bear. The conquistadores called the tribes *Pueblos,* the Spanish word for "towns." The Pueblo culture reached a climax in the Four Corners area — where Colorado and Utah meet Arizona and New Mexico—from the 10th through the 13th century. Then flourished the architectural wonders of Canyon de Chelly and Mesa Verde: penthouses of stone and masonry clinging to cliffs like swallows' nests.

Toward the last quarter of the 13th century, a drought haunted the southwest. Nomadic tribes may have begun to drift down from the north, and

the Pueblo people moved southeast to the Rio Grande and its tributaries. Only the Hopi, then as now, inexplicably hung on to their mesa-top villages in northeastern Arizona, where there are no permanent watercourses. The Hopi village of Oraibi was humming with life 500 years before the English settled Jamestown. It still is.

When Fray Marcos de Niza, the first European to view a pueblo, saw the Zuni village of Hawikuh from a high hill in 1539, he thought that he had found the fabled Seven Cities of Cibola. The Spanish harbored an old legend that told of seven cities, rich in gold and jewels, settled by oppressed Christians from Moorish Spain. De Niza's report to the Spanish viceroy describing a town "larger than the city of Mexico," its houses inlaid with "turquoise stones, of which there was a great abundance," brought Francisco Vasquez de Coronado up from Mexico. He led an army prepared to seize the treasure-laden cities. But the friar's tale proved to be exaggerated; either he had seen the town from a great distance or he had not seen it at all, relying on the accounts of friendly Indians.

Instead of gold and jewels Coronado found a "little, crowded village . . . crumpled all up together"—this was Cibola! The Zuni warriors stood ready to defend their town. They sprinkled sacred cornmeal in a line and warned the Spaniards not to cross. Coronado was reluctant to start a fight, but when a shower of arrows struck his ranks, he attacked. Stones and arrows were no match for Spanish armor and harquebus.

After plundering the town's food stores, the conquerors set out for Acoma and Tusayan, the ancient land of the Hopi. The Spaniards turned eastward to explore along the Rio Grande, still hoping to find the elusive golden treasure.

Coronado's expedition provided a glimpse into traditional Pueblo ways, many of which live on today in the more conservative villages. The Spaniards saw young men living in underground council chambers—kivas—and women plastering their adobe houses and grinding corn. The chronicler Castañeda wrote: "A man sits at the door playing on a fife," the women grind and sing, "moving the stones to the music. . . ." He noted that some marriages were arranged by village elders, that the groom wove a blanket to place before his bride; he admired the Indians' glazed pottery, cotton cloth, and "cocks with great hanging chins"—turkeys.

The men of the pueblos put in long hours cultivating corn, beans, squash, and cotton. Later they learned from the Spanish to plant wheat, melons, chili peppers, and fruit trees. Hunting parties stalked deer and antelope, and communal rabbit hunts were organized in most villages.

Varieties of tobacco grew wild in Pueblo country. Smoking the dried leaves in a "cloud blower" —clay pipe—was ceremonial rather than pleasurable or relaxing. Youths could smoke only when they proved they were good hunters. At Isleta Pueblo, near present-day Albuquerque, this meant killing a Navajo, the Pueblos' traditional enemy to the north. Most adult males also performed religious and secular duties in the kiva, from which women were usually excluded.

Black-haired Pueblo matrons, wrapped in dark blankets fastened to leave the left shoulder bare, fashioned pots of coiled clay or bent over stone slabs baking *piki*, a paper-thin bread. Women enjoyed a privileged place in society, especially among the Hopi, where they owned the houses and fields. Children became members of the mother's clan and inherited property through her.

Pueblo marriage was monogamous, although divorce and remating were (continued on page 169)

Serpent Messengers Summon the Rain Gods

Fearsome painted priests of the Snake Society, faces blackened with soot and chins daubed with white clay, perform a Stone Age ritual to bring rain and an abundant harvest to the parched Hopi mesas. One, a live rattlesnake clamped in his teeth, circles the village plaza four times followed by a "hugger," who soothes the serpent with a feathered wand. On the sidelines other priests undulate, growling a chant that seems to come from the bowels of the earth.

About a dozen priests dance with snakes, then cast them in the plaza. The pile of reptiles, writhing "like soft, watery lightning," is sprinkled with cornmeal by Hopi women. Runners grab as many snakes as they can hold and go off in the four directions, releasing their charges in the desert. The Hopi believe their "elder brothers" will crawl down to the underworld and intercede with the rain gods.

The origin of the ceremony is unknown, but a prehistoric cult of the "plumed serpent" may have spread north from Mexico. According to Hopi legend, Tiyo, the Snake Youth, learned the mysterious rites in the underworld, then returned to earth with a beautiful Snake Maiden as his wife. In Hopi belief, all members of the snake clan are their descendants.

The spectacular dance is the climax of a 16-day ceremony held in August; only a few white men have witnessed its secret kiva rites, in which priests feed the reptiles pollen and wash them in yucca suds. How the Indians handle the snakes without harm (about a third are poisonous species) is uncertain. Theories abound; most likely, priests allow the rattlers to strike objects in the kiva before the ceremony. Hopi snake handlers, remarkably free of fear, do not believe the reptiles will bite a man with a pure heart; but if a bite does occur, "snake medicine" heals the wound.

Throngs of tourists, as well as neighboring Indians, view the sacred drama each year; cameras have been banned since the early 1900's to protect the rite from further commercialism. More often than not, visitors have scarcely left the mesa when the skies open up and the rain comes, renewing life and faith in the ancient pueblo for another year.

JOHN RUNNING

The Rites of Spring:
A Pueblo Prayer Drama

"Let the heavens be covered with banked-up clouds. . . . Let thunder be heard over the earth." Corn dancers make the centuries-old plea for rain and fertility at San Ildefonso, a Tewa pueblo in New Mexico. Crowned with crimson parrot feathers and draped with prized cowrie or conus shells from the Pacific, the male dancers leap and stamp to wake up the spirits. They carry gourd rattles and—to ward off witches—wrap their moccasins in skunk fur. Their evergreen finery, thrown in the river at ceremony's end, will appease the *Shiwana*, the rain-cloud people.

Gentle "earth mothers" shuffle barefooted in black *manta* and *tablita*, Spanish words for the ancient blanket dress and tiara worn by Pueblo women. A decorated pole symbolizes the fir tree the people climbed to escape the underworld. An onlooker (right) wears traditional dress and high white "puttee" moccasins.

All Rio Grande pueblos stage a Corn Dance, usually in spring, sometimes on the village saint's day. Villagers may attend a Catholic Mass before the ritual dance, reflecting co-existent Indian and Christian belief.

Prayers for a Bountiful Life

That all living things may "be fruitful and multiply," the Pueblos stage their ritual dramas. An annual round of dances seeks to ensure not only rain and plentiful crops, but also an ample supply of game and even the continued increase of humankind.

"The abundance of game appears infinite," reported Fray Alonso de Benavides, a Spanish missionary who visited the Rio Grande pueblos in the 1600's. In those days Pueblos hunted in the surrounding hills; some ventured east to the Great Plains. Such forays, always filled with danger, were wrapped in ritual and taboo.

Then as now, the pueblos staged a winter ceremony so that the Mother of Game would have many children, and to propitiate the slain animals' spirits. At a Tewa pueblo in New Mexico, the Hunt Chief calls the costumed "deer" and other animals in from the hills. They run in winding, snakelike patterns toward the village, led by the chief. In aboriginal times he was a powerful priest who decreed when the hunt should begin and end. When they reach the plaza, the deer dance rhythmically, bending over willow sticks that resemble forelegs. After special rites in the kiva they emerge and another dance begins, this one lasting all day. Dressed in comic costumes, two "Apaches" patrol the dance and burlesque those famous hunters. As a finale the deer run away, chased by women of the village, who take their captives home and feed them. The women receive meat in return. Traditionally, a dancer not caught by sundown will turn into a real deer.

Even today, hunting has its own mystique. The dead animal, wrapped in an embroidered blanket and adorned with beads, is an honored guest in the hunter's home. Deer antlers rest on housetops, blessed with meal and hung with prayer feathers. Village dogs wait in vain for the bones, which are ritually consigned to the Rio Grande lest the animal's spirit be offended.

At Puyé Cliffs, near Santa Clara Pueblo, the Basket Dance promotes fertility and abundance. Maidens holding traditional basket plaques kneel before boys decked with boughs; using musical rasps carved by a male partner, the girls accompany the singing and dancing. A winter rite whose origins are lost in remote antiquity, the dance now is performed for tourists.

168

Court jester and mediator with the spirit world, the *kossa* invokes supernatural gifts at Tewa ceremonies to protect the pueblo from enemies. In ghostly black-and-white makeup, hair tied in two "horns" flagged with cornhusks, the sacred clowns mask their serious purpose and delight villagers with pantomime and ribald horseplay. Power to increase fertility in man or beast gives the spirits license to joke obscenely. The ritual dancers pretend they are invisible.

fairly frequent. A Hopi husband who found his possessions stacked outside the door knew that he was not expected to return. At Taos and Acoma, adultery was punished by public whipping.

If a boy wanted a girl to be his bride, he would make a "bundle" for her—clothing and fine white buckskin moccasins, which he left on her doorstep. If they were accepted, so was he. When a wedding followed, there were elaborate festivities, with an exchange of gifts by the two families.

The peaceful Pueblos, content in their close-knit village life, went to war only when necessary —to defend themselves or to avenge a raid by enemy Indians. Tewa warriors sang to their wives:

So we have bad luck for we are men.
You have good luck for you are women.
To Navajo camps we go, ready for war.
Farewell!

Their weapons were arrows, clubs, and stone knives; from their belts hung a bag of *pinole*— meal made from roasted corn, rations for the journey. The war priest held ceremonies for as long as three nights to guarantee the expedition's success and the warriors' safe return.

At Zuni, the powerful Bow Priests controlled warfare and the rituals that would lead to victory. Their power came from the twin children of the sun, who in mythic times led the Zuni to victory over their enemies.

The Pueblo warriors would attack at dawn, rushing on surprised enemies as they came stumbling out of their shelters. They took a few scalps, gouging out a small, circular piece from the top of the head. When attacking from a distance, they shot arrows, sometimes tipped with rattlesnake venom. Before a counterattack could be organized, the warriors fled, hurrying through enemy country, back to the pueblo. If they were

carrying scalps, they did not enter but camped outside, for a scalp was dangerous and full of supernatural power. The scalp must be cleansed and then it became a friend, bringing good instead of evil. Zuni warriors who had taken scalps took part in a dance ceremony, becoming initiated members of the Cult of the War Gods, pledged to defend the village against all enemies.

In Coronado's time, about 90 pueblos were inhabited. Today there are only 30; the others were abandoned because of chronic drought, intertribal warfare, or conflict with the Spanish. From Taos, the northernmost pueblo, the Rio Grande descends rapidly and the valley opens up until the mountains of the west recede into the distance. Along here for approximately a hundred miles, like beads on a crooked string, are located the pueblos dependent on the Rio Grande and its tributaries. These villages are strikingly similar on the surface, but the people speak four mutually unintelligible languages. Located farther west in desert and mesa country are the "western" pueblos—Acoma, Laguna, Zuni, and the Hopi villages.

All the towns, from Taos to Hopi, whether built of sandstone on bluffs or of adobe on the banks of the Rio Grande, have one common characteristic: They blend with their surroundings. The Pueblos learned to build this way, to be architecturally unobtrusive, during the long centuries when they lived in every habitat from treeless desert to timbered mountain slopes.

In 1598 both the western and the Rio Grande pueblos again felt the heavy hand of Spanish imperialism. The conquest and colonization of New Mexico began under Juan de Oñate, who ruthlessly put down opposition to his program. Acoma resisted. Its inhabitants "spent all that night in huge dances and carousals, *(continued on page 174)*

Burnished by golden sunsets for a thousand years, Acoma Pueblo sits on its fortress rock nearly 400 feet above the New Mexico plain. Ancient Acomas

descended tortuous toehold trails to fields below. Now "Sky City," survivor of Indian attack and Spanish *entrada*, lives on in traditional serenity.

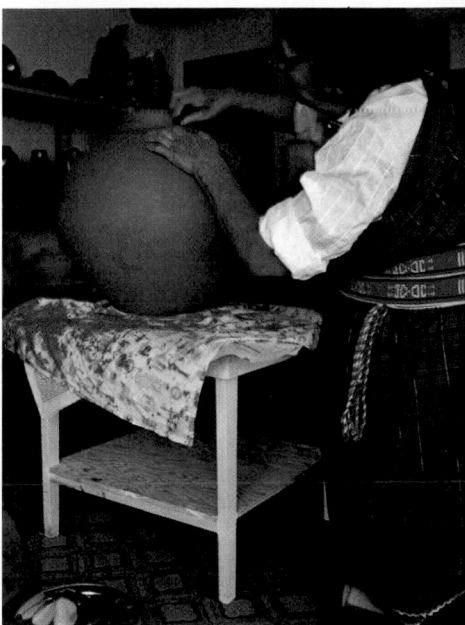

"Clay is selfish; each kind must speak for itself," says Tewa potter Margaret Tafoya of Santa Clara Pueblo. With nimble fingers she shapes pots much as her ancestors did 1,000 years ago. Digging clay from nearby hills, the potter sprinkles cornmeal in the pit to propitiate Clay Mother, who has "given her flesh." Proper mixing of clay with sand may take a week, then ropes of moist clay build coil on coil. (New World Indians never used the potter's wheel.) Under skilled hands, the shape of the pot gradually emerges. Dried, sanded, coated with a thin red "slip," and polished to a high gloss with a smooth stone, the pot is ready for painted motifs, applied with a brush or the chewed end of a yucca blade. Firing in the open with cakes of dung as fuel is the final step. If the fire is smothered, a chemical process turns the pot black.

Surrounded by her exquisite red and black polished ware, Margaret Tafoya knows her craft will survive awhile longer: Six daughters are potters.

MARTIN ROGERS

shouting, hissing, and making merry, challenging the army to fight," wrote a Spanish observer. Though the pueblo, high on its mesa, was invulnerable to attack by Indians, it could not withstand Spanish gunfire. After three days of fierce resistance, Acoma surrendered.

The other pueblos in New Mexico submitted peaceably and the Franciscan friars could begin the "harvest of souls." The Indians' native religion, which had been the focus of life for centuries, was suppressed, their "idolatrous" ceremonies forbidden, transgressors whipped or executed. As a result, the friar in charge of the missionary program reported in 1630 that 90 chapels had been built in as many towns, and that 60,000 Indians had been converted to Christianity.

Native rites went underground, and the Pueblos went to Mass, but only to please their oppressors; the Indians did not understand a god who came down to earth offering eternal life. Their own religion was more practical: Special priesthoods existed to insure a successful hunt or a bountiful harvest, to cure disease, or to vanquish enemies. Pueblo ceremonies were more elaborate than those of any other Indians north of Mexico.

Though the Pueblos shunned violence, the many injustices suffered under Spanish rule were intolerable, and in 1680 the villages, even the distant Hopi, successfully united to cast off the Spanish yoke. The revolt was a stunning though temporary defeat for the Spanish. Fourteen years passed before New Mexico was reconquered, and during that period the Indians went back to native ways, repudiating everything foreign, exulting in their freedom to worship the old gods. By 1694 a new governor, Diego de Vargas, had subdued the Indians again and restored the church. The priests, however, were fewer in number now and lacked authority to suppress Pueblo rites.

Out of 33 friars assigned to the province, 21 had been killed in the rebellion. Among the Hopi, only one mission was reestablished. Christianity languished, but survived.

Today, Pueblo festivals often combine traditional Indian dances and Christian pageantry, especially on the patron saint's day assigned each village by the missionaries. A visitor may see a deer dancer wearing antlers leave the plaza and enter the church, shaking his rattle. The sound mingles with the music of a Christian hymn, and the Indian worshipers are pleased. Many Pueblos are Catholic communicants, keep sacred images in their houses, and recite prayers in Spanish; but the old ways are not forgotten.

The Pueblo Indian's ancient religion still pervades his life. He believes that all things—animate and inanimate—have a place in the cosmos. The center of the cosmos is *sipapu*, his ancestors' place of emergence from the dark underworld. For the Tewa, the center is a lake in Colorado; for the Zuni, it is on the edge of their own ancient village. But all Pueblos have a place of emergence, bounded by sacred mountains in the four cardinal directions. Within these boundaries life must be harmonious, regulated, under control, the mind free of evil thoughts; religious rituals must be performed correctly, according to tradition. If this is done, the supernaturals will dispense the blessings of life.

Like their prehistoric ancestors, the chiefs of religious societies meet in the kivas to purify themselves and perform dances to keep the rain falling and the crops growing. In this harsh land where insufficient rain may mean starvation, the undulating rhythms of nature govern existence, while personal milestones like birth, puberty, marriage, and even death receive scant attention.

Mimbres bowl
c. 1150

Tesuque jar
c. 1890

Pima jar
c. 1885

Santa Clara
jar c. 1880

Zuni bowl
c. 1885

Hopi bowl
1967

Zuni canteen
c. 1880

San Ildefonso
bowl c. 1920

Zuni olla
c. 1885

Zuni bowl
c. 1880

The Potter's Art

Dancing whirlwinds, clouds, birds and beasts of desert and mountain fired the imagination of southwestern potters. Ceramics reached the Hohokam and Mogollon peoples about 300 B.C., probably by way of Mexico. Women kneeling in humble shelters in the Mimbres Valley of New Mexico painted graceful designs of rabbits, bears, turtles, and figures of fantasy—and achieved a pinnacle in prehistoric art. Archeologists ponder: Was this embellishment the inspiration of a single genius who founded a school that vanished with her? Mimbres bowls buried with the dead were "killed" —a hole punched in the bottom—perhaps to release the vessel's spirit into the next world.

Farther north, along the San Juan River about A.D. 400, the Pueblos' ancestors fashioned sun-dried bowls of clay and vegetable fiber; firing may have been accidental when a house burned. Later, clay tempered with sand or crushed potsherds formed water jars (ollas), mugs shaped like beer steins, and ladles. Some, unearthed at Chaco Canyon and Mesa Verde, have geometric and curving designs in black on white or red. The potter mixed paints, as she does today, from minerals and plants—ocher, beeweed, tansy mustard. A glaze technique, now lost to the Indians, brightened Zuni and Rio Grande Valley pots until 1700.

Pueblo pots had been principally household or ceremonial vessels. With the coming of the railroad in 1880, the Indians could serve their tortillas and venison stew on commercial ware and sell the handmade pots to the tourists. Today the craft flourishes; potters favor traditional motifs, yet seek new ways to make the clay sing. One artist dreams her designs; another studies museum pottery. A Hopi potter of the early 1900's revived an ancient style copied from potsherds picked up in nearby ruins. And Maria Martinez of San Ildefonso invented a new style—matte black on polished black.

At Zuni, where myth and tradition permeate life, the potter leaves a break in the line drawn around a jar's neck, believing her life would end if she closed the "road." Lifelike birds circle a Zuni bowl, but the Zuni olla's rainbird, all lines and circles, usually goes unrecognized. "Paint anything you like," the apprentice is told. "Only put it on straight!"

TOP: MUSEUM OF NEW MEXICO, SANTA FE. OTHERS: SMITHSONIAN INSTITUTION.
GORDON W. GAHAN AND JAMES P. BLAIR, BOTH NATIONAL GEOGRAPHIC PHOTOGRAPHERS

Mirror of the desert sky, turquoise set in silver adorns a Zuni artisan. His ancestors wore turquoise beads and earrings and—to ward off evil—encrusted cradles and doorways with the magic blue stone. In the 1880's Navajo and Zuni smiths mounted the gem in silver, often with a Spanish flair: the concha belt disks copied from spur buckles, petals of the "squash blossom" necklace from pomegranates, a Spanish heraldic motif. The crescent pendant hung from a horse's bridle.

Among the Hopi and Zuni, ceremonies center on the masked kachinas. Murals and carvings found in New Mexico attest that the kachina cult is at least 600 years old. Pueblos believe the kachinas are supernatural beings, spirits of their much-loved ancestors. At festival times, they borrow men's bodies and come down from their sacred mountains to visit the villages, bringing rain and fertility, awarding gifts, and enforcing discipline. Priests of the kachina cult, all adult males, don masks and impersonate the gods. In Indian belief, he who wears the mask of a kachina loses his own identity and becomes the spirit.

The people think of the masked gods as companions who come to the village to exchange favors. Prayer sticks decorated with feathers are planted at holy places—in fields and at springs—to carry prayers aloft to the spirits:

Now this very day
For the rite of our fathers . . .
We have prepared plume wands. . . .

Yonder from the north,
The rain maker priests . . .
Will make their roads come hither. . . .

With eagle's mist garment
With the striped cloud wings
And massed cloud tails
Of all the birds of summer. . . .

The Hopi kachinas come in December to celebrate the winter solstice, and again in February when the bean-planting ceremony, *Powamu,* reawakens the sleeping earth. For 16 days preceding the ritual, beans planted in the kivas are nurtured. They will sprout ahead of the planting season—symbolizing the power of the kachinas.

Powamu begins at dawn when the Crow Mother kachina, a majestic figure garbed in white, appears at the shrine on the edge of the village, bringing a basket of cornmeal. Suddenly other kachinas, splendidly arrayed in mantas and kilts, bright-colored sashes and freshly painted masks, scurry about. All the townspeople gather on housetops to watch. The kachinas enter the plaza and distribute gifts—bows and arrows, dolls, and baskets of sprouted beans for each household.

Later in the day, ogre kachinas—the *Nataskas*—wearing masks with long wooden snouts and brandishing saws or knives, threaten to carry off disobedient children. Wailing youngsters clinging to their mother's skirts are "ransomed" with offerings of cornmeal, piki bread, or freshly boiled corn-on-the-cob. Food collected in this way is distributed to the villagers and to the priests who spend much of their time in religious ritual.

At night, dancing kachinas perform inside the kivas. A loud stamping on the roof overhead announces their arrival; children peer upward in awe and anticipation as the spirits rapidly descend the ladder. To the sound of the sacred songs and sometimes to the hypnotic beat of drums, they stamp and gyrate rhythmically. Flickering firelight plays on costumes and glistening body paint. Grotesque shadows leap upward around the dancers. The onlookers are content to be there, halfway within the earth, watching. Nothing exists for them but the sacred drama.

A few years ago some friends and I were attending the *Niman,* or Home Dance. Then the masked gods perform for the Hopi people before returning to their homes in the San Francisco Peaks, distant but dimly visible to the southwest. The night before, we had camped below the Third Mesa villages; above us we could see the slender steeple of the ruined Old Oraibi Mission silhouetted against the sky. Now on the western horizon glowed a magnificent golden sunset, punctuated by ominous dark clouds. Being seasoned travelers in that country, we knew that the day following would be an unusual one.

The Niman is performed after the summer solstice, in July. The gods have danced frequently for the people for half a year now, and with this last dance they bid a dramatic and deeply moving farewell. The occasion is not without apprehension, for the Hopi must consider the possibility that the gods may not return, either the following year, or ever again. The last moments of the drama can be ones of almost pure religious insight. After years of observing the Hopi bid farewell to the gods, I did not have to understand their language to know that the elders were confessing to the gods on behalf of the people, acknowledging that they had been weak, forgetful of tradition, and disrespectful of their elders.

But they were also promising to try harder in the year ahead. The eyes of the old ones were not entirely dry as they implored the gods not to forget the people, to return. Finally, just before sundown, the masked gods filed southwest through the village to the edge of the mesa, in line with the mist-shrouded San Francisco Peaks. Many people followed the gods at a respectful distance until they disappeared over the horizon at the edge of the cliff. We followed too, caught up in the solemnity and magical power of the occasion. An old Hopi stepped in front of us. He told us: "No farther. You cannot go on. They are they, and we are we. They have their own ways and we of this world have ours."

I remembered as I watched these sacred Hopi ceremonies that they had been witnessed, centuries ago, by the Apache and Navajo, who had wandered into the mountains north of the Rio Grande by Coronado's time. At first there were few

"We will come as clouds ... to bless the Hopi people," sing the beloved ancestor spirits, the kachinas, whose legendary home atop Arizona's San Francisco Peaks looks out upon the sunbaked mesas. Here in a realm of plenty, the Hopi believe, the supernaturals feast on plump squash and melons and gather their ceremonial needs for six months of the year. Then they descend and enter the villages. A Hopi with a pure heart may someday join his ancestors on the snowy peaks.

TERRY EILER

peaceful contacts with these hunters and raiders from the northwest. Although the newcomers continued to raid for the next three hundred years, the Navajo, especially, would prove themselves willing and able to adopt Pueblo ideas and institutions, even to take Pueblo wives.

The Apache and Navajo are related to the Athapaskan tribes of northwestern Canada. About the year 1500, or perhaps earlier, small bands began to drift into the southwest, possibly taking a route along the eastern foothills of the Rocky Mountains. We know they were living in Gobernador Canyon, New Mexico, at least 400 years ago; remains of the Navajo's traditional dwelling, the hogan, have been found there.

Some of the newcomers settled along the Colorado-New Mexico boundary between the Chama and San Juan Rivers, later spreading south and west into today's Navajo country. The Tewa called them *Apaches de Nabahu*—enemies of the cultivated fields. It is easy to imagine these wild hunters raiding the peaceful Pueblo farmers, stealing corn and women, and disappearing again into their remote canyons. In historic times bands of Navajos raided the Tewa and Hopi villages at harvest time with such regularity that trails were worn into Navajo country.

No one knows when the Apache and Navajo separated, but long after the Navajo had settled down to farming and sheep raising, Apaches roamed the mountains hunting game and gathering wild food. Because of their roving life they had few possessions or crafts except waterproof baskets and knee-high moccasins of buckskin. Home was a skin tipi or a wickiup, a framework of saplings that could be thrown up in an hour.

In most Apache tribes the bridegroom went to live in his wife's community, but all Apaches showed respect for a mother-in-law by never speaking to her. This custom, shared with the Navajo, is a vestige of their northern origin.

A Spanish missionary described the Jicarilla Apache of New Mexico in the 1600's: "They are wont to have as many wives as they can support ... and upon her whom they take in adultery they ... execute their law, which is to cut off her ears and nose." The Jicarilla occupied mountainous country in northeastern New Mexico, and ranged eastward to Kansas. Their culture reflects contact with both Pueblo and Plains Indians.

Apache! The very word filled the air with foreboding along the frontier settlements of the southwest. The Chiricahua of southern Arizona and New Mexico gained renown as clever and ruthless fighting men. Before he could join that elite fraternity of warriors, the Chiricahua youth served a long apprenticeship. Games with the bow and arrow sharpened his skill, and sorties into the rugged mountains taught him survival in the wilderness. He learned to run four miles with a mouthful of water without swallowing. Apache warriors could travel as far as 70 miles a day, on foot, with very little water. At the age of 17, the youth was ready to join the council of warriors and share in the glories of the warpath.

The Western Apache, who ranged Arizona from Tucson to Flagstaff, would swoop down from a mountain fastness to raid Mexican ranches and Pima Indian villages, stealing supplies and driving off livestock. Stolen Spanish horses were valued as mounts or for transporting goods. Surplus animals were never wasted; the flesh might be cut in strips, dried, and eaten.

All over the southwest, Apaches waged a guerrilla war, often in reprisal for unprovoked attacks. "The whole land is at war with the widespread heathen nation of the Apache Indians," declared a

"The Kachinas Are Coming!"

The cry goes up in the dusty plaza of a Hopi village, and all eyes turn toward the edge of the mesa. First comes the sound of rattles and drums. Then—masked and costumed, following the "road" of sacred cornmeal sprinkled by the priests—the kachinas appear, living spirits of the dead and all the mysterious forces of nature. For six months they will live in the village and dance for rain and other blessings.

"Kachina" means three things: a spirit the Hopi believe in, a masked impersonator, and a carved and painted likeness—the kachina doll. Before a ceremony, fathers and uncles busy themselves creating the sculpture from blocks of cottonwood root, adding beak, ears, or horns, and bits of shell, feathers, or turquoise. Between dances the kachinas present the dolls, dangling from their wrists and fingers, to beaming children. To the Pueblos the dolls are not idols to be worshiped, but lessons to be studied; they hang on the wall at home as constant reminders. At age seven to ten boys and girls are initiated into the kachina cult and learn (if they did

not know) that the impersonators are their relatives and neighbors. Thereafter, boys may participate in ceremonies. Girls take less active roles, but also feel themselves part of the tribe's sacred tradition.

Most Pueblos recognize kachinas, but the Hopi pantheon is largest—more than 250. Supernatural beings encountered after the Hopi had emerged from the dark underworld, the spirits once lived with the people and taught them how to conduct ceremonials.

Kachinas take many forms—demons, ogres, animals, birds, or clowns (overleaf). Mudheads, the best-known Hopi clowns, entertain at ceremonies—mocking tourists, anthropologists, neighboring Indians, or themselves. Their guessing games and balancing acts please the crowd. In Zuni legend, punishment for incest left them coated with mud, hence the name Mudhead.

Some Hopi and Zuni craftsmen carve authentic kachina dolls for sale, varying in size from a few inches to two feet. The masterworks of the best carvers can be seen only in museums and private collections.

COLLECTIONS OF MARGARET KILGORE, JAMES T. BIALAC, SHARON N. JAMES, TOM AND GEORGIA MILLS; TERRY EILER

Clowns

Cloud-corn girl   **Blue Ho-te kachina**   **Tsuku clown**

Wolf kachina   **Mudhead**   **Hano Mana kachina**

missionary father in 1669. "No road is safe . . . everyone travels at the risk of his life. . . ."

When Apaches took scalps, they staged a wild victory celebration, dancing around a pole with the scalp on top. But fear of the dead kept the Indians from collecting them as trophies, and anyone who handled one used "ghost medicine" to protect himself from his dead enemy's power.

The Chiricahua are best known as the last American Indians to lay down their arms. They battled the Army and citizenry of the United States for nearly twenty years, striking with speed and stealth, then disappearing into their hideouts. Soldiers standing watch—even inside military posts—could expect ambush at any time. Disguised with branches, stripped naked, Apaches wriggled along the ground to within yards of their prey. They killed quietly and expertly with lance or bow, and then, as a cavalry officer put it, "scattered like their own crested mountain quail."

By the beginning of the 1800's, the Navajo, mounted on horses plundered from the Spaniards, had moved west into the land "between the four mountains"—a vast expanse principally in Arizona, about the size of New Hampshire, Vermont, and Massachusetts put together. There the Navajo flourished, counting their wealth in horses and huge flocks of sheep. Many of these were stolen from the corrals of white settlers or other Indians. Navajos ranged as far east as Nebraska, bringing back Pawnee slaves to exchange for more horses at the Spanish fair in Taos.

Navajo settlements were not towns like those of the agricultural Pueblos, but clusters of hogans in box canyons or at the base of cliffs. The women cultivated gardens or helped with sheepherding. Some kept slaves to do the menial work and give them more time to weave the woolen blankets for which the Navajo are famous. In the 19th century, Navajo men began making silver jewelry, an art they learned from the Mexicans.

Navajo craft designs, impressive as they are by themselves, have their roots in the traditional dry paintings of the Navajo religion. And the paintings, in their turn, are pictorial representations of the great sings or chants which make up the heart of Navajo religion. The chants—prayers, myths, and poetry rendered into song—are performed as curing rites. Each chant is concerned with specific illnesses. The Mountain Chant, for example, cures nervous disorders.

It would be impossible to understand the Navajo and their culture in relation to the ruggedly beautiful land without a sense of their chantways. Each of these long song cycles not only represents prayer and literature but also tells part of the Navajo creation story—a long saga about how the gods created the first people and brought them up from the underworld.

A pervasive feature is repetition; the message or power of the song peals outward, usually four times over, in gentle but insistently undulating rhythms. Since each song has its setting entirely within the Navajo cosmos, telling how one aspect of it came into being and was ordered by the Holy People, everyone who hears it understands a little better, from the Navajo point of view, how they feel about their life, their land.

I first gained an appreciation of the power of the chants during long nights beside a flickering campfire within Canyon de Chelly, and at the base of the giant spires in Monument Valley. As the words and repeated phrases of the Night Chant return to memory in the shadow of these towering natural formations, it is not difficult to understand why so many of the songs tell of sacred journeys of the Holy People, traveling from place to place

A green giant with spiny arms that may reach 50 feet, the saguaro cactus yields its crimson fruit to a Papago grandmother. For centuries her tribe has harvested the figlike fruit at "saguaro harvest moon," the beginning of the Papago new year. From it they make jam, candy, syrup, and—for a summer rain ritual—wine.

Father Kino, a Jesuit missionary, visited the Papago homeland in southern Arizona in the 1600's. He found the tribe and their Pima cousins farming irrigated land and gathering wild food. They still do.

In July, whole families camp out in Saguaro National Monument where the government permits the traditional harvest. With a picking pole made from the skeleton of a dead saguaro, women rake off the fruit, scoop out the juicy meat, and drop the pod on the ground, face up. This, they believe, will entice the rain gods to speed the summer rains.

CHARLES O'REAR

Balancing a basket of juicy saguaro fruit, a Papago picker heads for her camp in the Arizona desert. There pans, ollas, and sieves are set out for a cooking bee. The fruit in its flowerlike pod is the size of a hen's egg and filled with tiny black seeds—a treat for birds; sometimes they beat the Indians to the desert feast.

Over a hot mesquite fire, the fruit cooks while the women laugh and gossip. Juice is strained and then boiled until it becomes syrup; three pecks of fruit yield a half gallon of syrup. Many hands help remove seeds from the pulp, which can then be used to make jam. Seeds are ground for oil and flour.

After the harvest, each family contributes a jar of syrup. When the batch ferments, the people gather before the council house. The chief— "Keeper of the Smoke"—invites them: "Drink, friend! Get beautifully drunk! Hither bring the wind and the clouds." Eagerly the people drink, symbolizing the rain soaking the earth.

CHARLES O'REAR

Misty vale of enchantment, Havasu Canyon shelters the "people of the blue-green water," the Havasupai, who fled here by the 12th century, perhaps to escape enemies. Their paradise valley of plunging waterfalls lies in a deep gorge of Arizona's Grand Canyon. The tribe, numbering some 400, traces kinship to the Colorado River Yuman, whose shamans talked with spirits in dreams, receiving power and clairvoyance.

TERRY EILER

within the Navajo world. The deities are described in poetic images from nature:

In Tse'gíhi
In the house made of the dawn,
In the house made of the evening twilight,

In the house made of the dark cloud,
In the house made of the he-rain,
In the house made of the dark mist . . .
Oh, male divinity!

With your moccasins of dark cloud,
 come to us.
With your leggings of dark cloud,
 come to us.
With your shirt of dark cloud,
 come to us. . . .
With your head-dress of dark cloud,
 come to us.
With the dark thunder above you,
 come to us soaring.
With the shapen cloud at your feet,
 come to us soaring.
With the far darkness made of the dark cloud
 over your head, come to us soaring. . . .

The prayer is addressed to a mythical dark bird, "chief of pollen," one of many supernatural beings who dwell in Tse'gíhi, "among the rocks," south of the San Juan River. The lengthy prayers, committed to memory by a singer, or medicine man, are invocations to the Navajo gods whose help is sought. If the rite is performed correctly, the patient will overcome the evil causing his illness, so that once again he "walks in beauty."

The Navajo arrived in the southwest centuries ago with a simple culture and an economy based on hunting and gathering. From the beginning they have never missed an opportunity to acquire new skills and better ideas. Many of these ideas came

from the settled folk — the Pueblos — who were already in the southwest when the Navajo swept in from the north.

If you ask the Navajo where their people learned to weave, they will say "from Spider Woman, in the beginning." Actually, they learned after the reconquest of the 1690's, when refugees fleeing the Spanish streamed into Navajo camps. The Pueblos, who had been weaving for a thousand years, were good teachers; their Navajo pupils became the greatest weavers of the southwest.

Religion was influenced by the Pueblos, too. On long winter nights around flickering campfires, "when the snakes are asleep and the thunder silent," there was time to impart the intricacies of Pueblo myth and ritual, around which the Navajo have constructed the splendid pageantry of their religious ceremonials. But for the Navajo the ritual was performed not as a prayer for rain, but as a curing rite to bring the patient back in tune with the universe.

Taos Pueblo sits snugly at the southern base of a majestic sweep of mountains which culminate in 13,160-foot Wheeler Peak, highest point in New Mexico. The Taos people have the notion that they live at the top of the world because their sacred Blue Lake is located high on the rim of the mountains. Through this lake, according to their sacred teachings, emerged their ancestors from another world.

It has been a long-standing folk belief in Taos that if their people ceased to exist, the world itself would cease to exist. A village elder explained: "After all, we are a people who live on the roof of the world; we are the sons of Father Sun, and with our religion we daily help our father to go across the sky. We do this not only for ourselves, but for the whole world." (continued on page 195)

DAVID HISER

An Apache Way

Facing east, a ceremonial tipi rises under a wide New Mexico sky. The stage is set for the Mescalero Apache's chief religious festival—the girls' coming-of-age celebration. Centuries ago, the tribe roamed wooded foothills of their sacred mountain, Sierra Blanca, foraging for food. Some ranged farther south and east. Later the Mescalero raided Spanish corrals and rode east into the Staked Plains of Texas to hunt buffalo.

While the warriors hunted and raided, groups of women set out in search of the tribe's staple food—mescal. Armed with piñon sticks, they hacked off the plant's huge crowns, then, digging a cooking pit in the rocky soil, roasted them. (Mescalero means "mescal maker.") Back in camp women found more chores: They built shelters, fetched wood and water, sewed moccasins, made baskets, cooked, cared for children. A shrill and noisy group, they worked together to lighten the burden of incessant toil.

But a young Apache maiden had her time in the sun before the routine of married life began. At the age of 12 to 14 she starred in a four-day drama that would launch her properly into womanhood. The whole tribe gathered to share in the festivities.

Today as in aboriginal times, cattail fronds, symbol of renewal, carpet the entrance to the tipi; inside the girl kneels, clad in golden buckskin, the color of pollen. Attending shamans wail their high-pitched songs:

> . . . the rainbow moves forward, dawn maidens. . . .
> Beautifully over us it is dawning.

A "godmother" paints the young virgin with pollen from cheek to cheek, then pushes her toward a tray laden with ritual objects, which she circles four times. Every night the girl dances until midnight, while outside, her people dance and feast. On the last day a shaman blesses her, a sun symbol in his palm:

> The sun . . . has come down to the earth,
> It has come to her. . . .
> Long life! Its power is good.

Meekly the girl submits to the demanding rite; for if she behaves well on this day, the Apache believe, she will always be a good woman.

DAVID HISER

Dance of the Mountain Spirits

A bonfire stabs at the dark. From the east into the circle of light stamp five grotesque figures — swaying, posturing, brandishing striped wooden swords. Soon the dancers are challenged by another group, then another, all dancing and charging each other and the fire in wild, tumultuous freedom.

This is the Mescalero Dance of the *Gahe*, spirits who live in the sacred mountain and come forth to drive away sickness and evil and bring good fortune. Impersonators of the spirits wear black hoods of buckskin, sometimes adorned with strength-giving abalone shells or turquoise. Towering headdresses, painted with sacred symbols—a cross or star—have horns of yucca to symbolize game protected by the spirits; eagle feathers float from streamers tied above the elbow.

Rooted in Apache lore, the Spirit Dance resembles masked Pueblo ceremonies. The government suppressed Apache rituals in the 1890's; today the Mescalero puberty rite and Spirit Dance are woven into a single spectacle, held annually in the shadow of Sierra Blanca.

A stormy cloudscape gathers at Ship Rock, landmark of the Navajo's traditional homeland in northwestern New Mexico. The Indians call the ragged monolith *tse bit'a'i*, rock with wings. In mythic times, Navajos pursued by enemies gathered atop the rock; suddenly it rose and sailed across the sky, taking its passengers to safety. Today, Navajo ponies graze in the shadow of the hallowed pinnacle.

TERRY EILER

Taos is divided by a mountain stream into parts called North Pueblo and South Pueblo. The council of religious elders which rules the tribe is drawn equally from both halves and governs impartially. In aboriginal times, the Taos people farmed on their grassy plateau and hunted in the mountains. Through a narrow pass to the east they traded with the Plains Indians. They have always been known for their leatherwork, especially moccasins and drums, as well as for golden-hued pottery.

I would like to try to impart a sense of the unchanging rhythm and nature of life at Taos by describing a visit of my own there. It was just before dawn in the first week of spring and I recall waiting for the sunrise by the multistoried buildings of the old village. First light came with the gradual unfolding, then evaporation, of dark pink shadows on the five stories of North Pueblo, which faces the sunrise almost squarely at this, the beginning of the planting cycle.

I began to discern the texture of the adobe face on this massive apartment building several centuries old. I could see the semicircular streaks made by the hands of the women who periodically replaster the building. These streaks harden as the plaster hardens, and because the mixture—pink desert clay and black river-bottom earth mixed with straw and chaff to prevent cracking—is so strong, it takes several years of moisture and wind to smooth out the surface.

As the sun's first rays shone over a great gap in the mountains, men robed in colorful blankets appeared on the upper stories of North Pueblo. Some stood and peered intently in the direction of the sunrise. I wondered about their thoughts and feelings. Were they grateful to Father Sun for granting them yet one more day of life? At Taos one learns quickly not to pry into such matters, but I have often imagined since that the silent figures gazing off into the distance were reciting a prayer to greet the rising sun, like the one my grandfather taught me when I was a boy:

O, our elders,
this is the name bestowed on me,
when I was presented to you at dawn,
four days after birth.

O, our elders,
you who have never become mortal beings,
who have no reason to worry,
*   no reason to be lonely,*
*   no reason to weep,*
*   no reason to be sad,*

I, a child of darkness,
come forth on this dawn to feed you,
with the sacred cornmeal of tradition,
and to offer you this,
my humble morning prayer.

May you, our elders,
keep meadows and mountains alive,
with grass and with game.
And may I continue
to be accepted and loved.
May I catch up with that
for which we always seek,
long life and abundance.

As the sun stood free of the mountains at last, another blanketed figure appeared on the rooftop. This was the town crier, who shouted the pueblo governor's orders for the day to the now-awakened village. This ancient institution has been more than a quaint survivor in Taos, for in the pueblo the elders have not permitted electricity or telephones. The Taos people would like to keep out encroaching civilization, *(continued on page 200)*

Transitory tapestry in sand, a Navajo dry painting
calls forth divine gifts of healing. A sick child seated in
the magic circle absorbs the power of the golden sun god
and the eagle. Feathers of the majestic bird, sacred to the
Navajo, radiate to the four directions, one feather for
each song in the curing chant. As the medicine man sings,
the patient relives the trials of a long-ago hero cured by
the gods. "Happily my head becomes cool," she may sing at
ritual's end, "impervious to pain I walk."

The medicine man, with helpers, works for hours to create
the magic picture, trickling crushed sandstone, pollen,
or charcoal taken from a tree struck by lightning. No models
exist but those inside his head. Like a stained glass window,
the intricate design makes the Holy People visible.
But by sunset its ephemeral beauty must be scattered to
the winds lest evil spirits come and make mischief.

The Navajo "singers" know at least 35 major curing chants,
each with its own songs and dry paintings; for one of these,
more than 500 songs must be memorized. A patient's family
hosts a "sing," and hundreds of Navajos gather to share the
blessings. Modern medicine marvels when there's a cure, but
the principle is old: Mind and body are one. The Navajo
treat the patient, not the illness; the ritual will bring him
back into harmony with himself and the world.

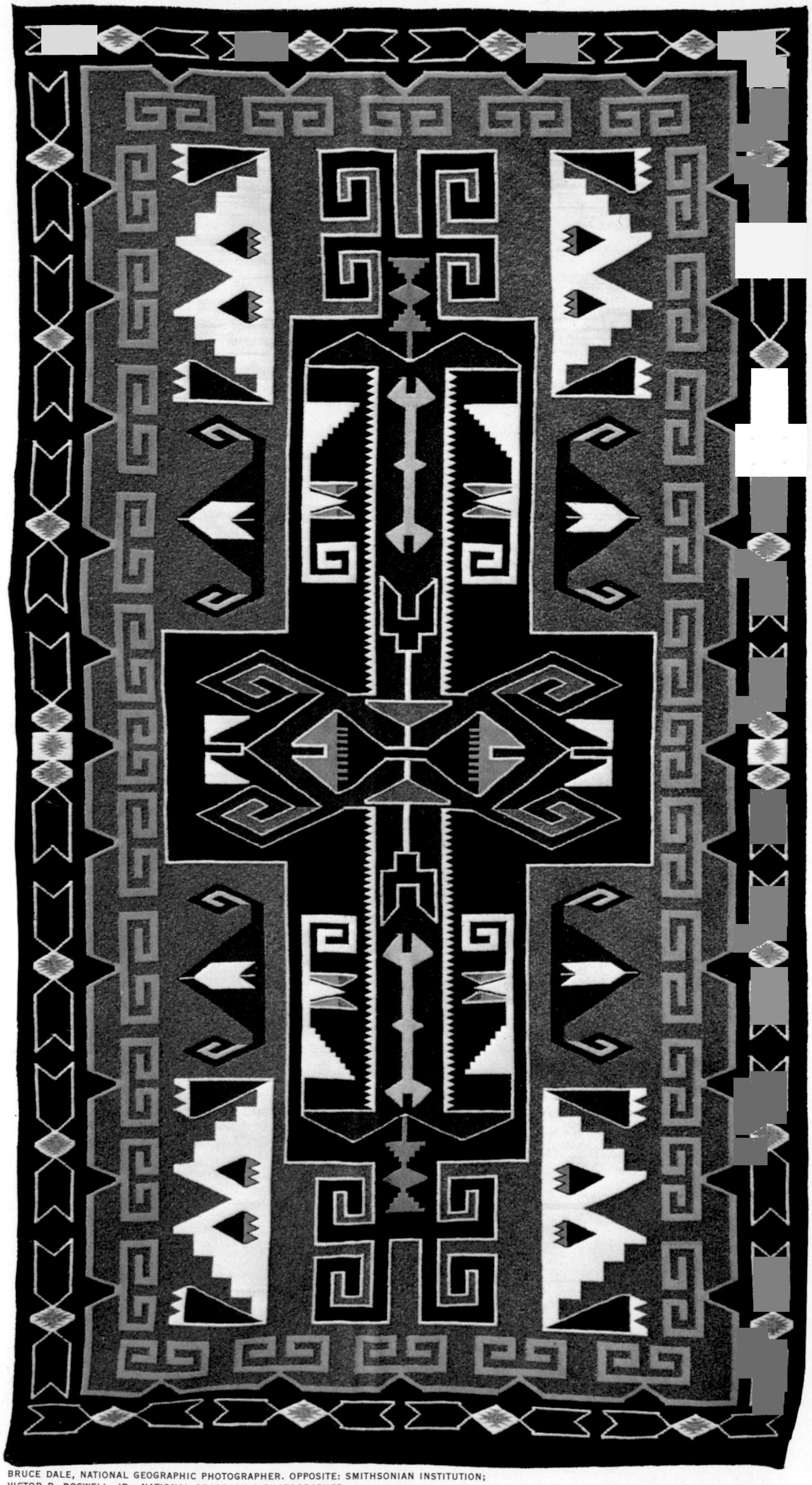

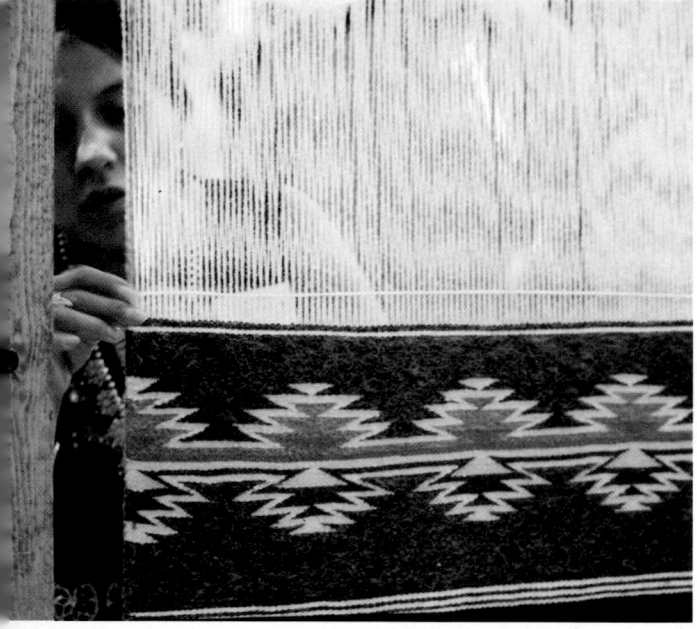

Weaving her own trail of beauty, a Navajo woman shapes a masterpiece in wool. She works a loom of prehistoric Pueblo origin; makers boast such rugs are so close-woven they can hold water.

Early craftsmen made striped "chief's blankets" to wear and to trade as prestige symbols. Indigo dissolved in fermented urine made a good blue dye, but native reds were poor. When bayeta flannel—English baize—found its way into Navajo country, weavers patiently unraveled the threads to make crimson blankets with diamond or zigzag designs. One (lower right), made c. 1870, is from a golden age of Navajo weaving.

A fringed rug reflects the era of commercial yarns and dyes. With an eye on the tourist, traders had turned blanket into rug by 1890. Recent trends back to native dyes and patterns raise quality and prices—this brown-toned rug from Teec Nos Pos sold for $3,500. Traditional designs emerge from the weaver's memory—always, it is said, with a break in the pattern, an escape route for the maker's spirit.

BRUCE DALE, NATIONAL GEOGRAPHIC PHOTOGRAPHER. OPPOSITE: SMITHSONIAN INSTITUTION; VICTOR R. BOSWELL, JR., NATIONAL GEOGRAPHIC PHOTOGRAPHER

but pickup trucks parked in the narrow streets and tourists snapping pictures are common sights. By the time the crier appeared, I began to detect the aroma of half a thousand fires of cedar and piñon wood wafting onto the plaza, intermingled with the scents of boiling coffee, tortillas, and beans cooking on the stoves.

The signs of a community reawakened were continued by the appearance of several elderly women on the plaza. Each had one or two buckets in hand. As they made their way to the stream to get water, I noticed that some were bent over with age; others were blind. Yet all moved in a leisurely way, first to the stream, then back again.

I also watched some woodchoppers, and they too had this same leisurely rhythm. Each would take a few hefty swings, then pause to joke with a neighbor, or look up at the mountains or sun. Something only they could perceive along the sky-line beyond the pueblo seemed to interest them. This could not be more different from the hustle and bustle of modern communities. I felt then, as I always do on such occasions, a profound sense of antiquity, a feeling that I was in the presence of something timeless.

On a previous visit I had been taken to the top of North Pueblo by a man I was visiting. Our families had been friends for generations; otherwise I would not have been extended the rare privilege of viewing the sunrise from "the roof of the world." As we stood there, my host, an older man, gazed out over the eastern horizon for a long while. Then he observed, with a slow sweeping gesture over the whole of that mountainous distance, "Some things will never change, must never change." I nodded in agreement, a little closer to understanding just why it is that the Taos people feel their own destiny so closely bound up with the rhythm and the very health of the cosmos.

Sunset gilds the lofty apartments of Taos Pueblo, nestling in New Mexico's Sangre de Cristo Range. Legend tells of a chief who led his people to the foot of the mountains; where an eagle dropped two plumes beside a sparkling stream they settled. First inhabitants may have been refugees from Mesa Verde 700 years ago. In ancient times Taos pulled up its ladders, showing enemies a blank adobe face; today it still shields its Indian heart, shutting out the world's clamor.

MARCIA KEEGAN

Fishermen and Foragers of the West

Robert F. Heizer

In the early 19th century an Englishman trading along the continent's northwestern coast made one of the native chiefs a magnanimous offer —to take him on a visit to England or "America." To the trader's surprise, the chief declined, "as he considered we were slaves—even our chiefs— who were always doing something from necessity, and as we were always at work for a living. 'I have slaves,' said he, 'who hunt for me—paddle me in my canoes,—and my wives to attend upon me. Why should I wish to leave?' "

Here was no aboriginal poverty pocket, the trader was given to understand. One of the most aristocratic, richest Indian cultures north of Mexico flourished in the Pacific northwest—a land of salmon and cedar, potlatch and totem pole— where only the weak were meek and the highborn man who inherited wealth dutifully flaunted it.

Ancient patterns of the culture are broken now. But the matrix—a lush natural setting—remains. "Nothing to the eye but immense ranges of mountains or impenetrable forests.... In some places the country appears to be level on the coast, but still the eye soon finds itself checked by steep hills and mountains, covered ... with thick woods down to the margin of the sea."

Written nearly two centuries ago, this description of the steep and abrupt northwest coast of America still holds for the 1,500-mile stretch from Yakutat Bay, Alaska, to Cape Mendocino, California. North of the Strait of Juan de Fuca—marking the United States-Canada border—hulks of partly submerged mountains form the rugged islands of British Columbia and Alaska. Warm currents flowing along the Pacific margin produce a relatively mild climate with much rain.

Stand at water's edge when sea fog broods over a tree-quilled cove and it is not hard to imagine an Indian village nestling there, unchanged from

Forested isles dot a silvery swath along the northwestern rim of the continent, wild tangle of sea and land that cradled one of North America's most lavish and colorful Indian cultures. Riches of both realms were there for the harvesting. Seas teemed with fish and mammals. Shores yielded game and fruits such as red huckleberry in season. Beaches so abounded in shellfish, including meaty-stalked goose barnacles, that it was said, "When the tide goes out, the table is set."

ENTHEOS

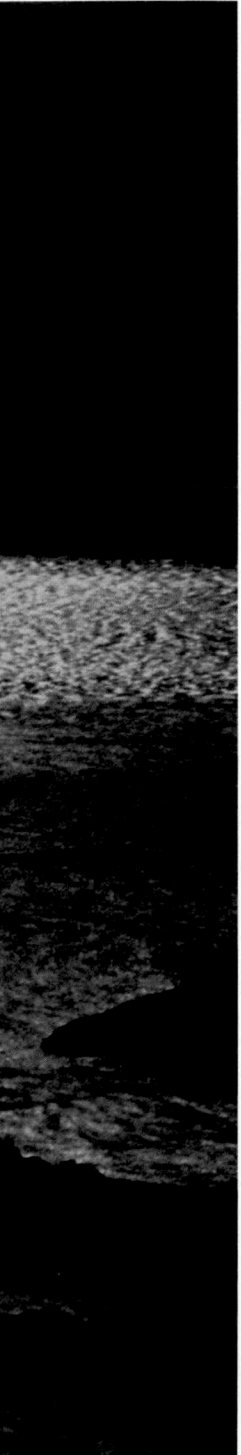

the days of English trader John Meares' first visit: Rows of low, multifamily houses tier the slope, the soft gray of weathered cedar planks blending into the mist; huge dugout canoes wait beyond the reach of the tide; and stocky, dark-haired men in cone-shaped hats and raincapes of woven bark— perhaps landbound and bored for weeks on end— plead in song for a break in the weather:

> *Don't you ever, you up in the sky,*
> *Don't you ever get tired*
> *Of having the clouds between you and us?*

In this rocky and rainy coastal strip there are few extensive beaches. But wherever a river delta or a protected inlet broke the phalanx of forest, there the native people settled, taking an abundant livelihood from the streams and ocean. From Yakutat Bay to Mendocino—in an area of 176,000 square miles—an estimated 150,000 Indians lived at the beginning of the historical period. There were dozens of tribal groups, quite separate, yet the conditions of nature under which they lived and their responses were sufficiently alike to define a distinct cultural unit. The larger tribes, by language groupings, included the Tlingit in southeastern Alaska; Haida of the Queen Charlotte Islands; Tsimshian, Kwakiutl, and Salish on the mainland; Nootka on Vancouver Island; and Chinook along the lower Columbia River. A number of smaller tribes held the coastal area from Washington south into California.

Maritime specialization deeply affected all aspects of the culture—material, social, spiritual. Villages of sturdy houses were sited with an eye to a beach where canoes could be drawn up. Tools and implements included a vast array of devices for fishing and for hunting sea mammals. And the religion, both rituals and deities, centered on aquatic creatures that were the staff of life.

formulas and fish lore carried it like an honored guest to an altar, sprinkled it with sacred eagle down or red ocher, and made a speech of welcome followed by songs and prayers. Then he cooked the fish in a ritually prescribed way and gave everyone a taste. After the sacrament, fishing could begin in earnest, though all bones were put back into the water so they could return to the Salmon House for reincarnation. A few weeks of feverish activity in early autumn would yield enough salmon—filleted, smoke-dried, and stored—to free the people of any serious food quest during the wet, stormy winter months.

Similar rituals honored the first herring and eulachon—a small fish so rich in oil that, dried, it could be burned from end to end like a candle—and other species that spawned in the rivers and inlets. Deep-water cod and halibut could be taken with hook and line at any time of year. Ocean and shore yielded abundant shellfish and edible kelp. Sea mammals provided both food for the larder and furs for special-occasion robes and for trade. The sea is the "great market to which these people resort," said Meares, who set up a trading post among the Nootka in the late 1700's.

In addition to the summer village on the beach, many tribes had a winter seat at the head of a protected inlet or back in a fjord sheltered from the lash of storms. Rough terrain and dense evergreen forests with an obstacle course of fallen timber, shrubs, and vines beneath the canopy discouraged overland travel. There were few trails. Most people traveled by canoe rather than on foot. The heavy framework of both winter and summer houses was stationary but planks for the roof and walls moved with the occupants. As soon as the herring began to school in the sounds in early spring and it was time to move to the seaside, men would lash the house planks between two large

Fish was the main article of diet, salmon the mainstay. Each year salmon streamed up rivers to spawn in such numbers they seemed immortals bent on a mass sacrifice of their bodies for the Indians' benefit. If the Salmon Beings were treated with respect, people believed, their spirits would return to the Salmon House under the sea, acquire new bodies, and make the sacrificial run again.

All along the coast from Monterey Bay north Indians held some sort of first salmon ritual. Its basic purpose was a kind of game management since, as part of the rite, provision was made for enough salmon to ascend and spawn to ensure their return. How conscious the Indians were of this conservation aspect we do not know, but the rite must have developed with this idea in mind.

The first fish taken at each important fishing site was considered the leader whose command the other fish obeyed and so was given the most elaborate attention. A ritualist versed in secret

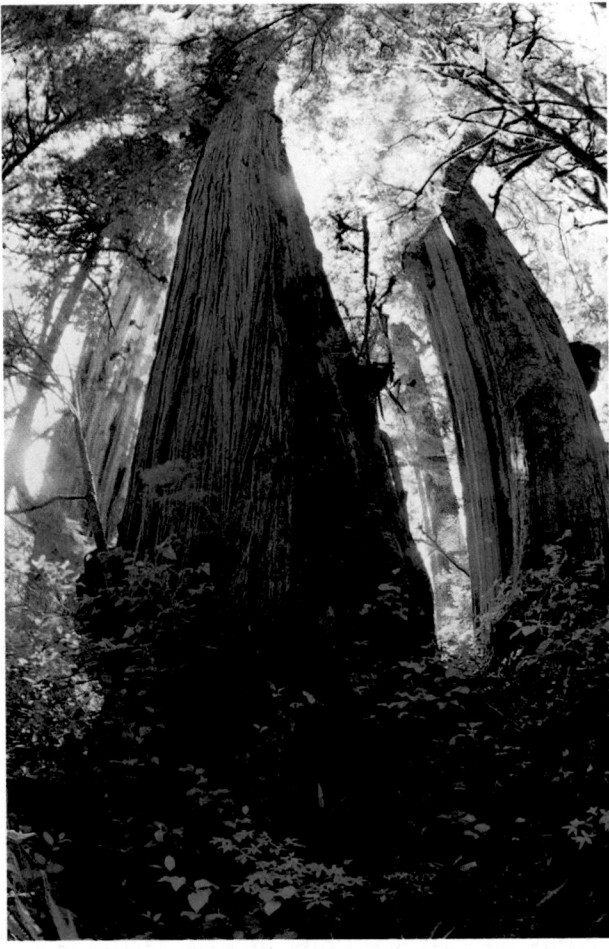

Majestic cedars wanted to be used. That was why, by Indian reasoning, cedar wood was so soft and straight-grained, so readily split into house planks or carved into totem poles, tools, or utensils. The bark, too, had a multitude of uses—from baskets and clothing to whaling ropes. Sang the Kwakiutl woman to the compliant, all-purpose tree:

Look at me, friend! I come to ask for your dress,
For you have come to take pity on us;
For there is nothing for which you cannot be used....
Long-life maker...

Dense forest yielded the knot-free giant for a fine canoe, its size determined by use. Felled and rough-shaped with fire and adz, the hull was towed to the village beach. A master canoe maker steamed it for the delicate task of spreading the beam. At last—finely balanced, fitted, and polished with sandpapery skin of a shark—the craft was deemed ready for long voyages or for food-gathering near the village.

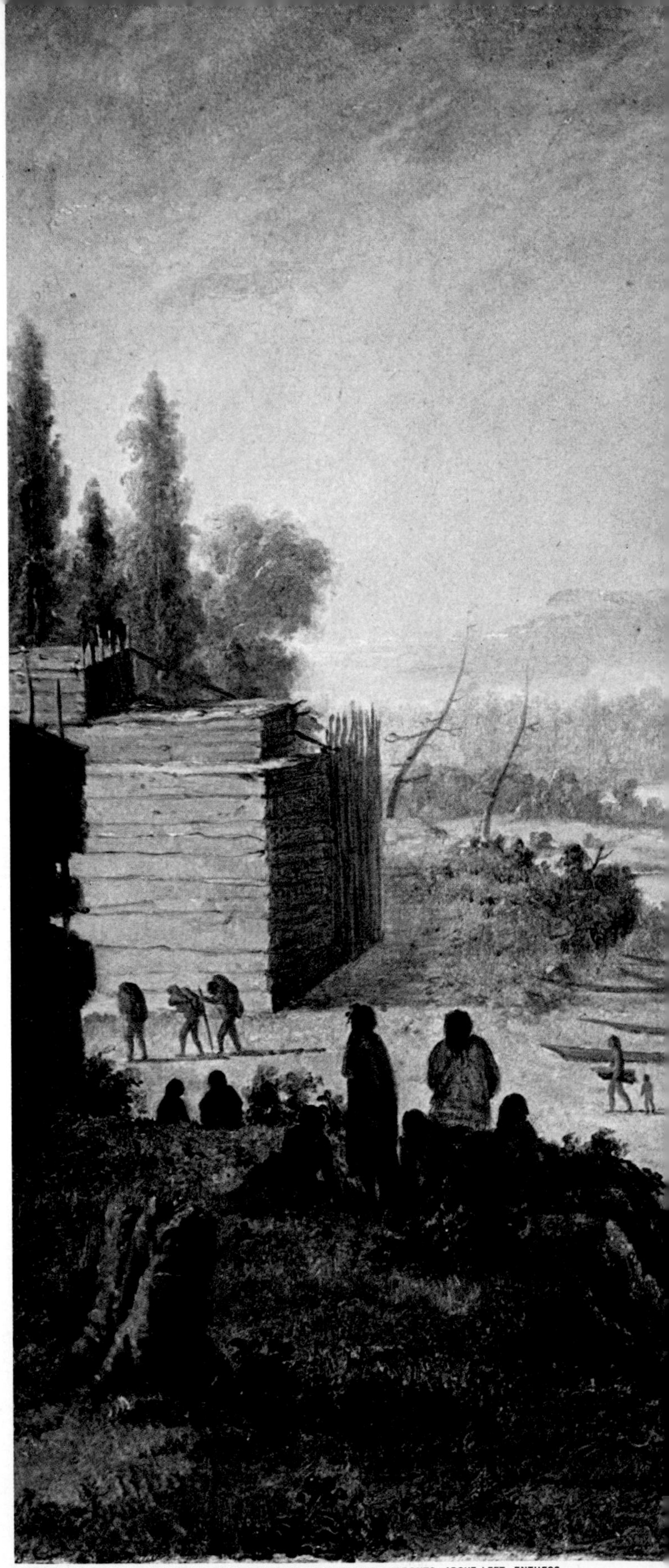

A SALISH VILLAGE, BY PAUL KANE, C. 1847; ROYAL ONTARIO MUSEUM, TORONTO. ABOVE LEFT: ENTHEOS

Cavorting killer flashes armed jaws that lock on snacks of fish or banquets of blubber. Like the Nootka chief whose woven spruce-root hat depicts a sea chase, the ferocious mammal hunts the gray whale as food. Whether in awe or empathy, coast clans frequently chose Killer Whale as totem.

canoes. Onto the makeshift catamaran the family piled its mats and baskets, spears and harpoons, its storage boxes filled with blankets and dishes, clam digging sticks, tumplines, fishhooks and lures, duck nets, traps, chisels, knives and adzes, ceremonial masks and costumes, magic charms and amulets, the children's toy tops and kelp-stem popguns, along with whatever dried salmon and eulachon oil might be left after the winter's marathon ceremonials. Then paddlers shoehorned into their places in the canoes, and everybody else piled on and hoped the unwieldy craft would float.

Next after Herring-spawn Moon—March—in the Nootka calendar came Wild Goose Moon when geese, ducks, and other waterfowl clogged the Pacific flyway, winging north for nesting. Then it was Getting-ready-for-whaling Moon.

The Nootka stand out as the most intrepid sea hunters of the north Pacific coast. Their territory was the west side of Vancouver Island. A colonial offshoot, the Makah, had migrated south to the tip of the Olympic Peninsula before the advent of the white man, and the Makah also were renowned whalers. A search for better sea hunting may, in fact, have motivated their southward move.

A local chief controlled the property of his kin group, the village sites, fishing rivers, berry patches, hunting grounds, beaches, and the sea as far out as his people fished and hunted. Whaling carried so much prestige that the chief always organized the hunt. He alone usually had wealth enough to make and equip the 30-foot canoes and the authority to direct the eight-man crews. The main weapon was a long-shafted harpoon of yew wood

with a shell tip and two bone barbs, called "man" and "woman." Fastened to the detachable head was a 600-foot rope of cedarbark with four inflated sealskin floats tied on at intervals.

In May when seas were calm and the California gray whale was running off the coast, the chief would announce a whaling expedition. When the gear was stowed and all was ready the men—nude, with their faces painted black—carried the boats to the water. A little before sunset they set out for the whaling grounds, ready to begin the hunt at dawn.

The slender craft cut the waves soundlessly. In single file, the chief's boat first, the Nootkas approached the whale from behind as it lazed along the surface, keeping to its left side and out of its line of vision. Waiting for just the right instant, the steersman gave the signal and the chief, standing in the bow, plunged the harpoon with all his might, aiming for a spot just behind the flipper. Now came the most dangerous moment. Everything had to move like clockwork. As the harpoon struck, the first paddler threw out the first float. The chief ducked to avoid being hit by the harpoon shaft as the whale rolled and thrashed in pain, preparing to sound. In turn, paddlers eased out floats two, three, and four while the other crewmen turned the boat sharply to port to clear the powerful pendulum of the tail flukes and let the line pay out smoothly. A slow getaway might end in a smashed canoe and death to a crewman.

Once the whale submerged, the boats gave chase. Floats on the line served to tire the animal and helped the whalers gauge its depth, its direction, and the strength of its efforts to loosen the

**Tlingit hook for halibut;
of wood with bone barb**
PEABODY MUSEUM, HARVARD UNIVERSITY

**Haida ladle carved
of horn; shell inset**
SMITHSONIAN INSTITUTION

"Were I to affix a name to the people of Nootka," Captain Cook wrote in 1778, "I would call them *Wakashians;* from the word *wakash,* which was very frequently in their mouths. It seemed to express applause, approbation, and friendship." On visits with the friendly villagers Cook took along artist John Webber, who made this detailed drawing of a house interior.

Several families live together. As mealtime nears, steam rises from a cooking box where seafood boils around hot stones. Roof openings let out the smoke and admit light and air. On overhead racks fish dry for winter storage. Platforms for sleeping and sitting line the plank walls. Wooden chests hold spare clothes, masks, and decorated bowls and spoons. Fishing tackle—U-shaped halibut hooks, salmon spears, nets and traps—is strewn about the house.

At ease but curious, Nootkas watched the artist at work. Not above a bit of friendly bargaining, one man covered the carved house posts with mats until Webber bartered all the buttons off his coat for the privilege of sketching them.

GLENBOW-ALBERTA INSTITUTE, CALGARY

embedded harpoon. Each time it surfaced, the canoes closed the distance and more harpoons were planted, forcing the huge mammal to dive and flee without enough breathing time. Its dives grew shorter. Wounds and the drag of floats sapped its strength. At last, perhaps hours after the first strike and miles from shore, the quarry became exhausted. The hunters immobilized it by slashing the great tendon of the flukes. Then while the whale floundered helpless they dealt the death blow, plunging a bone-tipped lance to the heart.

Towing the prize to the village beach could be as laborious as the hunt itself—grays weigh up to 40 tons—and hazardous if the sea was high. A diver slit the whale's jaws and tied its mouth shut with the tow line to keep out water. The crews sang towing songs praising the village and telling the whale what a royal welcome awaited.

Mere humans could not expect to overcome so mighty an animal as the whale without supernatural help. Regardless of his skill, no responsible chief took blubber and glory for granted. Months in advance he and the first lady began ritual training to win cooperation of the whale spirits: continence, icy baths at night during the waxing moon, and not eating the flesh of land animals. A few days before the hunt, crewmen also took up the ritual. If the hunt proved unsuccessful or unduly arduous it meant that someone had been weak, wanton, or lazy and had broken training.

A special attraction was thought to exist between the whale and the chief's wife. While the canoes were at sea, the first lady had a part to play at home. Acting the role of a docile whale willing to be killed for the Nootkas' benefit, she lay immobile in bed until word came that the chief's harpoon had found its mark. When the shaft of his harpoon broke free, messengers who accompanied the hunt retrieved the shaft and carried it back to the village and stood it over the chief's bed.

Beaching a whale, usually at high tide, called for high celebration with songs and speeches. Eagle-down adorned the whale and chief whaler. The chief's special cut of the carcass was not regarded as meat but as a visitor to his house, to be honored. The chief then distributed portions of the blubber as his largess, giving fathom-long slices from choice or not-so-choice parts of the whale in the order of the recipient's importance.

Northwest Coast Indians stood medium to tall, with broad chests and wide shoulders. Faces were broad with low concave noses; complexion ranged from light to medium brown. Actually less heavily pigmented than they appeared at a glance, they were out-of-doors people who exposed their bodies to the sun.

The mild climate required little in the way of clothing. In good weather men went naked; women fashioned animal hides or shredded bark into skirts, often worn without tops. Woven hats and conical capes of bark—sometimes edged with fur—shed the rain. People rarely used footgear. Early explorers noted Indians walking barefoot in the snow without complaint. Men of some northwest coast and California tribes grew beards and mustaches, a feature that Capt. James Cook noted as unusual among the aboriginal peoples he had encountered on his travels.

The first recorded contact between Europeans and Northwest Coast Indians was in 1741 when Vitus Bering, a Dane employed by Russia, anchored in Tlingit territory. Neither of two small boats sent ashore ever came back. Indians killed the crews and burned the boats for the metal they contained. Then in 1774 Spaniard Juan Perez skirted the coast but had only ephemeral contact with the Nootka. Of far (continued on page 225)

EDWARD S. CURTIS

Portraits of a Passing Era

"My dear Mr. Curtis:

I regard the work . . . as one of the most valuable . . . any American could now do . . . making a record of the lives of the Indians. . . . You have begun just in time. . . . The Indian, as an Indian, is on the point of perishing."

To picture the "vanishing race in all its glory" was the formidable task that photographer Edward S. Curtis had set for himself. The urgency reflected in President Theodore Roosevelt's letter seemed justified at the time. Defeated in battle, their great chiefs demoralized or dead, lands and freedom stripped away—this was the plight of the native Americans whose traditions Curtis had set out to record in pictures and text.

In Seattle in the 1890's Curtis made his first Indian pictures of Princess Angeline, daughter of Chief Seattle for whom the city was named. Aged and poor, she welcomed the dollar he gave her to pose digging clams. Forty thousand pictures and thirty years later, field work for the 40-volume series would be complete. From Mexico to the Arctic, plains to the Pacific, Curtis focused his magic boxes on tribe after tribe.

His 1910 trek among Northwest Coast Indians was largely by boat, first down the Columbia River, then along the coast of Washington, and finally in British Columbia. Often putting in 20 hours a day, he handled his own boat, made pictures, collected data, and—lacking money to pay wages—cooked for his crew.

For the privilege of photographing a forthcoming Kwakiutl ceremony, Curtis was given the task of collecting the human skulls and bones and female "mummy" his hosts needed for the ritual. His interpreter's wife obligingly led Curtis to her family graveyard and spoke to her dead relatives as he took up their remains.

On Vancouver Island he had made the portrait of Chief Yakotlus (left). Later Yakotlus lay dying—a victim of *eka*, or sorcery, his relatives believed. They asked Curtis as the chief's friend to head an investigation. Finding "evidence" of the sorcerer's guilt, the Indians burned his house, though Yakotlus was beyond help.

Volume by volume, the last in 1930, *The North American Indian* appeared in print, full of sensitive evocations of aboriginal America, caught from life or reenacted by a generation who remembered it.

Geared for the most perilous of hunts, a Makah whaler
lugs harpoon, line, and floats down to the beach. With the
20-foot staff too heavy to cast, he must stab the whale
from alongside. A gifted harpooner needed magic as well
as might; by purification ritual he sought harmony with
the whale spirits. The right snatch of song to gentle the prey
toward shore meant prestige and the prize cut of blubber
for the whaler, much food and oil for his village.

Fruits of a season's sea hunting, fishing, and gathering—
preserved and stored—left months of leisure for feasts and
ceremonies. Traveling to a distant village for winter dances,
costumed Kwakiutls limber up as canoes move into port.

A bizarre bird with a taste for human flesh swoops from the gloomy winter skies and abducts a young victim; so begins a Kwakiutl myth-drama. The youth—heir to a Hamatsa role in the Dance Society—later is found in the woods running wild. Possessed by the spirit of the cannibal-bird, he cries *"Hap, hap*—Eat, eat" and hops about snapping at would-be rescuers, society members. They seize and carry him to the dance house.

Flickering shadows from the central fire, tunnels, secret rooms, hollow-kelp speaking tubes, and other props of stage magic help to mystify the audience as dancers garbed for their inherited roles enact the drama of kidnap, possession, and exorcism to initiate the novice. Dousings with sea water or fish oil, smoke baths, and bites of meat from a "mummy" calm Hamatsa's cannibalistic cravings. But the frenzy recurs; he hops out for a bite to eat—from someone's arm.

Quasi-religious ceremonies reached their zenith with the round of dances held in the cold wet months when supernatural spirits were thought to be most active. Among the Kwakiutl Curtis visited, the dance hosts fed villagers as well as invited tribes. When feast fare ran low, the new-fledged Hamatsa grew tame. A potlatch confirmed his new status and it was all over but paying the bills— a canoe or 200 blankets to each person bitten.

EDWARD S. CURTIS

EDWARD S. CURTIS

Bowman, shaman, artisan, chief—persons from all walks
of Indian life posed for Curtis' cameras in the dress of their
forebears. Button-embroidered trade blanket—formal wear—
and carved staff signifying his right to make speeches
identify Hamasaka as a man of status. The Kwakiutl chief
at Fort Rupert in 1910 was also the principal Hamatsa.
By his own count, he had partaken of 32 mummy feasts.
Bark capes and waterproof spruce-root hats sheltered
both men and women from rain—up to 200 days per year.
In fine weather men went naked except for ornaments;
women wore skirts of vegetable fiber that did not lose shape
when wet, and dried quickly. The most successful people
in northwest coast society were quite often the cleanest.
Ritual bathing was a way of attaining spirit power for
any important undertaking—including curing the sick.
The seeker ate sparingly, practiced continence, and during
the waxing moon bathed in icy water, singing, praying, and
scouring the body with branches to rid it of human taint.

Smoke, song, and dancing feet allay a catastrophe in the skies. As a monster slowly swallows the moon during an eclipse, Kwakiutl villagers raise a clamor beside a smoldering fire meant to make the monster sneeze and disgorge its lunar meal.

EDWARD S. CURTIS

224 **Age-old answer to an energy problem: Kwakiutl man twirls a wood spindle between his palms, creating friction against the dry board below, and prays, "Please come, fire." Villagers tried to keep at least one fire burning so coals could be borrowed; traveling men carried a long coil of rope smoldering at the end, so the laborious fire drill was seldom needed.**

greater consequence was Captain Cook's sojourn with the Nootka. In 1778 during his third and final voyage with the *Resolution* and *Discovery,* he collected some sea otter pelts. When his ships reached Canton, after Cook had been killed by Hawaiians, the Chinese paid handsomely for the soft, lustrous furs. Thus began a fiercely competitive trade that drew a dozen ships a year to the coast until the once plentiful sea otter was nearly extinct.

The Indians were avid traders. A vessel at anchor near a village would soon be surrounded by a flotilla of canoes filled with men and women and their items for trade. Exchange was never by a set-price system, Meares noted, but took the haphazard form of reciprocal giving of "gifts" until both sides were satisfied. For "copper, iron, and other gratifying articles," the Nootka men "took off their sea-otter garments, threw them, in the most graceful manner, at our feet, and remained in the unattired garb of nature on the deck. — They were each of them in return presented with a blanket, — when with every mark of the highest satisfaction, they descended into their canoes, which were paddled hastily to the shore."

Local chiefs handled the bargaining, but their wives also took a hand and at times vetoed deals that displeased them.

In exchange for their furs the Indians at first preferred items made of metal, either knives, chisels, and adzes, or strap metal they could make into tools. According to Cook, one man offered to trade him a five- or six-year-old child for a spike nail. Meares once declined the grisly offering of a severed human hand. Brass buttons from the officers' coats also were popular — Indians turned them into nose rings. And once they learned that firearms — unlike their own arrows — could kill an enemy despite his thick leather armor, the coastal people wanted muskets and ammunition.

Meares, learning that his Nootka friend Maquilla planned war on an enemy to the north, decided to aid the chief's cause by lending him firearms. "Indeed we felt it to be our interest . . . if necessity should compel them to battle, that they should return victorious." In 20 war canoes, each with 30 men, they "moved off from the shore in solemn order, singing their song of war. The chiefs were clothed in sea-otter skins; and the whole army had their faces and bodies painted with red ocher, and sprinkled with a shining sand, which, particularly when the sun shone on them, produced a fierce and terrible appearance.

"The battles . . . are we believe inconceivably furious, and attended with . . . barbarous ferocity. They do not carry on hostilities by regular conflicts; but their revenge is gratified, their sanguinary appetites quenched, or their laurels obtained by . . . sudden enterprize. . . ."

Some two weeks later Maquilla brought back the guns, baskets filled with the heads of slain enemies, and a booty of sea otter skins.

Early relations between whites and the natives were friendly, but soon the Indian groups were competing fiercely with each other for the traders' favor, and the traders vied with each other for the Indians' best furs.

Though not so highly prized as sea otter, pelts of bear, fox, marmot, and other land animals also found a ready market with the seagoing merchants. To supply this demand, the Tlingit began to act as middlemen, plying the river trails between interior tribes and the ports of call. An ambitious Tlingit from the coast would go so far as to marry extra wives in the inland groups in order to gain the special trade advantages due a kinsman. The original wife back on the coast usually took the position that she would be foolish to object to her husband's temporary polygamy when it meant he could bring home more furs.

Firearms not only made intertribal wars more deadly; such weapons also reduced the onesidedness of Indians' dealings with white traders. One observer, Edward Bell, wrote in 1792: "Their former weapons, Bows and Arrows, Spears and Clubs are now thrown aside & forgotten. At Nootka . . . everyone had his musket. Thus they are supplied with weapons which they no sooner possess than they turn against the donors. Few ships have been on the coast that have not been attack'd. . . . and in general many lives . . . lost on both sides."

In 1803 an American trading ship, the *Boston*, was attacked in Nootka Sound and all but two of the crew murdered. John Jewitt, ship's armorer, and John Thompson, sailmaker, were captured by Chief Maquina and "employed at slavery" for more than two years before they were rescued. Jewitt was kept busy making weapons. He writes in his diary that he made his Indian master particularly happy when he forged some iron whaling harpoons of European type which did not draw out so easily as wooden ones. Maquina had a good whaling season. His fortunes and his reputation soared. Other Nootka chiefs wanted Jewitt to make harpoons for them but Maquina, zealously guarding his newfound success, did not allow it.

U nder the northwest coast system of social ranking, each villager was born to his specific status, high or low. Each rank comprised a loose social stratum. At the top were chiefs, few in number, possessing great influence, and functioning as the heads of lineages.

Next came the nobles—younger brothers of a chief and other highborn persons. A third group, commoners, made up the mass of society. A commoner might be a social nobody who fished and

On scaffolds over foaming falls of Oregon's Deschutes River, Indians keep an ancient rendezvous with the salmon. Homebound from the sea, one leaps—out of the maelstrom into a dip net. Traffic in salmon, at times fin-to-fin, includes the chinook, coho, and sunset-vivid sockeye.

DICK DURRANCE II, NATIONAL GEOGRAPHIC PHOTOGRAPHER. BELOW: ENTHEOS

hunted for the chief in return for part of the proceeds, or he could be quite important if he were an excellent warrior, a skilled woodcarver, or a master canoe maker.

At the bottom were slaves, usually women and children taken captive in wars or raids on other tribes. In some groups, slaves numbered as high as 20 percent of the population. They did menial labor for their master, such as carrying water and firewood, and contributed to his store of food. In return he gave them protection so long as it pleased him to do so. Slaves were mere chattels, pieces of property that the master could sell, give away, or kill on some special occasion to show that he could afford to waste valuable belongings.

Although social position was inherited, an individual could begin to use his titles and privileges only after they had been validated in the public ceremony called "potlatch." The Kwakiutl potlatch is the best known. But other northwest coast tribes had the institution in basically the same form. The word potlatch comes from the Chinook trade jargon and means "to give." The giving of gifts to guests at a potlatch made them formal witnesses to the titles and privileges.

Winter was the social season; with larders full, the people had time for lengthy feasts and ceremonies. The overt reason for giving a potlatch might be to celebrate a marriage, the accession to office of a new chief, the ransom and social redemption of a war captive, or the birth of an heir. Whatever the occasion, the host group used the assembly to display its wealth and hereditary rights such as songs, dances, crests, and titles.

As guests arrived, each was addressed by all his valid titles and seated according to protocol. At a large gathering, remembering who was who posed a challenge. Among the southern Kwakiutl all members of a local kin group, or *namina*, held

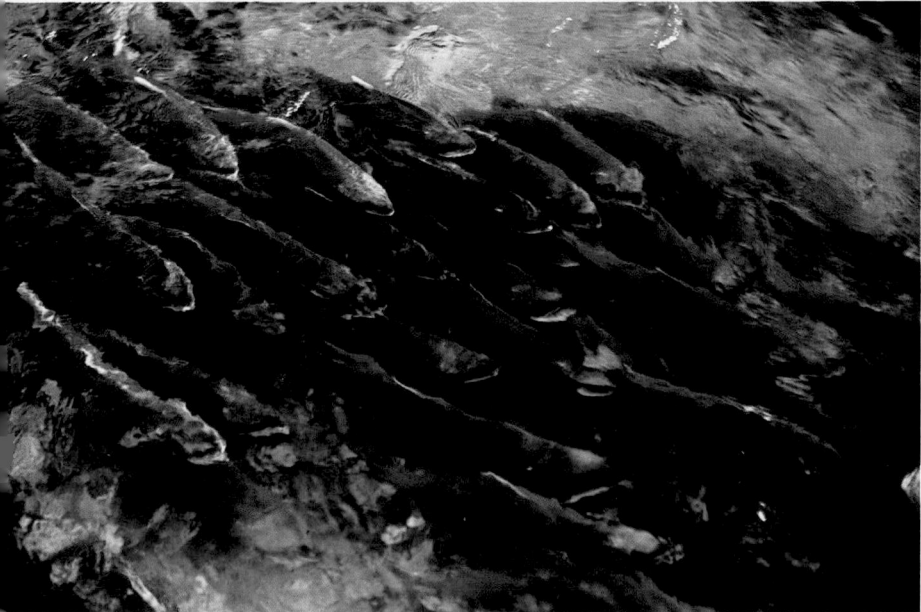

As salmon return generation after generation to spawn
in native rivers, so came Indians to ancestral fishing places.
An 1855 treaty with the U. S. Government guaranteed
perpetual rights to such sites as Kettle Falls on the Columbia,
now drowned in backwaters of Grand Coulee Dam.

individual rank in a hereditary order or precedence. Their word for chief is *gialaxa*—"first to
come down." The original ancestor of a namina,
in the Kwakiutl's mythical history, descended to
earth in the guise of a supernatural being—raven,
thunderbird, or other animal—then removed his
mask and costume to assume human form. The
ranking chief inherited the responsibility for his
kinsmen along with titles and property. Each lesser position in the hierarchy, created in antiquity,
descended in its own direct line.

In all social occasions, hosts observed the
order of precedence with absolute correct-
ness, much as a Washington hostess at a
state dinner must seat guests according to diplomatic, military, or social ranking.

The business part of a potlatch comprised an intricate and extended show-and-tell. The host
group performed its songs and dances, reciting
the origin myth and history of each. The speaker
named and introduced all persons in the namina
entitled to use those privileges. New names from
the owned stock of titles were bestowed upon
particular honorees. All this somewhat resembled
a university granting an honorary degree or a government awarding an official decoration.

The distribution of presents to the guests also
followed a rigid pattern. The first and largest gift
went to the highest ranking visitor; the second and
next largest gift to the next in rank, and so on
down the roster. A speech glorifying the giver accompanied each presentation. The potlatch was
thus an ego trip for the chief of the host group.
Since his kinsmen also brought goods to be given
away, they shared in his glory.

In pre-white times it took years to assemble
enough canoes, coppers, and handmade blankets
for a grand potlatch. The booming fur trade soon

"FALLS OF THE COLVILLE" BY PAUL KANE, C. 1846; ROYAL ONTARIO MUSEUM, TORONTO

Flatheaded meant "free" among the Chinook and Salish. Babies of slaves were
denied the year-long beauty treatment—a board tied to the infant's padded skull—
that permanently flattened the foreheads of tribal members. With babies bound to
cradleboards, mothers' hands were free for weaving. Blankets from the looms
of Coast Salish used wool from a now-extinct breed of dog. The domestic canines,
shorn like sheep, belonged to the wife and were a measure of her wealth.

BLANKET-WEAVING, AND COWLITZ MOTHER AND CHILD, BOTH BY PAUL KANE, C. 1847; ROYAL ONTARIO MUSEUM, TORONTO

flooded the area with cheaper goods, such as barrels of flour, bolts of cloth, Hudson's Bay Company blankets, rum, guns, and cash.

Social pressure to potlatch increased along with the opportunity. Native populations were decimated by introduced diseases and by their own greater efficiency in war through use of firearms. Each death of a high-ranking person left his titles vacant, so that the need to perform the validation ceremony grew with the rising death rate.

Late in the 19th century potlatching escalated into an intense form of rivalry. Two men, each claiming to be the rightful heir to a certain title, would try to outdo each other in alternate potlatches. During the proceedings a claimant tried to demean his rival and prove his own greater worth by a more lavish giveaway or by destroying more goods—smashing canoes to bits, burning blankets, or tossing great quantities of valuables into the sea. Eventually, the guest chiefs could end the contest by recognizing the claim of one rival. If not, one rival—the host with the least—would go bankrupt and lose by default.

Canadian law, urged by missionaries intent on Indian "progress," tried to put a stop to the giveaways. A provision of the Indian Act as revised in 1885 reads: "Every Indian . . . who engages in or assists in celebrating the Indian festival known as the 'Potlatch' . . . is guilty of a misdemeanor, and shall be liable to imprisonment."

Storm-lashed battlements rising hundreds of feet from the ocean floor flank the land of the Haida. The tallest and best red cedars—gift of drenching winter rains—grace the Queen Charlotte Islands, 155-mile archipelago stretching north to "fifty-four forty," the line between Canada and Alaska. View is toward Langara, the northernmost island, across Cloak Bay where islanders learned nuances of white man's commerce: three hundred prime sea otter cloaks—hence the name Cloak Bay—for some iron "toes," or adzes. Bold and energetic, the Haida already had their sea-girt world well in hand, raiding and trading hundreds of miles along the mainland in dugouts hewn from giant cedars with stone- or shell-tipped tools. Now the news in canoes was longer—up to 70 feet—and speedier than paddlepower's two to six knots. Inspired by traders' "flying canoes" such as the one Nootkas incised in a Vancouver Island petroglyph, Haidas added sail to their keelless craft.

ENTHEOS

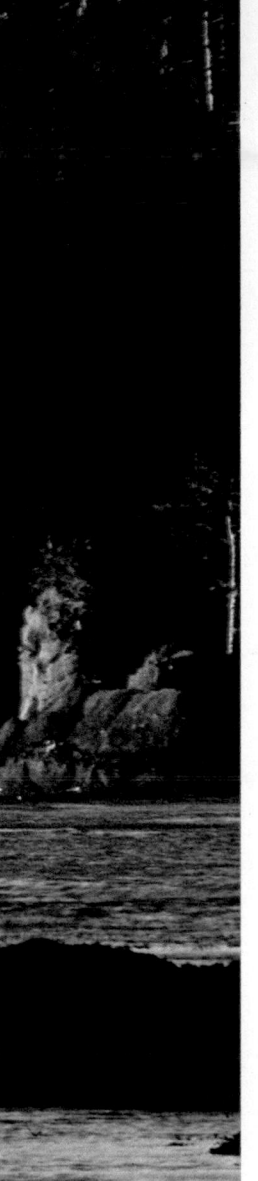

Enforcement of the law was another matter, particularly in outlying areas. For some Kwakiutls, devising ways to foil the authorities added new interest to the potlatch. An ingenious host, for example, might take his potlatch door-to-door, visiting the homes of successive groups of guests rather than risk one large assembly. Eventually, the law was dropped from the books.

The northernmost Tlingit, neighbors of Eskimo peoples, in Yakutat Bay used the umiak and the bidarka, skin-covered Eskimo boats, as well as the coastal dugout canoes. Another feature of Eskimo culture which the Tlingit adopted was a casting stick for the darts that they used in hunting sea mammals.

Alone among Northwest Coast Indians, the Tlingit wore clothing shaped to the body. Men wore a breechclout, like tribes in the colder interior where they traded, and buckskin shirts and trousers with attached moccasins.

The Tlingit were famous for the so-called Chilkat blanket, an elaborate robe woven of wool from the mountain goat. Though women did the actual weaving, they followed patterns drawn on cedar boards by men of the tribe. Men also hunted the goats—three per garment—and made the loom, consisting of two upright poles connected at the top by a crossbar from which warp strings hung. Weavers made each panel or decorative element separately, then stitched them together. Chilkat blankets, the glory of early northwestern textile art, are still made in the traditional manner.

"Paintings everywhere, everywhere sculpture, among a nation of hunters," marveled Étienne Marchand, visiting the Queen Charlotte Islands, land of the Haida, before the turn of the 19th century. In his *A Voyage Round the World 1790-1792* he penned one of the earliest descriptions of a totem pole, the carved pillar at the entry of a Haida house on Langara Island:

"This opening is made in the thickness of a large trunk of a tree which rises perpendicularly in the middle of one of the fronts of the habitation, and occupies the whole of its height; it imitates the form of a gaping human mouth, or rather that of a beast, and it is surmounted by a hooked nose, about two feet in length, proportional in point of size, to the monstrous face.... Over the door is seen the figure of a man carved in the attitude of a child in the womb ... above this figure rises a gigantic statue of a man erect, which terminates the sculpture and the decoration of the portal.... On the parts of the surface which are not occupied by the capital subjects, are ... figures of frogs or toads, lizards and other animals, and arms, legs, thighs, and other parts of the human body."

Totem poles, the hallmark of northwest coastal art, were never intended to evoke religious awe. They represented, rather, a pride in ancestry. The main theme was the depiction of supernatural beings: animals, humans, and monsters which were wholly imaginary or composed of parts of different animals. These supernatural beings represented the ancestors who originated the clan or lineage. Only the descendants of a clan founder could use these emblems—often called crests because they serve much the same purpose as heraldic designs on European coats of arms.

The artist emphasized certain body features to identify each of the stylized creatures: the spread wings, earlike plumes, and curved beak of Thunderbird, two big front teeth and cross-hatched tail of Beaver, long, straight beak of Raven, or the dorsal fin of Killer Whale. Parts of the design were repeated symmetrically. Carvers were specialists; the noble entitled to display the crests hired the carver who made the pole to extol his family tree.

Stately totem poles portico the picturesque Haida village of Skidegate in this 1878 photograph.

Emblems of a bygone epoch crumble into the dank soil of the forest. Bear muzzle molders near an abandoned Haida village; birds nest in a thunderbird's skull. After a ceremonial raising, Indians left poles to the elements. The famed Tsimshian "Hole-in-the-Sky" survives *in situ;* museums collect and mend others. A few Indians practice the old arts, as at 'Ksan workshop in central British Columbia.

House portals were only one use of totem poles. Other carved pillars might support a house roof, serve as grave markers—and perhaps as coffins—or glorify the chief who owned a beach. Houses were impressively large and had names to match. Modesty no virtue, Haida chiefs advertised with such house names as "The-Clouds-Sound-Against-It-As-They-Pass-Over" and "The-House-Chiefs-Peeped-At-From-A-Distance-Because-It-Was-Too-Great-To-Let-Them-Come-Near."

Canoes of these island-dwellers—"Vikings of the Pacific northwest"—represented the peak achievement on the coast in boat building. Shaped with fire and adz from a single red cedar tree, a Haida dugout often exceeded 50 feet—longer than some Viking boats—with a beam of 7 or 8 feet. Such a canoe could carry an entire war party or tons of cargo. European sailing ships inspired the coast people to supplement paddle-power with sail, unknown to them earlier. They traded for canvas or else wove cedarbark mats for sails. With masts and sails, the keelless, rudderless canoes could run before the wind but lacked the stability to tack or turn.

For the 1908 Seattle Exposition, a Haida master craftsman carved an authentic war canoe such as his ancestors might have used on a slave-taking foray to the Puget Sound country. Sixty-six feet long and beautifully decorated, the craft took eight months of hard work. At last it was complete. A schooner would tow it, with the owner aboard, to the mainland for shipment to Seattle.

As the two boats entered the open waters of Dixon Entrance a tumultuous gale blew up. The towing line parted. Schooner and canoe lost sight of each other. When the schooner's captain managed to battle his way to Prince Rupert, he found the canoe snug and safe in port. Her Haida maker had

ADELAIDE DE MENIL

ENTHEOS

ENTHEOS

ADELAIDE DE MENIL

ENTHEOS

ADELAIDE DE MENIL

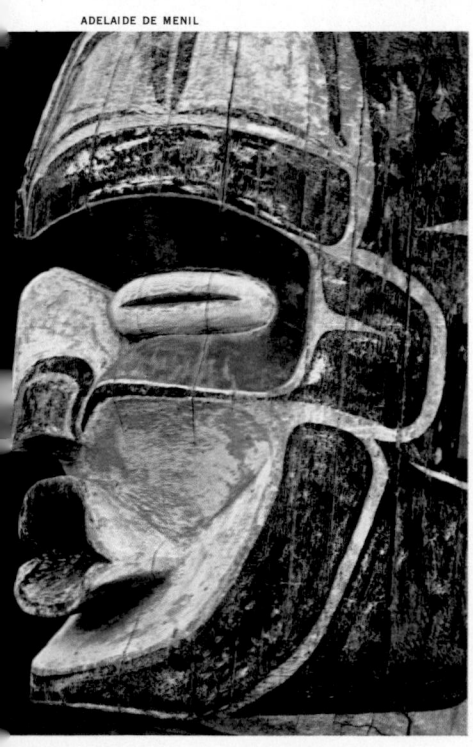

Fledged with moonlight and mist, gulls wing low over rippled waters of Queen Charlotte Sound. Storms and incessant rains kept the coastal Indians close to home and fireside day after dreary winter day—and culture profited. In a sense, foul weather was the mother of Northwest Coast Indian art.

hoisted a sail and—the wind being right—bettered the schooner's time by many hours.

Tribes with skilled carvers of their own appreciated the excellent Haida canoes. Each summer Haidas made a trading trip to the mainland and up the Nass River into Tsimshian territory.

The lower Nass was one of the spawning rivers of the eulachon, and the Tsimshian were chief purveyors of its "grease," a highly prized foodstuff. As shoals of the tiny eulachon, or candlefish, silvered the surface, the Tsimshian raked them from the crests or netted them with a funnel-shaped *yakatl*, quickly filling their canoes. Ashore, they emptied the fish in pits to rot and went back for more. To render the oil they dumped the partly decomposed fish into wooden boxes, added water, and boiled them by dropping in heated stones. They skimmed off the oil as it rose. Grease was a favorite food—butter, sauce, gravy—served at festivals and given as gifts by all northwest coast tribes. I have tasted eulachon oil and class it one of the gamiest foods ever concocted.

A beach camp where the oil was rendered in quantity could be smelled ten miles downwind. The most important grease camps were at Red Bluff on the Nass. At trying time groups of grease-hungry Indians—Haida with canoes and chewing tobacco, Tlingit with blankets and large copper plaques—came to trade with the Tsimshian. Red Bluff became a hubbub of haggling, enlivened by fights, like as not. The Tlingit had little use for the Tsimshian and would just as soon fight as bargain, so long as they got the grease. By one means or another, the rank riches were distributed and the delegations, trailing a certain aura, paddled away.

Chinook-speaking tribes held the lower Columbia River valley and thus became proprietors of the phenomenal salmon resources of that river. A

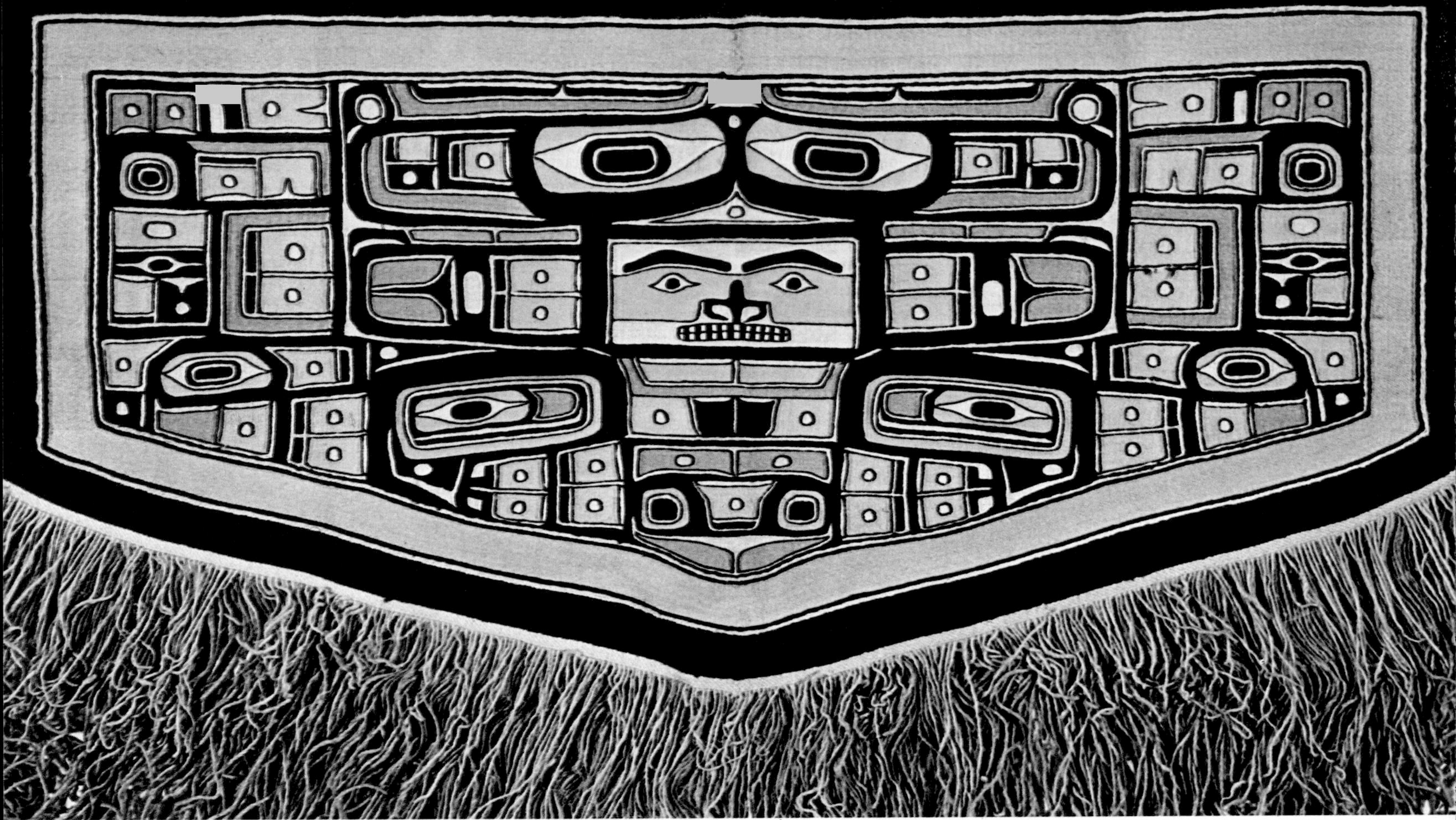

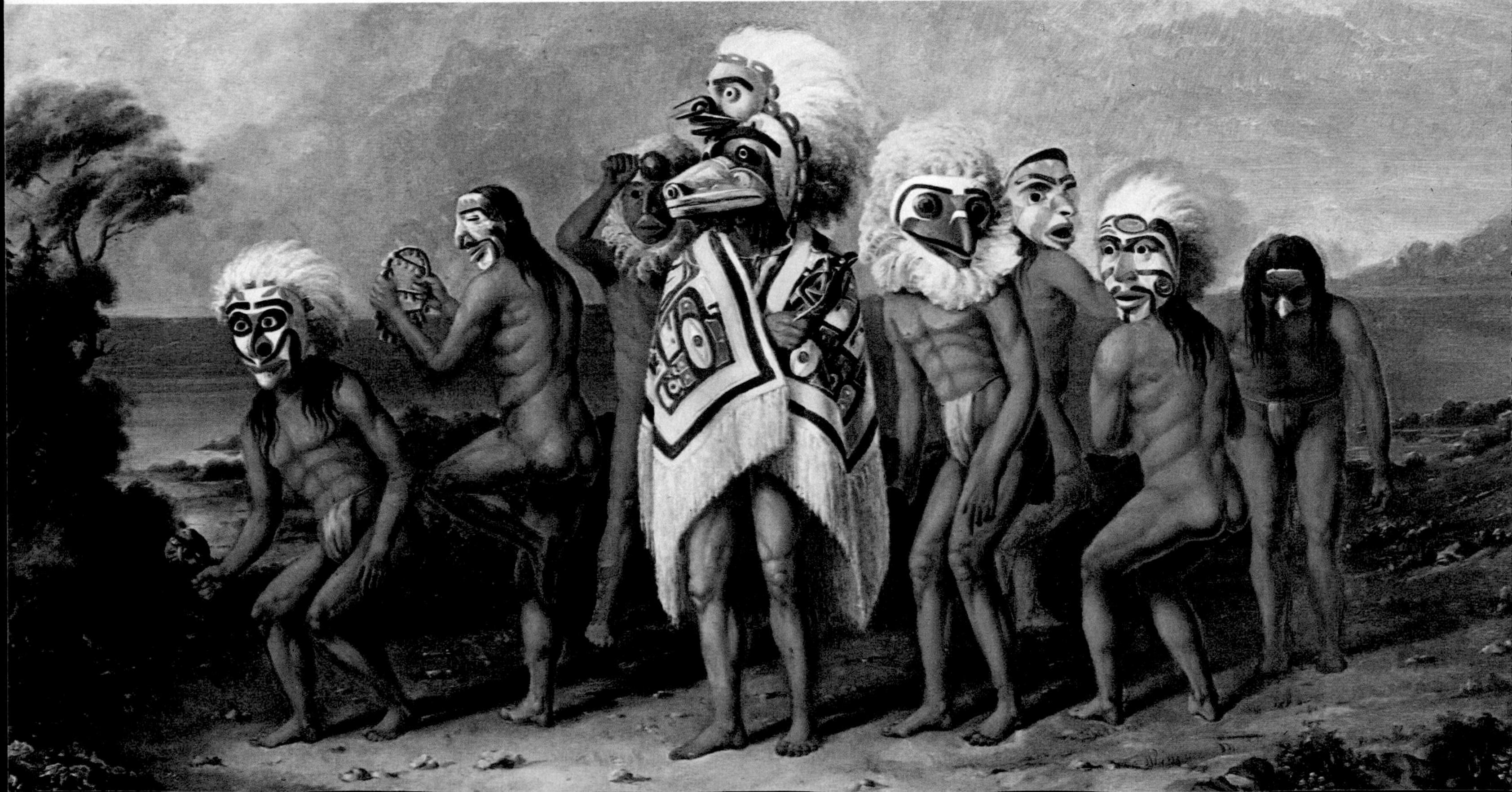

Wardrobe of a well-dressed Tlingit chief might boast an elaborate ceremonial cloak of mountain goat wool woven by women of the Chilkat subtribe. The prized robes—a year in the making and patterned with stylized parts of animals that served as clan crests—once were traded widely. In Paul Kane's painting, "Medicine Mask Dance," a Chilkat blanket and masks of various tribes adorn Salish dancers.

large Chinook population—about 25,000—presumably reflects the abundance of this nutritious protein food. Tending huge basketlike traps and fencelike weirs, set below cataracts that the fish had to leap, the Chinook filled their own needs and also caught an immense surplus for trade.

Long before its "discovery" by whites, Indians used the Columbia as part of a trade route to and from the Great Plains. The lower river also was strategically located between the coastal tribes of Washington and British Columbia and the peoples to the south in Oregon and California. At the rapids of The Dalles, where canoes had to portage, Chinooks set up a thriving marketplace. Indian traders from the north, south, and east came to exchange slaves, furs, and dentalium shells—used as ornaments and money—for dried salmon.

After Robert Gray's momentous stopover in 1792, the mouth of the Columbia became a regular port of call for trading ships. Chinooks prospered as middlemen, shuttling pelts and slaves downriver in exchange for guns, ammunition, beads, knives and axes, brought upriver to The Dalles.

Customers who did not know standard Indian tongues did business in the "Chinook jargon"—probably of Chinook origin since words of that language predominate. Nootkan and Salishan words, and during the historic period many French and English words, were incorporated. In the heyday of the Chinook merchants the jargon served as *lingua franca* from Alaska to California.

Westward on the heels of Lewis and Clark came the trappers and the settlers. An epidemic of "ague fever," probably malaria, brought a population crash in 1829. By 1855 disruption of Chinook culture went into the terminal phase: the few hundred survivors were sent to reservations in Oregon.

The basic northwest coast type of culture flourished as far south as the northwestern corner of California. Details varied. Redwood, for example, took the place of cedar. The Yurok, Hupa, Tolowa, and Karok tribes of the lower Klamath River did not potlatch or carve totem poles. But, responding to a similar environment of river, forest, and sea, they built plank houses, developed woodworking tools and skills, traveled by dugout canoe, and tapped the awesome salmon runs.

Here as farther north, wealth and status went hand in glove. Food was plentiful so men had time to dream of piling up riches: strings of dentalium shells, knives flaked from obsidian, red scalps of the pileated woodpecker, rare furs. The ultimate treasure: the skin of an albino deer.

To get rich required not constant hard work but training rituals. Men devoted hours to sweat baths and prayer. They slept in the sweat-house apart from their wives and money except in the summer, when people slept outdoors. Sexual activity in the presence of wealth would cause it to flee the house, the Yurok believed. Wealth objects, which came from nature, all had spirits that would be attracted to the ritually pure man. One day a white deer might even stand still before a good man's bow.

Dentalium shells served as money all along the coast. The shells, which the Kwakiutl harvested from the sea, tended to increase in value as they were traded farther and farther from the source. While some northwest tribes very casually evaluated the shiny white shells, the Yurok devised a precise system of grading them by quality and length. Yurok men, in fact, had marks tattooed on their upper arms for measuring dentalium strings.

These thrifty Indians of northwestern California worked out a sophisticated legal code under which all possessions and personal privileges had an exact value in goods. Every violation of

Fascinating faces of animals, mythical monsters, and real people enhance treasures from the Tlingit tribe. The carver's art went to war with the wary chief who hid his own vulnerable head inside a burly helmet. Clan crests adorn a "copper"—a wealth symbol inflated in value each time it changed hands—and other ritual and useful objects. A favorite totemic figure was wily Raven, culture hero whose trickery put sun, moon, and stars in the sky and set a chaotic world in order.

Ceremonial "copper" of beaten metal; painted, incised with bear crest

BROOKLYN MUSEUM

Wooden battle helmet with carved portrait

AMERICAN MUSEUM OF NATURAL HISTORY, NEW YORK

Chief's wooden raven rattle
used in lieu of speaker's gavel
ROYAL SCOTTISH MUSEUM, EDINBURGH

Copper sea-bear mask; shell
inlays, fur ears and ruff
MUSEUM OF PRIMITIVE ART, NEW YORK

Shaman's mosquito headdress; walrus
whisker antennae, shell inlays
MUSEUM OF ANTHROPOLOGY AND ETHNOGRAPHY, LENINGRAD

Scarlet scalps from pileated woodpeckers on a band of white fur headline the finery of a Hupa Jumping Dancer. Displaying treasures of the tribe—feathers, furs, shells—men standing abreast jumped in time to slow, plaintive chants. The Jumping and Deerskin Dances, held on the same sacred spots each autumn, were part of an intricate pattern of magic and dance meant to renew the world for the coming year.

EDWARD S. CURTIS

personal or property rights had its price in dentalium strings. Some typical Yurok valuations:

A house, 3 strings.

A fishing place, 1 to 3 strings.

A tract bearing acorns, 1 to 5 strings.

A slave, 1 or 2 strings.

For the killing of a man of standing, the cost was 15 strings. A common man was worth 10 strings.

Whether an offense was intentional or accidental had no bearing on the penalty, nor did the age, sex, or previous record of the guilty party. Only the fact of damages was considered. These California tribes were touchy, quick to take offense, and forever involved in some legal dispute.

A person of wealth or status could press a claim more vigorously than a poor man could. A guilty person who could not pay up became the slave of the man he owed. If he refused servitude, he could be killed with full social approval.

One gets the impression that life in these tribes may have been interesting—not to mention profitable—if you were an important person with wealth, but that persons lacking these advantages may have led a pretty miserable existence.

A commoner might rise in status and perhaps get rich from fees by becoming a shaman. In northwest California, but not elsewhere, more women than men became healers. What made people sick were "pains," pairs of small, animate objects which flew invisibly through the air. The shaman attempted to draw the pains from a patient's body into her own and then to expel them. To gain healing power a candidate fasted, prayed, and danced in some remote spot. If she was lucky a spirit helper appeared and gave her a "pain" to practice on. Over a long training period she swallowed and vomited the object until she could produce it at will, with impressive songs and dances, when making a house call on a patient.

One Yurok shaman's account of how she got her power starts: "For several summers I danced . . . on a peak. . . . It looks out over the ocean. Then at last while I was sleeping I dreamed I saw the sky rising and blood dripping off its edge. . . . Then I saw a woman standing in a doctor's maple-bark dress with her hair tied like a doctor. . . . The woman reached up as the edge of the sky went higher and picked off one of the icicles of blood, said 'Here, take it,' and put it into my mouth."

The sky edge in the shaman's dream refers to the Yurok picture of the earth as an island in the ocean with the sky covering land and water like a dome. In tribal mythology the edge of the sky rises and falls into the ocean, causing breakers. While the shaman's dream only repeats the myth, it is taken as proof of the reality of the myth.

A number of beliefs could be cited to show that Yurok logic draws a hazy line between everyday and mythical worlds. People did not talk to dogs, for example, because the dog might speak back and the person die. According to tribal myth, in prehuman times animal spirits ruled over the earth and dogs did converse. Later, when they turned the earth over to men, animals no longer used speech. But the taboo on talking to dogs persisted.

Also, the Yurok never drank the water of the Klamath River: Someone upstream could have thrown a dead dog into the river, poisoning it. It was not lethal chemicals they feared but a supernatural contamination that could injure or kill.

The leaves of wild tobacco plants were never smoked because they might have been growing over a grave and become tainted by the corpse. Yet the Indians would collect and sow seeds of those wild plants—on a spot known not to be a grave—and then smoke the cultivated leaves.

Honoring her Yurok heritage, Geneva Mattz of Crescent City, California, preserves her ancestral home beside the lower Klamath River. Once her grandmother's domicile, the sturdy redwood house is entered by squeezing through a round hole closed with a sliding plank. Family heirlooms and baskets of her own making surround Mrs. Mattz as she prepares *kegoh*, acorn meal mush. Cooked by stirring with hot stones, the acorns provided a good source of protein, fat, fiber, and carbohydrate.

DAVID HISER

Such beliefs seem to amount to an obsession that the world was hostile and filled with invisible dangers. Everyday life and special events required prayers for success. A dozen or more religious ceremonies and dances, meant to renew the world for the coming year, began with a priest reciting a formula. One important Hupa ritual began:

"It will be pleasant weather everywhere in the world. . . . Everything will be as it should be. The good food will come again; it will grow again. By means of it the people will live happily. This sickness which the people used to have they will have no more. This that the people used to be sick with, blow out to sea with you, O wind."

Edged by the Pacific and the Sierra Nevada, central and southern California lay beyond the pale of northwest coast influence. Gentle like the climate, more than a hundred Indian groups spoke diverse tongues—yet lived in peace. Not unity but variety characterized the culture. Ritual, tools and utensils, and means of gaining a livelihood differed from place to place.

How do we account for such diversity? Under the "fish-trap" theory, anthropologists view California as a cul-de-sac into which peoples of different speech and customs migrated. Finding the land pleasant and fruitful, they stayed. If we accept the hypothesis and its implications, it can be argued that the early California Indians had solved one of mankind's most vexing problems— how to live in peace with other nations.

In central California, food was abundant and varied: acorns, seeds, roots, berries, game, fish, and fowl. If one resource failed, another filled the need. Each tribal group staked out a territory that included several "life zones"—areas where vegetation and wildlife varied because of differences in elevation, soils, or temperature and rainfall. The

Thunderous surf pummels a stony headland on California's sun-gold Monterey coast. Peaceful foragers inhabiting the Pacific strand assimilated into the Spanish mission culture, losing their own. Of such tribes as the now-extinct Esselen, no trace remains but fragments of language.

DECLAN HAUN

practice shows that these people, who used resources of their lands in common, were fully aware of the dangers of over-dependence on wild foods produced in a single zone. The adjustment of such territories between groups implies long occupation, perhaps for centuries.

The common political unit was the tribelet—3 to 30 neighboring villages. Unlike the northwest coast's strong emphasis on rank or class, California society was more egalitarian—though being rich or poor meant something among most groups. The tribelet's acknowledged leader lived in the largest village. He exercised no real authority; he was simply a man whose counsel was followed because he was considered wise.

Contemptuously labeled "Diggers" by white adventurers and settlers, California Indians were advancing toward a complex level of culture when the Spanish and then Americans assumed power. True, dress and houses were simple, but complicated rituals of some religious cults featured beautifully costumed dancers. And the fine basketry of the Pomo ranks among the world's best.

In 1542 gold-seeking Spaniards under Juan Cabrillo first set sail to the unknown seas north of Mexico. Cabrillo found the Chumash of the Santa Barbara area friendly and helpful. However, they possessed no precious metals. Not until 1769 did the Spanish begin to occupy coastal California. Indians played a vital part, furnishing manpower for the chain of Franciscan missions, the only settlements for about half a century.

Several Indian groups were named for missions, those holding what is now Los Angeles for Mission San Gabriel. The Gabrielino originated a moralistic cult that centered around a deity named Chinigchinich. The cult spread widely; even Indians serving the missions practiced it secretly. Devotees

Unsinkable boat, fishing float, house thatch, a mattress
to lie on, coarse baskets, headgear, footgear—whatever the
need, raw material might come from the tule patch.
One widespread use for the rushes which grow 15 feet tall
was the *balsa;* California tribes used this cigar-shaped raft
made of bundles of tules for crossing lakes and rivers.
Fine basketry was the art in which far western groups
excelled. Unsurpassed for variety of techniques and patterns,
Pomo weavers overlaid entire pieces with bits of shell,
brilliant feathers, or beadwork (below). When using
horizontal bands in the design, a Pomo weaver left a break
in the pattern—so as not be struck blind. Not so the Yokuts;
human figures encircle a shouldered museum-piece,
tufted with top-knot feathers of the California quail.
Nature-colored materials—peeled willow, black bracken root,
redbud bark—and 100,000 careful stitches went into the
masterpiece of a Washo artisan, Datsolalee. She called it
"We assemble to discuss the happy lives of our ancestors."

252

taught initiates an ethical code whose precepts included truthfulness, honor and charity for the aged, and respect for one's in-laws.

Animal messengers of Chinigchinich would punish transgressors of the code—a painful death at the hands of the bear, mountain lion, or raven. The faithful, conversely, could expect to live long and pleasurably. One of the moralistic sermons ends: "And when you die you will be spoken of as those in the sky, like the stars. Those, it is said, were people who went to the sky and escaped death. And like those will rise your soul."

Before white settlement, the California Indians numbered about 300,000. By 1834, when the missions were secularized, of the 83,000 Indians who had lived in and served the missions, only 20,500 were still alive. Numerous tribes were extinct.

The 1849 gold rush brought on a brutal confrontation between the fortune-seekers and the Indians who lived in the Sierra Nevada foothills and along northern California rivers. By 1870, more than 50,000 Indians of this region had died from bullets, disease, and starvation. In 1910 the California Indian population hit a low of 20,000, then rose slowly to today's nearly 100,000. Of these, about 40 percent are mixed-blood descendants of original California natives.

East of the Sierra Nevada lies the Great Basin, arid, deficient in vegetation and animal life, and—even today—thinly populated. It took the greatest ingenuity to stay alive in the "Great American Desert." In good weather Indians of the Basin wore little or no clothing. Where mosquitoes were bothersome, people rolled in the mud for a coating to protect the bare skin. In winter they wrapped up in robes of rabbit fur.

Their diet included almost everything edible: grass seeds, bulbs and roots, insects, rabbits, and rats. A staple food was pine nuts, but piñon trees did not bear every year. In an environment where everyone had to do his utmost at every opportunity to get something to eat, the distinction between rich and poor did not exist; a truly egalitarian social system operated. Each summer several families joined forces to forage. They combed the territory, harvesting grass seed here, digging bulbs there, hunting rabbits in one valley, huge swarms of grasshoppers in another. One method of capture was to build a fire in a pit. While it burned down to coals, the Indians spread out and encircled the insect swarm. As they beat the bushes, they tightened the circle, forcing the grasshoppers into the coals to roast like peanuts.

All food beyond their immediate needs they carried to a winter camp in a sheltered canyon or a cave. Through the winter—often months of bitterly cold weather—the group rationed food carefully and huddled around fires to keep warm.

In 1859, a Captain Simpson of the Corps of Topographical Engineers encountered a Shoshone in eastern Nevada. He wrote: "I asked him if his country was a good one. He said it was. He liked it a good deal better than any other. I asked him why. Because, he said, it had a great many rats."

Rich or poor, on shore or desert, the Indians respected the American wilderness because they lived as an integral part of it, as one creature among others, and were intimately bound to it through their beliefs and mythology. The Shoshone had one way of saying that he liked his country. Though they would have phrased it differently, we can be sure that California and Northwest Coast Indians felt an equally strong attachment to their homeland.

And that deep regard for country, in my estimation, shows that the aboriginal societies of the west were successful ones in human terms.

Horsemen of the Plains

John C. Ewers

Coronado's conquistadores, exploring the southern plains in the spring of 1541, marveled at Indians unlike any the Spaniards had seen in the familiar pueblos of the southwest. These Indians did not grow maize. They killed strange, shaggy wild cattle with bows and arrows, and they butchered the beasts with wooden-handled flint knives. They did not build houses but lived in tents made from the hides of their prey.

They pursued the great herds across the grass-lands and "have no permanent residence any-where," a Spanish chronicler reported. "Troops of dogs" moved with them, dragging tent poles and bearing burdens. The skins of the cattle, as the Spaniards called the bison, gave not only shelter but also clothes and shoes, rope and wool. They made thread of the buffalo's sinews, awls of its bones, jugs of its bladder. Even the dung was used —for fires, "since there is no fuel in that land."

These strange Indians seemed to live on buffalo meat, roasting it over the dung fires or eating it raw: "Taking it in their teeth, they pull with one hand, and in the other they hold a large flint knife and cut off mouthfuls.... They drink the blood just as it comes out of the cattle...."

From the chronicle emerges a picture of an aboriginal culture; we see ingenious, nomadic buffalo hunters making a living on the plains as they had for thousands of years, with no domesticated animals other than dogs. To us, though, something is missing from the picture: Where is the horse?

The image of the American Indian that persists in our minds is this: a tall Indian, clad only in a feathered bonnet, breechclout, and moccasins, astride a horse. Indians of other areas may protest that a brave on horseback does not truly symbolize their particular tribal cultures. But this heroic image does personify the picturesque Plains Indians during that relatively brief yet highly

Linked by rawhide rope and destiny, a captor and his prize forge a historic partnership: the horse and the Plains Indian. Seized as booty or gained in trade, the horse lifted nomads from long-trod paths to a tradition of mounted hunters and warriors. Earthbound no more, the Indian of the plains rode the trail to a new—and more complex—way of life.

dramatic time when they were at the height of their power. In that period—after they had acquired the horse and before they lost their tribal independence—they were among the finest horsemen and ablest mounted warriors in the world.

The Indians who first saw Coronado's conquistadores more likely feared than coveted the four-legged creatures from the white man's world. The awe the Indians must have felt is echoed in an 18th-century account of a Cree's first sight of a horse on the northern plains. The old Indian told a white trader how, about 1730, he and other young warriors had trekked to a fallen horse, killed by an arrow in a battle with a tribe that was mounted.

"Numbers of us went to see him," he remembered, "and we all admired him. He put us in mind of a stag that had lost his horns; and we did not know what name to give him. But as he was a slave to Man, like the dog, which carried our things, he was named the Big Dog."

The story also illustrates how knowledge of horses spread across the plains, tribe by tribe. There is no historic foundation to romantic tales of strays from Coronado's expedition providing the first horses to the Plains Indians. Rather, the slow and prolonged process is a classic example of what anthropologists call cultural diffusion. Mounted Indians appeared in northern Mexico in the latter half of the 16th century, and later around Spanish settlements in the southwest. But two centuries would span the time between Coronado's exploration and the acquisition of horses by distant tribes on the northern plains.

As the Big Dog came into their lives—undoubtedly by intertribal trading—the Plains Indians were transformed from plodding followers of the buffalo into a pastoral people concerned with the

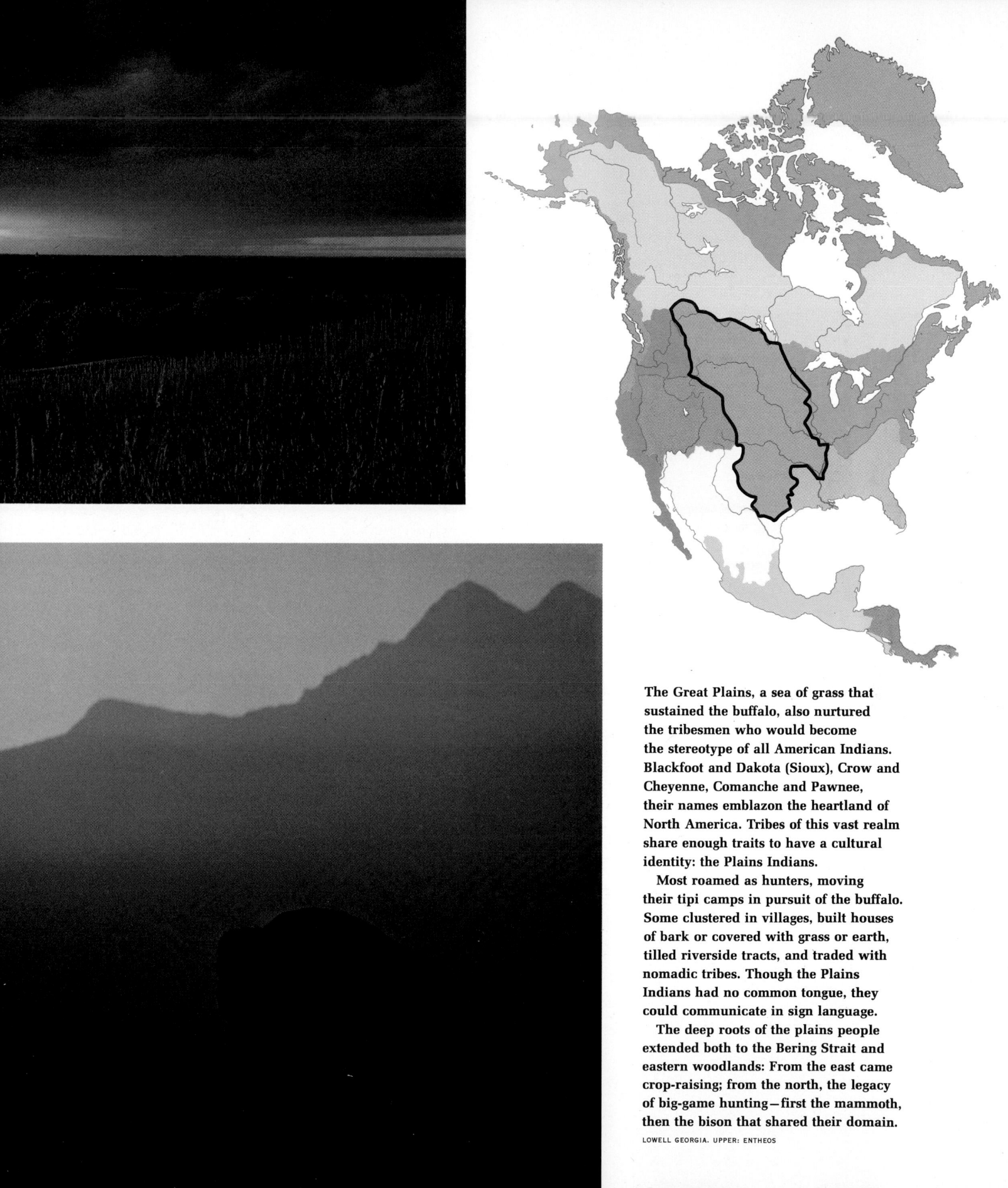

The Great Plains, a sea of grass that
sustained the buffalo, also nurtured
the tribesmen who would become
the stereotype of all American Indians.
Blackfoot and Dakota (Sioux), Crow and
Cheyenne, Comanche and Pawnee,
their names emblazon the heartland of
North America. Tribes of this vast realm
share enough traits to have a cultural
identity: the Plains Indians.

Most roamed as hunters, moving
their tipi camps in pursuit of the buffalo.
Some clustered in villages, built houses
of bark or covered with grass or earth,
tilled riverside tracts, and traded with
nomadic tribes. Though the Plains
Indians had no common tongue, they
could communicate in sign language.

The deep roots of the plains people
extended both to the Bering Strait and
eastern woodlands: From the east came
crop-raising; from the north, the legacy
of big-game hunting—first the mammoth,
then the bison that shared their domain.

"THE BUFFALO HUNT" BY CHARLES WIMAR, 1860; WASHINGTON UNIVERSITY, ST. LOUIS. RIGHT: "BUFFALO HERD GRAZING" BY GEORGE CATLIN, C. 1832; ROYAL ONTARIO MUSEUM, TORONTO

Buffalo hunters race alongside their quarry, horses and riders melded into centaurs. Each man knows his best shot—from the left for a lancer, from the right for a bowman, who draws to plunge his arrow "to the feather." The gun-wielder will work like a bowman, firing the flintlock perilously close to his target. Stalking in wolfskin was a tactic in pre-horse days. One of the hunters portrayed here is apparently George Catlin himself, sketchpad in hand.

breeding, daily care, and protection of large herds of domesticated animals. With the horse came new values, a new standard of living. Families began to measure their wealth in horses. Tribes would reckon their history from the time they acquired the horse. What went before were the dog days, "when we had only dogs for moving camp."

What we know about those dog days has been put together from old Indians' reminiscences recorded by white men in the 18th and 19th centuries and from elderly Indians who lived in our own century and remembered parents' and grandparents' accounts of life without the horse. I met some of them when I was the first curator of the Museum of the Plains Indian in Montana, in the 1940's. One of my best sources was Weasel Tail, who died in 1950, when he was about 90 years old. As a young man, he had managed to go deeper into the past by talking to old Indians, such as Victory All Over Woman, who related stories her grandparents had told her, and Two Strikes Woman, a reputed centenarian whose father passed to her the memories of his grandfather.

This chain of memory leads us back to the time of a pedestrian society adapted to the movements and habits of the Indians' prey, the buffalo. The strategy of the hunt called for a tribe to separate into bands, each made up of 20 to 30 families, many probably with blood ties. During most of the year the hunting bands moved from camp to camp, in the wake of millions of buffalo that ranged in great herds across the grasslands.

On the move, a camp of several hundred Sioux flows in an old pattern with horses added. Once the nomads walked, with their dogs pulling goods on small travois. Now braves who earned horses ride them, and horsepower varies among families. Some may have several horses. The poor, owning only one, overload it with passengers and freight. The poorest, lacking any, still trek under heavy burdens.

"SIOUX INDIANS MOVING THEIR TENTS" BY GEORGE CATLIN, C. 1832; AMERICAN MUSEUM OF NATURAL HISTORY, NEW YORK

When a band moved camp, scouts set out ahead, watching for game or enemies. All able-bodied men and women, along with all children big enough to keep up, walked. Mothers bore infants on their backs. Men, carrying only their weapons, protected the flanks and rear. Women, children, and dogs formed the center of the moving camp. Each family transported its own belongings. The tipi, a conical lodge made of poles and buffalo-hide cover, was the heaviest family possession. It was hauled by dogs.

I estimate that a strong dog could drag about 75 pounds on the Indians' carrier, the A-shaped, wooden travois. This weight limit would keep the size of the lodge cover, and thus the size of the lodge, to around six or eight buffalo cowskins. The rest of the goods—furnishings and household utensils—were lashed into bundles or put in skin sacks. These burdens went on the travois or on the backs of the dogs or women.

The dogs were not good pack animals. They fought, chased rabbits, or took off to lap up water in nearby lakes or streams. Their antics slowed down the march, as did the burdened women and the old and feeble. The latter usually were carried on a special litter made by lashing cross-poles between two travois pulled by a pair of dogs. If a march had to speed up for some reason, the aged and the infirm might be abandoned. At best, marchers could not expect to make more than five or six miles a day.

When camp was set up, the hunt began. Henry Kelsey, first white known to have met Indians on the northern plains, told of the hunt in 1691: "... when they seek a great parcel of them together they surround them ... which done they gather themselves into a smaller Compass Keeping ye Beasts still in ye middle and so shooting ym."

This was still one of the methods about 1750,

262

Lodgepole pines, standing tall in Glacier National Park, retain in their name the memory of how they served Indians. Women who prepared poles for the tipi, or lodge, preferred this pine; its gradual taper from base to top lessened the need to pare it. At a Crow Indian fair in Montana, men begin what was once a chore for women, the erection of the family's mobile home. They lash together two of the four foundation poles. (Some tribes used a tripod array.) After the basic poles are raised, others are laid in the four-pole crotch so that they interlock. This completes the conical house frame. The cape-shaped cover is wrapped around them, its base pegged down, its ends joined by wooden pins. As buffalo waned, so did skin tipi covers; by the 1870's the government was providing Crows with canvas, still used here. Women, who competed as tipi-makers, sometimes decorated exteriors. Modern yarn-tipped dangles recall ornaments of porcupine quills wrapped about rawhide strips.

The tipi (from the Dakota *tipi*, "they dwell" or "dwelling") differed from the wigwam, a bark- or mat-covered hut of eastern woodland Indians. A home for all seasons, the tipi resembled a cone, tilted so its open top was a vent, not a hole that would let in rain. Tipis ranged from portable ones 12 feet in diameter to more permanent 30-foot family lodges whose 20 poles encompassed 700 square feet of ground.

NICHOLAS DEVORE III. ABOVE LEFT: DAVID S. BOYER, NATIONAL GEOGRAPHIC STAFF

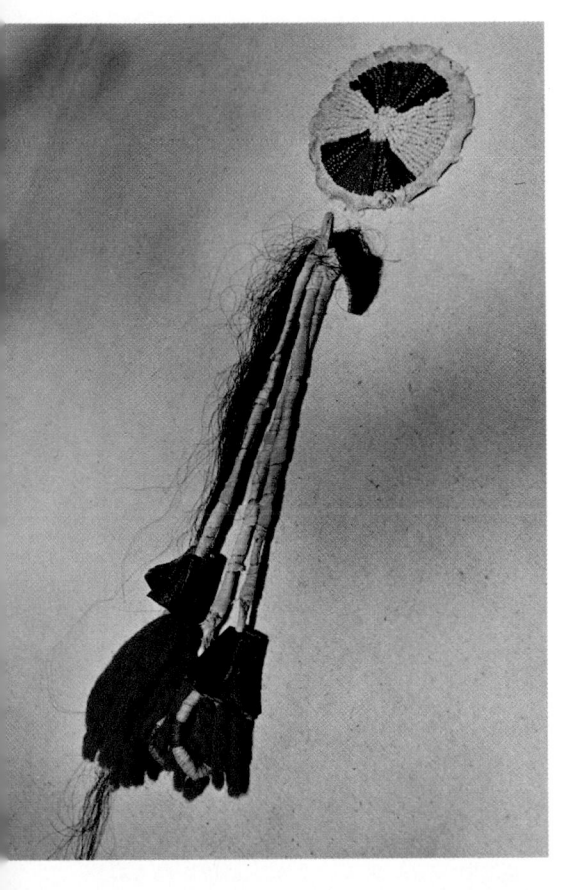

Rawhide, wrapped wet to dry and shrink in viselike grip, binds scraper and maul.
KIOWA MAUL, IOWA SCRAPER, 19TH CENTURY; SMITHSONIAN INSTITUTION

according to Weasel Tail, who told what he had learned of those days before the Blackfoot got the horse. "After swift-running men located a herd of buffalo," he recounted, "the chief told all the women to get their dog travois. Men and women went out together, approaching the herd from downwind. . . ." The women placed their travois upright in the ground, spacing them like fence posts and tying them together to form a semicircular barricade. The women and dogs hid behind it while two men upwind from the herd stampeded the animals toward the fence. Other men closed in, forcing the buffalo together—to mill as they neared the flimsy barrier with its frightening chorus of shouting women and barking dogs.

Now the men rushed, shooting arrows and plunging lances into the maelstrom. After the kill, the chief counted the dead animals, divided the meat equally among families, and allotted the hides. Women hauled the meat to camp on travois.

In late fall, as the buffalo headed to wooded areas for the winter, the Indians of the dog days changed their tactics. They felled trees and, usually at the bottom of a hill, made a crude three-sided corral, studded with sharpened stakes set at an angle so the points would impale buffalo that tried to break out of the corral. At the base of the hill the Indians laid poles smeared with manure and water. When the mixture froze, it created a surface too slippery for the animals to tread if they attempted to escape by climbing out.

Before the men of the camp began driving a herd into the corral, supernatural power—"medicine"—was invoked by the owner of the beaver medicine bundle. He took sacred "buffalo stones" from the bundle, prayed, and sang: "Give me one buffalo or more. Help me to fall the buffalo."

After the herding and the kill, the camp chief supervised the division of the meat. "While butchering, the people ate buffalo liver, kidneys, and slices of brisket raw," Weasel Tail recalled, for his own memory reached back to the last buffalo drives of the 1870's. Two young men took choice pieces to the beaver bundle owner "who had remained in his lodge during the slaughter, but whose power had brought success in the hunt. Each man who killed a buffalo was given its hide and ribs. The slaughtered animals were cut into quarters which were divided among the families in the camp. Each family, whether it was large or small, received an equal share."

The hunting tradition is much older on the plains than the cultivation of corn, beans, and squash. Even so, members of Coronado's expedition who met the buffalo hunters also saw semipermanent settlements of farming tribes. In the great bend of the Arkansas River, in what would become Kansas, the explorers visited a series of about 25 "well settled" villages. In some clustered as many as 200 houses, most of them round and covered with grass.

The villagers raised abundant crops, part of which they traded for meat and hides brought by nomadic hunters. Four decades later, other Spaniards saw a similar trade: Plains Apaches bringing to eastern Pueblos "articles of barter such as deer skins and cattle hides for making footwear, and . . . meat in exchange for corn and blankets."

Assiniboin hunters north of the Missouri River still did not have the horse in 1738, but they killed enough game that year to feed themselves

The Bounty of the Buffalo

Before tipis shrouded in buffalo skins, Comanche women work on fresh hides of the animal that enwrapped the lives of Plains Indians. To them, the buffalo gave its all: from its flesh, food; from its skin, shelter and clothing; from its bones and sinews, the raw materials of tools and weapons. Its meat was the staff of life for the nomads, who rarely fished or trapped; consumption often averaged three pounds per person per day. Infants and toothless elders sucked sustenance from juicy tidbits. Other choice dishes: tongue, brains, raw liver, kidneys, sausage made by filling intestines with pounded meat and marrow; a dessert of berries and blood.

The underscrapings of hides, softened in boiling water, were used as flour for berry cakes. Meat and marrow grease formed ingredients of pemmican, a trail food stored in bags made of unborn calves' skins; in lean days the grease-soaked bag was eaten. Dried strips of lean flesh were packed with layers of fat, peppermint, and berries into a rawhide envelope—the parfleche (right). Misnamed by Frenchmen who apparently saw it as a shield (parer, "parry"; flèche, "arrow"), it was a folded piece of rawhide. Women painted geometric designs, their brushes porous buffalo bones. Men, using tufts

of buffalo hair, painted large blank areas on lodge covers. Pigments in pre-trading days came from mineral sources; buffalo gallstones supplied a yellow.

"Green" rawhide lashed stone and metal tools to handles (opposite); long, seasoned strips became rope. "Soft-dressed" hides were fleshed—rid of fat—on the ground or on racks (above), then scraped; women softened them by rubdowns with brains, liver, and fat. Thick, shaggy hair was left on winter hides—the Indian's overcoat, wrapped around the body hair-side in. Old, smoke-softened lodge covers were cut up to be recycled as shirts, breechclouts, dresses, and moccasins. Sinews became thread, bow strings, and cord to bind arrowheads and feathers to shafts.

From horns came spoons, powder flasks, ladles; from a paunch, a bucket. Hair was stuffed in saddle pads or braided for bridles and halters. Even the skeleton served: Through eye sockets rawhide was drawn to strip it of hair. Bone tools fleshed hides and straightened arrow shafts. Children sledded on rib-bone runners. And they grew up in a culture whose range nearly coincided with that of the buffalo. Swaddled at birth in its soft, warm skin, they would ever be touched by it—even in the winding sheets of death.

266

Skilled hands bring to life a lost art, evoked by the ghostly
mask of a warrior's horse. Porcupine quills, flattened by biting,
are wrapped around hide strips for decorating possessions.
Modern dyes supplant colors that came from the living land.
Quills gave way to glass beads, easier to work, brightly
hued—but "dead," said those who cherished the old art.

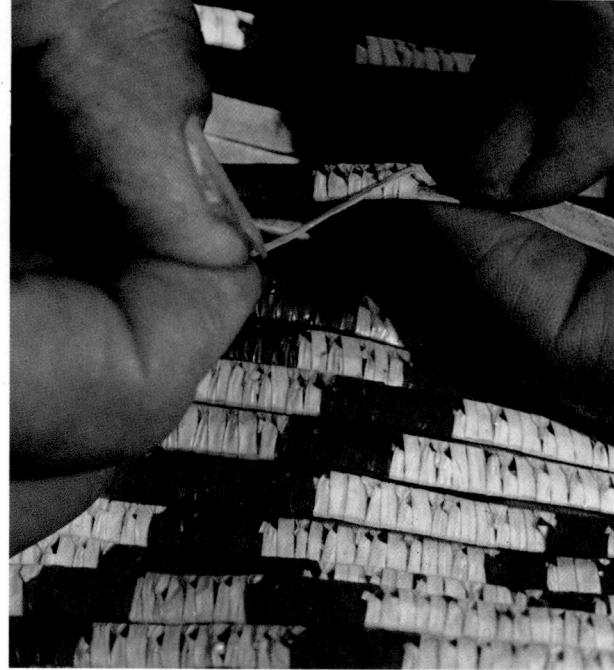

and provide buffalo products for trade. That winter Pierre de La Vérendrye, a French fur dealer, accompanied Assiniboins to a busy trade center—fortified Mandan villages on the Missouri. His records tell of villagers exchanging corn and beans "of which they have an ample supply" for "dressed skins trimmed and ornamented with plumage and porcupine quills, painted in various colors, also white buffalo skins."

The Mandan, La Vérendrye noted, "are sharp traders and clean the Assiniboin out of everything they have in the way of guns, powder, ball, knives, axes, and awls"—goods that the nomads had acquired through contact with the white man.

The aboriginal trade pattern encouraged both nomadic hunters and village farmers to produce more than they needed. But not all of the intertribal contact was peaceful. From elderly Blackfoot Indians in 1787, the English trader David Thompson obtained a lively account of their warfare with the Shoshone on the northwestern plains about a half-century earlier. In those days before the horse, the greatest damage was done when a large force surprised, attacked, and massacred a small hunting camp of 10 to 30 lodges.

The men were all killed and scalped, the women and children captured. The women probably became the wives of the victors, and the children were adopted into the conquering tribe.

Sometimes the tribes fought larger battles with opposing forces of nearly equal size, numbering in the hundreds. The warriors were content to form lines facing each other, barely within arrow range. Kneeling behind rawhide shields three feet in diameter, they shot arrows at each other until darkness came; the battle usually ended in a stalemate with few casualties on either side. The principal weapon in such warfare was the longbow, which came up to the chin of a standing bowman. Warriors on both sides also carried lances, knives, and clubs. But these shock weapons were wielded only if one side so outnumbered the other that the larger force seized the advantage and closed with the enemy.

Logic supports the view that intertribal trade rather than raids must have been the initial method of diffusion of horses from tribe to tribe; Indians with no riding experience would hardly have stolen their first mounts. The historical record offers us some dates that pinpoint the

268

Buffalo and Indian, lashed by winter, bend to the fierce
wind of the northern plains, where the woolly hide of one
became the coat of the other. A Crow woman carries
firewood to her tipi in a Montana river valley. A buffalo
finds grass beneath snow in Yellowstone National Park.
If ice coats the snow, bison will bloody their muzzles
trying to break through to food. Unlike horses, they are
not adept at pawing for grass through ice-crusted snow.

Indians of northern tribes usually left the open plains
in the late fall, setting up winter camps that sometimes
stretched for miles along broad, timbered river valleys.
They scattered their tipis amid the trees. Bands with large
herds of horses might move several times to find new
grazing patches and stands of cottonwood, whose bark became
fodder and whose stripped branches provided firewood.
When snow lay deep, horses floundered and were useless;
some froze to death. Men then reverted to hunting afoot,
driving buffalo into hobbling drifts or stalking deer, elk, or
mountain sheep. Severe winters thwarted even small-game
hunting, and the bands subsisted on stores of dried meat.
But starvation ever threatened; in 1846 the Assiniboin, after
devouring their horses and dogs, resorted to cannibalism.

Counting the long dark days on notched sticks,
Indians sought signs of winter's end: the burgeoning embryos
in slain buffalo cows, the cracking of the river's ice,
the northward flight of geese. Then at last came the answer
to an ancient prayer: "May I see the spring!"

Snow masks a thief—and soon blots out his tracks—as he enters an enemy camp on a horse raid. He will steal horses one by one, leading them from owners' tipis to other raiders beyond the camp. His rawhide lariat, thrown around his prize's neck, is a halter; its loop hitched on the horse's lower jaw, it becomes a bridle. A stolen horse was kept from straying out of its new herd by tying it to a gentle mare, neck to neck. Or bits of their hocks were rubbed onto each other's nose as a scent bind.

PAINTING BY W. LANGDON KIHN, 1944

acquisition of the horse by various tribes. During the 1650's Spaniards were trading horses to Plains Apaches at Pecos in exchange for their Wichita slaves. In 1687 white men in east Texas watched Indians lancing buffalo from horseback. In 1739 French traders saw horses brought to Mandan villages by nomadic Indians, presumably from farther south. Tribes of the northwestern plains had the horse before Anthony Henday—the first white man to visit the Gros Ventre—accompanied some of them on a buffalo hunt in 1754 and praised their skill as horsemen. Surely the Crow on the Yellowstone had owned horses for several generations before the first white man penetrated their country in 1805. By 1800 the horse frontier reached the northeastern border of the Great Plains.

To the nomadic tribes the horse was a godsend. Indeed, most of my aged Blackfoot informants offered mythological explanations of how their tribe had been blessed with this gift. Horsepower enabled Indians to move farther, faster, and with much heavier loads. Packing 200 pounds on its back or hauling 300 pounds on a travois, a horse could move four times the burden of a heavily loaded dog and could travel twice as far in a day. And the horse could save lives. A Pawnee chief told a French trader in 1724 of his tribe's desperate need for the horse—because "our wives and children die under the burden" of moving camp. The aged and infirm, transported on horse-drawn litters, also better survived the rigors of travel.

Since the horse could drag longer and heavier lodgepoles, Indians could erect larger homes. Now 11 or 12 buffalo hides were needed to cover the average tipi. Today's trailer campers will recognize what happened next: The ability to carry more belongings dramatically changed the Indian campers' way of life.

Dried meat and tallow in greater quantities filled the parfleches slung on packhorses or lashed to the bigger travois. The parfleche—an envelope of waterproof rawhide—was part of the richly decorated luggage that began to come into fashion. Chokecherries and berries, picked in the fall and dried for winter use, were carried in buffalo calf-skin bags. Trail lunches of pemmican (thin slices of buffalo meat, dried, cooked, pounded fine, and mixed with melted fat and berries or cherries) were packed into bags hung from the saddles of the horses that the women rode.

A new household industry sprang up: Women made and decorated wooden, rawhide-covered saddles and fancy, rawhide harnesses. The women also fashioned dress clothing that would make the wearer look impressive on horseback, on ceremonial occasions, or when paying visits to other tribes.

Traditional ways of buffalo hunting were abandoned in favor of the chase on horseback. The new technique required no new weapons. Yet a single hunter on a fleet horse could kill three or four buffalo at close range, obtaining enough meat in a day to feed his family for months.

The horse could outrun the swiftest buffalo, but when the pursuer closed for the kill, the skills of both horse and rider were tested. And so trained, long-winded, intelligent buffalo horses—buffalo runners, they were called—became prized possessions. And their selection and training became important activities for the men of the tribe.

As the amount of time needed for hunting drastically decreased, men found more time on their hands for feasting, ceremonies—and warfare over horses. Since only a few hunters were needed to supply meat for a band, other young men could raid enemy camps for horses or join war parties.

Mounted warfare rendered the static, pitched

battles of the dog days obsolete. The big shield, the longbow, the rawhide body armor—all of which would impede a warrior on horseback— were discarded in favor of a smaller shield, a shortened bow, and men and horses stripped for action. Charging down upon the enemy, mounted Indians wielded their shock weapons in man-to-man fighting. Casualties were high, but close combat offered greater opportunities for men to acquire war honors, which were graded according to the degree of courage required to win them.

My older informants agreed that the taking of an enemy's weapon—especially a gun—earned the highest Blackfoot war honor. Scalping an enemy brought honor of the second rank, and the capture of a horse from an enemy honor of the third rank. Though some Indians said the killing of an enemy warrior should outrank the taking of a scalp, others did not even mention killing as a recognized honor. After all, a gun or arrow could kill from a safe distance; a man might scalp an enemy slain by someone else. Possession of booty was taken as proof of man-to-man courage. In fact, *namachkani*, the Blackfoot term for war honor, meant "a gun taken."

Another superlative deed was "coup," or the touching of an enemy. When warriors "counted coup" they would also accept for scoring the capture of an enemy's ceremonial pipe, war shirt, war bonnet, shield, or bow. A wound in battle rated as only a minor honor, though a disabled warrior was well cared for by his people.

The horse raid, which could last for weeks, became the most common kind of war action. The objective was horses, not the taking of scalps or the killing of enemies. Like the commandos of World War II, horse raiders depended upon stealth, surprise, and swift escape.

Members of a Blackfoot raiding party were volunteers, usually four to 12 young men. Raiding offered sons of poor families their best chance for economic security and social advancement. Their

Bloodied weapons stab the torchlit night as Teton Sioux warriors celebrate
victory with a scalp dance, their choreography conjuring the battle.
Women, here waving grisly trophies, were given other proofs of hand-to-hand
combat: severed limbs, later tossed to the dogs. Unlike stealthy horse sorties,
scalp raids might enlist hundreds of men seeking vengeance and glory.
A Sioux (below) shows off a feat of horsemanship impractical in battle.

leader was a mature man whose past successes inspired confidence in his ability to lead his group to an enemy camp, capture horses, and return with all his followers.

The night before the raiders are to set out they drum on a piece of buffalo rawhide and sing their war songs. The words drift through the camp. "... *Girl I love don't worry about me. I'll be eating berries coming home. ...*" Other young men who wish to be taken along on the raid join in the singing. As the singers move about the camp, friends and relatives give them presents of food and moccasins. The raiders check their war medicine bundles and their weapons. They will leave on foot at dawn.

A war medicine bundle contained objects that were sacred symbols of the owner's "powers," bestowed by supernatural forces. Ask where he got his war medicine and a Blackfoot would almost always name an elder: "Three Suns gave me an owl feather for my hair." Another says, "Tail Feathers gave me a coyote skin painted red to wear around my neck. A coyote sees a long ways and never misses what he goes after." Or, "My father gave me a song and the skin of a blackbird which I tied on my head." Most war medicines consisted simply of a feather or a bunch of feathers worn in the hair. Light and compact, feathers were practical objects for travel.

Let us follow our raiders now as they leave their camp. They move out at a steady pace, in no particular order, stopping occasionally to rest and smoke. They will walk about 25 miles a day for a few days. But, as they near enemy territory, they advance more cautiously, traveling at night and hiding out by day. Each man carries extra moccasins, an awl and sinew for repairing them; one or two rawhide ropes, each with a honda, or eye, at

A widow mourns her warrior-husband, laid to rest beyond

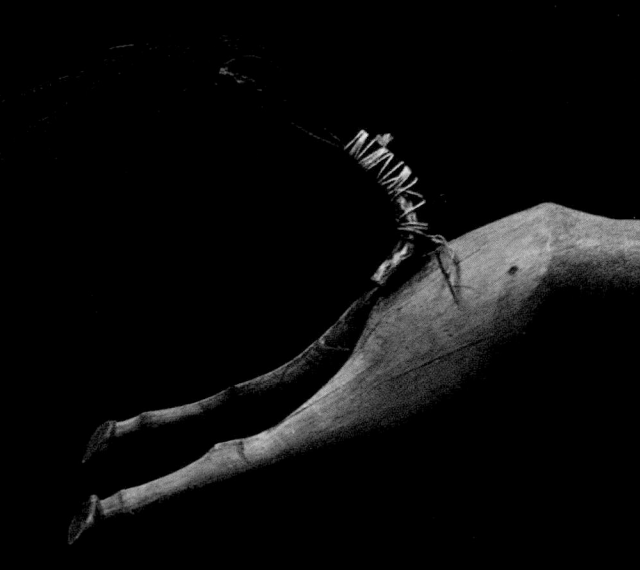

"OFFERING TO THE DEAD WARRIOR" BY WILLIAM CARY, C. 1880; GILCREASE INSTITUTE OF AMERICAN HISTORY AND ART, TULSA. WOOD-FRAME, RAWHIDE-COVERED SADDLE, FROM THE COLLECTION OF RALPH L. WILLIAMS. SIOUX HORSE FIGURE; ROBINSON MUSEUM, SOUTH DAKOTA HISTORICAL SOCIETY

animals' reach, his horse sacrificed to serve him in the afterlife.

Effigy with red-marked wounds honors
a horse that survived valorous combat.

Woman's saddle also served children,
lashed in to ride alone by age five.

Tales Told at a Glance

An Indian's appearance was a chronicle for friend or foe to read. A single feather on a Dakota spoke of deeds in battle (left). The buffalo-horn, eagle-feather war bonnet of Four Bears, second chief of the Mandan, proclaimed him one of the tribe's finest warriors. His shirt told a saga. The heads drawn above black lines say, *I killed or scalped many enemies*—a statement punctuated by fringes of human hair. The painted hand reports his slaying of a foe in hand-to-hand combat. The red wooden knife in his headdress and his reddened lance say, *I have killed with these weapons*. To show how, he drew—with watercolors given him by a visiting white artist (page 282)—the gory climax of his fight with a Cheyenne, one of five enemy chiefs he said he killed. After both cast their guns aside, he parries a knife by grabbing the blade with his left hand, and, ignoring his spouting wound, raises a battle ax.

The drawing, says Dr. Ewers, shows the influence of white painters on traditional Indian art. Earlier works—cartoonlike figures on hides (page 278)—were crude. The author believes Indian artists were "not idle dreamers but active warriors," typically a man, like Four Bears, "who enjoyed picturing the most exciting, heroic, and memorable of his rich experiences."

Killed an enemy

Cut throat and scalped

Suffered many wounds

Fourth to strike a fallen foe

Fifth to strike

"MAH-TO-TOH-PA, FOUR BEARS," BY GEORGE CATLIN, 1832; SMITHSONIAN INSTITUTION.
"THE ARTIST FIGHTING A CHEYENNE CHIEF" BY MATO-TOPE, 1834; NORTHERN NATURAL
GAS CO. COLLECTION, JOSLYN ART MUSEUM, OMAHA

one end for forming a lasso; a small pipe and tobacco; his personal war medicine; perhaps a whip and a wolfskin. A man's belongings are wrapped in an old lodge cover, a piece of rawhide, or a trade blanket, rolled, tied with rawhide rope, and carried on his back. In a bag worn over one shoulder is a pack of dried meat or pemmican.

The raiders carry no shields, lances, or war clubs. Their weapons are bows and arrows, sometimes guns, and knives sharp enough to cut firewood and timber for temporary shelters. These "war lodges" will be built as the raiders approach the enemy camp. They will spend a few days there, killing enough game to live on for the rest of their journey. The lodge, made of timbers covered with brush and bark, will conceal their fire and serve as a fort in case of surprise attack and as a base for scouts, who, usually camouflaged in wolfskins, seek out the enemy.

"It was in winter," Weasel Tail recalled, "when I helped to make my first war lodge. More than 20 of us went to steal horses. . . . I took my wife along. My wife said she loved me, and if I was to be killed on a war party she wanted to be killed too."

He told of the building of the lodge, the killing of buffalo and drying of the meat for provisions. Scouts were sent out to search for the enemy and his horses. Then, late one afternoon, they returned, "zigzagging and circling down a hill in the distance, a sign that they had seen the enemy."

The raiders piled up sticks near the lodge and danced around them as the leader went out alone to meet the scouts. When he led them back, he kicked over the pile of sticks. "All of us scrambled for them," Weasel Tail remembered. "We thought that whoever got the first stick would be the first to take a horse. . . . Toward evening our leader told

Painting History on Hides

In the annals of Indians, buffalo skins are pages and drawings are words—"pictorial shorthand," the author calls it. The painter, "more historian or biographer than artist," produced works that give modern scholars clues to the past. The earliest known Plains Indian buffalo-robe record is this one collected by Lewis and Clark in 1805; it depicts a battle between Mandans and enemy tribesmen about 1797. The 44 warriors on foot and the 20 mounted men wield bows and arrows, lances and firearms; the 15 guns and a pistol reveal white trade.

Tribal history was often recorded by Sioux on hide records called "winter counts" (perhaps because *winter* designated a year). On the Rosebud Sioux Reservation in South Dakota, Kills Two, a Brulé medicine man, paints the year 1926—the 131st year arrayed on the hide before him. The count begins at the top, where hooflike symbols mark 1796, "Winter of Horse-Stealing Camp," when snowbound enemies spent their time raiding each other. A year might be chronicled by a drawing of a cosmic event—a meteor shower (1834), a solar eclipse (1870)—or a human one: the killing of an enemy (1815), the arrival of whiskey (a jug for 1822). In one year, 1829, nothing special happened and so nothing was painted. With the appearance of traders in 1800, the hide is increasingly dominated by the white man (usually symbolized in a black hat) and his legacy: smallpox (spotted Indian), checkered blankets, silver dollars (small circles). In 1868, when whites were wiping out the buffalo, the government issued denim for lodge covers; 1868 became "Blue Tipi Year." A train killing an Indian marks 1912. But amity ends the record: In 1925 Indian and white hail a new bridge. In 1926 the reservation loses a respected official. His unhatted symbol says, "This year a good agent left."

"BIG MISSOURI'S WINTER COUNT"; NEBRASKA STATE HISTORICAL SOCIETY, LINCOLN.
PAINTED BUFFALO ROBE, C. 1800; PEABODY MUSEUM, HARVARD UNIVERSITY

Monument to the Mandan, a reconstructed summer village commands a Missouri River bluff. Mandans wintered in similar earth-covered lodges set amid river-bottom trees. Between the lodges stands an "ark," remembrance of the mythical wooden tower ancestors built to save themselves from a deluge. Nothing could save Mandans from white man's smallpox, which struck the tribe in 1837 and nearly wiped it out.

SLANT INDIAN VILLAGE, FORT LINCOLN STATE PARK, NORTH DAKOTA; ROBERT W. MADDEN, NATIONAL GEOGRAPHIC PHOTOGRAPHER

us to start for the enemy. . . ." The raiders reached the camp under cover of night.

Before dawn Weasel Tail was close enough to hear "someone talking in the Sioux language," apparently "telling the people to let their horses out of the corral to feed. . . . I caught one of the horses, put my war bridle on it, and rode to where my wife was hiding, without being noticed. I told her to mount it and I would try to get another horse for myself. . . . I saw another, a fine horse with a feather on his head and another in his tail. I caught it. It was a good riding horse. I looked around and saw another horse that looked good to me, roped it and led it. As soon as I got back to my wife, I told her, 'Let's go!'"

Weasel Tail did not mention any casualties on this raid, but he did in other war stories he recounted to me. Horse raids accounted for more deaths than did the far less frequent pitched battles. But as long as the nomadic life based on buffalo hunting persisted, these dangerous escapades remained a young man's surest road to social status. The excitement, the winning of war honors, and the possession of horses meant so much to some men that they went out 40 or more times before they retired from raiding.

Horses were individually owned, and wealth was measured in the number of them that a man or family possessed. Middle Sitter (nicknamed Many Horses), head chief of the Piegan Blackfoot, was said to have owned more than 500. He was renowned for his generosity and often lent horses to the poor. But his tribe averaged only eight to ten horses per lodge, and some families owned none.

Rich men were expected to help the poor by lending horses for hunting and moving camp. A man of wealth with a good war record could become a chief if he shared his horses. A stingy warrior got no recognition as a leader. "When peo-

ple want a chief," an old Indian named Lazy Boy once told me, "they select a good-hearted man."

From my interviews with elderly Indians and from other historical sources I can envision what the "horsepower revolution" meant to the average family in a nomadic tribe in the mid-19th century. Our hypothetical family would include two grown males, three adult females, and three children. I estimate that a family of this size should have had one horse to carry the lodge cover and its accessories (a draft screen or lodge lining, anchoring pegs, pins to fasten the opening), a load weighing about 200 pounds.

The family would need two more horses to share the 380-pound load of 19 lodgepoles; two to carry meat, food, and equipment; three more to bear the women and infants and pull travois; two riding horses for the men, and two buffalo runners for hunting—a total of 12 horses. A well-balanced herd would also include four or five additional horses to replace losses and to give the family a sense of security.

But we know that the average family did not have that much stock; the person-horse ratio was nearer one-to-one. So our hypothetical family had to cut corners by overloading horses, making do with fewer riding and hunting mounts, and continuing to use dog travois.

Some families were worse off. Weasel Tail told of a poor Blood Indian who owned only one horse. His lodge cover was the upper part of a rich man's discarded cover. His lodge was so small there was no room to hang a tripod and kettle inside it. When camp moved, he and his wife walked. She led the horse, which pulled a travois loaded with the couple's scant baggage. The children rode on the horse's back, on top of other baggage. Dogs dragged short lodgepoles. (continued on page 286)

Paintbrush Historians

On canvas and on sketchpad, two artists in the 1830's limned a cultural high noon, a way of life that was at its zenith. When George Catlin set up his easel amid Mandan warriors to paint Four Bears (page 276), and when Karl Bodmer spent days re-creating the interior of a lodge, they found a vigorous people. Disease later struck the tribe; what the artists recorded lived on.

Catlin was a Philadelphia portraitist beckoned westward by a desire to portray "man, in the simplicity and loftiness of his nature." He followed the Lewis and Clark trail for 2,000 miles up the Missouri, creating 135 works along the way. Superstitious Sioux, amazed by his ability to capture human beings on canvas, hailed him as a powerful medicine man. But once he had to flee when his magic triggered a murder: A warrior, watching him paint a three-quarter view of a rival, mocked the sitter as half a man and in a fight killed him. Catlin also painted a Blackfoot brave, though he boasted of eight white scalps he had taken.

Bodmer, a young Swiss, accompanied Alexander Phillip Maximilian, prince of a small German state, on a two-year expedition. The first scientist and artist in Blackfoot country, they witnessed an Indian battle there; Bodmer drew it while the prince took pot shots and tried to get a victim's skull for study. A chief said he had survived because of good medicine—his pre-battle portrait. Bodmer, like Catlin, immortalized Four Bears, who, with Bodmer's watercolors, created one of the first Indian pictures in that medium (page 277).

Despite perils—and sometimes frozen colors—Bodmer produced about 400 works. A master draftsman, he mirrored life. His village scene (right) reproduces bullboats down to their willow frames. Dr. Ewers calls Bodmer's lodge interior (top right) "one of the most satisfying and informative pictures ever made of an Indian subject." (Catlin was sometimes inaccurate, as in the sketch above; Mandans did not live in tipis.)

Other artists—such as Peter Rindisbacher, who left some 100 works, though he died at 28, and Albert Bierstadt, portrayer of the Rockies—recorded the Old West. But to Catlin and Bodmer, Dr. Ewers gives the credit for "establishing the Plains Indian as the typical American Indian in the minds of millions...."

"INTERIOR OF A MANDAN INDIAN EARTH LODGE" AFTER KARL BODMER, 1833; RARE BOOK DIVISION, NEW YORK PUBLIC LIBRARY. BELOW: "MIH-TUTTA-HANGKUSCH, A MANDAN VILLAGE" AFTER BODMER, 1833; COLLECTION OF MR. AND MRS. PAUL MELLON. LEFT: FROM "NORTH AMERICAN INDIANS," VOL. 1, BY GEORGE CATLIN

Men of a Mandan warrior society, wielding lances, clubs, and guns, weaving amid imagined foes, mimic the frenzy of battle. Two of the bravest wear full

"BISON DANCE OF THE MANDAN INDIANS" AFTER BODMER, 1834; COLLECTION OF MR. AND MRS. PAUL MELLON

buffalo heads, emblems of their resolve never to retreat during a battle. The spectacle stirs the villagers, who are protected and policed by such societies.

The family owned no dress clothing and could transport very little food.

A wealthy family of average size owned 30 to 50 or more horses. The favorite wife (rich men usually were polygamous) rode a horse that also carried her husband's personal belongings in bundles over the horns of her fancy saddle. In her double saddlebag she carried his dress clothing. Each of the other wives rode either a saddle horse or one pulling a travois. Ample supplies of food, along with the components and furnishings of one or more large lodges, were distributed among many horses, none of them heavily loaded.

Besides easing the rigors of moving camp, at least for the rich and the middle classes, horses came to perform many roles in the social life of the Plains Indian. They became standards of value in trade, and high stakes in gambling. Horse races replaced foot races as popular sports. Gifts or exchanges of horses were involved in arranging marriages. Sometimes a murderer could avoid punishment by giving horses to the family of his victim. Horses were slain at the grave of a dead warrior as assurance that he would not be left afoot in the spirit land.

So the horse, which literally lifted the Plains Indian off his feet, was much more than a larger dog or an animated tool. Its presence became felt in so many aspects of Indian life that it brought a true cultural revolution, not just a revolution in transportation. In dog days gardening tribes had enjoyed less arduous, more secure lives than did the nomads. But the possession of both buffalo horses and riding horses enabled the aggressive hunters to become the dominant tribes.

The Crow, Cheyenne, and perhaps the Arapaho and Gros Ventre, abandoned their fields and villages, converting to (continued on page 293)

Playing for Keeps

Two Hidatsa youths run through a winter village, playing a game called hoop-and-pole, perhaps making believe they pursue foe or quarry. In one version, a hoop of ash wood was covered with rawhide, woven to make a small hole in the middle—"the heart." When a player speared the heart, he chased his opponents until he hit one with the hoop. That one rolled it back, shouting, "There is a buffalo returning to you!"

Such play, widespread in North America, taught skills of the hunt and battle. So did a wild ball game in which as many as 300 young men, divided into two teams, chased a ball between goals set a quarter of a mile or more apart on a prairie or frozen river or lake. Hands could not touch the ball—a round knot of wood, a rag-filled buckskin bag, a hide-covered clay sphere. Like hockey players, they slammed the ball, and sometimes each other, with curved sticks. Though spoilsports might run to the sidelines for weapons, elderly umpires usually kept order. They also minded the stakes, which players piled up to bet on the game: moccasins, bows and arrows, even horses. Some games tested skills; in one, archers competed to see how many rapidly fired arrows could be kept aloft simultaneously.

High stakes—perhaps even an offer of slavery to an opponent—were risked on many games. Some women were so addicted to gambling that they wagered household goods, children's clothes, and husbands' possessions—a bet that could win the bettor a beating.

One game's variations looked to whites like a merger of dice and poker. Its markers—bone, pottery, or shell disks; beaver or woodchuck teeth; walnut shells; peach or plum stones—were incised or painted, sometimes only on one side. They were either thrown by hand or tumbled in a basket (right), their array the basis for scoring. Playing in turn, gamblers might toss six plum stones, four in a spotted "suit," two in a striped. If one tossed all blanks, his "hand," like a straight flush in poker, beat four of a kind. Three spotted and two striped, like a full house, topped three of a kind.

For non-gamblers, there were toys, such as tops and ring-and-pin (right), a courting game. The closer to the pin you impaled a deer-foot bone, the higher your score. And, if you wanted to make the game interesting....

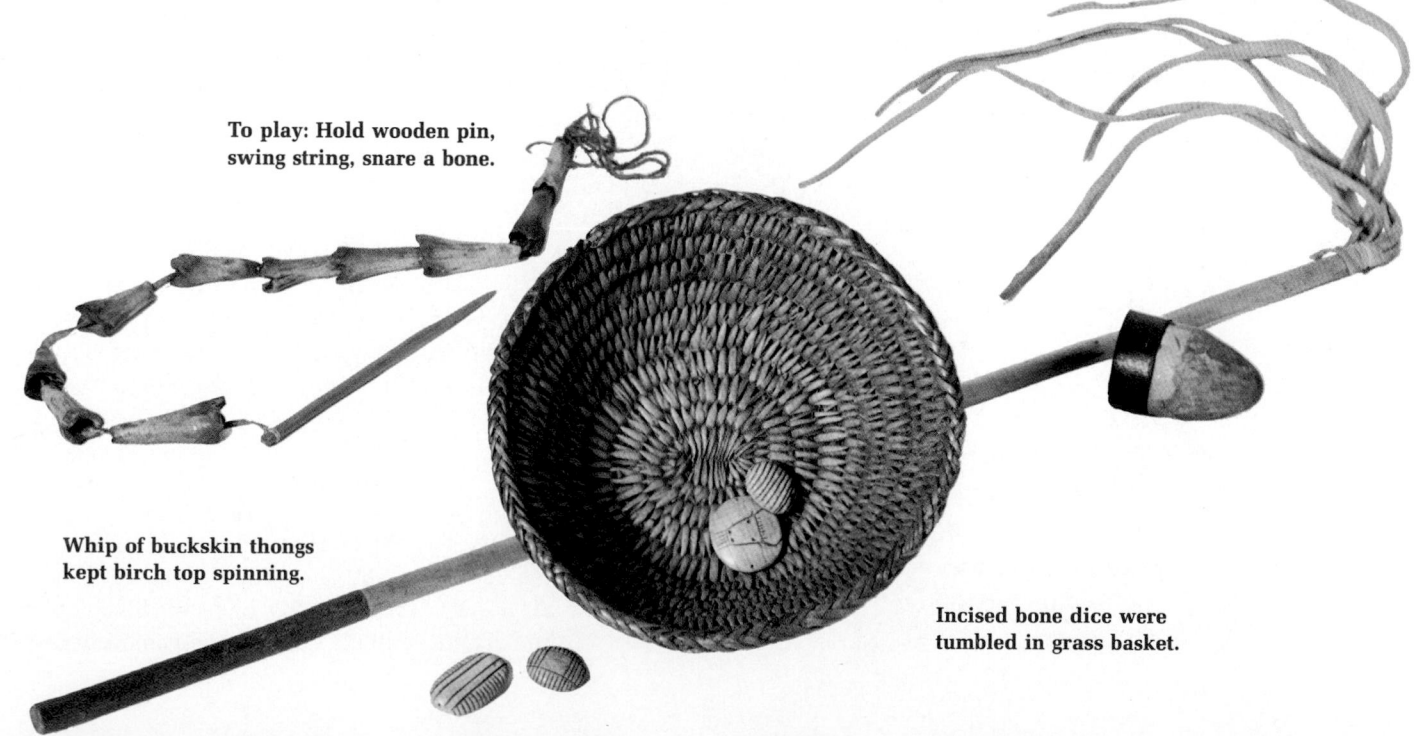

"WINTER VILLAGE OF THE MINATARRES" [HIDATSA] AFTER BODMER, 1834; COLLECTION OF MR. AND MRS. PAUL MELLON. MANDAN DICE, SIOUX RING-AND-PIN, 19TH CENTURY; SMITHSONIAN INSTITUTION. BLACKFOOT TOP, 1942; COURTESY JOHN C. EWERS. PHOTOGRAPH BY JOSEPH H. BAILEY, NATIONAL GEOGRAPHIC STAFF

To play: Hold wooden pin, swing string, snare a bone.

Whip of buckskin thongs kept birch top spinning.

Incised bone dice were tumbled in grass basket.

288

The trading post—shopping center, social hall, pawn shop, rendezvous for hunting bands— lured Indians to the goods and the ways of the white man. Here Indians banked, getting credit in advance of the winter hunt. They sometimes deposited valuables—"a motley array of medicine-bags, drums, rattles, lances, saddles, and other articles useful and ornamental"—for loans against their accounts. The Piegan, who feared the spirits of the dead, brought the bodies of leaders to a post, where traders served as undertakers. Hostile tribes sometimes used the posts as neutral grounds, gathering in truce for trade. Indian girls married traders, and visiting families joined in holiday parties that rollicked on for days and nights.

At flag-flying Fort Pierre, portal signs (above and below) advertised hunt-and-barter commerce to the Teton Sioux tribes around it. Amid their tipis, women prepare prime trade goods: buffalo robes. Other women outside the stockade play the shinny game, a shin-bruising ancestor of hockey. Though Indians living around the post were friendly, the whites had ample small arms and blockhouses adapted for cannon. About 100 traders, interpreters, clerks, and their families lived inside the post; the manager had the gabled house. Erected in 1831, Pierre was built for profit, not war. But soon after this scene was painted, owner Pierre Chouteau sold out to the U. S., which placed here the first military post on the Missouri in the Dakotas. Nearby a new Pierre would rise, destined to be a capital.

"VIEW OF FORT PIERRE" BY FREDERICK BEHMAN, 1855; NATIONAL ARCHIVES

Trade beads cascade upon traditional cradleboard.

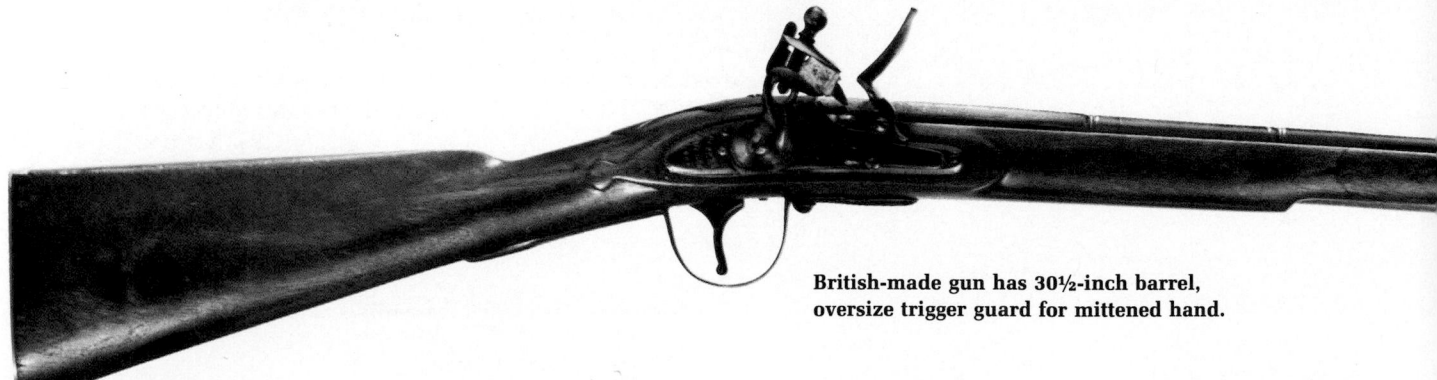

"THE TRAPPER'S BRIDE" BY ALFRED JACOB MILLER, C. 1840; JOSLYN ART MUSEUM, OMAHA

British-made gun has 30½-inch barrel, oversize trigger guard for mittened hand.

Hard soles and complex
designs in small beads date
moccasins to late 1800's.

Oldest known Plains Indian
quill-and-bead art adorns dress.

Red stone Sioux pipe has
a bowl inlaid with lead.

Trading Away Tradition

The father gives the bride away—for $600 worth of the groom's goods—in a transaction that symbolizes Indian-white dealings forged by trade. Marriages between traders and daughters of chiefs often resembled business mergers, for both sides had economic stakes in the union. Marriage to a trapper also could mean security for a bartered bride. To keep her, commented the painter of this nuptial scene, the trapper would have to provide "a dress, horse, gorgeous saddle, trappings, and the deuce knows what beside."

Indians, says Dr. Ewers, had a heritage of intertribal trade and, as horse traders, had "all of the keen bargaining sense that term has come to imply." Mandans added 100 percent markups on their goods. In the early 19th century an Indian might pay 12 beaver pelts to a white for a gun—such as this .60-caliber, smoothbore flintlock (left). The gun might pass through the hands of several bargainers until an Indian in a distant tribe acquired it at a cost eight times the original barter value. Blackfeet tried to keep whites from trading guns to small, unarmed tribes.

Trade beads, which had to meet Indians' size and color specifications, blossomed on buckskin that once bore only natural trimmings. An ankle-length Mandan dress (left), collected by Lewis and Clark, displays old and new: rows of traditional quillwork plus traders' beads, brass disks, and hemline janglers. As trade flourished, so did beads, covering such articles as cradle-boards and moccasins. The latter retain their old style, but hard-leather soles may be white-inspired.

On a decorative pipe, one Indian—his medal probably signifying a prominent chief—serves liquor, a status symbol. White men plied customers with alcohol. The pipe, carved from a single piece of stone for a curio-collector clientele, suggests the end of an era.

Bartering would persist into reservation times. But when whites introduced cash transactions, the new money economy baffled and exploited the keenest Indian trader. Even a robber could be a victim: A warrior plundering a wagon train ignored gleaming gold and silver coins. He saw no point to "buttons without eyes."

292

The first thunder of the spring has rumbled in the sky and now Blackfeet gather in the holy tipi for the annual sacred ceremony: the opening of the medicine pipe bundle. The keeper holds aloft the pipe, richly hung with ermine skins, scalps of woodpeckers, porcupine quillwork, and eagle feathers. Around coals wafting the scent of burning sweet grass, men and women pray and sing some of the 300 songs handed down for this rite. Afterward, the women will prepare a feast.

SCULPTURE (ONE-FIFTH LIFE-SIZE) BY ROBERT M. SCRIVER, 1969; WHITNEY GALLERY OF WESTERN ART, CODY, WYOMING; DICK DURRANCE II, NATIONAL GEOGRAPHIC PHOTOGRAPHER

"I am the Thunder Maker," said the giver of the pipe long ago. "You have seen my great power." Indeed, with his every puff there came a peal of thunder. "This Pipe is all powerful. It shall protect you and your People." And so it went before them on the march, protecting them from the lightning that comes with the thunder and can kill man or beast. Surely a man would die if he should break a vow he makes upon the holy Thunder Medicine Pipe.

nomadism under pressure from mounted aggressors. The largest and strongest nomadic tribes—the Comanche, Blackfoot, and Teton Sioux—took possession of some of the choicest hunting grounds on the plains. The Mandan, Hidatsa, and Arikara, longtime residents on the Missouri, remained sedentary. But their fortified villages were surrounded by mounted tribes that either attacked them at will or made temporary peace to obtain garden produce in return for surplus meat and hides. And penned in their villages, the farming tribes suffered great losses from more insidious enemies: smallpox, measles, and other plagues of the white men.

While Plains Indians traded horses northward and eastward from the Spanish southwest during the 18th century, they also dealt in inanimate objects from the white man's world, bearing them southward and westward from peripheral English and French outposts. These trade goods, accepted or modified by their recipients, became another factor in the reshaping of Indian culture before the mid-19th century.

The plains tribes had been extensive traders before they met the white men, as shown by archeological finds of marine shells from the Pacific and Gulf coasts in prehistoric village sites on the Missouri in the Dakotas. In historic times the Indians also knew what they wanted, and they did not have to be cajoled into trading for their wants: deadlier weapons, sharper tools, and more durable kettles than they could make from the materials of their own country. They were no less attracted to the milder tobacco, colorful glass trade beads, and woven cloth they received in return for their furs and buffalo robes.

No other manufactured article was more coveted by the Plains Indians than the gun, although

From Pipestone National Monument in Minnesota comes a pipe carved by skills and tools older than the white man's steel. The artisan finds a piece of catlinite, a red stone named after the painter, who visited the quarry. With flint and obsidian he traces an outline of the pipe and cuts it out. He then shapes and drills with flint. A cloud of rock

ROBERT W. MADDEN, NATIONAL GEOGRAPHIC PHOTOGRAPHER

they feared it when they first heard the muzzle-loading flintlock fired. The Sioux could not understand this noisy metal rod that discharged a deadly missile so fast that the eye could not follow its flight. Believing there must be a spirit within the gun, they called it "medicine iron." But fear of the gun was short-lived.

Equal exchanges of one gun for one horse occurred in the early intertribal trade. Then, as white traders began doing business directly with tribes of the plains, the beaver pelt, and later the buffalo robe, became standards of value for all articles the whites offered. At Hudson House on the Saskatchewan River in 1795 a dressed beaver pelt would bring an Indian 12 iron arrowheads or a pound and a half of gunpowder or two bayonets (used as lance heads). A flintlock gun would cost him 9 to 12 beaver pelts, depending upon the length of the barrel. By 1850, the price for a gun at Fort Union, near the mouth of the Yellowstone River, was ten buffalo robes.

Plains Indians wanted a light, cheap, serviceable weapon. They got it in the Northwest trade gun, furnished with a large guard around the trigger so that it could be pulled by a mittened finger. The Indians retained the silent arrow for hunting and used the gun primarily in warfare; a warrior speeded up reloading by carrying lead balls in his mouth and spitting them down the barrel. To lighten the gun he cut several inches off the barrel; the excess iron was used to make arrowheads and tools. Old gun barrels were transformed into skin-dressing tools, tobacco pipes, or courting flutes. (These were traditional signaling devices used by lovers. With one, an ardent swain could play musical secret messages to a maiden in her family's tipi: "I am watched. Remain," for example, or "Meet me tomorrow.")

dust tells him his two drillings are true. Now George Bryan—Standing Eagle—will round off and polish. An Ojibwa who married into a Sioux pipe-making family, he demonstrates an art that began to fade when metal tools arrived. But smoking endured, a Sioux once said, "Because this pipe is us. The stem is our backbone, the bowl our head. The stone is our blood, red as our skin."

The introduction of trade goods produced drastic changes in handicrafts. Metal arrowheads, lance heads, tomahawks, and axes; files, awls, needles, and scissors—the new goods rendered traditional weapons and tools obsolete. As metal kettles appeared, pottery-making ebbed and eventually disappeared even among sedentary tribes.

Indians learned to use chisels and files to make arrowheads from barrel-hoop iron—though they often hit the chisel with a stone, not an iron hammer. They made pipe-drills from scrap metal, dug pith from ash-wood pipestems with heated rods.

Members of the Lewis and Clark expedition, wintering near Mandan villages in 1804-1805, discovered their Indian neighbors were "extravagantly fond of sheet iron" for making arrowheads and skin-dressing tools. The party's blacksmith traded pieces of a burned-out stove; for each four-inch-square chunk he was given eight gallons of Indian corn. He was kept busy that winter forging iron battle-axes in exchange for more corn. And by 1811 some Arikara women were cultivating their cornfields with iron-bladed hoes.

Clothing styles seem to have changed during the fur trade period, partly due to white influence. Men of the Upper Missouri tribes probably did not adopt the breechclout until cloth was introduced. Moccasins with separate rawhide soles may have been unknown among Plains Indians before they saw white men's shoes. Women's fashions were also transformed. In the north, women had been wearing a long slip made from the skin of a deer or mountain sheep and supported by shoulder straps; full, separate skin sleeves were added in cold weather. On the southern plains, where the climate was milder, a woman's basic body garment was a buckskin miniskirt; Wichita women painted or tattooed their breasts. For special occasions and in winter a southern woman donned a short pon-

cho made from a single deerskin with a hole cut in the center for the head. Then, as the 19th century progressed, in the north appeared the long buckskin dress that cloaked the upper arms, and tribes in closest contact with the advancing frontier of white settlement began covering up in cloth garments adapted from white styles. The earliest photographs of Plains Indians, taken in the mid-1840's, show Iowa men and a woman wearing calico shirts and trade blankets.

At scattered posts throughout the plains many a chief's daughter became the bride of a prominent trader in a marriage that brought the bride security and her father special favors from her white husband. The clerks and common laborers at the posts also took Indian wives. Their marriages contributed growing numbers of Indian-white children to tribal groups. By the early 19th century communities of mixed-bloods were established. The best known were the Métis of the Red River Valley of Manitoba. They wore colorful cloth garments garnished with floral designs, grew crops, and conducted well-organized, months-long buffalo hunts whose kills numbered in the thousands. They brought home the meat in squeaking, horse-drawn, two-wheeled carts—1,210 of them loaded with 1,089,000 pounds of meat in one epic hunt. On their hunting trips the mixed-bloods triumphantly fought off war parties of full-blooded Sioux.

Pioneer missionaries, stationed at or near the trading posts, sought to make Christians of Indians—with little success. The gulf between Christian and Indian beliefs could not be bridged easily or quickly. A Catholic missionary found this out when warriors came to him eager to be baptized, but on their terms. They told him they looked upon baptism as a powerful war medicine that

Only this Oglala Sioux knows what
his mind and faith have summoned to
this hill. His pipe pointed skyward,
the skull of the life-giving buffalo
at his feet, he evokes the mystique
of the vision quest. Rites varied
among tribes, but the purpose ever
was the same: a plea, a seeking for
an infusion of supernatural powers.

They came through the medium of
animals and natural forces. For an
Oglala, perhaps a buffalo would bring
them. And in thanks a man prayed
to *Wakan-Tanka*, the Great Mystery:
"You have taught us Your will through
a four-legged one, so that Your people
may walk the sacred path...."

Indians who described the vision
quest to whites could recount its steps:
Purify mind and body by passing
through the smoke of pine needles.
Go to a hilltop. Stay for days, fasting,
praying to the powers of earth and
sky, to the Grandfather of All.
But the experience itself—the coming
in a waking vision of a power in the
guise of man or animal—was beyond
the reach of words. Even the man
who had the vision might go to elders
for interpretation. To a Crow, a vision
of the sun was rare; it augured great
power as a medicine man—but a short
life. The sun was chief of sky beings,
his helper the eagle. The moon, which
appeared as male or female, offered
long life. Moon's helper was the owl;
the sky's was thunder; the evening
star's, the buffalo. Earth, chief of
all trees and mother of four-legged
animals, was aided by rats, snakes,
and mice. Any chief or helper might
be the benefactor, the bringer of
the power that would mold a life.

EDWARD S. CURTIS

Towering image of earth touching sky, Chief Mountain in Glacier National Park called men whose quests for visions took them to a lofty stage. Others sought bare hilltops, lakesides, sites where they could be alone with their searching souls. What they found they transformed into the tangible—a medicine bundle, a medicine shield.

The bundle contained a miscellany of objects—animal skins, sacred stones, feathers—related to a vision. Only its owner could fully delve its mysteries. But his shield proclaimed his vision. The power it radiated was beyond that which warded off arrows. He did not always take his medicine shield to war; he might wear miniatures of it about his neck or in his hair.

Rotten Belly, a Crow chief, is said to have got his (below) from Thunderbird, though the sexless figure suggests the moon. Cloth—red, the color of life—drapes a crane's head and body, eagle's feather, deer's tail. He believed the shield guided him in war. Legend says on the eve of battle in 1834 it told him he would die. History records his death in that year.

BUFFALO-HIDE SHIELD, C. 1785; MUSEUM OF THE AMERICAN INDIAN, HEYE FOUNDATION, NEW YORK. RIGHT: DAVID S. BOYER, NATIONAL GEOGRAPHIC STAFF

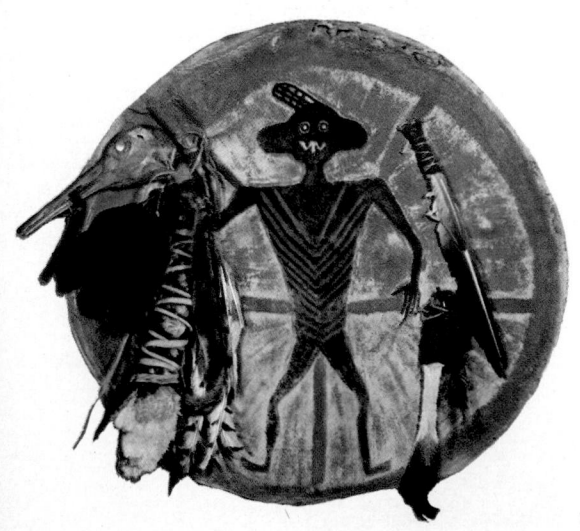

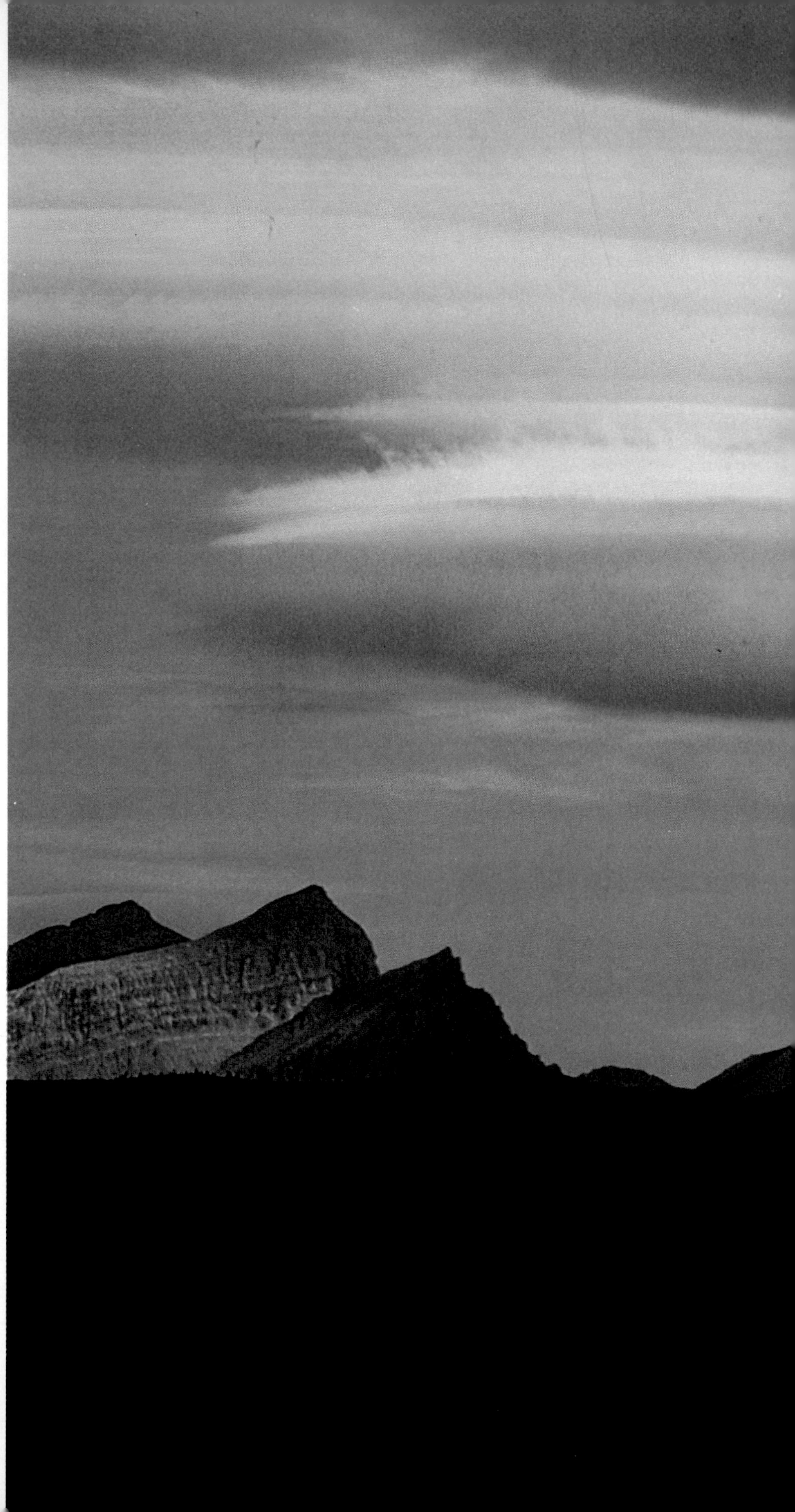

would help them to "conquer any enemy whatsoever." The priest refused to baptize them.

Plains Indians clung to their traditional belief that supernatural powers of the sky, the waters, and the land surrounded them and that these powers were far stronger than the natural powers of man. Sun and thunder were mighty sky spirits. Beaver and great serpentlike monsters were underwater ones. The Indians believed that birds, mammals, reptiles, and amphibians also possessed supernatural powers and that these powers could be communicated to human beings.

A young man sought this gift by going alone to a bare hilltop or other isolated spot. There he fasted and called upon all the powers of sky, earth, and water to take pity upon him. "Hear, Sun," he might ask. "Hear, Old Man; Above People, listen; Underwater People, listen." He fasted and thirsted until, exhausted, he slept.

If he were fortunate, the power would come in a vision. An animal, a bird, or some force of nature, such as thunder, appeared to him, usually in human form, and offered him some of its power. The spirit—a man-bird apparition of a hawk, say —showed him certain sacred objects and told him how they should be made, cared for, and manipulated to bring him success and protect him from harm. He would henceforth see the hawk as a medium of the vision spirit, and he would keep in his medicine bundle a cluster of feathers or some other manifestation of the hawk.

The supplicant also received sacred songs, face-paint designs, and instruction in the rituals and taboos associated with the ownership and use of that power. Thereafter the man had the right to paint a likeness of his supernatural helper on the cover of his tipi and on the front of his shield. He could also transfer some power to other men who failed in their quests for visions or whose own powers had not proved helpful.

Men who obtained their powers from the same source formed cults and performed ceremonies honoring their benefactor. The Bear Cult flourished in many tribes. Bear power was considered particularly potent in war and in the curing of ills. Cultists' face paintings resembled claw scratches, and some members carried into battle sharp, double-edged knives with grizzly-jaw handles. These men were thought to be short-tempered and dangerous—just like bears.

Wolf power also especially served in warfare. War songs were "wolf songs." Raiding-party scouts wore wolfskin disguises. Elite Comanche warriors were called wolves. These brave men carried straps of wolfskin with which they tethered themselves to pegs on the battlefield, determined to die rather than retreat.

The Sioux, Crow, and Assiniboin sought elk power as a love medicine. The Sioux called their courting flutes "elk whistles" because they had heard the bull elk in rutting season calling females with his flutelike whistle. Indians preserved the umbilical cords of their children in small, decorated cases shaped like turtles, snakes, and lizards because these were considered long-lived creatures that would endow their sons and daughters with long lives.

Beaver men—"those who have powers over the waters"—kept the huge Blackfoot beaver bundle, which contained not only the "buffalo stones" invoked in the hunt but also the skins of many animals and birds. The beaver man also kept the tribal calendar, counting the months and foretelling spring. When food was scarce, the people asked him to open his huge bundle and perform his buffalo-calling ritual. To learn all its songs and acts in their proper sequence was an intellectual

To the throb of pain and drums, men dance before the sun in the climax of a solemn rite once performed by most plains tribes. It begins with purification in a sweat bath. A medicine man slits a man's chest and slides a skewer through the flesh. Then, blowing an eagle-bone whistle and tethered to a central pole, the dancer begins tugging until the skewer is torn away. The torment fulfills a dancer's sacred vow. The Sun Dance, like other Indian religious rituals, was denounced by whites.

PHOTOGRAPHED BY RICHARD ERDOES IN SOUTH DAKOTA, 1971

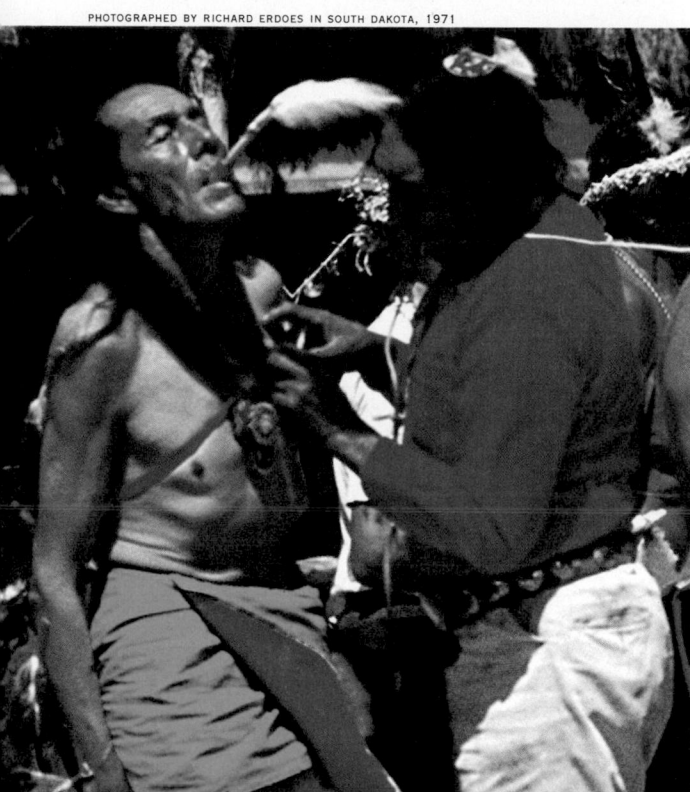

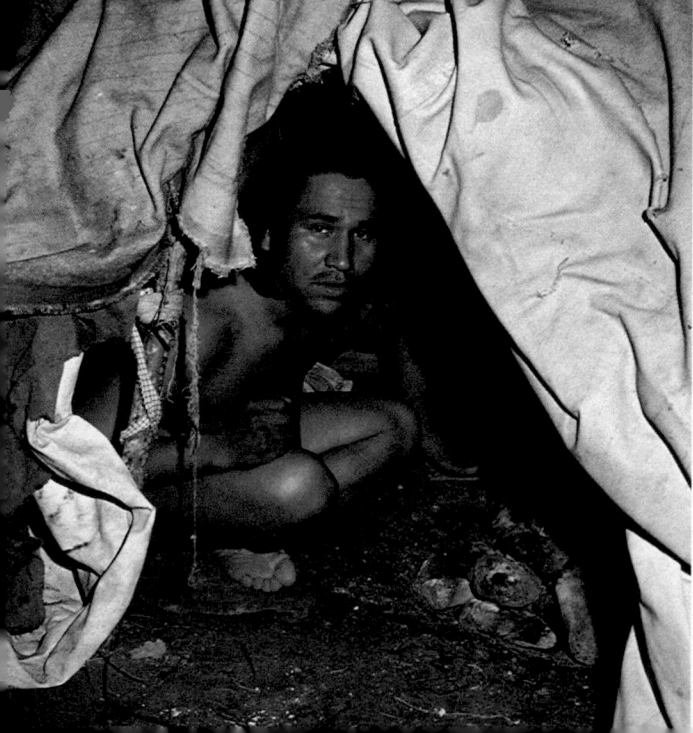

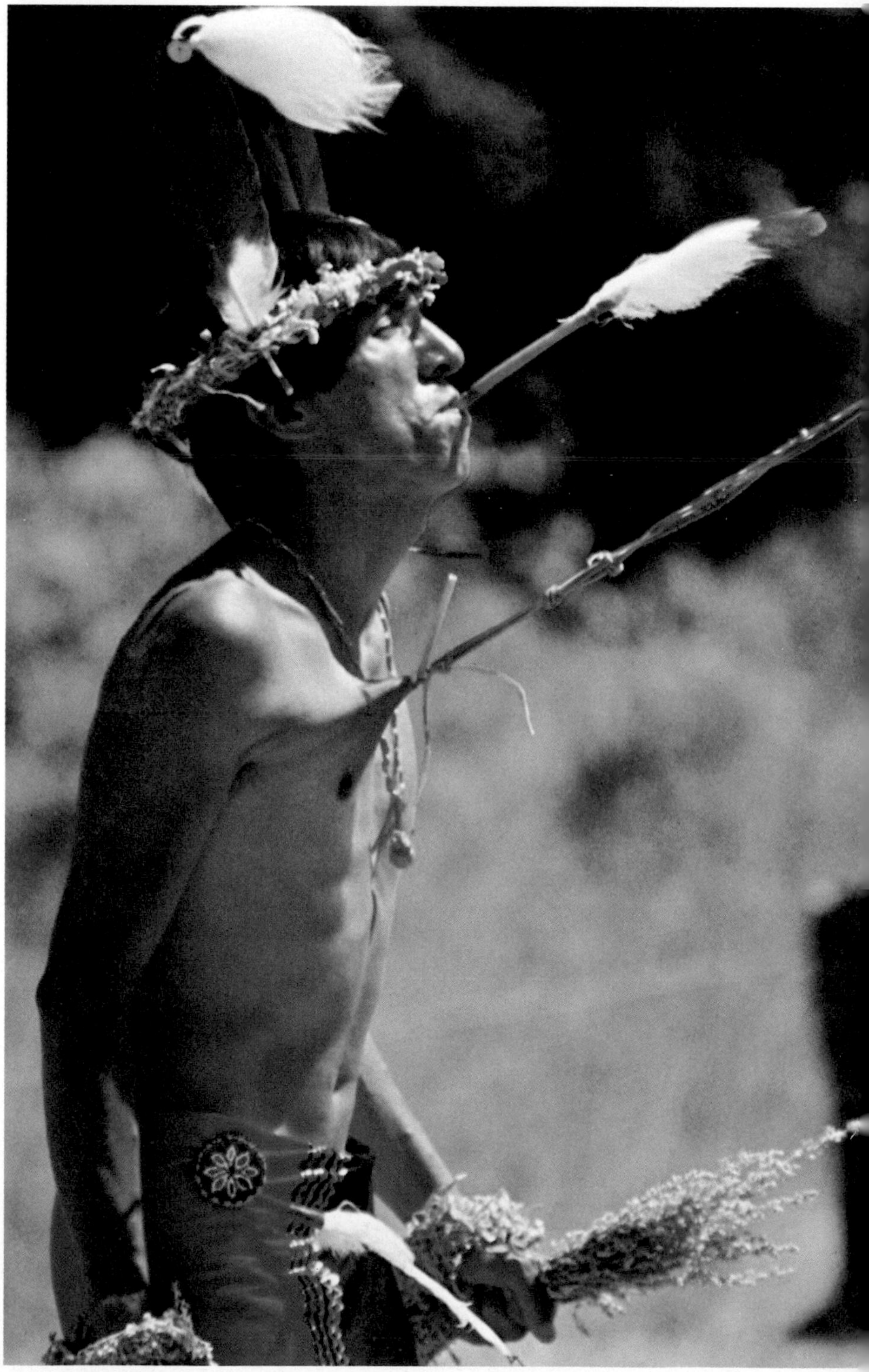

Young Mandans hang by their skewered flesh, bodies weighted by buffalo skulls strung to other wounds. Prodded by older warriors, they spin in agony. Once down, each will lose one or two fingers to the hatchet brandished by the masked elder. Catlin, first white to see the entire rite, heard them cry out—but not in pain: They begged the Great Spirit for strength to endure, for more trials awaited them.

"MANDAN TORTURE CEREMONY" BY GEORGE CATLIN, C. 1832; AMERICAN MUSEUM OF NATURAL HISTORY, NEW YORK

feat. An old beaver man taught the ceremony to a younger man to pass it to the next generation.

For many tribes of the plains, the major tribal ritual during the mid-19th century was the Sun Dance, which served to thank the sun for past favors and to petition for protection and future blessings. Details of the long, complex ceremony differed from tribe to tribe, but for the Blackfoot the leading role was played by a woman known as the medicine woman of the Sun Dance. She had solemnly vowed to perform the mission if a loved one survived some illness or peril. Only a virtuous woman could qualify to conduct the sacred rites.

Preparations for the dance began in the spring when a messenger went from the medicine woman's camp to inform other bands of her promise. In early summer, when the bands assembled for the tribal buffalo hunt, relatives of the medicine woman collected bull buffalo tongues. Small pieces later were distributed to certain women. Holding the pieces, facing the setting sun, the women prayed for the welfare of their loved ones, and then buried the morsels.

The climax of the Sun Dance came with the women's ritual and the building of a medicine lodge. Its center pole, a tree chopped down by a man who had killed an enemy, was lowered into a hole at the direction of the medicine woman. If the pole did not stand erect, she would be accused of not being as virtuous as she said she was. When the pole was up, her role ended, and the men of the tribe began a round of dances and ceremonies. Young men who had made vows to the sun were presented in the medicine lodge to fulfill them.

In 1947, I heard such a vow come from the lips of an old Blood Indian named Heavy Head. He was telling me about the Sun Dance, and he began by recalling how and when he had made his

Led out of the medicine lodge "with the weights still hanging to their flesh and dragging on the ground," the young men now stumble and fall before Catlin's recording eye. Each is tied between a pair of painted runners who pull their charges around dancers circling the sacred "ark" (page 280). Spectators may jump on the skulls to quicken the tearing away of the bloody burdens. Freed, a youth lies like "a mangled corpse . . . his life again entrusted to the keeping of the Great Spirit." Catlin was told of only one initiate who died in all tribal memory. Those who unflinchingly endured the torture and won the Spirit's aid were destined to become Mandan leaders.

The test of faith and courage ended the Okipa, an elaborate four-day annual ceremony that preserved tribal unity by dramatizing Mandan traditions and assured survival by luring buffalo. *Okipa* (look alike) men, wearing buffalo robes and heads over their painted bodies (above), mimicked the beast in ritual dancing. Others portrayed the beaver (left) and creation: night's defeat by earth's first day (below).

"THE LAST RACE" BY GEORGE CATLIN, 1832; SMITHSONIAN INSTITUTION. CATLIN DRAWINGS, C. 1832; COLLECTION OF MR. AND MRS. PAUL MELLON. LEFT: WESTERN AMERICANA COLLECTION, YALE UNIVERSITY LIBRARY

306

"PAWNEE INDIAN COUNCIL" BY SAMUEL SEYMOUR, 1819; BEINECKE RARE BOOK AND MANUSCRIPT LIBRARY, YALE UNIVERSITY.
"YOUNG OMAWHAW, WAR EAGLE, LITTLE MISSOURI AND PAWNEES" BY CHARLES BIRD KING, 1821; SMITHSONIAN INSTITUTION

On western plains and in eastern cities, Indian and white man begin their crucial confrontation. In council under an alien flag, Pawnees agree that soldiers' stolen horses will be returned and the thieves flogged. Visiting the East, Indian leaders parley and pose. In a portrait that illumines their strength, a weapon looms over a token of peace—and a symbol of the new masters of the Indians' world.

promise to the sun. About to enter an enemy camp to steal a horse, he had looked up to the moonlit sky and prayed, "If I have good luck and get home safely, I shall be tortured at the sun dance." When he told me his story, six decades after he lived it, he still bore the scars of his ordeal.

"Rawhide ropes," he remembered, "were brought out from the center pole and tied to the skewers in my breast—right side first, then left side. Red Bead grabbed the ropes and jerked them hard twice. Then he told me, 'Now, go to the center pole and pray for your vow to come true.' I walked up there. I knew I was supposed to pretend to cry. But oh! I really cried. It hurt so much....

"I leaned back and began dancing, facing the center pole. It felt just like the pole was pulling me toward it. I danced from the west toward the doorway of the lodge and back. Then, when the skewers didn't break loose, the old men realized that the incisions had been made too deep. Red Bead cut the outside of the incisions so they would break loose. As I started dancing again the left side gave way and I continued dancing with only my right side holding. Then an old man, Strangling Wolf, got up from the crowd and... jumped upon me. The second rope gave way and I fell to the ground.

"The three old men cut off the rough pieces of flesh hanging from my breasts. They told me to take these trimmings and the sagebrush from my wrists, ankles, and head and place them at the base of the center pole as my offering to the sun. This I did. Then I took up my robe and walked out of the medicine lodge alone...."

The Indians' fear of harmful powers often inspired dread of natural phenomena. Deaths from drowning may have made them terrified of underwater spirits. Plains Indians avoided lakes where these monsters lived; before crossing deep rivers or swift streams, they besought the spirits to allow safe passage. The widespread taboo against eating fish may have been associated with fears of the underwater spirits.

Plains Indians also dreaded the thunder, which they visualized as a giant bird carrying in its talons arrows that it hurled earthward as lightning—a power that could kill men. When a Blackfoot hunting band moved camp, the sacred object that gave protection from thunder, the medicine pipe bundle, was borne on the back of a fine horse at the head of the line of march.

The religious beliefs of the Plains Indians may have helped them live in cautious harmony with nature—but not at peace with their fellow man. They sought supernatural power to protect them from their enemies and to bring them victories. Indeed, some medicine men were famed for their powers to kill or maim members of their own tribe whom they or their patrons disliked. The Cree were especially feared for their witchcraft. Benevolent and malevolent symbols hung from the center pole of the Teton Sioux Sun Dance: the rawhide figure of a buffalo, which the Teton depended upon for life, and the figure of a man—the enemy, whose power to harm the tribe had to be controlled for the tribe's survival.

By the mid-19th century the white missionaries —Catholic and Protestant distinguished by their clerical garb as "Black Robe Medicine Men" and "Short Coat Medicine Men"—had made few inroads on the age-old beliefs and practices of the Plains Indians. But in other ways the white man had greatly changed Indian life since Coronado's time. Aided by the horse and gun, the nomadic tribes had become the dominant people of the plains. Intertribal wars raged continually, threatening some of the smaller villages and hunting peoples with extinction. The Blackfoot, Sioux, and Comanche had grown strong and confident of their supremacy in their vast hunting grounds. There were still millions of buffalo on the high plains.

For several generations those Indians had known and dealt with whites. They looked on the white man as a trader, not an enemy. The whites had brought many useful and attractive goods, and had married Indian women. White men were few. There was no need to fear them.

Not many Indians of the plains had any conception of the great and growing numbers of whites on the farms and in the cities and towns to the east. Small delegations of Indians occasionally were invited to visit Washington, Philadelphia, and New York. But who could believe the tales they told on their return?

A white man who traveled among the southernmost tribes in mid-century wrote: "I tried to convince a Comanche of our numerical superiority by representing the whites as the spears of grass on the prairie, and the Comanche as the few mesquite trees scattered on the surface; but all I got for my pains was an intimation that he thought I was a fool; and that the Great Spirit would not do such an injustice to his friends, the Comanche."

By 1850 white-topped wagons bound for California and Oregon had passed up the Platte Valley in such numbers that they gouged a trail through Sioux and Cheyenne hunting grounds. During the summer of '43 more than 1,000 emigrants passed Fort Laramie on that route, which the Indians called the Great Medicine Road. The whites knew it as the Oregon Trail. Sioux at the fort watched the long wagon trains and decided that the white man had moved his Big Village. An Oglala chief pointed to the east and asked if there could be any whites still living there.

Mormon wagons stream toward a ferry to cross the wide Missouri in 1856.
The streams became a floodtide that washed across the plains as settlers rolled west
to claim Indian land. "The Great Father has . . . left me nothing but an island,"
Red Cloud, the great Oglala Sioux chief, told federal officials in 1870. "Our nation is
melting away like the snow on the sides of the hills where the sun is warm,
while your people are like the blades of grass in spring when the summer is coming."

"KANESVILLE—MISSOURI RIVER CROSSING—1856" BY WILLIAM HENRY JACKSON, 1937; SCOTTS BLUFF NATIONAL MONUMENT, NATIONAL PARK SERVICE

The Clash of Cultures

D'Arcy McNickle

A proud Assiniboin journeyed east in 1831, the white world's wonders to behold. He returned a kid-gloved dandy, walking "like a yoked hog" in high-heeled boots. At St. Louis, George Catlin noted the telling before-and-after. Although the drama of Indian wars held center stage, subtler tragedies such as this eroded the heritage of untold generations.

AH-JON-JON, THE LIGHT, GOING TO AND RETURNING FROM WASHINGTON
BY GEORGE CATLIN, 1832; SMITHSONIAN INSTITUTION

In the bitter winter of 1831 the French traveler Count Alexis de Tocqueville stood on the banks of the Mississippi at Memphis and watched a band of Choctaws crossing to take up new lands in the confines set aside as "Indian Territory." They had been forced from their homes in the east by the U. S. Government.

Tocqueville wrote: "The Indians had their families with them, and they brought in their train the wounded and the sick, with children newly born and old men upon the verge of death. They possessed neither tents nor wagons, but only their arms and some provisions."

As the Indians filed into the boats that would take them forever from their ancestral domain, there was "no cry, no sob . . . all were silent. Their calamities were of ancient date, and they knew them to be irremediable."

The pathetic spectacle moved Tocqueville, but he shrewdly perceived its deeper meaning. The Indian tribes of North America, he wrote, "have been ruined by a competition which they had not the means of sustaining. They were isolated in their own country, and their race constituted only a little colony of troublesome strangers in the midst of a numerous and dominant people."

Yet that "little colony" had one great strength to cling to: the dynamic of Indian life which, against all defeats and humiliations, still tries to gather up the pieces and maintain a moral order, a harmony between man and his universe. For a living society is always an extension of its past. And the clash of cultures between red man and white was essentially a continent-wide effort by tribal groups to hold fast to the values and lifeways which had evolved in the course of centuries of New World adaptation.

Since the first crossing of the Bering land bridge, human occupation of that New World had spread

from the Arctic to Tierra del Fuego. Every climate, every terrain between those continental extremes had been tested and men had come to terms with what they found. The accommodation which made possible survival in unfamiliar and sometimes harsh and hostile lands was a natural process—like that of a plant population expanding its tolerance for strange soils and growing seasons. No massed invasions occurred: When migrating groups came together unexpectedly, they sometimes blended. More often they drew away from the encounter and kept identities distinct.

So natural was the spread of human habitation across two continents that the contours of the land were little changed. Streams ran clear in channels of their own making. Burden carriers followed a web of trails and waterways that led everywhere and made the land a familiar place. A Pawnee Indian boy knew of "no reason why he should hesitate to set out alone and explore the wide world." To the Huron, the world itself was just an island carried on the back of a turtle that swam in a primeval sea.

The white men who came afterward on voyages of "discovery," finding a countryside so seemingly unadulterated by man's presence, could only conclude that the New World was but casually occupied—and by a race more brutish than human. Certainly, they felt, there was no serious moral obstacle to the displacement of that race.

The French explorer Jacques Cartier on his probe of the St. Lawrence River in 1536 reported to his king, "By what we have seen and been able to understand of these people it seems to me that they should be easy to tame."

The Europeans who came to discover, and later to conquer, were motivated by experience which differed profoundly from that of the people who had accommodated themselves to the wide range of two continents. The Spanish, first to come in numbers, had just completed a centuries-long conquest of the Moors in their own Iberian Peninsula. Their forceful entrance into the New World was in effect a continuation of that old struggle between Christians and infidels. As one scholar has pointed out, they "were armed with an ideology that included the medieval theory of the 'just war' of Christians against infidels and the thinking of the Renaissance about the relations of 'prudent men' with barbarians."

Thus while Columbus found Arawaks of the Caribbean "a loving people, without covetousness. . . . their speech is the sweetest and gentlest in the world," the Spanish colonists did not hesitate to put them to work on farms or in mines. The Indians, scorning such toil, fled or perished.

When missionaries protested the abuse, the Spanish crown faced a dilemma: allow the forced labor to continue and receive constant criticism, or stop it and bring bankruptcy to the colonists and loss of revenue to the crown. The crown sought to satisfy both sides. The governor of the Indies was instructed to compel the Indians "to gather and mine the gold . . . to till the fields"; but the reason given was to cure their "idleness" and to facilitate their conversion to Christianity by having them associate with the colonists.

Armed with such logic, the Spanish went on to conquer much of South and Central America and to settle Florida, California, and the southwest.

English settlement in the north came a century after the Spanish, but religious imperialism had not abated. Thus John Winthrop could declare in 1629 ". . . the whole earth is the Lord's garden,

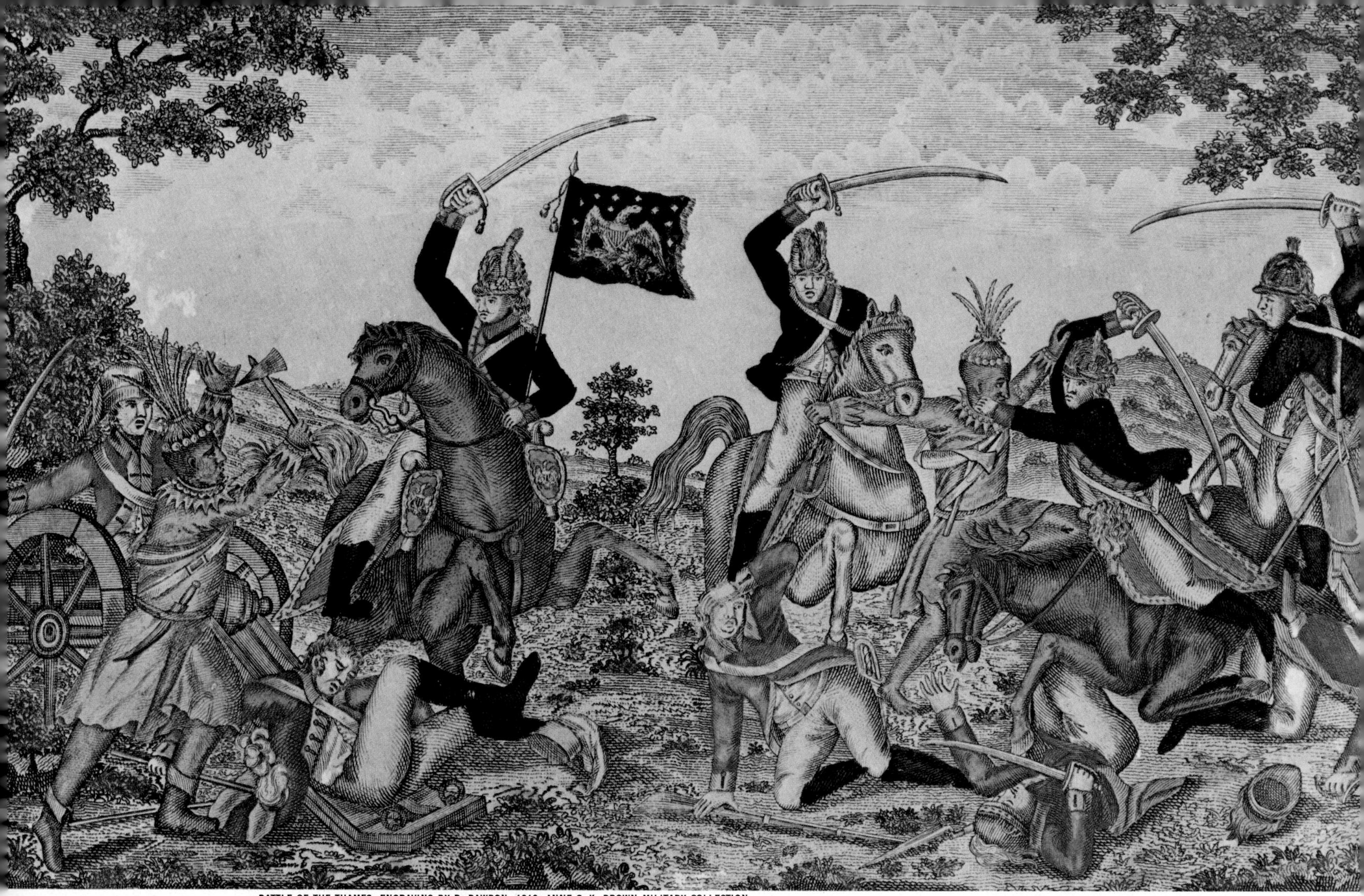

BATTLE OF THE THAMES, ENGRAVING BY R. RAWDON, 1813; ANNE S. K. BROWN MILITARY COLLECTION, BROWN UNIVERSITY LIBRARY. BELOW: ENGRAVING AFTER A PENCIL SKETCH, C. 1808; SMITHSONIAN INSTITUTION

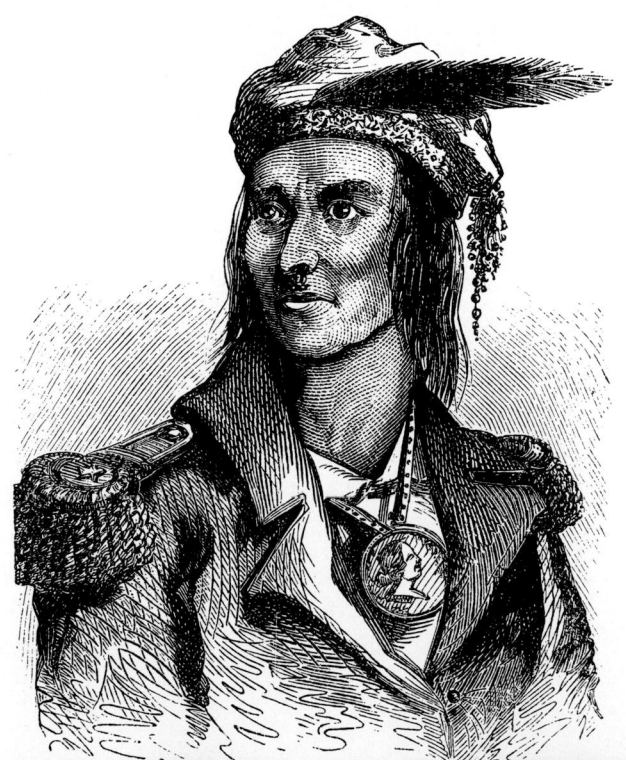

Routing a British and Indian army beside Ontario's Thames River in 1813, saber-wielding U. S. troops felled gifted warrior-statesman Tecumseh. They accomplished more than they knew. The Shawnee chief had sought to weld an array of woodland tribes into a unified power against the expanding young republic. Leaderless, the campaign fell apart.

Tecumseh dreamed of building a free Indian nation without white ways and vices, patterned after his Prophet's Town on the Tippecanoe River. Seeking the goal, he could be blunt. He crowded William Henry Harrison, Indiana territorial governor and future President, to the end of a council bench. Thus whites crowded Indians off their lands, he explained.

When the War of 1812 erupted, Tecumseh spurned American advances and joined the British. They made him an officer and gave him a uniform (right); an eagle feather topped its red cap. But he died in the fringed buckskins of his people.

Campaign sloganeers long remembered the respected chief. "Tippecanoe and Tyler Too," chanted supporters of Harrison (who sacked Tecumseh's village) and his running mate John Tyler. Richard M. Johnson, an officer at the Battle of the Thames, ran for Vice President in an earlier election with "Rumpsey, Dumpsey, Colonel Johnson Killed Tecumseh."

and He hath given it to the sons of Adam to be tilled and improved by them." Declarations such as these, repeated across the years from metropolitan center to wilderness hamlet, bred among the whites a mythology of invincible righteousness.

Popular understanding, perpetuated by conventional American history books, viewed the Indian reaction in images of bloody warfare—the tomahawk and scalping knife. But in fact Indian tribes across the continent acted in positive ways to reach accommodation with the incoming stranger. The Indian experience had placed at the core of Indian life a respect for what each man stood for; warfare was not the initial or usual reaction to intrusion.

At Jamestown the chief Powhatan chided Capt. John Smith for the aggressive behavior of the colonists. "My people," the captain's account reported him saying, "dare not come to bring you corne, seeing you thus armed with your men. . . . What will it availe you to take that . . . you may quietly have with love, or to destroy them that provide you food? What can you get by war, when we can hide our provision and flie to the woodes, whereby you must famish, by wronging us your friends?"

Confederacies and states like the one Powhatan led had been formed or were in the process of forming before Europeans flocked into the New World. The coalitions joined groups sharing similar cultural practices. But, except for Powhatan's state, they were not closely organized political units; rather they were a web of autonomous villages, each maintaining its own boundaries and independence of action. And they brought together for ceremonial or social occasions large numbers of people in a renewal of group identity.

Powhatan's state resorted to war only when sharpened English aggressiveness made any other

course impossible. After Powhatan's death, his half-brother Opechancanough hurled his tribesmen upon the English in 1622 and again in 1644, crippling the colony on each occasion. The ultimate reprisal was devastating, and what had begun as an effort by Indians to find peaceful accommodation ended in near extermination.

In the southeast the Creek confederacy whose towns de Soto had encountered maintained a kind of armed neutrality, avoiding domination by any of the competing European powers. Then, after the Revolutionary War, pressures against the tribes intensified. Under their mixed-blood chief, Alexander McGillivray, the Creeks turned to President Washington and negotiated a treaty which confirmed their boundaries but also acknowledged themselves to be "under the protection of the United States." Georgians coveting Creek lands were incensed by what they considered a betrayal of their interests. But McGillivray's tribal opponents felt even more distressed to find themselves acknowledging the superior power of the United States. As the Creeks were to discover, neither pledge of protection nor guarantee of territory had any enduring meaning. The Indian Removal Act of 1830 swept them from their ancient homeland as if no promises had been put on paper.

In the northeast the powerful Iroquois confederacy pursued its objective of domination in trade and war. No pawns of the contending Europeans, the Iroquois nations had leagued first with the Dutch and then with the English to prevent the French from winning control of the fur trade and the territory which produced the pelts. But the Revolutionary War proved disastrous for the league. Three of the tribes, the Mohawk, Cayuga, and Seneca, supported the British. The Oneida and Tuscarora, officially neutral, actually aided the rebelling colonies. The Onondaga sent war

On "the trail where they cried," forlorn Cherokees under armed escort reach Indian Territory, now Oklahoma. In 1838, 16,000 were herded from beloved southern uplands; some 4,000 perished along the way. Andrew Jackson, defying the Supreme Court, pushed Indians west to open land for whites.

parties to both sides. Having thus dissipated the strength which they once drew from united action, the Iroquois were unable to resist the westward drive of settlers that followed Britain's defeat.

Confederacies that formed solely to resist European encroachment — usually in a last-ditch effort to save a deteriorating situation — fell apart as quickly as they began. The tradition of the autonomous tribe was too strong. But one such league left a bloody trail on New England soil. That union was forged by Metacomet, known to the colonists as King Philip, son of the friendly Massasoit. His Wampanoags had helped the Pilgrims survive the difficult early years, then found their lands encroached upon and tribesmen summarily punished for "trespassing."

Philip, only 24 when he succeeded to leadership, became convinced the English must be driven from the country. The Indian population in New England stood then at about 10,000; the English, 75,000. Philip sought the support of other tribes. He was only partly successful, but when war came in 1675 warriors fell on 52 of 90 settlements, killing hundreds, disrupting the economy. But desertions and betrayals—and the colonists' switch to Indian ways of fighting—sank the uprising. Philip's head went on display in Plymouth.

Across the continent at about the same time another confederacy similarly flared and died. Pueblos of the southwestern Indians were autonomous religious states, with control lodged in a variety of ritual societies. Through a century of Spanish domination they had held fast to religious traditions already a thousand years in the making. But repressive measures grew so brutal that tribal leaders—the best remembered a man named Popé—secretly united the villages for rebellion. In 1680, despite a last-minute leak which

"THE TRAIL OF TEARS" BY ROBERT LINDNEUX, 1942; WOOLAROC MUSEUM, BARTLESVILLE, OKLAHOMA

Robt. Lindneux
1942 ©

White man's whiskey and diseases destroyed Indian life and lifeways as effectively as the gun. Plains Assiniboins with their tipis and woodland Ojibwas with bark-covered lodges drain a keg of Hudson's Bay Company rum on the Red River of the North. Artist Rindisbacher's "frolic" scarcely hints at the hangover of mayhem that often followed.

"A DRUNKEN FROLIC AMONG THE CHIPPEWAYS AND ASSINIBOINES" BY PETER RINDISBACHER, C. 1820; U. S. MILITARY ACADEMY MUSEUM, WEST POINT

Old World killers like smallpox cut down roving tribes, emptied villages. In western Canada traders resold blankets stripped from dead Bella Coolas; the cost included 200 more Indian lives. Among the Sioux a pocked figure (opposite) on a "winter count" hide noted a disastrous year. To an eastern colonist an epidemic among "Salvages" was evidence of God's "wondrous wisedome."

almost brought the conspiracy to a premature end, the villagers rose, burned churches, killed missionaries, attacked garrisons and settlements.

Then the confederacy disintegrated. The Pueblos were never a warlike people; they had no genius for military organization and aggressive action. But they had made their point, and restoration of the Spanish regime 14 years later brought a more tolerant policy.

If the French left a less sanguinary record in their occupation of the New World, the reasons stemmed from a different logic of self-interest. Colonization was never strongly promoted; a string of settlements and posts could maintain the lucrative fur trade, and the wilderness be kept for its riches. The same economic goal prompted the French to seek tribal alliances rather than conquests. Almost from the beginning the French sent young men to spend a season or so in an Indian camp and invited young Indians to winter with the French. Thus communication between the two peoples was encouraged—a rare thing in days of early contact. And the French gained access to fur lands in the interior without tribal displacement or wars of annihilation.

Nevertheless, the fur trade profoundly affected Indian cultures and strengths. Old skills were lost as dependence developed on the trader's steel axes and knives, bolts of cloth, iron pots. Introduction of the gun made the Indian a more efficient hunter —sometimes so effective that game became disturbingly scarce. The trade also changed tribal warfare, making it deadlier and more decisive.

Along with such goods came alcohol. "They will pawne their wits, to purchase the acquaintance of it," one European said. Too many Indians for centuries would find among the dregs in a barrel disaster for themselves and their people.

Finally, the fur trade occasioned explosive wars between tribes vying for trapping grounds, and between the French and English, each with their Indian allies. The conflicts would lead to destruction of some tribes, the unsettling of many.

By the time the United States came into being, most tribes had had some contact with white men, and each of the parties had formed some ideas about the other. Now, as their old French and English trading partners departed, the Indians looked with suspicion on the emerging nation and the designs it might have for putting settlers on their land. They sensed that the years ahead would prove critical.

Their suspicions had basis. With the Revolution behind, settlers searched out mountain gaps and westward-flowing rivers, pouring into the Ohio country and other areas across the Appalachians.

Strong voices in the new government called for seizing the land of tribes which had allied themselves with the British. But a more moderate view prevailed and the early Congresses followed the English policy of treating the tribes on a nation-to-nation basis and respecting their lands.

The Northwest Ordinance, adopted by the Continental Congress in 1787 to provide for the organization of the Ohio country, assured: "The utmost good faith shall always be observed towards the Indians; their lands and property shall never be taken from them without their consent; and in their property, rights and liberty, they never shall be invaded or disturbed, unless in just and lawful wars authorized by Congress...."

These were respectable legalisms with a worthy history, but more important in shaping U. S. policy was lust for land and white attitudes toward the Indians. Many whites viewed the Indians as lacking the potential for full participation in human society. It was seriously questioned whether they could ever be civilized.

Even goodly missionaries cast Indian character in odious terms. A Jesuit, working among the Hurons in 1710, complained, "They hold tenaciously to their native belief or superstition, and on that account are the more difficult to instruct. For what can one do with those who in word give agreement ... but in reality give none?"

Father Joseph Neumann, after 50 years among the Tarahumara Indians of northern Mexico, acknowledged failure with bitterness: "... with these stony-hearted people.... The seed of the gospel does not sprout, or if it sprouts, it is spoiled by the thorn of carnal desire...."

Fur traders also drew vicious portraits. Alexander Mackenzie wrote of the Athapaskans he met along the river that now bears his name, "They are a meagre, ugly, ill-made people, particularly about the legs, which are ... covered with scabs."

Santee Sioux rose in 1862 to terrorize the settlements of southwestern Minnesota. A petty quarrel over stealing eggs sparked the smoldering bitterness of reservation life into the deadliest attack on white settlers in two centuries; hundreds were slain. Scenes from a lecturer's panorama depict the warriors bypassing a friendly farmer, killing a mother and daughter. Swift trials condemned 306 Indians; Lincoln spared all but 38, who swung simultaneously from a gallows at Mankato.

PANORAMA OF THE MINNESOTA MASSACRE BY JOHN STEVENS, C. 1868; MINNESOTA HISTORICAL SOCIETY; TIME-LIFE PICTURE AGENCY

Eyes dull with fatigue, Minnesotans who escaped the Sioux fury in '62 rest in flight. Among them are missionaries and teachers, alerted by an Indian friend to the onrushing wave of pillage and massacre. Citizens of the new state cried vengeance; few heeded Episcopal Bishop Henry Whipple's plea for "reform of an atrocious... system, which has always garnered for us the same fruit of anguish and blood."

MINNESOTA HISTORICAL SOCIETY

Such comments reflected a clash of values and an unwillingness or inability of one side to see virtue in the other. The Europeans, framed by a different set of traditions, failed to understand the complexities of Indian beliefs and adaptations. Moreover, they felt no need to try.

For their part, Indians saw little reason to sort out the intricacies of the white man's life or abandon the familiar and proven. Thus an Arikara, telling trader Antoine Tabeau that his tribe followed the principle of "he who has divides with him who has not," could challenge: "Why do you wish to make all this powder and these balls since you do not hunt? Of what use are all these knives to you? Is not one enough with which to cut the meat? It is only your wicked heart that prevents you from giving them to us. Do you not see that the village has none? I will give you a robe myself, when you want it, but you already have more robes than are necessary to cover you."

Said Tabeau, baffled, "All the logic... in the world [is] thrown away against these arguments."

Unfortunately for the Indians, who on their own had settled two continents, the Europeans had the technology and very soon the power to impose their view of reality. Whites saw the Indians as but casual and impermanent occupiers of the soil with no notion of ownership, no instrumentalities for recording or transferring title; they roamed over the land as did beasts of the forest, and constructed no permanent settlements.

Indian country was universally referred to as "Indian hunting ground" and Indians described as "nomadic hunters." The fact that Indians had been cultivating the land long before the first Europeans arrived was ignored. Even as early settlers robbed artifacts from the great mounds of the mid-continent, they explained away the marvels as works of a superior race that had vanished.

Ignorance of Indian community life and subsistence patterns only partly explains such conceits. More enduring was the idea that the taking of Indian land and putting it under white cultivation served a higher human purpose. As John Quincy Adams argued: "... what is the right of a huntsman to the forest of a thousand miles over which he has accidentally ranged in quest of prey?... Shall the lordly savage not only disdain the virtues and enjoyments of civilization himself, but shall he control the civilization of a world?"

Indian history, however, is more than a history of Indian-white relations and the dislocations resulting from that relationship. Indians reacted to the incoming white man, but they also reacted to the total environment, as any society does. In spite of the pressures exerted by the military, by government agents, missionary workers, and educators, Indian communities accepted what they could use—the horse, the gun, fabric in place of skins—and rejected what posed a threat to the moral order by which they lived. Resistance took a variety of forms—at first alliances, then movements seeking solutions based on native experiences and ideologies.

In 1763 the Ottawa leader Pontiac pursued a vision of restoring an Indian world. The white man's ways were to be rejected—his teachings, his goods, especially his alcohol and the vices it incited. Pontiac welded a union of tribes northwest of the Ohio River and captured a chain of British forts. But his uprising failed when the tribes pulled back. Tribal autonomy partly dictated the action, but in fact tribes in battle had no organized supply lines and little opportunity to live off the land. Once provisions ran out they had no choice but to break off and go home, where they had families to feed.

324

Penned in a mist-hung Fort Snelling stockade, peaceful Sioux await their fate in the wake of the Minnesota rising. Though innocent of bloodshed, they were resettled in Nebraska, where descendants live today. Hostiles who had eluded capture slipped into Canada; with them went four-year-old Ohiyesa, in later life the famed author and physician Charles A. Eastman. The bloodstained ground became a no-man's-land as fearful whites deserted 23 counties. Long years went by before settlers returned.

In November 1868 Custer and the Seventh Cavalry burst out of a blizzard to destroy a sleeping Cheyenne camp on the Washita River. Among the Indian dead: Black Kettle, survivor of Sand Creek (page 336). Thus did the Army answer attacks on burgeoning traffic west—ordering tribes on the southern plains to newly assigned reservations and opening an unprecedented winter war of extermination on those who disobeyed.

"ATTACK AT DAWN" BY CHARLES SCHREYVOGEL, C. 1900; GILCREASE INSTITUTE OF AMERICAN HISTORY AND ART, TULSA

Half a century later the great Shawnee leader Tecumseh and his brother Tenskwatawa, the Prophet, put together an even more broadly based alliance. It too had a messianic impulse. Tecumseh's planning was on a scale never before attempted by an Indian leader. He traveled from the Canadian border to Florida, from Missouri into New York State. Everywhere he urged tribes to hold together, to keep to old ways, above all to retain their lands. "Sell a country!" he exclaimed, "Why not sell the air, the clouds and the great sea, as well...?" As he journeyed, nature added portents: A comet flamed; the earth shook with a great quake felt from Missouri to the Atlantic.

Tecumseh's brother allowed a premature test of strength on the Tippecanoe River in 1811, his lost battle blunting the Indian drive. But Tecumseh pushed on, seeing in the War of 1812 "a chance ...such as will never occur again." His forces fought alongside the British, on two occasions destroying large columns of Kentuckians. But in a critical battle on the Thames River in 1813 the British commander fled, leaving troops and Indians without generalship. Tecumseh was killed and his Indian allies scattered. With the defeat in 1814 of Creeks in the south who had responded to Tecumseh's vision of a restored native America, the strategy of the confederacy collapsed. No such effort on so large a scale was ever tried again.

Until the 1830's no major break occurred to alter the relationship between the autonomous tribes and the developing nation. True, there had been war, tribes had been pushed from their seaboard homes, and much of the Ohio country had been overrun. Yet damaging as these losses were, tribal life remained essentially intact. And for many tribes, most of North America remained an island carried on the back of a turtle.

The first blow was the Indian Removal Act of 1830, which gave President Andrew Jackson the authority to arrange for the eastern tribes to pack up and move west of the Mississippi. The law specified that he could act only with the Indians' consent, that the Indians would be paid for their land and given new territories in the west to which they would hold perpetual title.

The act reverberated like a thunderclap on tribes wedded to ancestral realms. A Choctaw leader had protested, "In a few years, the American will also wish to possess the land west of the Mississippi." No matter: Jackson was in a hurry. The Southeastern states were beginning their cotton boom; some had already passed laws curtailing Indian rights and letting whites seize their lands.

The peaceful Choctaws departed first, then the Creeks. The Cherokees, having adopted many of the white man's ways, took their case to court. In a landmark decision by the Supreme Court, Chief Justice John Marshall affirmed the tribe's rights: "The Cherokee Nation ... is a distinct community, occupying its own territory, with boundaries accurately described ... and which the citizens of Georgia have no right to enter, but with assent of the Cherokees themselves, or in conformity with treaties, and with the acts of Congress."

Jackson ignored the ruling. "John Marshall has made his decision, now let him enforce it," he is reputed to have said. When Cherokees tried to withhold their consent, troops were dispatched to their homes and negotiations concluded at bayonet point. The Cherokees departed.

Within ten years the Eastern states were cleared also of Chickasaws and Seminoles—some 60,000 people in all taking the "Trail of Tears" to the newly created Indian Territory. Along the way thousands perished of hunger, cold, illness, and sorrow. Only the Seminoles resisted as a group,

Weary of war—between the states, between red men and white—
the government sent forth apostles of peace to the plains.
Under a billowing tipi canopy at Fort Laramie, illustrious
warriors gathered to parley: Spotted Tail, Pawnee Killer,
Man-Afraid-of-His-Horse, William Tecumseh Sherman,
Alfred H. Terry, William S. Harney. In 1868 they agreed
to end all war "forever." Red Cloud of the Oglala Sioux
demanded more than words. He had fought the Army to a
standstill; not until the soldiers backed off the Bozeman
Trail did he come in, make peace, and settle on a reservation.
Others held out. Sitting Bull, Crazy Horse, Gall clung to
the freedom they cherished—up north of Laramie, where the
Powder and the Rosebud and the Little Bighorn flowed.

From a crude stockade thrown up by fur traders in 1834,
Fort Laramie swelled with the westering tides to become
the most famous stopover on the Oregon Trail. Here at the
confluence of the Laramie and North Platte Rivers paused
Marcus Whitman, Frémont, Brigham Young and his Mormons,
forty-niners. During the Civil War "Galvanized Yankees"—
paroled Confederates—manned it. The fort was deactivated in
1890, the year census takers declared the end of the frontier.

NATIONAL ARCHIVES. LEFT: "FORT LARAMIE" BY ALFRED JACOB MILLER, 1837;
WALTERS ART GALLERY, BALTIMORE

and in their Florida swamps they fought a war that lasted from 1835 to 1842 and cost the United States 1,500 soldiers. The Seminole population there was reduced to a scant 500.

Ohio River and Great Lakes tribes were also rounded up—Ottawa, Potawatomi, Shawnee, Delaware, Kickapoo, Winnebago, Peoria, Miami, and finally the Sauk and Fox who made a last stand under Black Hawk in Illinois. All were sent out of their homes to lands beyond the Mississippi.

The 1830 Removal Act was followed rapidly by other unilateral measures: creation of an Indian Affairs department with an overwhelming bureaucracy, assumption of power in the internal affairs of the tribes, granting to U. S. courts the right to supersede tribal authority in cases involving a white man. Treaties which in the early years of Indian-white association had expressed mutual friendship and trust were now succeeded by treaties serving primarily as instruments for separating the Indian from his land.

The opening up of the Oregon country and the discovery of gold in California brought the blazing of transcontinental wagon roads and building of forts to protect them. The Indians had to be pushed north and south of the lines of travel. Some tribes—among them the Delaware, Shawnee, Kickapoo, Sauk, Fox, and Winnebago—were moved repeatedly. Each time they drew less acreage and usually poorer lands. Such removals allowed no time for a tribe to adjust to a new environment. Tribes from the Great Lakes, used to an economy that included fishing, hunting, and gathering, found the waterless plains a forbidding habitat. The horse Indians of the plains were thrown into fierce competition with displaced tribes even as the buffalo began to disappear. Starvation became a constant visitor.

The government reacted by issuing rations. This in turn provided a lever for pressuring tribes into compliance with official policy: the threat to withhold food. A more disastrous course of action could hardly have been devised, since the dependency fostered by the ration system wasted the energies and spirit of the people. A race which had survived for millenniums by adapting to environmental challenges was immobilized.

Wastage of human capacity was accompanied by population decline. Native America had been free of killer diseases known for thousands of years in the Old World. One theory suggests that Arctic cold provided a "germ screen" that eliminated harmful organisms as migrant populations wandered across from Asia. Physical anthropologist Ales Hrdlicka wrote in 1910 that "the condition of the skeletal remains, the testimony of early observers, and the present state of some of the tribes ... warrant the conclusion that on the whole the Indian race was a comparatively healthy one." But all this changed rapidly as diseases brought by the white man—smallpox, typhus, cholera, tuberculosis—struck peoples lacking immunity.

Smallpox was the deadliest killer. Epidemics raged over thousands of miles. In 1837 the American Fur Company's supply steamer brought smallpox up the Missouri along with its cargo of food, clothing, blankets, medicines, and tools for the trading posts. The Assiniboin lost whole villages; the Blackfoot were reduced by a third; the Mandan population was cut from 1,600 to 150.

Disease was not the only cause of population decline. In California the number of Indians would plummet by 90 percent—the result largely of slaughter by early miners and settlers. Gen. George Crook would (continued on page 336)

On the plains they long roamed free, buffalo flow across a set of alien tracks. They stop a train but cannot stop progress. There was not room enough for the buffalo, which sustained the Indian, and the iron horse, which sustained the white man. Before he came, some 60,000,000 buffalo ranged the continent. Soon after he began to spread, he saw them "in numbers—numberless," on plains that "were black and appeared as if in motion." By 1800 hardly any bison existed east of the Mississippi, though an estimated 40,000,000 still darkened the plains. Hired hunters launched the slaughter to get meat for railroad builders—who often laid tracks on herds' traditional paths. Buffalo Bill Cody boasted of 48 kills in 50 minutes, 4,280 in 18 months.

Slayers often took only the tongue, a delicacy, and left the carcass to rot. Hide dealers shot as many as five animals for each skin taken. About 40,000 hides, a month's supply from one shipper, lie stacked at a Dodge City, Kansas, shipping dump (right). Military leaders endorsed the slaughter, which made starvation a strategic weapon. By 1900, the nation's wild bison numbered 39—all in Yellowstone National Park, where 1,600 live today. About 50,000 survive in other havens.

"HELD UP" BY N. H. TROTTER, 1897; SMITHSONIAN INSTITUTION. RIGHT: H. F. SCHMIDT

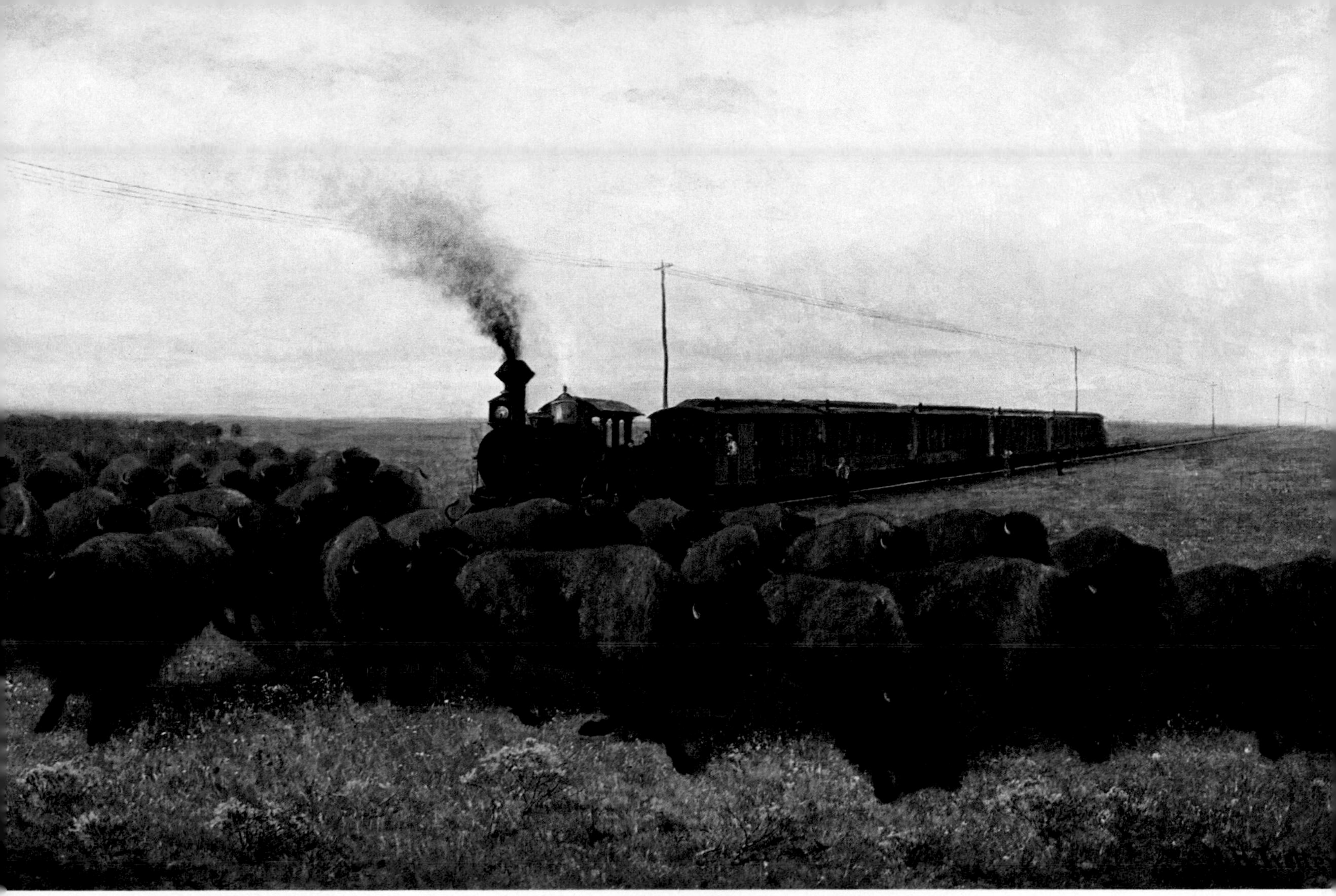

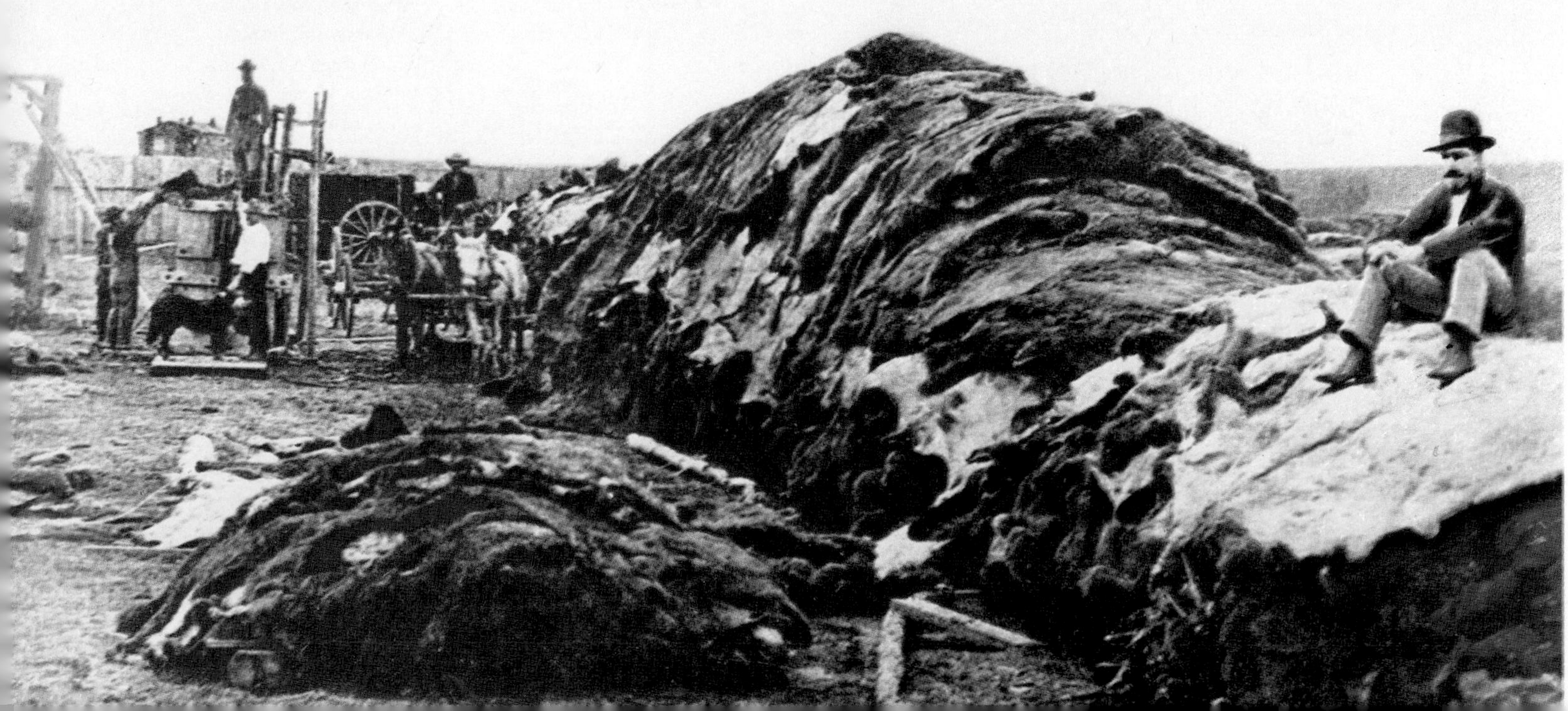

Misfortunes of war reunited Cheyenne bands in the soul-stifling enclaves of Oklahoma. Southern Cheyennes, scarred by the slaughter on the Washita, seethed as the great hunts, the laden travois, the winter encampments became a memory. When the northern Cheyennes arrived, dispirited exiles from the Montana grasslands, their southern kin scorned them as "fools." They found food scarce, malaria rife. To foil hot, dusty winds, the newcomers ringed tipis with brush. Above all, the northerners were homesick; a desperate 300, under Dull Knife and Little Wolf, headed back, skirmishing with soldiers, raiding homesteads. In Nebraska one group led by Dull Knife chanced into the hands of Fort Robinson cavalrymen. Freezing in prison, dreading a return to Oklahoma, the Indians broke out and were cut down—though their chief slipped free. Little Wolf's band made it to Montana and signed on as Army scouts. A nation aroused by their suffering set aside a reservation on the Tongue River. There Dull Knife and Little Wolf lived out their days. There, too, the buffalo soon vanished. But the Cheyennes were home. And still are.

NATIONAL ARCHIVES

Gold "from the grass roots down"—tidings of Custer's 1874 reconnaissance of the Black Hills pealed over the western Dakota plain.

ROBERT W. MADDEN, NATIONAL GEOGRAPHIC PHOTOGRAPHER

Denied lease or title, hordes of gold-hungry whites took by trespass land sacred to the Indians and theirs by both heritage and treaty.

later recall, "It was of no unfrequent occurrence for an Indian to be shot down in cold blood, or a squaw to be raped by some brute. Such a thing as a white man being punished for outraging an Indian was unheard of."

Like the Indians of the east, the Indians of the Pacific northwest and California rose in resistance. To no avail. "I thought if we killed all the white men we saw," one Modoc chief explained, "no more would come. We killed all we could; but they came more and more. . . ." In time, the white man was as firmly anchored on the west coast as in the east; the pressure now would fall on tribes that roamed the plains and the southwest.

Again, treaties preceded disaster. Pact upon pact called for land cessions and boundary guarantees. Violations of the guarantees fired hatred. Greedy white men, hot-blooded young Indians out to prove their manhood — the rubbing of two cultures ruled out peace.

An incident near Fort Laramie, Wyoming, in 1854 wrote a libretto that would ring in a chorus of violence across the plains. A westering settler complained that Indians had killed his cow. A young lieutenant led a detachment of soldiers to a Sioux camp. An argument followed, then shooting. The 30 soldiers were annihilated. The Army in reprisal attacked a Sioux camp at Blue Water Creek, slaughtering 86 men, women, and children.

And so it went. The Civil War interrupted the United States' westward push and drained off energies as well as soldiers, but there was little peace in the Indian lands. In 1862 the Santee Sioux, chafing under white injustices, rose in anger and fell without warning on Minnesota settlements and farms. Two years later in Colorado whites held a massacre of their own. Militia raised to counter bands attacking wagon trains and ranches slashed through a peaceful camp of Cheyennes at Sand Creek. The commander returned to Denver a hero — with scores of Indian scalps.

Not until months later did a congressional committee ferret out the truth about the "heroic" battle: "It scarcely had its parallel in the records of Indian barbarity. Fleeing women holding up their hands and praying for mercy were shot down; infants were killed and scalped in derision; men were tortured and mutilated."

In New Mexico and Arizona meanwhile, Kit Carson was dispatched to round up tribes feared for their raiding: the Mescalero Apache and the Navajo. With orders to kill any who resisted, he tackled the Mescalero first, herding them to a desolate tract 40 miles square called Bosque Redondo, in New Mexico. Then he turned to the Navajo, burning their crops, chopping down their peach orchards, penetrating their canyons. They too took the "Long Walk" to Bosque Redondo.

With the end of the Civil War, westward migration gathered momentum. The Homestead Act permitted settlers to obtain title to a quarter-section of public land for a nominal fee. Discharged soldiers, land-hungry townsmen, and a tide of European immigrants swarmed into the prairies. New wagon roads were opened. Railroaders made plans to link the coasts, and promoters gained land grants as a means of financing construction.

Now the government turned sternly to the task of forcing the Plains Indians to quit their buffalo lands and settle on reservations. The reservations were lands the tribes retained for themselves as a subsistence base after ceding to the government a much larger acreage out of their aboriginal territories. But popular white concept viewed it as "giving" lands to the Indians for homes and cultivation. In the process the government got greater control over Indian lives.

Grim testimonial to the horror of plains wars, hunter Ralph Morrison lies near
Fort Dodge, Kansas. Roving Cheyennes killed and scalped him in 1868.
Scalping, known in the Old World since the time of Herodotus, was far from universal
among Indians. Nor was it always fatal; live captives often survived the mutilation.
Whites encouraged it. In 1764 Pennsylvania offered 134 pieces of eight "for the
scalp of every male Indian enemy above the age of ten"; for females, only 50.

To the Sioux, the tree-straggled stream was the "Greasy Grass River"; the Crow and the Seventh Cavalry they served as scouts knew it as the "Little Bighorn." On a hot June day in 1876 it saw the battle that brought death—and immortality—to George Armstrong Custer. A Civil War general in his 20's when Mathew Brady took this picture (left), he had a colonel's command when Indian wars swirled over the plains. Boldly (or rashly—his tactics stirred unending controversy) he led

THOMAS NEBBIA. LEFT: MATHEW BRADY; NATIONAL PARK SERVICE

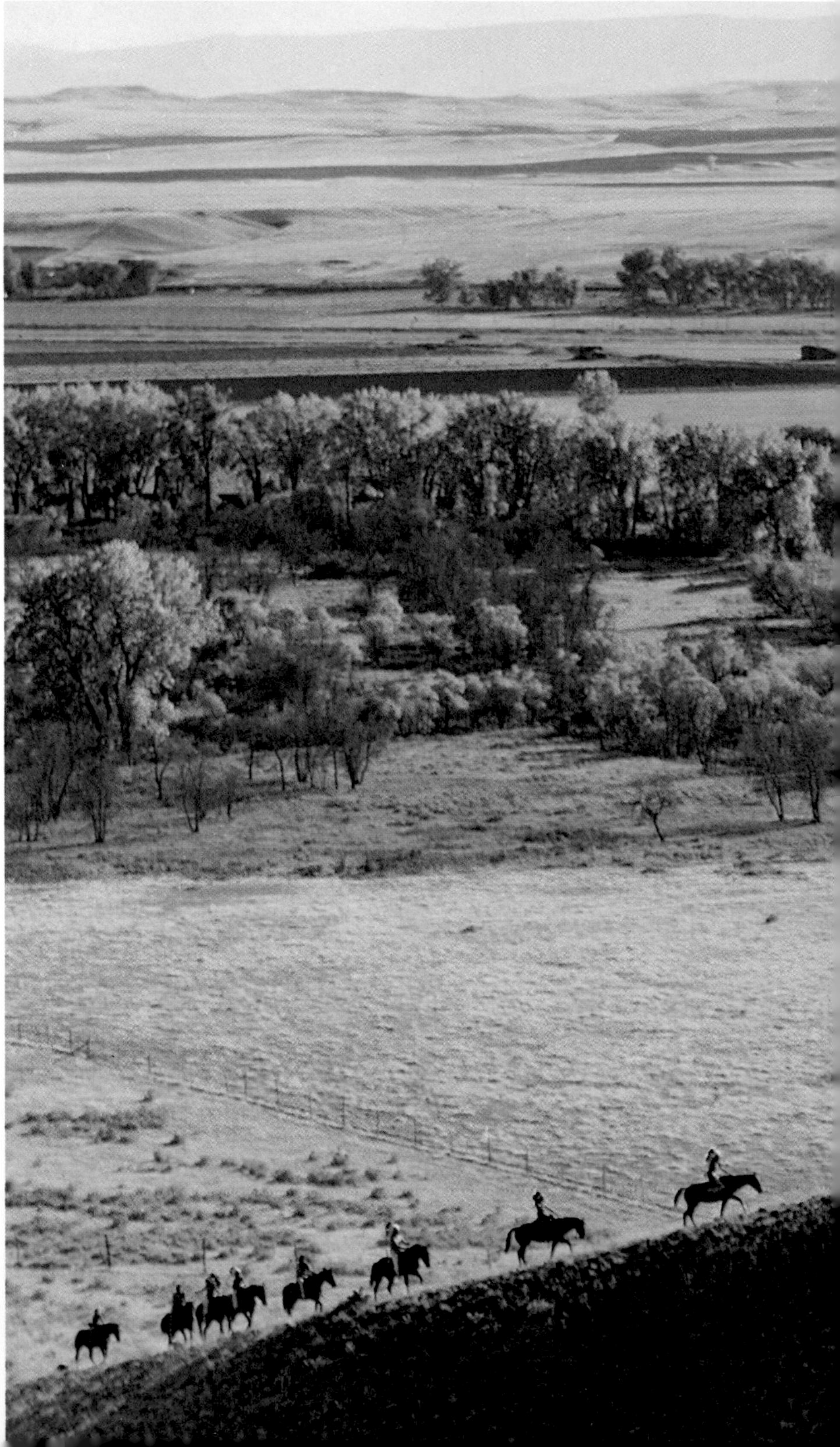

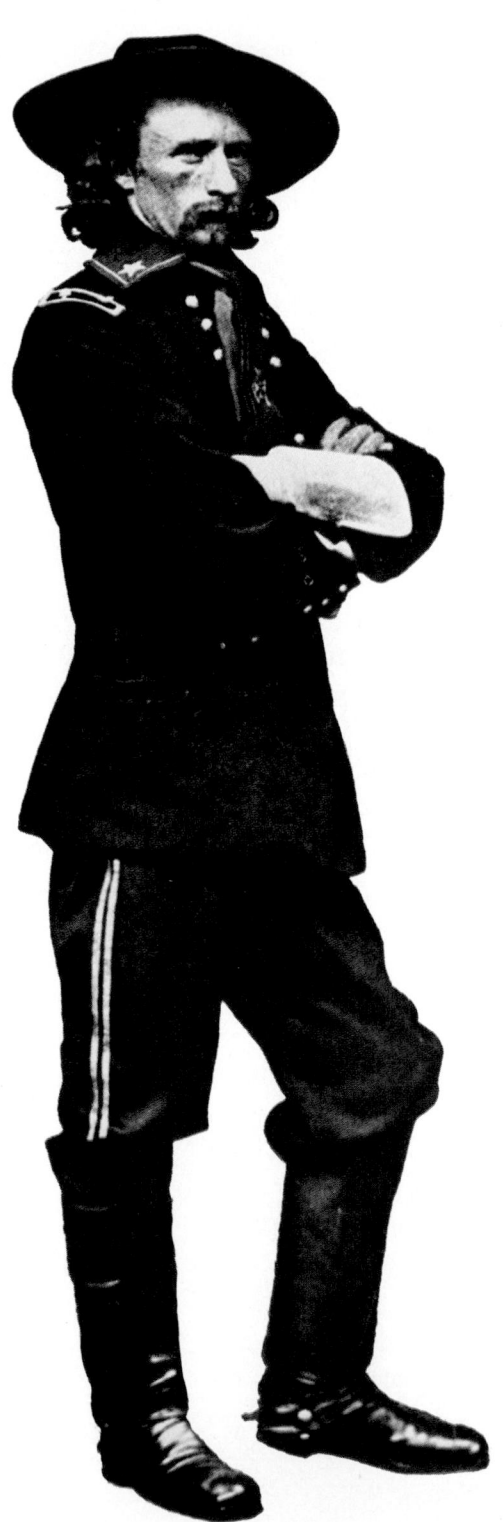

his detachment against an enemy encampment. Warriors among the 12,000 Sioux and Cheyennes gathered there swarmed over the hill and ravine where Custer made his stand. The fury of battle lasted no more than an hour; troopers died to the last man. Recalled an Indian witness: "The blood of the people was hot and their hearts bad, and they took no prisoners that day." Now the Montana site is a national monument, carved from the Crow reservation where horsemen file over Custer's hill.

Cheyennes, Comanches, and other peoples of the southern plains were pressured first; by 1875 they had been forced on reservations. In this campaign a frontier phrase became indelibly linked to Gen. Philip H. Sheridan. A Comanche told him, "I am a good Indian." Sheridan's reputed reply: "The only good Indians I ever saw were dead."

Suppression of the Indians of the northern plains proved difficult. Government agents had sought guarantees of peace along wagon trails and railroad routes in the region. Offered annuities, some tribes agreed, but not the Oglala Sioux under Red Cloud. The new Bozeman Trail crossed their best hunting lands.

Red Cloud protested by harassing forts and wagon trains. The Army soldiered on. In the most famous engagement Capt. William J. Fetterman (who boasted he could lead 80 men through the whole Sioux nation) led precisely 80 men from Fort Phil Kearny to rescue a wood-cutting crew. Against orders, he galloped after the Indians, and into an ambush. His detachment was annihilated.

In 1868 the government abandoned its forts, and Red Cloud signed a treaty of peace. The Indians were assigned a reservation comprising half of South Dakota and also a vast "unceded Indian territory" in Wyoming and Montana. Agencies were set up. Some of the Sioux settled near the agencies, but most roamed the "unceded" lands and visited the agencies only for rations.

The arrangement worked for a few years. Then in 1874 the seeds were sown for the last and greatest of the plains wars. That year Lt. Col. George A. Custer led an expedition into the Black Hills of South Dakota. He confirmed rumors of gold, and miners and opportunists rushed in.

The Black Hills, sacred to the Sioux, lay on their reservation. When asked to sell, they refused;

Best-known of Indian battles, Custer's fight has inspired more than 960 paintings. This, done by artist Paxson after years of research, is considered one of the most accurate. Custer fell with bullets in head and breast. Said Sitting Bull, whose medicine roused warriors that day, "I tell no lies.... Those men who came with 'Long Hair' were as good men as ever fought."

friction increased. To bring the tribes to heel, the government ordered all bands roaming the "unceded" lands to report immediately to reservation agencies. The order arrived in midwinter. Many of the Indians ignored it; such a move was impossible, even had they chosen to obey.

The government now had an excuse for war.

In May 1876 Brig. Gen. George Crook led an army from the North Platte River to round up the bands. Indian and soldier met at Rosebud Creek, each force numbering about 1,300. The Indians attacked, Chief Crazy Horse urging on his men with the cry, "Come on, Dakotas, it's a good day to die." Soldier and Indian fought from midmorning to midafternoon; then the Sioux began to drift away. "They were tired and hungry, so they went home," one warrior later explained. Crook claimed a victory but had to withdraw to await reinforcements and another campaign.

The Indians retired to an immense camp, perhaps the largest the plains had ever known, on the Little Bighorn River. Great leaders were there—Sitting Bull, Gall, Crazy Horse. A vast pony herd grazed nearby; the grass was green; there was dancing at night.

General Crook's force was only one of three sent after the Sioux and their Cheyenne allies. Two other columns approached from the north. Col. John Gibbon led one, Custer the other. Brash, confident that any number of Indians would flee before the Seventh Cavalry, Custer decided not to await Gibbon's column. Incredibly he divided his 615-man force into three attack units. With one he struck toward the heart of the great camp.

Gall, Crazy Horse, and Two Moon fell on these 215 men "like a hurricane . . . like bees swarming out of a hive," eyewitnesses recalled. "The smoke of the shooting and the (continued on page 347)

342

By Word and Deed in Freedom's Cause

Antagonists in war lie together in peace at a green valhalla in Fort Sill, Oklahoma. A rise called "Chief's Knoll," highest point in the national military cemetery, holds the graves of nearly a score of Indian leaders. Around them rest men who fought as bluecoats on the southern plains.

Fort Sill sprouted in 1869 as an Army base and Indian agency center overseeing a new reservation. That reserve had been formed two years before in treaties signed at a great council of southern tribes on Medicine Lodge Creek in Kansas. A thousand tipis—Comanche, Kiowa, Arapaho, Cheyenne, Kiowa-Apache—rose there. Such noted chiefs as Black Kettle, Ten Bears, Little Raven, Satanta, and Stumbling Bear attended and ratified the treaty terms. The Indians expected peace in which to hunt buffalo, but it never came. Settlers pressed in, white hunters slaughtered herds, angry warriors raided and scalped. Then Army columns hounded the "hostiles." By 1878—Indian leaders dead, buffalo vanished—quiet reigned on the southern plains. And words of the Comanche Ten Bears rang hauntingly: "I was born upon the prairie, where the wind blew free and there was nothing to break the light of the sun. . . . I lived like my fathers before me, and, like them, I lived happily. . . . But it is too late. The white man has the country which we loved. . . ."

Eloquence came naturally to Indians. Theirs was an oral culture: Children grew up to oratory and tribal legends told around campfires; young men developed word skills in coup-counting speeches; adults polished phraseology in council talks, religious ceremonies, negotiations with other tribes. And so a chief could stir his people, or impress whites, with rhetoric. But emphasis on talk had drawbacks: On occasion traditions of tribal autonomy and the right to speak delayed decisions at moments critical for action.

The white man's challenge produced a long roll of great Indian leaders who sought to stem the tide or to work out adaptations. Their records are history. And though a plaque at the entrance to the Fort Sill cemetery notes the "valor . . . in freedom's cause" of soldiers lying there, Indians too fought for freedom.

*"I think I am a good
    man, but . . . all over
the world they say
      I am a bad man"*

Short and stocky, his eyes "like two
bits of obsidian with lights behind
them," Geronimo led a band of Apaches
in a life that alternated between
sojourns on arid reservations and
fugitive spells in mountain hideouts
—from which lightning raids spread
panic along the southwestern border.
His Apache name, Goyaathle, means
"One Who Is Yawning." Mexicans called
him by the Spanish word for "Jerome."

Mexican troops who killed his wife
and children earned his undying hatred.
He turned against Americans after,
reported a government study, "acts
of inhuman treachery and cruelty
made [the Apaches] our implacable
foes." Said Geronimo, "I never do
wrong without a cause. . . ."

Yielding at last, he was carted off
to an eastern prison—an Army band
playing "Auld Lang Syne." He spent
his last years at Fort Sill, with
such interludes as riding in Theodore
Roosevelt's inaugural parade and
appearing at the 1904 World's Fair.

"You have taken our land and made us outcasts"

Tatanka Iyotake—Sitting Bull—counted his first coup at 14, won leadership as a warrior and medicine man of the Hunkpapa Sioux, foresaw success at the Little Bighorn. That vision came at a Sun Dance where he sacrificed 100 pieces of his flesh. To escape the roundup that followed Custer's defeat, he led some 2,000 Sioux to Canada. Hunger drove them to surrender in 1881.

But Sitting Bull nursed rock-hard hostility. Once, honored speaker at a last-spike ceremony, he said, "I hate all the white people. You are thieves and liars." His interpreter, dismayed, mumbled platitudes. The chief got a standing ovation. He died in 1890— shot while being arrested during the ferment of the Ghost Dance movement.

"Are . . . sacred graves to be plowed for corn? Dakotas, I am for war!"

A meteor flamed in the skies the year he was born, and so he got the name Maȟpiya Luta—Red Cloud. He was 43 when the Civil War ended, a chief who never gave up trying to preserve old ways for his Oglala Sioux.

Shrewd, called by a U. S. general "as full of action as a tiger," he put such pressure on the road to Montana goldfields that emigrants and freighters quit using it; forts along it couldn't get wood or hay without sending out a strong guard. At last the Army withdrew; Sioux gleefully burned the forts. "Red Cloud's War" is counted the only one against the U. S. that Indians won. After it the chief kept his word to live in peace, once going to Washington for the medal from President Grant he wears here.

346

*"My heart is sick
    and sad. From where
the sun now stands
    I will fight no more"*

His tribe could boast that since
Lewis and Clark first encountered
their friendliness in Oregon country
no Nez Perce had ever killed a white
man. Even when treaties were broken
and settlers crowding into their lands
sparked ugly incidents, they had
avoided retaliation. Now, in 1877,
his band summarily given 30 days
to move to a strange reservation in
Idaho, young hot-bloods lashed back
with murderous raids. The old boast
ended, but a 15-week fighting trek
began that blazoned forever the name
of one leader, Chief Joseph. To the
Nez Perce he was Hinmatówyalahtqit—
"Thunder Coming Up Over the Land."
Shepherding women and children,
the little band fought more than a dozen
engagements and dodged four Army
columns in a 1,700-mile attempt to
reach Canada. The tribe's poignant
story prompted an observer to write
that Chief Joseph "in his long career
...cannot accuse the Government...
of one single act of justice."

EDWARD S. CURTIS

dust of the horses shut out the hill. . . . and when we came to the hill there were no soldiers living . . . Long Hair lay dead among the rest.''

The defeat stunned a white United States celebrating its centennial and holding a world's fair at Philadelphia. To the Indians, scattered and spending the days in hunting, dancing, and feasting, it seemed the best of summers.

But with winter a reinforced U. S. Army converged on the tribes, fought skirmishes, destroyed camps, forced the Indians into impossible positions. Yet even when tribes surrendered and submitted to reservations, the Indians found tragedy and death their companions. In 1878, after a year of ''sickness, misery and bitterness'' in Oklahoma, a band of northern Cheyennes broke away. They sought to return to their old lands, ''where their children could live.'' Overtaken by soldiers, a chief said: ''We do not want to fight you, but we will not go back.'' The troops opened fire.

But the band escaped, reached Nebraska, then split. One group of 149 met a party of soldiers and agreed to a parley at Fort Robinson. There they faced an ultimatum: Go south or go hungry. Court records tell what happened next: ''In the midst of the dreadful winter, with the thermometer 40° below zero, the Indians, including the women and children, were kept for five days and nights without food or fuel, and for three days without water. At the end of that time they broke out of the barracks.'' Troops hunted them down.

Other groups had their torments. Modocs led by Captain Jack, refusing reservation life, holed up in lava beds near Tule Lake, California, in 1872 and fought off the Army for months. In 1877 the Nez Perce, hoping to end a war precipitated by their own young men, began an epic flight to Canada. They were caught 40 miles from the border.

Not until 1886 did the last of the holdouts—

Geronimo and his Apaches—give up. The great guerrilla fighter had fled the reservation amid rumors that he was to be hanged. With only a small group of warriors, encumbered by their families, he led the U. S. Army on an exhausting chase into the mountains of Mexico. At one time some 5,000 soldiers marched manfully after no more than 18 men, 13 women, and 6 children. Persuaded to parley, Geronimo accepted an offer of transfer to a new reservation, a land of woods and water. Instead his band of 498 went to prison. Within three years a fourth of them had died. General Crook, sent to investigate, attributed the mortality to ''homesickness, change of climate, and the dreary monotony of empty lives.''

During these years of war and suppression the government made its final repudiation of the nation-to-nation relationship under which tribes had sought to hold the white man's society at arm's length. In 1871 Congress abolished treaty-making powers of the tribes and indicated that the government's public servants could make better decisions for the Indians than Indians could make for themselves. The ultimate device for fostering dependency had been discovered.

Constricted in their lands, pressed by military forces, many Indians turned to spiritual movements. In the 1870's and '80's the cult of the prophet Smohalla spread throughout the northwest. A member of a tribe related by language to the Nez Perce, he experienced a vision, then urged a return to Indian ways, preaching that the white man's exploitation ruined mother earth. ''You ask me to plough the ground! Shall I take a knife and tear my mother's bosom? . . . You ask me to dig for stone! Shall I dig under her skin for her bones? . . . You ask me to cut grass and make hay and sell it. . . . But how dare I cut off my mother's hair?''

No 305.
SIOUX INDIANS.
GETTING THEIR BEEF RATIONS
PHOTO & COPYRIGHT, BY—
J. A. ANDERSON. 1893.

A more enduring expression of Indian genius was the emergence of the Native American Church, a religion based on the sacramental use of the "button," or tip, of the peyote cactus, which induces visions and meditative states. This movement, essentially religious but possessing political strength as well, reflects the ability of a people to create for itself a habitable universe in a hostile environment. Where tribes faced intolerable choices for survival, peyote entered as a new way, bridging the traditionalism of the Indian past with elements of Christian compassion.

Efforts such as these, arising out of ancient disciplines concerned with folk survival, were scarcely understood for what they were. The Sun Dance of the plains tribes was banned as a "savage" spectacle, and missionaries and government agents relentlessly attacked the peyote religion.

But it was the Ghost Dance ritual of the prophet Wovoka, a young Paiute, that triggered the final bloody crushing of Indian resistance. Wovoka's message, borne from his home in the Nevada desert by disciples, began to sweep across the plains in 1889. Soon village after village of Sioux began to perform his "Ghost Dance" with its promise of a return to old ways in a world from which whites would have been erased by a flood.

The dancing appalled and frightened whites. One commented, "A more pernicious system of religion could not have been offered to a people ... on the threshold of civilization." Another wired Washington, "Indians are dancing in the snow and are wild and crazy. . . . We need protection. . . ."

Army troops fanned out to round up the Ghost dancers and to settle them near their agencies. Among the last to be caught was a group of about 350 Sioux under Big Foot. They were led to a military camp at Wounded Knee Creek. An incident triggered gunfire, and cavalry carbines and rapid-fire cannons rent the camp. When firing ended, more than 150 Indians—men, women, children—lay dead. Others fled or crawled off wounded.

The handful of survivors were taken to shelter in the nearby Pine Ridge Episcopal Mission, still hung with greenery from a Christmas service a few days earlier. The words of Chief Red Cloud serve as an epitaph: "We had begged for life, and the white men thought we wanted theirs."

In what is now the United States, an Indian population that may have numbered 1,850,000

Butchered beef on wagon beds and missionaries in Sunday black accented
reservation life for Plains Indians in the 1890's. Extermination of the buffalo
brought Indian dependency on government rations — and kept tribes at home.
At first cattle were turned loose to be shot by riders in a piteous version of old hunts.
Then came the ignominy of agency queues. Church work on reservations echoed
a 1609 admonition to offer "savage people . . . the meanes to save their soules. . . ."

The End of the Dance

"Dance," the prophet said; "everywhere, keep on dancing." This would hasten the day when the world would be renewed, the white man destroyed, the game brought back, and the Indian restored to happiness with all his kin. Because it promised a return of the dead, whites called it the "Ghost Dance." Wovoka, a Paiute, framed the belief after a revelation that came when he was ill with a fever during an eclipse of the sun. Whites took the rite for a war dance, not noting that women participated (right). And they overlooked Wovoka's tenet for the new life: "You must not . . . do harm to anyone. You must not fight. Do right always."

Ghost Dance rituals among the Sioux triggered such white alarm that troops were sent. One confrontation brought the massacre at Wounded Knee in 1890. A camp led by Big Foot was being searched for arms. An Indian, Black Coyote, resisted. Another Sioux would later recall that Black Coyote fired his gun; soldiers ringing the camp "returned fire and indiscriminate killing followed." Even fleeing women and children were cut down. Bodies frozen in the South Dakota cold were stacked like cordwood in a common grave.

ARAPAHO GHOST DANCE, JAMES MOONEY, 1893; SMITHSONIAN INSTITUTION.
LEFT: MONTANA HISTORICAL SOCIETY

Snows of Wounded Knee his shroud, Big Foot finds the frozen peace of death. The Sioux chief, ill with pneumonia, was camped under a flag of truce when a tragic incident loosed the slaughter which cost his life. But it ended too the long list of wars the Indian fought to keep his ancient ways.
SMITHSONIAN INSTITUTION

when Columbus arrived had dwindled to less than a quarter of a million at the time of Wounded Knee. But the tales of lives lost, battles fought, and atrocities committed by white man and red in the intervening centuries obscure and demean the human dimension. Such tales, enshrined in history books, perpetuate stereotypes which stand in the way of understanding.

The Indian wars make for sensational reading, but more important is the story of the Indian will to survive and to preserve his own sense of a moral order. The Indian fought when he had to, and fought well even when outgunned. But the harmony he prized as the proper relationship between man and his universe was not achieved in battle. Men cleansed themselves after combat; the peace chief, not the war chief, invariably ranked first in tribal councils. This view of the moral order and the good life still persists. The ravages of disease, the decimating wars, the reservation confinement have not destroyed it.

The thread of continuity which bound the Indian experience together, through time and across geographical space, was the vision of a native America free of domination by the outsider—the white man. Tribal prophets had dreamed of this, and as often as their dream was demolished by gunfire and by burned-out villages, other prophets dreamed it again. Ten thousand years of growing up with the land had made the dream; five hundred years of denial would not extinguish it.

It lived as a dimly felt reality in every Indian community; it flared to intensity when oppression was most brutal. It remains a force in Indian society today. Only such a dream can explain why it is that tribal Indians are still adapting to strange soils and harsh social climates, still striving to make the continent fit for human habitation.

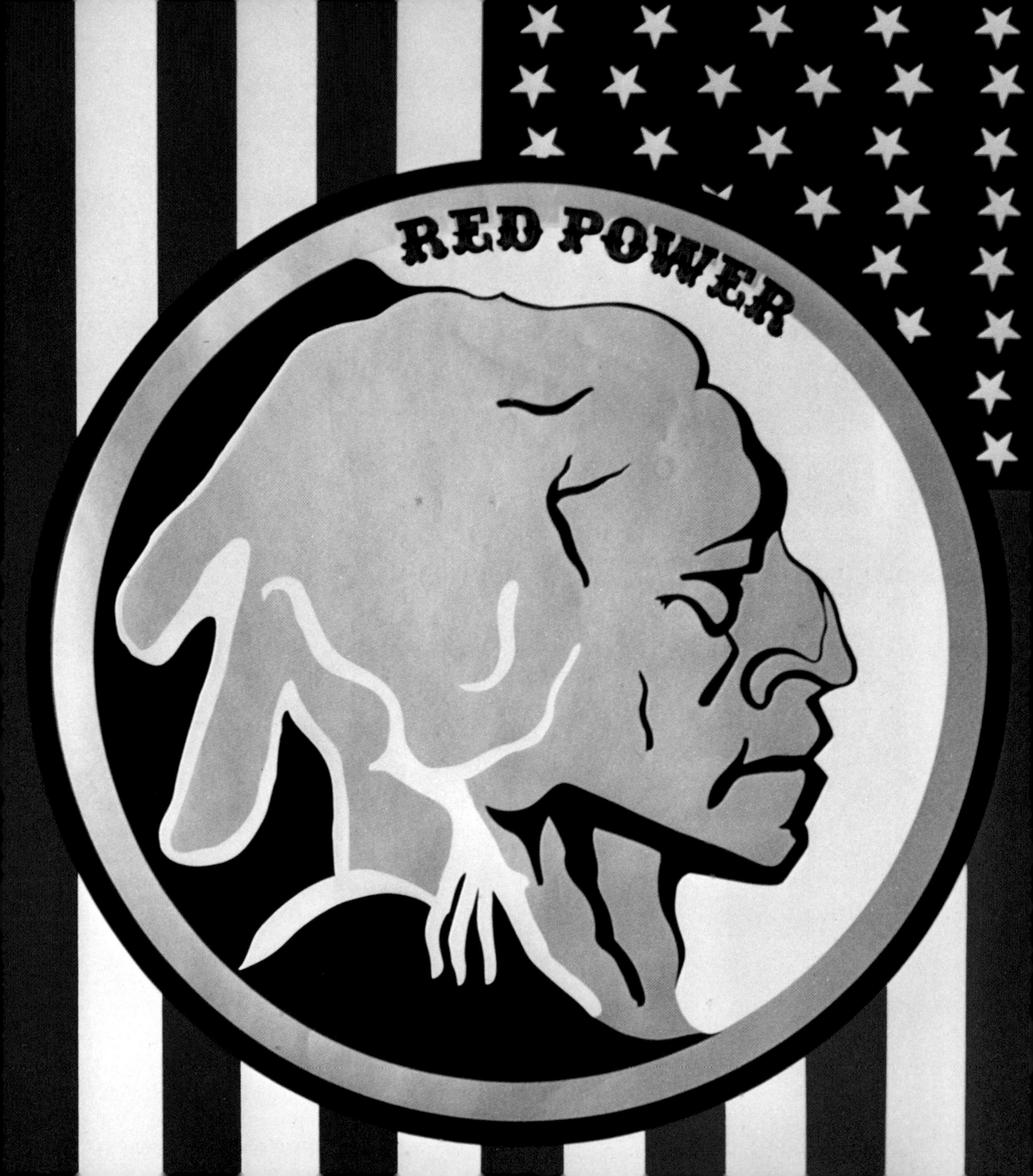

From Wounded Knee to Wounded Knee

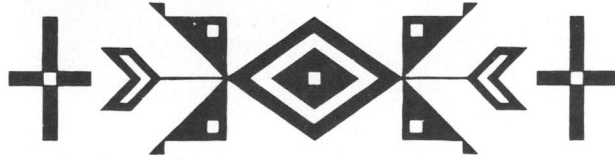

Vine Deloria, Jr.

The Indian and the buffalo—two sides of the same coin—
faced a similar oblivion. Now the Indian banners forth his
determination to shape his own future in the land of the red,
white, and blue. Slogans fuel the struggle—some blunt
and defiant, others arrow-sharp like the title of the author's
1969 best-seller, *Custer Died for Your Sins*.

JIM DOMKE

On a fall day in 1969 the desolate turtleback rock of Alcatraz came alive. Chill sea winds swept the sounds of laughter and song, drumbeat and defiance out across golden San Francisco Bay. To the cracked walls and rusting barbed wire of the abandoned federal prison, symbol of despair and isolation, came people driven by despair and isolation: Winnebago, Sioux, Blackfoot, Apache, Navajo, Cheyenne, Iroquois; city people, reservation people, horse people, sheepherders, fishermen, hunters of the Arctic.

Indians of all tribes, they called themselves. The island is a part of sacred mother earth, they said, wrongfully taken from their forefathers, and now surplus to the white man's needs. Here they would build a spiritual center, an ecological center, a training center. With smiling words they offered "the Great White Father" $24 in glass beads and red cloth, the sum that Peter Minuit paid the Manhattan Indians for *their* island in 1626. And with utmost gravity the Alcatraz occupants resolved, "We must forever survive as Indians."

For 19 months government agents parleyed, warned, threatened. Then they moved in and cleared the island. Other sites would be claimed —ancestral Pit River Indian lands in California; Fort Lawton, Washington; a lighthouse near Sault Sainte Marie, Michigan; Mount Rushmore in the Black Hills. Soon blood would flow at Wounded Knee again. And white Americans would no longer shake their heads and say, "We didn't even know there were any Indians left."

There weren't supposed to be any left. A century ago a West Pointer wrote for his class in ethics: "We behold [the red man] now on the verge of extinction . . . and soon he will be talked of as a noble race who once existed but have passed away." The cadet was George Armstrong Custer. Scarcely 50 years later anthropologist Franz Boas

Conquered Indians looked for a silver lining in vain. The aboriginal Americans remain the poorest of minorities; 1970 census-takers found two out of five Indian families living in poverty. This house at Pine Ridge has no plumbing; water must be hauled to it; white cattlemen lease the fields. Progress is slow and fitful. New houses, paved roads appear. Into a blighted life a health worker (opposite) can bring a ray of sunshine—all the brighter when he, too, is one of the people.

concluded that the Indian had "vanished comparatively rapidly." And why not? "This great continent could not have been kept as nothing but a game preserve for squalid savages," wrote Teddy Roosevelt as the guns fell silent on the plains.

When fighting stopped in the last quarter of the 19th century, surviving Indians, surrounded on remnants of former domains, had become strangers in their own land. Most histories have been content to leave them there. But on their reservations the tribes still held title to a total of some 139,000,000 acres—a realm that stoked the land lust of homesteaders, miners, railroad boomers.

Further, too many tribes clung to old ways that were incompatible with the way of life Indians would have to adopt in order to survive. In the light of today's understanding, the old cultures do not seem quite so primitive or barbaric. But to white men of a century ago the inheritors of those cultures appeared shiftless and forlorn. In the Yankton Sioux villages, the agent reported, the people refused to give up such "injurious habits" as "frequent feasts . . . heathenish ceremonies and dances, constant visiting. . . ." Reformers, finding a trace of humanity in these creatures, wanted to "civilize" them. One way or another, the centuries-old patterns of Indian life were doomed.

The magic of private property, which had been so beneficial to white society, was seen as the light to guide the Indians' way to a civilized state. Humanitarians deplored the government practice of moving tribes whenever land they occupied proved to have some value. Better to give each Indian a piece of land he could call his own and no longer push the tribe from one valley to another.

Even before the wars had ended, the agitation had begun to put Indians to work on individually owned farmsteads. In vain did Chief Ouray of the Utes protest, "We work as hard as you do. Did you ever try skinning a buffalo?"

Red Cloud, the unconquered Oglala Sioux chief, had accepted the white man's peace but not his ways. "You must begin anew and put away the wisdom of your fathers," he bitterly counseled his people. "You must lay up food and forget the hungry. When your house is built, your storeroom filled, then look around for a neighbor whom you can take advantage of and seize all he has."

At an 1885 conference addressed to Indian problems, Senator Henry Dawes of Massachusetts, a leading reformer, told of a visit to one of the Five Civilized Tribes in what later became eastern Oklahoma. He had found no paupers, the tribe did not owe a dime to anyone, it had its own schools

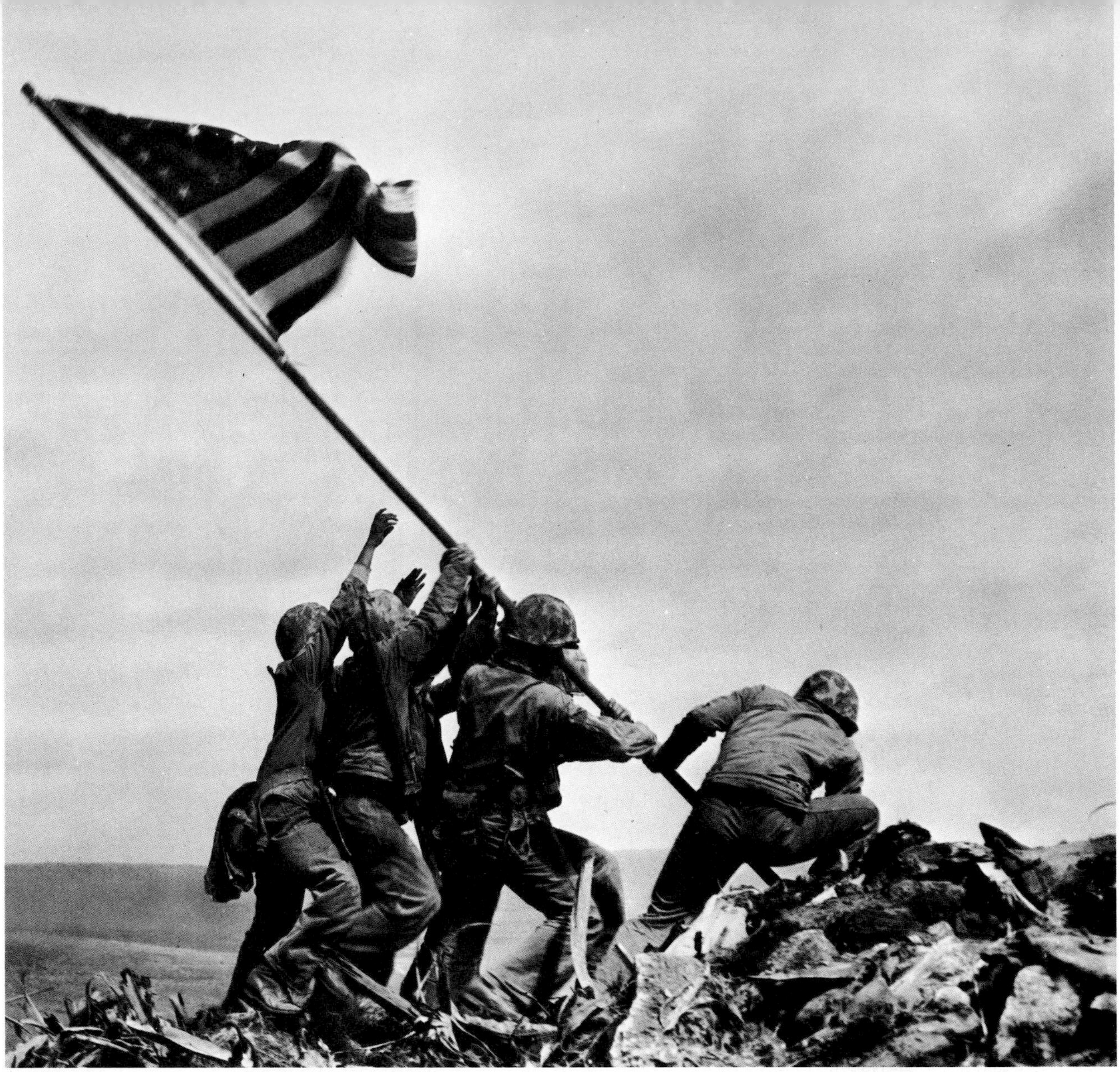

RED MOON SERVICE CLUB
SEMPER FIDELIS
Pfc. Dixon Lone Elk

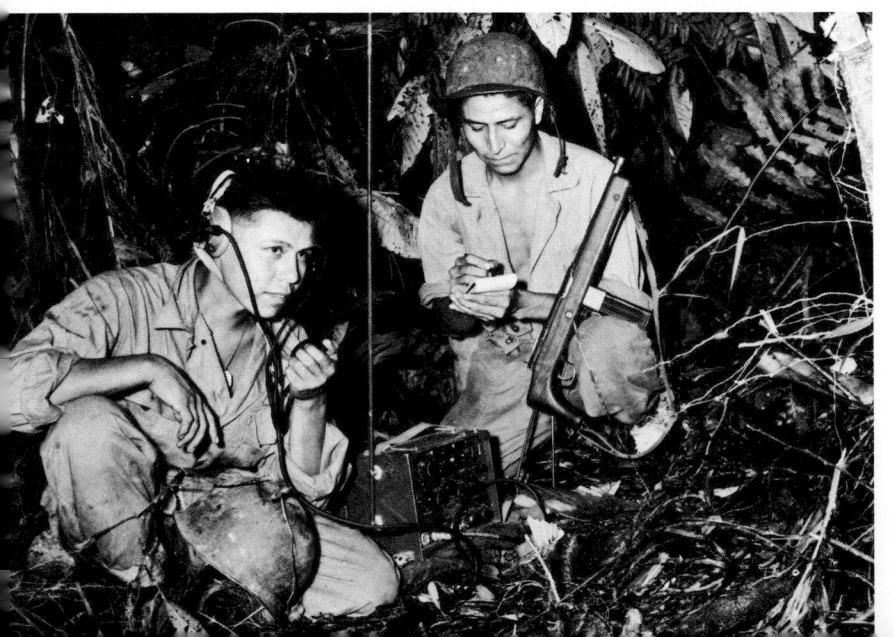

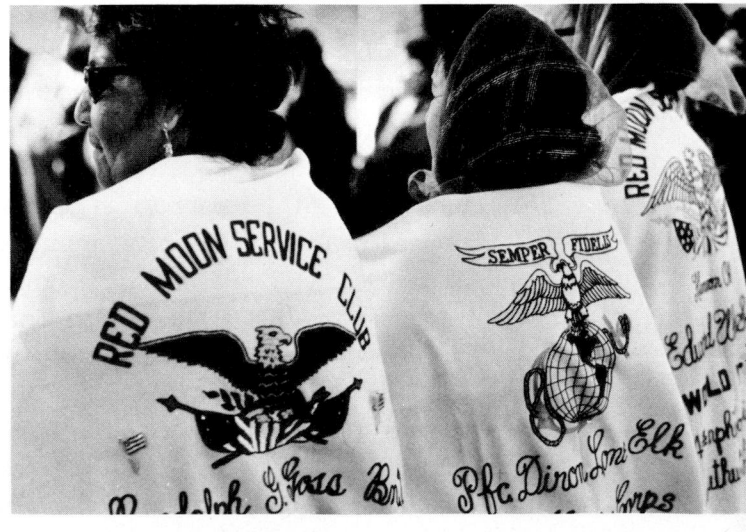

and hospitals. "Yet," he concluded, "the defect of the system was apparent. They have got as far as they can go, because they own their land in common. . . . There is no selfishness, which is at the bottom of civilization."

Two years later the senator's enthusiastic leadership triumphed with the passage of the General Allotment Act—one of the most significant laws in American Indian history. Under the Dawes Act, as it was also known, tribes would have their communal lands divided—a quarter section (160 acres) to the head of a household, smaller tracts to individuals. What remained of a tribe's lands after allotment would be bought from the Indians by the United States and opened to white settlement.

While the law *allowed* the government to negotiate with tribes for the breakup of their reservations, administrators interpreted the statute as *requiring* such allotments. Often disregarding the suitability of the land—whether desert, rocky highland, woodland, or semiarid plain—government negotiators pressed on.

The impact on Indian holdings was devastating. Members of the Iowa tribe of Oklahoma retained a total of 8,568 acres after allotment, while 207,174 acres were declared "surplus"; the Cheyenne and Arapaho of Oklahoma lost five-sixths of their four-million-acre reservation. Other tribes suffered in like proportion. Even on the allotted lands troubles proliferated. Minors away at boarding schools couldn't farm their tracts; old Indians simply refused to farm, preferring the traditional hunting life even with game virtually gone. When someone asked Chief Washakie about farming on the Wind River Reservation in Wyoming, the old Shoshone snapped, "God damn a potato!"

No matter. The lawmakers had a remedy. Indians could lease their allotted acres. So the value of learning to farm successfully, of hard work and

self-reliance, disappeared as Indians became idle, and often absentee, landlords.

In time, inheritance grew into a nightmare. On my own Standing Rock Sioux Reservation in the Dakotas, one 320-acre tract was owned, in 1959, by 183 heirs. Helen White Bird held one of the smallest shares, 3,124/115,755,091,200ths of the tract—or about .4 of a square foot!

Friends of the red man well knew, as Senator Dawes remarked, that you could not take an Indian "by the nape of the neck" and turn him into a farmer overnight. The reformers hoped that contact with white farmers would hasten the process. Above all, they insisted, schools would rescue the young from a disintegrating culture, even if the old were too far gone.

Education had long been a bone of contention between red and white. Ben Franklin recorded how Indian leaders firmly rejected one offer of schooling in the 1700's: "We have had some experience of it: Several of our young people . . . were instructed in all your sciences; but when they came back to us, they were bad runners; ignorant of every means of living in the woods; unable to bear either cold or hunger; knew neither how to build a cabin, take a deer, or kill an enemy; spoke our language imperfectly . . . they were totally good for nothing."

Yet the Europeans continued to press their educational theories on the tribes, and eventually developed a widespread system of boarding schools run by government agencies or, more often, by missionary groups eager to raise young Indians as members of their denominations.

The farther from home the school the better. A hostile chief was unlikely to go on the warpath with his children a thousand miles away. And the children would more easily shed the influence of their native surroundings. "Indians," an educator observed, "have no home life anyway."

One Indian who had attended boarding schools in the 1860's vividly recalled the experience in later life: "When we entered the mission school . . . we encountered a rule that prohibited the use of our language, which rule was rigidly enforced with a hickory rod, so that the newcomer . . . was obliged to go about like a little dummy until he learned to express himself in English.

"All the boys in our school were given English names, because their Indian names were difficult for the teachers to pronounce. Besides, the aboriginal names were considered by the missionaries as heathenish. . . . And so, in the place of Tae-noo-ga-wa-zhe came Philip Sheridan, in that of Wa-pah-dae, Ulysses S. Grant."

The rigidities lingered even into our own time. Many a child never made it home for vacation, spending the summer doing chores at the school or working for white families nearby. On skimpy budgets that at one point stood at 11 cents per student per day, the diet often consisted mainly of starches with little fresh fruit or vegetables; tuberculosis flourished.

"Indians are good with their hands" was the guiding philosophy. So the curriculum was aimed primarily at training in skills, with boys learning trades such as carpentry and the girls a version of home economics completely foreign to their homes in Indian country. Some schools made a great ceremony of teaching Indian girls how to serve afternoon tea. There was no lack of instruction about the backwardness of "blanket Indians."

Filling such schools might require extraordinary methods, often little short of kidnapping. Cavalry Lt. Richard H. Pratt, who believed that the Indians' best hope lay in total assimilation into white society, in 1879 started the Carlisle Indian School in Pennsylvania—with contributions from a "Civilization Fund" obtained from the sale of Indian lands out west. On one occasion Pratt went recruiting for students among Apache prisoners in a Florida camp. When no one responded to the overtures, Pratt lifted the arms of 62 "volunteers" and shipped them off to Pennsylvania.

In time Carlisle gained national prominence, particularly through the football exploits of the incomparable Jim Thorpe. The Chilocco School in Oklahoma and Haskell Institute in Kansas eventually came to rival Carlisle as the prestige schools in the federal system.

Unquestionably the boarding schools played their part in the assault on Indian communal strength, identity, and self-respect. Yet in one way they produced a surprising counter effect. Some graduates came away with a deeper awareness of the Indian plight, and they were among the first to see hope for their people in a national unification of the tribes. The sense of having survived a government school lingered among many, and had a unifying force not to be underestimated.

Around the turn of this century the ax of allotment finally fell on the Five Civilized Tribes: the Cherokee, Choctaw, Chickasaw, Creek, and Seminole. Since the time of their forced migration to Indian Territory in the early 19th century, they had established well-organized republics, with a substantial number of wealthy people. Some of the tribes had better educated citizenries than did the adjacent states.

When the clamor arose to abolish the tribal governments and allot the lands, traditionalists in the tribes resisted. For Cherokee religious leaders the long dark age foretold by ancient prophets of the tribe was at hand. A minor rebellion broke out among the Creeks; many fled into the hills rather

UNITED PRESS INTERNATIONAL. BELOW: © STERN MAGAZINE

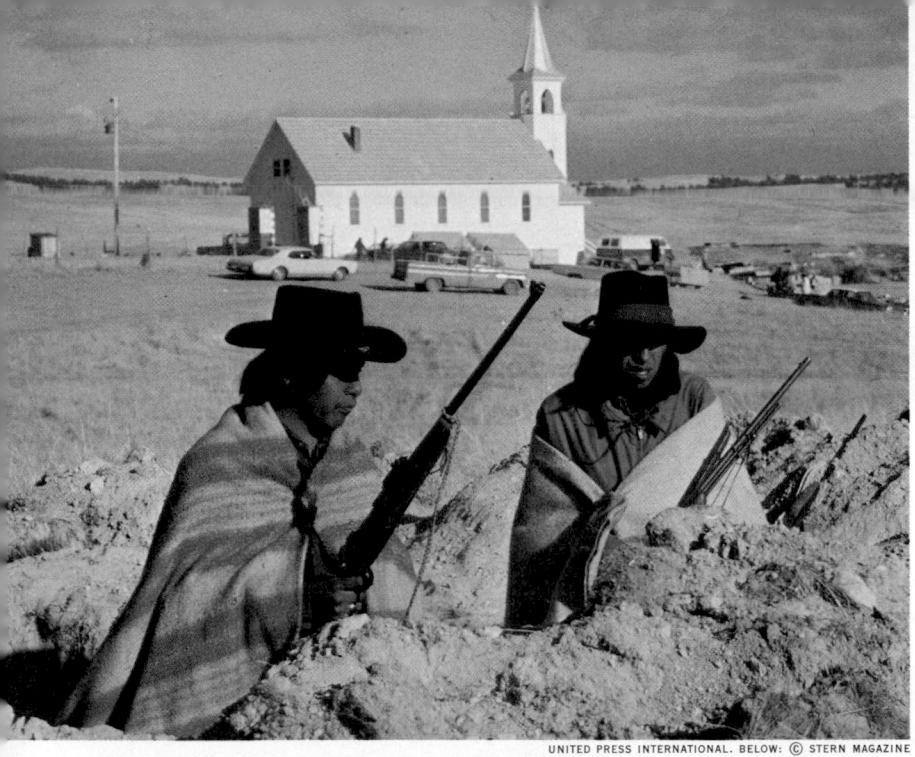

Out of sight, out of mind, skeletons rattling in America's closet for a century, Indians flared into the public eye as the mood of the 1960's roused the discontented of the earth to confrontation everywhere. Tipis sprouted from the rock of Alcatraz in San Francisco Bay when Indians laid claim to a speck of the continent they'd lost. On this abandoned prison island, the invaders noted with acid wit, they enjoyed all the comforts of home on the reservation.

The scene was grimmer, the people angrier, when militants captured the Sioux hamlet of Wounded Knee. Guns barked; threats thundered across the land. The government, shying from battle, negotiated a peace through tension-filled months. In the century since the great massacre here, the federals had learned the uses of patience. For many Indians, patience had run out.

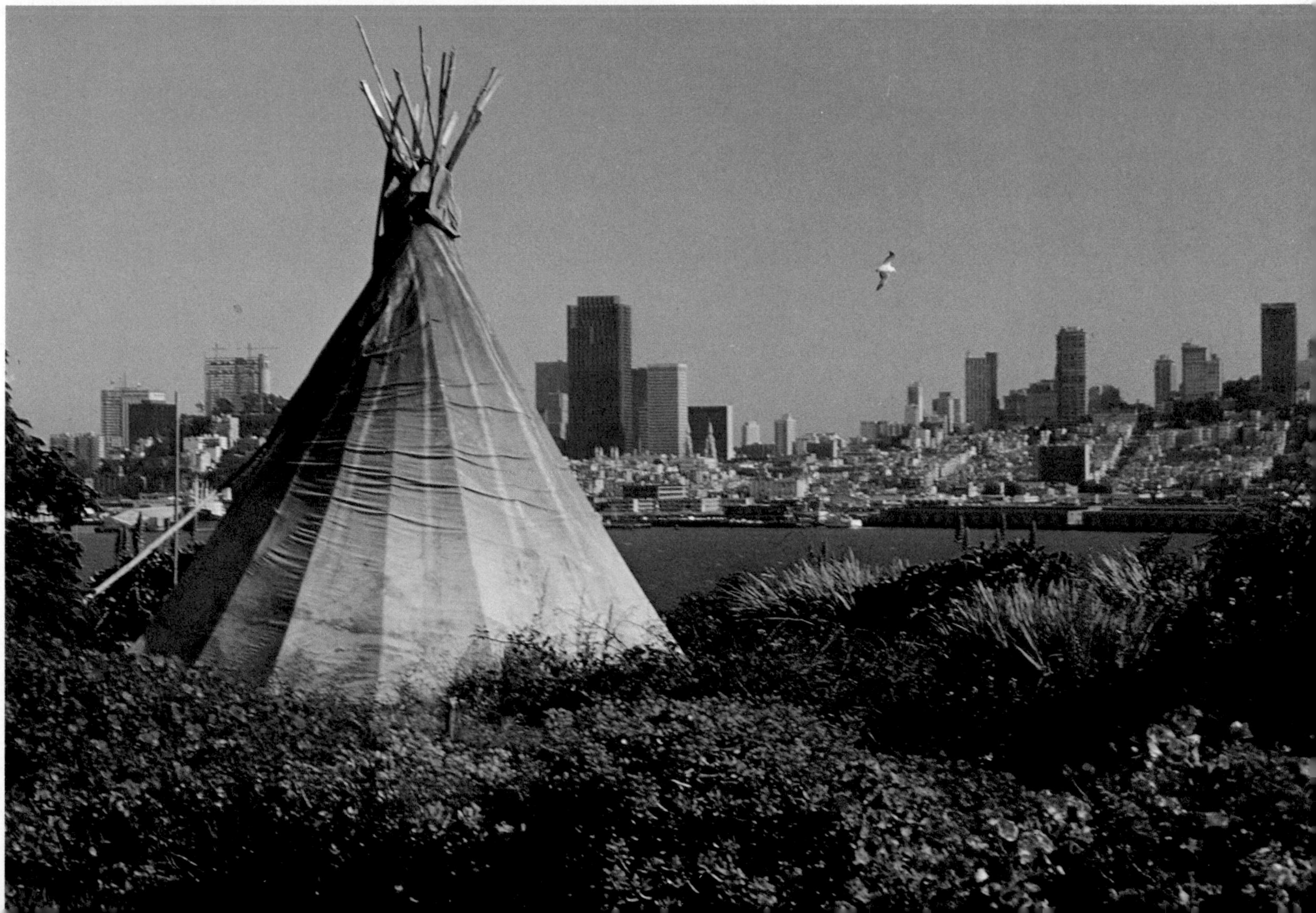

Heroes of the past, demons of the present highlight a
high school program in the San Francisco area. Like urban
Indians in dozens of cities, young activists here pursue
their cultural and political reawakening through a variety
of media. An Ouray disc jockey broadcasts a weekly Indian
show over the student-run radio station at the University

JIM DOMKE

of California; newspapers chronicle the latest happenings in Indian causes. Beyond these hums the invisible network of the moccasin telegraph. "It's hard to explain," says Vine Deloria. "One morning I attended a closed hearing in Washington, D. C. When I called a friend in Colorado during lunch, he told *me* what went on at the meeting. The word just gets around."

than touch a pen and accept an allotment. For nearly a decade Bureau of Indian Affairs officials chased the Creek fullbloods, trying to get them to take their parcels of land.

Choctaw fullbloods wanted to sell their allotments and move to South America. Jacob Jackson, their spokesman, explained to a Senate committee: "Surely a race of people, desiring to preserve the integrity of that race, who love it by reason of its traditions and their common ancestors . . . may be permitted to protect themselves, if in no other way than by emigration." Whites had left Europe to avoid intolerable conditions; the Choctaw sought the same privilege. Jackson's plea, along with those of others, fell on deaf ears.

For the Five Civilized Tribes had made a fatal mistake in allowing whites to live on their lands. Now the Indian population of some 50,000 was outnumbered by more than twice as many whites; pressure by whites for a clear title to lands they occupied carried the day. In 1907 Indian Territory was merged with its western neighbor, Oklahoma Territory, into the new state of Oklahoma.

By then a quarter of a century of misplaced zeal, greed, and chicanery had shrunk the tribal lands in the United States by more than half. Some Indians had reaped the expected benefits as independent husbandmen; some others had actively connived against the interests of their people. Not all the loss was due to allotment. Right-of-way laws let railroads cut swaths through reservations. And the policy of President Theodore Roosevelt, which enshrined him in the hearts of conservationists, gobbled up millions of acres of Indian lands in new national parks and forests. In New Mexico, Taos Pueblo saw its beautiful highland shrine, Blue Lake—"this proof of sacred things we deeply love"—placed in Kit Carson National Forest, ostensibly to protect it from development.

"Super Indian #2 (with ice cream cone)" portrays the paradoxes of Indian life—torment and humor, tradition and hip style—that inspire Fritz Scholder. Part Luiseño (a California mission tribe) and pioneer of Indian pop art, Scholder feels "the good vibrations of an emerging generation of Indian sculptors, actors, writers, dancers, and historians who will rewrite the history of the West."

PAINTING BY FRITZ SCHOLDER, 1971; COURTESY OF SUSAN T. AND JOACHIM JEAN ABERBACH

Soon cabins and trails and parties of campers, with the attendant litter, invaded the evergreen forest around the lake, an insufferable desecration to the Taoseños. They pleaded for more than half a century, rejecting an offer of money at one point, before they won back their holy lake. But several other sites revered in Indian religious tradition remain locked in federal preserves.

The tide engulfing the Indians seemed irreversible. Then a minor lawsuit involving the sale of liquor to Indians stemmed it. The status of the Pueblo people of New Mexico had always been different from that of other Indians. When Mexico ceded the territory in 1848, the United States confirmed the Pueblos' land titles and offered full citizenship to them and to the Mexican people who chose to remain. But as "full citizens" the Indians found their lands without even the skimpy protection of federal guardianship, and became easy prey for land grabbers.

Federal law forbade the sale of whisky in Indian country. Did it apply to Pueblo communities? In *Sandoval v. United States* the Supreme Court in 1913 ruled that the Pueblos were under federal protection—meaning not only the liquor laws but also the laws protecting them against squatters.

New Mexico seethed as thousands of property "owners" suddenly found themselves on shaky ground. Senator Holm Bursum of New Mexico sided with them in what became a classic legal confrontation of the new West. In 1922 he offered a bill to resolve conflicting claims by putting the burden of proving land ownership on the Pueblos.

The Indians were stunned when they heard of it. "We must unite as we did once before," said one, recalling the great rebellion of 1680, when the Pueblo people drove the Spaniards from the land. A council of 123 headmen from 19 tribes convened at Santo Domingo Pueblo, in a traditional one-room home of darkened beams and white walls festooned with red and blue dried corn, dried meat, and red chilies. "The time has come," the council declared in a memorial to the American people, "when we must live or die."

John Collier, a diminutive social worker filled with admiration for the Indian spirit, was there, recorded the drama, and went on to spearhead a coalition that included the General Federation of Women's Clubs. They aroused the nation, buried the Bursum bill, and in its place won passage of a law that made the squatters prove the legitimacy of their claims. In time some 3,000 were removed from Pueblo lands. Instead of vanishing, the Pueblo people had proven durable and hardy, eager to protect their tribal legacies.

A new era of reform gathered force, fed largely on the shattered myths of the old reforms. If individual ownership of property had any validity as a civilizing force, one would have expected Oklahoma to provide the prime examples. The Five Civilized Tribes had had long years of exposure to the complexities of white society, and the discovery of oil had blessed the state with lucrative resources. Yet here the worst abuses piled up, decades after the reservations were abolished.

To keep Indian land allotments from passing quickly into white ownership, the law restricted the sale of these tracts. But men bent on plunder found ways to surmount such barriers. Adult Indians found themselves declared incompetent by local courts and in need of guardians. Minors became wards of the courts. Oil-rich Osages were shot, poisoned, blown up in their homes; the Indians were terrorized by 24 unsolved murders in a three-year period. Wills turned up in which Osages for some reason left their estates to local politicians instead of their families. "To 2,000

Indian faces, Indian rhythms knit communal bonds on the crowded powwow circuit. Stars like Steve Charging Eagle (far right) make the rounds, war dancing for prize money. Traditionally powwows—the word comes from an Algonquian term for "conjurer"—were held to cure disease, ensure success in battle or the hunt. Coming together, sharing, reaffirming old ways—a powwow still makes good medicine.

ROBERT W. MADDEN, NATIONAL GEOGRAPHIC PHOTOGRAPHER

Osages," wrote Collier, ". . . in 16 years following 1915 there was paid out in cash, by the government, $265,000,000 in royalties from Osage oil. Ninety percent . . . went 'down the wind' of ruined Osages and corrupted and corrupting whites."

Fresh studies filled volumes with evidence that Indians remained a battered lump in the melting pot that was America. In a six-year investigation, begun in 1928, United States Senators found the same dismal pattern at one reservation after another: whites in control of rich resources, Indians struggling to eke out a living. On the Klamath Reservation in Oregon, the Bureau of Indian Affairs trained whites to supervise timber cutting, but kept Indians out of the training program. Coolidge Dam in Arizona had been built to water the Gila River Reservation; whites farmed the irrigated fields, while Pimas and Maricopas virtually stripped the reservation bare, chopping trees to sell as firewood. On the northern plains white-owned cattle grazed Indian-owned land.

Half-forgotten outrages seemed to rise from the mists of history to shock the Senate investigators. At Lawton, Oklahoma, they discovered the Fort Sill Apaches, descendants and survivors of a band of 750 Chiricahuas brought east when Geronimo surrendered. The band had been held in prison status for more than 20 years, then freed. Investigators queried an Apache spokesman, Asa Daklugie:

"At the time Geronimo surrendered you had among the peaceable band a number of men enlisted in the army known as scouts?"

Daklugie: "Yes, sir."

"Were they taken prisoners as well?"

"Yes, sir."

". . . . Some of these men who were prisoners for all these years, former scouts, are drawing pensions from the government?"

"Yes, sir."

"Indicating a judgment on the part of the government that at no time should they have been considered prisoners. . . ?"

"For 26 years."

". . . . Why was it that the government treated the peaceable Indians in the same way they treated the Geronimo band who were enemies?"

"That is what they would like to know and I would like to know that myself."

With the New Deal in 1933 came a new Commissioner of Indian Affairs, that tireless gadfly John Collier. A generation ahead of his time, he visualized the revival of aboriginal cultures among people who had been reduced to survival tactics. In Collier's grand concept, Indians would generously cede their allotted lands to new tribal governments which would build a new Indian society.

Such sweeping reforms were too much for Congress, too much even for many Indians who misunderstood and opposed the plan. The fullbloods, protested George White Bull, a Sioux from the Standing Rock Reservation, were "just getting accustomed to the allotment system."

Collier salvaged parts of his dream in the Indian Reorganization Act of 1934, though not enough to give the tribes fully functioning governments. But the long nightmare of allotment was ended; indeed the law provided funds for expanding Indian holdings. It also granted development aid which enabled the tribes to embark on ventures that were previously impossible. Perhaps more important, the law granted Indians the cherished freedom of religion; no longer did the old people have to perform traditional rituals in hiding.

The experiments in tribal self-government had barely begun when the tremors of World War II rocked the land and the people. Reservation

Font of faith wrested from Taos Pueblo, Blue Lake sparked
a 65-year crusade — and a new understanding of the mystic
link between Indian life and land. When Taoseños regained
their mountain-girt shrine in 1971, says author Deloria,
they scored the greatest Indian success of the last century.
ART KANE

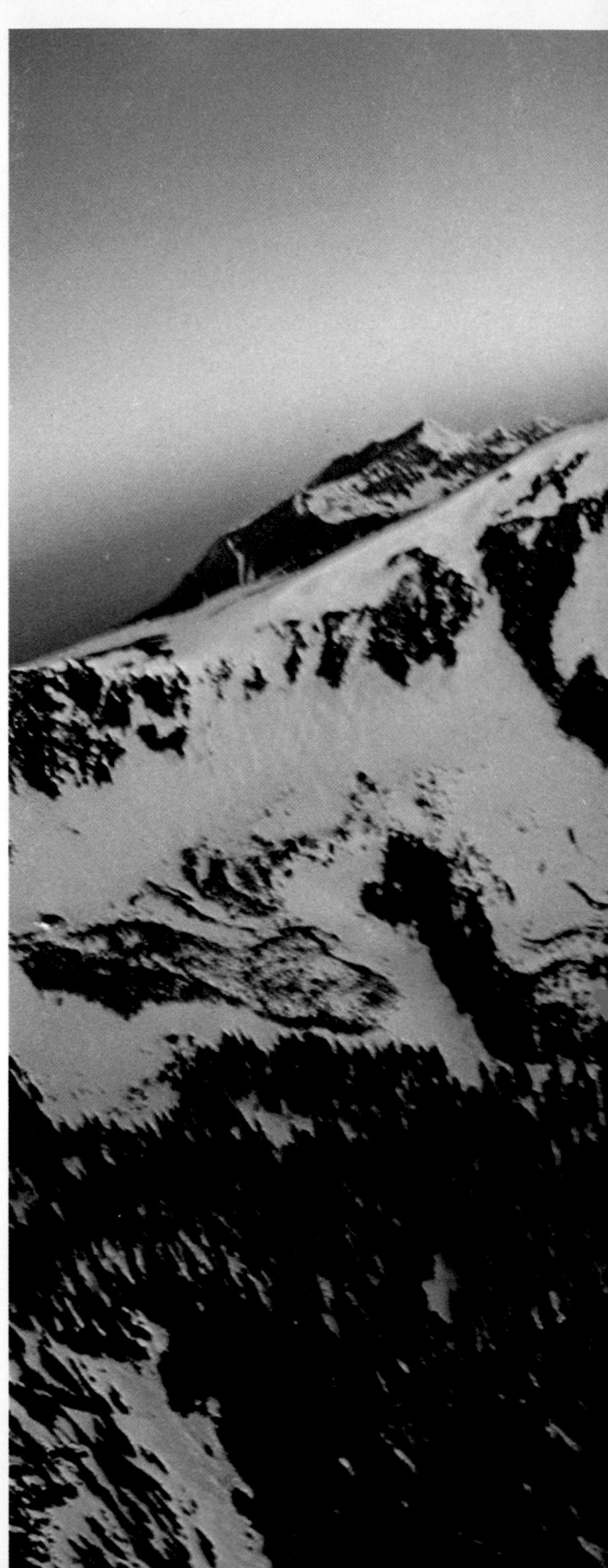

Indians who had resisted farming for decades glad-
ly grew crops because the victory gardens had a
purpose — winning the war — and were not simply
another arbitrary command of the Indian agent.
Thousands left their homes to man the war plants
in Los Angeles, Seattle, San Francisco, and San
Diego, many to remain and raise a new generation
without a memory of reservation life. With the
precedent set for moving off the reservation to
seek work, more and more Indians headed for
urban centers. Before long nearly every large city
had its Indian community.

Pearl Harbor sparked the ancestral warrior
spirit, calling forth a flurry of Indian volunteers.
Eventually some 25,000 served. A Creek and a
Cherokee, Ernest Childers and Jack Montgomery
of the famed Thunderbird Division, won the Congressional Medal of Honor in Europe. Gen. Clar-
ence Tinker of the Army Air Corps, an Osage, died
in the Pacific. Ira Hayes, a Pima Marine, helped
raise the flag at Iwo Jima, and a Pawnee, Brum-
mett Echohawk, a renowned expert in hand-to-
hand combat, trained commandos. Some Indians
chafed under the tedium of military routine. They
had come to fight, not to sit around, cut grass,
and clean latrines. So they simply went home.

Pursuing their new religious liberties, a number
of tribes had conducted ceremonies for departing
warriors. When the veterans returned, purification rites welcomed them back into the tribal fold.
"Let the War of the Whites be now forgotten," in-
toned a Navajo elder. "Let the white way of life,
and death, be now cast out of you."

Many a homecoming soldier found reservation
life harsh and stagnant, and, unable to make his
way in the white world either, drifted about, aim-
less and bitter. Others came back from the war
convinced that vigilance and participation were
the first responsibilities of citizenship. They

With $10 million in the tribal till and a sawmill in the black,
Menominees of Wisconsin faced rosy prospects in the 1950's.
Then came termination—a plan to cut federal ties and
let Indians fend for themselves. Baited with cash payments to
obtain their consent, termination ensnared the tribe, turning

looked out on the war clouds gathering on the domestic horizon and prepared to confront them.

Suspicious lawmakers who saw a subversive foreign influence in the effort to revive Indian culture drove John Collier from office. Before he left the Bureau of Indian Affairs, however, Collier encouraged his Indian employes to organize for the defense of tribal rights in the future. In November 1944, nearly a hundred Indians from across the land gathered in Denver, Colorado, to form the National Congress of American Indians, the first all-Indian national organization.

"We'd sent out invitations hoping that someone would come," recalled D'Arcy McNickle, a Flathead and one of the founders. "We didn't know if anyone would. So we just sat there in the hotel lobby and pretty soon it was filled with Indians. Where they came from we never did figure out."

The new group soon joined the successful campaign to establish the Indian Claims Commission. Hitherto, any tribe with a grievance over a broken treaty or a shady deal was forced to obtain a special act of Congress before the tribe could sue the government. Now the tribes could routinely file claims before the commission. By the time its statutory life—after four extensions—expired in 1978, it had heard more than 500 claims and made awards to tribal groups totaling some 800 million dollars. The issues were complex, and the Indians had many grievances.

More were piling up. While the claims law represented an act of national conscience, it also reflected the hope that the money awards would speed the day when costly federal services for Indian health, education, and welfare would end. In the postwar years the cry arose once again to "set these people free." The result: new laws to terminate the federal relationship with tribes that seemed able and were willing—or could be

persuaded—to go along. Indians knew only too well the humiliations of government wardship, but they also knew that it was inviting disaster to cut off federal financial and administrative support—and, with scarcely any experience, to plunge into the minefields of taxation, banking, corporate structures, and state bureaucracies.

The Menominees of Wisconsin, regarded as one of the more competent tribal groups, were among the first to be subjected to termination. They resisted, but they were especially vulnerable to arm-twisting. Early in this century the U. S. Forest Service had clear-cut a part of the Menominees' forest, causing enormous damage. (A clue to the thinking of that era came in 1917 when an assistant Indian Commissioner informed Congress that liquidation of Indian forests was a corollary to the process of liquidating the Indians.) In 1951 the U. S. Court of Claims awarded the Menominees $8.5 million for the old losses to their forest. To get any of the money distributed to themselves, the Indians needed congressional authorization. To get that, they were told, they'd have to take termination. And they did.

So the tribal government became a county government, and the reservation became Wisconsin's "smallest, poorest, worst educated, unhealthiest, and most undeveloped county"—as a study by Kirke Kickingbird and Karen Ducheneaux put it. A corporation, with non-Indians a majority of the board, ran tribal properties. The Menominee sawmill, which had operated profitably but primarily to provide employment, was automated to increase taxable revenue, throwing people out of work and onto welfare. Later, the mill caught fire. The fire engine couldn't start at first, but that hardly mattered; its hoses were found to be rotted —and useless. The mill was badly damaged. As the tribe reeled under its new burdens, federal and state costs went up, not down. The "freed" tribe was worse off by far. When a desperate hunt for revenue brought a plan to sell some 2,500 lakeside lots to whites, community dissent boiled over into a campaign to bring back the tribal structure.

Some 19 tribes lost federal support before the termination policy was finally terminated.

Another device to usher Indians into the American mainstream was "relocation." Under this experiment the government provided one-way bus or train tickets from the reservations into cities and helped the relocated families get settled and find jobs. Some succeeded. For others the free ride merely meant a shift "from one pocket of poverty to another." Many found their way back to the reservations; the one-way ticket became a joke. When the conquest of space was still a dream, Indians thought it would be a safe bet to send veterans of relocation to the moon: "If they're Indians they'll find a way to get home."

When the United States declared war on poverty in the 1960's, Indians quickly volunteered. They were experts on poverty; on some reservations the unemployment rate ran as high as 80 or 90 per cent. By now Indians were also experts in the legislative process. In 1964 the National Congress of American Indians, which I later served as executive director, co-sponsored a conference on poverty which led to the inclusion of Indians in the programs. Soon tribes were deeply involved in projects under a variety of federal agencies, and antipoverty campaigns became a major force in reservation life.

The Red Lake Chippewa of Minnesota and the Gila River Pima and Maricopa of Arizona achieved lasting improvements in reservation housing. The Lummi of western Washington, who had been forced from their ancestral dependence upon the bounty of the sea to become reluctant farmers and berry pickers, developed a marvel of aquiculture, harvesting salmon, trout, and shellfish at their unique sea farm in Lummi Bay. Humor, a useful social lubricant at tribal gatherings for centuries, found its way into the poverty wars. Around the country job-seeking teen-agers could get help at their Neighborhood Youth Corps; young Uintahs and Ourays of Utah, however, applied at the Neighborhood Ute Corps.

To the Navajo, determined to chart their own future as a people, the poverty campaign brought more than money. Always before, the bureaucrats had decided how to spend federal funds for Navajos, noted one tribe member. "Then," he added, "the Office of Economic Opportunity comes along with 11 million dollars a year and asks Navajos how *we* think the money should be spent. Navajos were like a snake in a jar until OEO let the snake out. What happens when you free the snake? When he realizes he's free, he begins to move!"

Educated Indians were attracted to the challenge of the new programs, and to the tribal councils which ran them. High-level jobs in federal agencies opened to Indians. And the century-old dilemma of the Alaskan natives' land rights came up for decision. After prolonged debate Congress and the President granted the Eskimo and Indian people of the state eventual title to some 40 million acres and payment of a billion dollars. In Maine, a court in 1975 upheld tribal claims to lands covering two-thirds of the state—and set off legal jockeying that may take years to conclude.

The movement of Indians into higher education in the '60's had accelerated everything in Indian affairs. In 1960 some 2,000 Indians were in college; a decade later the total was 12,000 with several hundred in graduate (continued on page 380)

The Way of the Navajo

For countless generations, through the long nights of winter when no Lightning People are abroad, Navajo elders have passed their legends along to the young. It is still the Navajo way. Only the book is new.

The book is in the language of the *belagaana* because the Navajo have chosen to use white men's words, just as their ancestors adopted useful aspects of other cultures—the sheep, horse, and silversmithing from the Spanish, weaving and religion from the Pueblos. Some scientists think the diverse strains that shaped the Navajo people have produced a "hybrid vigor." Whatever the reason, "the indestructibles" can boast of a spectacular history of endurance and survival.

They had been brigands—and the victims of brigands —in the harsh pattern of southwestern life. Then, in 1864, Kit Carson herded some 8,000 of them on the "Long Walk" of more than 300 miles to the hellhole of Bosque Redondo. Here they withered until, in 1868,

7,000 survivors were freed to return to their homeland. Since then the Navajo have become the biggest and wealthiest of all tribes. Their numbers multiplied twentyfold. The 16-million-acre reservation, sprawled across Arizona, New Mexico, and Utah desert, is bigger than 10 states. Its oil, coal, and uranium have earned hundreds of millions of dollars. And the Navajo aim to control their wealth, the land, and their tribal destiny.

They learn the white man's words but do not forget the language of the *Dineh*—the People. Increasingly, they use it in schools where elders stay with the children and tell the winter tales in new dormitories.

Thus, in either tongue young Navajos learn of their sacred mountains, of First Man and First Woman. And also of the Twins who slew many monsters but were persuaded to spare some. So, while the Navajo multiply and blend new knowledge and industry into the Navajo way, Hunger, Poverty, and Lice Man yet stalk the land.

Of Wealth and Health
in a Harsh Land

Against the stark monoliths of Monument Valley, a Navajo woman shears her flock. Livestock traditionally measured a man's wealth and status; the *rico* had many, the *pobre* few. It is a poor man, said a Navajo maxim, who can see farther than his animals graze. So the flocks grew until the land, miserly at best with forage and water, could no longer sustain them. In the 1930's the Department of the Interior ordered flocks cut in half, and many a shepherd was forced to seek a wage-earning job that did not exist. Elders still rue the days when sheep and goats were shot by the thousands, and were burned in great mounds or left to rot.

About a sixth of the Navajo homes are hogans like the one opposite. The family piles bedding against a wall, hangs trinkets from beams; the door faces east because the Holy People long ago built the first hogan that way. Even Navajos with modern houses may have hogans for religious rites. The traditional one-room structure provides a snug and compact dwelling, but the lack of plumbing contributes to health problems. And one medical team reported that windowless hogans chinked against the winter cold made "ideal transmission chambers" for the bacteria of tuberculosis.

Modern medicine offers a full range of services, from surgical transplants at major centers to home visits in the hogans (right). Yet living conditions still produce a tuberculosis rate six times as high as for the nation at large, still threaten Navajo youngsters with wasting, stomach-bloating nutritional diseases like kwashiorkor and marasmus.

The people accept doctors but may rank them with the lowest of traditional healers, the herbalist who treats symptoms and gives temporary relief. The diagnostician ranks higher; his hands may tremble until, with supernatural powers, he discovers the cause of sickness. His prescription is administered by a singer or medicine man whose chants and rituals may last nine days. The singer heads the hierarchy because his powers seek to cure the underlying disharmony of body and mind and nature. Science no longer ignores such psychotherapy; the National Institute of Mental Health has financed the training of medicine men in Navajoland.

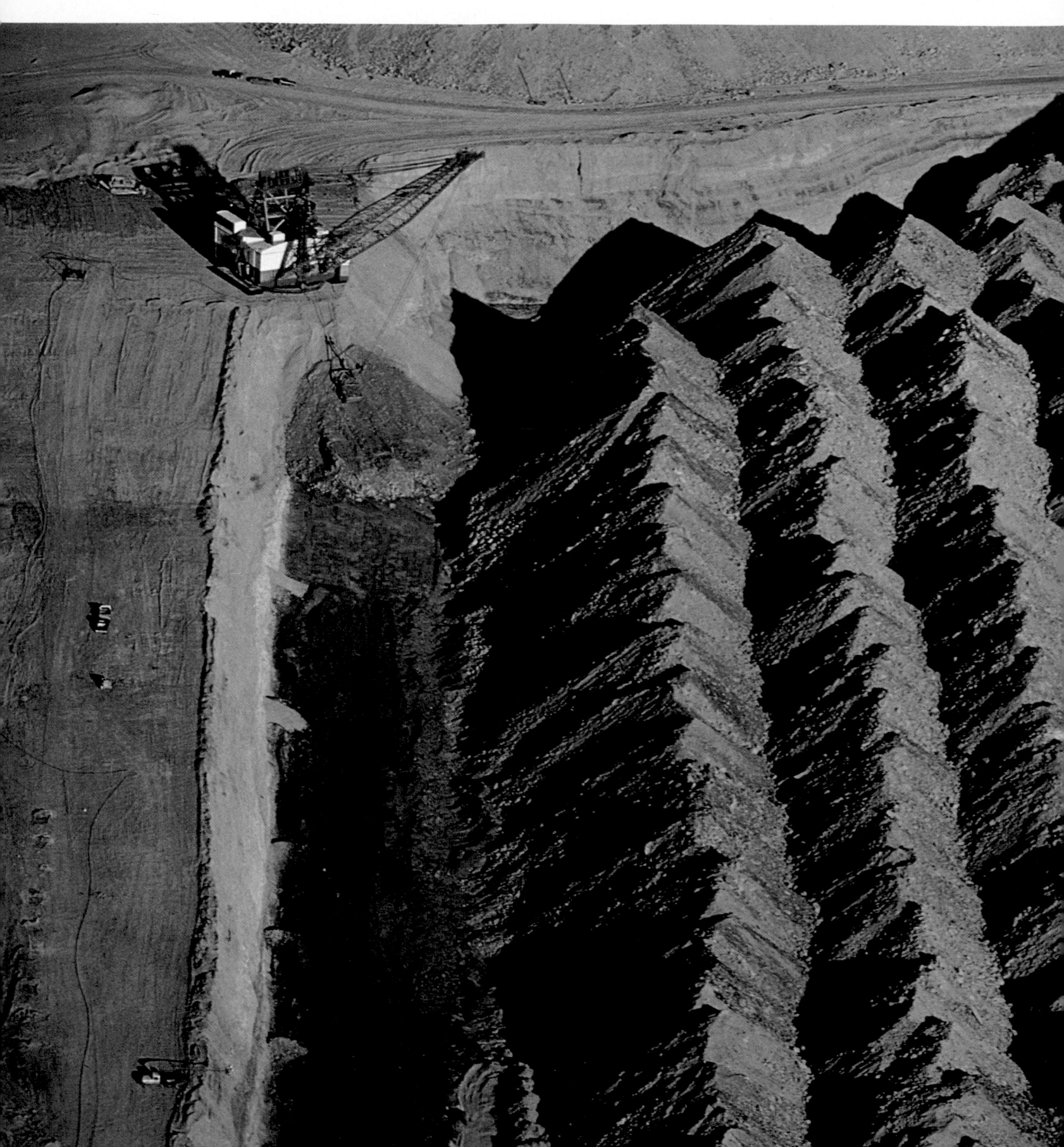

BRUCE DALE, NATIONAL GEOGRAPHIC PHOTOGRAPHER

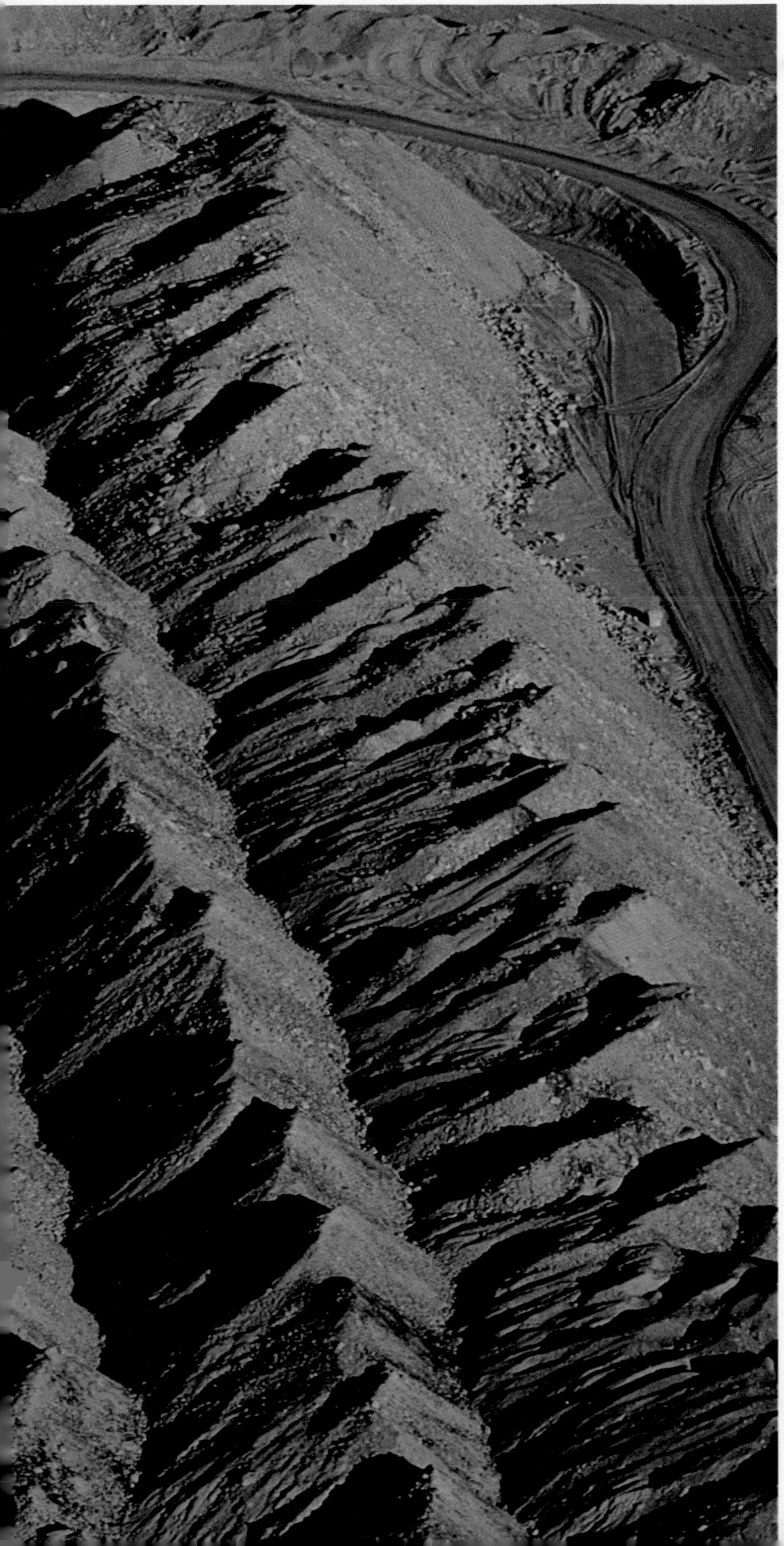

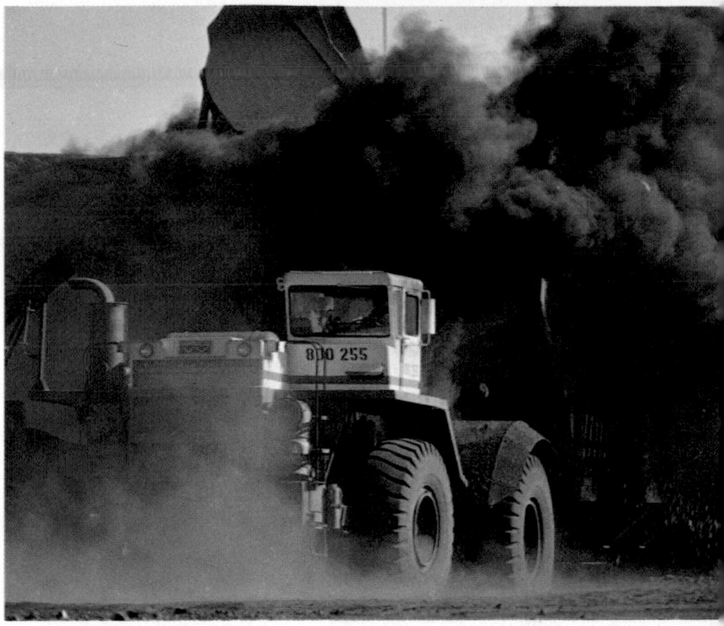

Coal Fuels a Controversy

Immense coal deposits generate power, wealth, and controversy in Navajo country. In the Four Corners region of New Mexico a dragline bares a seam in a billion-ton trove; a loader (above) kicks up a powdery cloud. The coal feeds a giant power plant nearby, one of several planned for the blue-sky country to appease the ever-growing power pangs of the Southwest and southern California. Mine and plant mean sorely needed jobs for hundreds of Navajos, millions for the tribal coffers. But what of the torn land, the smoke spewed from stacks? Controls cut down pollutants, and the land, say the mining firms, will be recontoured. Some Navajos doubt it: "They can never put it back the way it was." Others see no choice: "What are you supposed to do if you're sinking in quicksand and somebody throws you a rope? So it's a little dirty. Do you argue?"

At Black Mesa in Arizona both Navajo and Hopi reap the benefits and the anguish of strip mining. The mesa is the sacred Female Mountain of Navajo tradition; the Male Mountain lies nearby. Together they represent nature's balance. To the Hopi, whose reservation is surrounded by Navajo land, the mesa serves as a burial ground. In Hopi belief a great threat to man's survival has been prophesied. It will be borne by a new race of people, who will offer the Hopi false promises of progress. The prophecy tells of natural disasters to come, of three world wars. The last war will determine man's fate. Only the Hopi land will offer sanctuary; if it is despoiled, mankind will not survive.

TERRY EILER. OPPOSITE: BRUCE DALE, NATIONAL GEOGRAPHIC PHOTOGRAPHER

The "Long Walk"
to Navajo Nationhood

More and more the Navajo talk of themselves as a nation. Less and less does it sound like empty rhetoric. A few years ago the 74-member tribal council accepted the offer of the United States to let the Navajo run their reservation. Unlike other plans to "free" the Indians, this one would not relieve the government of its obligations. The local Bureau of Indian Affairs bureaucracy, with its budget of well over $100 million a year, would stay—but the tribe would control it.

The historic step was taken at Window Rock, Arizona, "capital of the Navajo Nation," and a symbol of change, resurgence, and tradition. To this site once came medicine men to fill woven bottles with water for the ritual which sought abundant rainfall. The council chamber (left) simulates the form of an eight-sided hogan. In Window Rock there are computers, a department store with glittering wares, a tribal museum, zoo, research library, the headquarters of the burdened health service. On the tribal flag and great seal, stylized rainbows encompass the people's sovereignty.

There are Navajo police, firemen, park rangers; a tribal utilities authority, an office of economic opportunity, a general counsel to advise on legislation or defend the tribe's land rights, and a legal aid service that can help a shepherd settle a dispute over his flock. Lawyers are held in high regard; Navajos see them as people who never lose an argument.

Indian educators from across the land have come to observe the Rough Rock Demonstration School, where Navajos hire and fire and set policy, where Indian parents are welcomed to the classrooms, and English is the *second* language. In 1968 Navajo Community College became the first institution of higher learning in the United States owned and operated by Indians.

At Shiprock, New Mexico, the tribe built a million-dollar electronics plant, which for a time provided jobs and training in new skills.

Lonely Frog Rock, which once looked out upon a handful of hogans and sheep nibbling the scanty vegetation, now echoes the whining saws of the Navajo Forest Products Industries mill and the bustle of the new town of Navajo, New Mexico, the first Indian-planned community (above).

"Moving from a hogan to a modern house," reports the *Navajo Times*, "means no more water to haul and no more wood to gather. . . ." Some three quarters of all reservation homes still have no running water. Less than a fifth of the 7,500 miles of roads are paved.

"We walked the 'Long Walk'," wrote the Navajo poet Jay DeGroat, "But the 'Long Walk' is not over. . . ."

Master fishermen for a thousand years, Lummis of coastal Washington pioneered new techniques of sea farming to harvest a two-million-dollar crop in less than a decade. Beginning in 1968, eager hands and minds, helped by government and private agencies, learned marine biology, built hatcheries, raced the tide to dike a 750-acre sea pond.

LOWELL GEORGIA

school. For the first time the tribes were not forced to go beyond their communities to find qualified professionals. By the 1970's a majority of Indian schoolchildren were enrolled in public schools. On the reservations Indian schools came increasingly under Indian direction. Faced with funding and accreditation problems, school leaders formed the Coalition of Indian Controlled School Boards, one of the most innovative groups ever to work in Indian education.

New courses in Indian languages, history, and art underscored the fact that the forces of cultural renewal unleashed in John Collier's day had intensified over the years. Indians thronged reservations for annual religious ceremonies and secular celebrations of dancing, feasting, and rodeo collectively called powwows. The Crow Fair and Oglala Sioux Sun Dance became major events of the Indian year. Almost every weekend some tribe, somewhere, had a gathering planned.

Often young college-trained Indians returned to the reservation in ignorance of their tribal traditions. They were not content to remain so, and were among the most determined to rediscover ancestral roots, to recapture the rich harmony: "You see, I stand in good relation to the earth. . . . to the gods. . . . to all that is beautiful."

With burgeoning pride many traveled the powwow circuit, caught the spark of the civil rights movement, and began to express a deep discontent with the dominant society. Some dreamed of returning to a pristine Indianness untainted by white contact; others thought revitalized tribal structures could help solidify recent political gains. Thus emerged a generation of activists dedicated to the renewal of tribal integrity and, if need be, the warrior tradition.

The first clash came with the "fish-ins" of Washington State in 1964. For years local Indians had

Indian workers nurse tiny oysters in tanks, count them in tubes, gather grown ones in barrels. Freshwater trout adapt to salt in holding tanks (below)—a process first used commercially here—then fatten in the food-rich sea pond thrice as fast as in nature. Now a Lummi aquiculture school trains other tribes who believe, as Lummis do, that "the water is our way of life."

protested state game laws that restricted Indian fishing rights guaranteed by federal treaty. Now, defying white laws, the fishermen, supported by the newly formed National Indian Youth Council, went out to fish the Puyallup, the Nisqually, and the Green Rivers. As police and wardens went after them, the men fought from their boats, and their families threw rocks from the shore. Dozens went to jail. "It was the first full-scale intertribal *action* since the Indians defeated General Custer on the Little Bighorn," declared Herbert Blatchford, the director of the Youth Council.

As the decade wore on, civil disobedience increased. With 1969 came the drama of Alcatraz. Indians who took part recalled it as a beautiful experience, a symbol of their need to retake the continent—in spirit if not in fact. But many of the invasions which followed it made little sense, lacking the kind of organized effort which might have made them successful. They were taken seriously only as long as the media found them interesting.

The younger leaders, impatient for change, gaining prominence—and notoriety—soon drew apart from the tribal establishments. Older leaders regarded the demonstrators as potential political rivals and lawless firebrands whose excesses might cut the pipelines of federal money. In turn the activists derided their Indian critics as "Uncle Tomahawks" and "apples"—red on the outside, white underneath.

As the 1972 election approached, an Indian caravan calling itself the "Trail of Broken Treaties" descended on Washington to demand new programs from Presidential candidates. Protest exploded into confrontation; Indians took over and vandalized headquarters of the Bureau of Indian Affairs during a tense week of occupation.

The gap of misunderstanding in Indian country widened as frustrated activists looked westward,

Once the scourge of intruders, White Mountain Apaches today greet guests with a warm *"Hon-dah—Come into my house."* The Sunrise Park Hotel, along with cattle and timber, may add vital income to the Arizona tribe. But the Apache also treasure a land unspoiled, a culture unfettered—wealth immeasurable.
DAVID HISER

and tribal leaders girded against assaults on their reservations. Early in 1973 trouble came to Pine Ridge, where dissidents had been sparring with the Sioux leadership. Armed Indians, spearheaded by organizers from the American Indian Movement, occupied the village of Wounded Knee.

The Oglala Sioux had known the glory of Red Cloud and Crazy Horse—and the agony of Wounded Knee in 1890. They had known, too, allotment and leasing, boarding schools, tribal government, health and poverty programs. Some had made the adjustment from the old way to the new, had even won power and affluence. But the rolling grasslands of Pine Ridge still displayed the signs of human wreckage: aimlessness, hunger, rutted roads, rusted jalopies, wretched housing, hopelessness soothed only by the hopeless remedy of alcohol.

For 71 days the militants held the hamlet, besieged by lawmen and the world press which made Wounded Knee II more famous than its predecessor. Sporadic gunfire crackled; two militants died, a marshal was paralyzed. Finally, federal officials negotiated a withdrawal, with the issues drowned in hatred, rhetoric, and media stunts.

In a real sense the past century of Indian existence had begun and ended at Wounded Knee. The bloody rout of 1890 gave tragic evidence that the old ways were gone; in their place came the challenge to Indians to adapt or vanish. The siege of 1973 had proved, at least, that they had done neither. In fact the Indian population had more than tripled since 1890, when it stood at 250,000.

And Indians seemed less inclined than ever to turn away from their ancient sense of the sacredness of earth and of tribal belonging. Their journey through history has not yet ended. They strive to prolong it, and to discover its meaning.

TOMORROW

We have wept the blood
of countless ages
as each of us raised high
the lance of hate. . . .
Now let us dry our tears
and learn the dance
and chant of the life cycle
tomorrow dances behind the sun
in sacred promise
of things to come for children
not yet born,
for ours is the potential of truly
lasting beauty
born of hope and shaped by deed.
Now let us lay the lance of hate
upon this soil.

Peter blue cloud

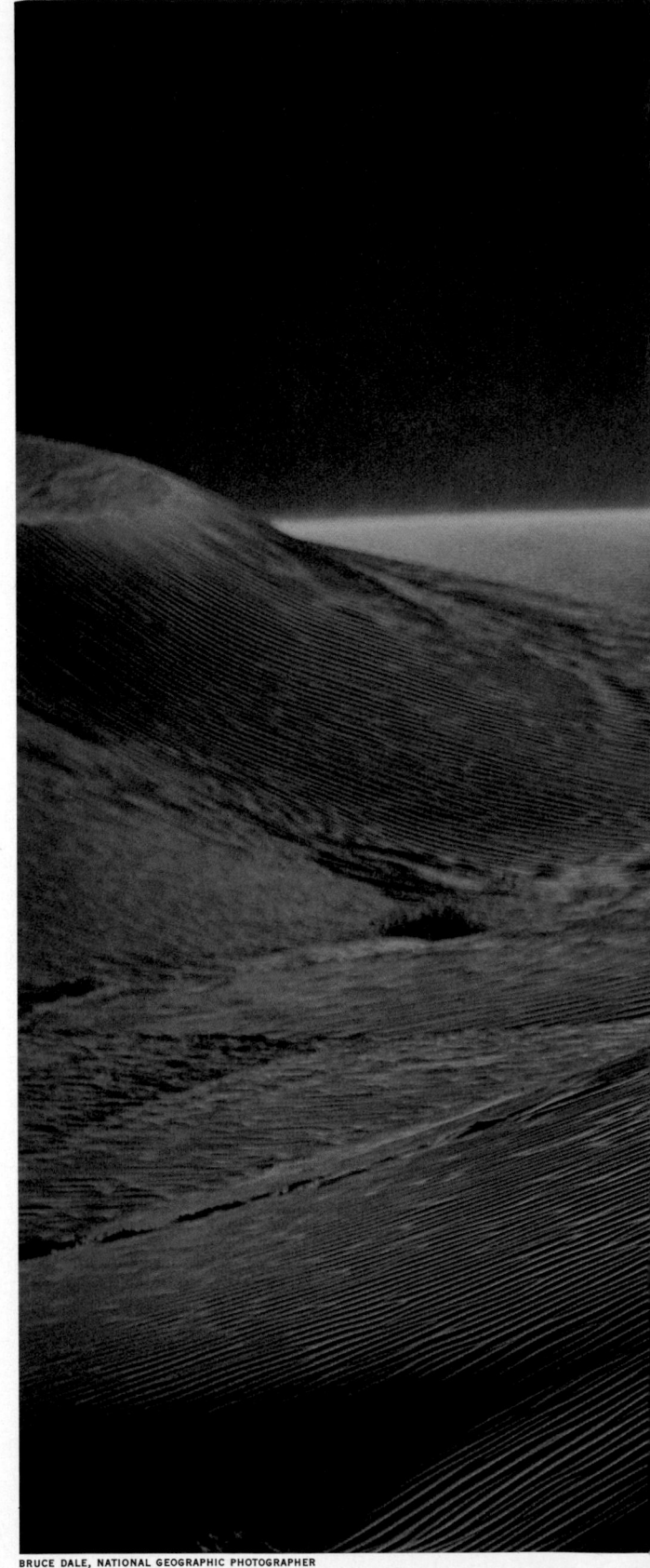

Tribal Supplement

This supplement lists all tribal groups of the United States and Canada shown on the book's back-pocket map. Each entry has a letter-number combination that corresponds to one in the map's border. Imaginary lines drawn from those keys intersect near where the entry can be found. From the location you can determine the culture area and book chapter covering the tribe's life-style.

For additional information carried in text references, consult the index.

Abenaki: Algonquians; like neighbor tribes, cite traditional origin to the southwest. *M16*

Abitibi: Algonquian band. *L14*

Accomac: Little known relatives of the Powhatan. *P16*

Achumawi: Called themselves *Ajumawi*, "River People." *M6*

Acolapissa: Small Muskogean tribe; united with Houma about 1750. *S13*

Acoma: Keresan pueblo. *Q9*

Acuera: Timucua tribe first mentioned by de Soto expedition. *S15*

Adai: Band associated with the Caddo. *R12*

Aglemiut: Skilled ivory carvers. *E4*

Ahtena: Athapaskans who turned back whites for nearly a century. Also called Atna. *F6*

Ais: Fishermen; scant record after 1703. *S15*

Akokisa: Atakapans; extinct after 1805. *S11*

Akwa'ala: *See* Paipai.

Alabama: Muskogean tribe friendly to French. Language closely related to Koasati. *R14*

Albany: Band of woodland Cree. *K14*

Aleut: *See* Atka, Unalaska Aleut.

Algonquin: Name, from the Maliseet, means "they are our relatives (or allies)." *M15*

Alsea: Small tribe, little studied. *L6*

Apache: Group of tribes speaking very similar Athapaskan languages. *Q9*

Apalachee: Once important Muskogean tribe, extinct by late 18th century. *R14*

Apalachicola: Hitchiti-speaking villagers; tradition says peace between them and Muskogee began Creek confederacy. *R14*

Arapaho: Algonquian speakers, allied to the Cheyenne. *P10*

Arikara: Farmers, earth-lodge dwellers, language closely related to Pawnee. *M10*

Arosaguntacook: Abenaki speakers driven into Canada in 1720's. *M16*

Assateague: Algonquians related to the Nanticoke and Powhatan. *P16*

Assiniboin: Large Siouan tribe speaking Nakota variety of Dakota; in Canada called "Stoney," perhaps from custom of using hot stones to boil foods. *L10*

Atakapa: Means "man eater" in Choctaw; language distantly related to Muskogean. *S12*

Atka Aleut: Great sea hunters; language remotely related to Eskimo. *B1*

Atna: *See* Ahtena.

Atsina: *See* Gros Ventre.

Atsugewi: Small tribe; language closely related to that of the Achumawi. *N6*

Auk: Tlingit group occupying gold field where Juneau was established in 1880. *G6*

Avoyel: Middlemen in Gulf flint trade. *R12*

Aztec-Tanoan: *See* Tano.

Baffin Land Eskimo: Many scattered bands; speakers of Inuit, or eastern, Eskimo. *F15*

Bannock: *See* Shoshone.

Barren Ground: Band of woodland Cree. *K14*

Barriere: Subdivision of Algonquin. *M15*

Bayogoula: Language perhaps like Choctaw; survivors of Taensa attack joined Houma. *R12*

Bear Lake: Closely related to Dogrib. *F9*

Beatty: Western Shoshone band. *P7*

Beaver: Nomadic plains hunters. *J9*

Beaver Hills: Plains Cree band. *K9*

Bella Bella: Kwakiutlan language; art styles like northern neighbors. *J6*

Bella Coola: Salishans who lived on river used as trade highway to interior. *J6*

Beothuk: Called "red men" for their heavy use of red ocher. Extinct by 1827. *K19*

Bering Strait Eskimo: Populous group; speak Inuit, or eastern, Eskimo. *C5*

Bidai: 1776 epidemic nearly erased this and neighbor tribes. *R11*

Biloxi: Spoke a Siouan language. *R13*

Blackfoot: Warrior tribe of northwestern plains. Algonquian language. *L9*

Blackfoot: Small band of Teton Sioux, not related to the Algonquian Blackfoot. *M10*

Blood: Algonquian Blackfoot subtribe. *L8*

Brulé: Band of Teton Sioux. *N10*

Caddo: Key intermediaries in early horse trading with northern tribes. Gave name to Caddoan language family. *R12*

Cahinnio: Caddo band; perhaps same group earlier known as Tula. *Q12*

Cahokia: In Illinois confederacy. *P13*

Cahuilla: Occupied diverse region of desert, mountains, valleys; language in southwestern family known as Aztec-Tanoan. *Q7*

California Athapaskan: Distinct groups speaking related languages; culturally similar to Yurok. *N5*

Calling River: Plains Cree band. *L10*

Calusa: Extinct by mid-1700's. *T15*

Cape Fear: Perhaps affiliated with the Waccamaw. *Q15*

Caribou Eskimo: Central Eskimos dependent on caribou rather than sea mammals. *G11*

Carrier: Interior Athapaskans; culture influenced by coastal neighbors. Supposedly

named from custom of a widow carrying her husband's ashes for three years. *J7*

Catawba: Large tribe whose language branched off from Siouan. *Q15*

Cayuga: Iroquois tribe. Sided with British during Revolution; afterwards major part of tribe moved to Canada. *N15*

Cayuse: Ravaged by 1847 smallpox epidemic; some of remnant merged with Nez Perce. *M7*

Central Eskimo: One of four divisions of speakers of Inuit, or eastern, Eskimo. *F11*

Chakchiuma: Small tribe; absorbed by the Chickasaw and Choctaw in the 1700's. *R13*

Chatot: Pressed from homelands to Mobile Bay, then Louisiana; unknown by 1817. *R14*

Chaui: Pawnee band. Their head chiefs outranked all other Pawnee chiefs. *N11*

Chawasha: Small tribe allied to the Chitimacha. *S13*

Chehalis: Group of small tribes of Coast Salishan stock. *L6*

Chelan: Spoke same Interior Salishan language as the Columbia. *L7*

Chemakum: Small tribe almost exterminated by constant war with neighbors. *L7*

Chemehuevi: Noted for traveling great distances swiftly on foot; language related to that of the Utes. *P7*

Cheraw: Met by de Soto. Hostile to colonists. No trace after 1760's. *Q15*

Cherokee: Language split from northern Iroquoian about 2000 B.C.; pop. in 1650 about 22,000. *Q14*

Cheyenne: Algonquians met by Lewis and Clark. Pushed onto plains from Minnesota homeland by Sioux and Ojibwa. *N10*

Chiaha: Hitchiti-speaking tribe in Creek confederacy. *R14*

Chickahominy: Algonquians; less under Powhatan's control than other tribes in his conquest state. *P16*

Chickasaw: Pop. about 8,000 in 1650; speak same language as Choctaw. *Q13*

Chilcotin: Probably migrated from farther north in late prehistoric times. *J7*

Chilkat: Tlingit tribe. *G6*

Chimariko: Tiny tribe of Hokan linguistic stock. Lived in 20-mile canyon along Trinity River. *M5*

Chinook: Gave name to Chinookan language family. Groups near mouth of Columbia R. sometimes called Lower Chinook; upriver tribes bore individual names. *L6*

Chipewyan: Largest subarctic Athapaskan group; name means "pointed skins," a reference to their parkas. *H11*

Chippewa: *See* Ojibwa.

Chiricahua: Most warlike of Arizona Apache. Geronimo a remembered chief. *R8*

Chitimacha: Noted basket makers; language

remotely related to Muskogean family. *S12*

Choctaw: Largest Muskogean group; skillful farmers. *R13*

Choptank: Little known Algonquians. *P16*

Chugach: Land and sea hunters; speakers of a language of Yupik, or western, Eskimo. *F5*

Chumash: Populous maritime tribes; spoke at least four related Hokan languages. *P6*

Cibecue: Western Apache band. *Q8*

Clallam: Salish tribe. *L6*

Clatskanie: Strong Athapaskan tribe; collected tolls from Columbia R. traffic. *L6*

Clatsop: Lewis and Clark named their Columbia R. post for these Chinookans. *L6*

Coahuiltec: Small, little known tribes. *S10*

Coast Miwok: May have greeted Drake's crew; formed a division of the widespread Penutian language family of the west. *N6*

Cochiti: Pueblo occupied since 1250. *R9*

Cocopa: Yuman tribe frequently raided by more warlike neighbors. *Q7*

Coeur d'Alene: Tribe of Interior Salishan language; French name means "awl heart"— said to be in reference to a trader. *L8*

Columbia: Also called Sinkiuse-Columbia. Language Interior Salishan. *L7*

Colville: Named for a Hudson's Bay Co. fort; spoke same language as Okanagan. *L8*

Comanche: Late arrivals on the plains; speak same language as the Shoshone. *R10*

Comox: On both sides of Strait of Georgia; language Coast Salishan. *K7*

Conestoga: *See* Susquehannock.

Congaree: Little known group, probably Siouan; remnants joined Catawba. *Q15*

Conoy: Algonquian tribe associated with the Nanticoke; also called Piscataway. *P16*

Coos: Small group speaking two separate languages, Miluk and Hanis. *M6*

Coosa: One of original Muskogee groups. Name also given to a Cusabo tribe. *R14*

Copper Eskimo: So named because they used native copper for tools, weapons. *F10*

Costanoan: Dispersed by Mexican settlement; spoke several Penutian languages. *N6*

Coweta: Muskogee tribe; head "war" town of Lower Creeks. *R14*

Cowichan: Major tribe in coastal division of Salishan language family. *K7*

Cowlitz: Tribe of Coast Salishan stock. *L6*

Cree: Populous tribe, widespread; language akin to Ojibwa. Early acquisition of guns gave it dominance over vast area. *K11*

Creek: Divided by river location into "Upper" and "Lower" groups. *See* Muskogee.

Croatoan: Algonquian tribe with which Raleigh colony supposedly took refuge. *Q16*

Crow: Siouans whose bird-name for themselves was mistranslated as "crow." *M9*

Cupeno: Also called Agua Caliente for hot

springs near their main village; language related to that of the Cahuilla. *Q7*

Cusabo: Group of small tribes totaling 600 people; little trace after 1750. *R15*

Dakota: Also called Sioux. Dialects varying in use of *d, n, l* distinguished eastern Dakota, central Nakota, western Lakota. *N11*

Deadose: Little known. *R11*

Delaware: Major Algonquian group; moved west as guides, trappers with white advance, dispersed to Ontario and Oklahoma. *N16*

Dogrib: Name from myth ascribing origin to union of a supernatural dog and an Indian woman. Language in Athapaskan family. *G9*

Duwamish: Coast Salishan tribe allied with Squamish; 1850's chief of combined tribes gave his name to city of Seattle. *L7*

East Greenland Eskimo: Long isolated; speakers of Inuit, or eastern, Eskimo. *D17*

Eastern Keres: With W. Keres, formed a bridge between Pueblo cultures along Rio Grande and those of the Hopi and Zuni. *Q9*

Eno: Small tribe, believed Siouan. *Q15*

Erie: Extinct Iroquoian tribe; little known except for disastrous 1650's war with Iroquois league. *N14*

Esselen: Small group of Hokan speakers; ranged mountains and disappeared early. *P6*

Etchemin: Poorly known Algonquian group; extinct by early 1600's. *M17*

Eufaula: Muskogee townsmen. *R14*

Eyak: Middlemen in copper trade between Tlingit and interior tribes; language related to Athapaskan family. *F6*

Eyeish: Caddo band. *R12*

Fernandeno: Gabrielinos located around mission San Fernando.

Flathead: Did not deform infants' heads but left them naturally flat on top, hence appellation. Also called Salish, which gave name to Salishan language family with Coast, Interior, and Straits divisions. *L8*

Fox: In central Algonquian language group; joined with Sauk after Black Hawk War. *N13*

Fresh Water: De Leon's 1513 landfall made in lands of this Timucua band. *S15*

Gabrielino: Lived around San Gabriel mission; language related to Cahuilla. *Q6*

Gitksan: Language nearly the same as Tsimshian; located on route used in trade for eulachon grease. *H7*

Gonaho: Tlingit group. *G6*

Gosiute: Roamed arid lands around Great Salt Lake; language related to Utes'. *N8*

Gros Ventre: Algonquians, also called Atsina. Tribal name in sign language—

hands-across-belly, for "always hungry"— mistranslated by French as "big bellies." *See also* Hidatsa. *L9*

Guacata: Unknown after 1763. *S15*

Guale: *See* Yamasee.

Haida: Populous tribe ravaged early by white diseases; language has slight similarity to Tlingit and Athapaskan. *J6*

Haihais: Branch of Bella Bella. *J6*

Haisla: Northernmost Kwakiutlans. *J6*

Halchidhoma: Yuman tribe. *Q7*

Han: Small Athapaskan tribe. *E7*

Hano: Tewa-speaking pueblo; established among Hopi after 1680 Pueblo revolt. *P9*

Hare: Athapaskan tribe which used Arctic hares for food and clothing; speakers of the same language as the Dogrib. *E8*

Hasinai: Caddo subgroup; known also as Tejas, or Texas, meaning "friends." *R12*

Havasupai: Farmers closely related to the Walapai, Yavapai. *Q8*

Heiltsuk: Kwakiutlan speakers. *J6*

Henya: Subtribe of Tlingit. *H6*

Hidatsa: Missouri R. farmers; sometimes called Gros Ventre, also Minitari, Rees. Language close to that of the Crow. *M10*

Hitchiti: Tribe of Creek confederacy; gave name to a Muskogean language. *R14*

Hoh: Quileute band. *L6*

Hokan: *See* Seri.

Hopi: Pueblo group; language nearer to Great Basin tribes' than to Pueblo neighbors'. *Q8*

Houma: Driven south by Tunica; language lost, may have been Muskogean. *R12*

Huna: Tlingit group. *G6*

Hunkpapa: Band of Teton Sioux. *M10*

Hupa: Athapaskans with life-style similar to that of the Yurok. *M6*

Huron: Populous Iroquoian confederacy shattered by war with Iroquois; one branch, with related Petun, fled west and became known as Wyandot. *M15*

Hutsnuwu: Branch of Tlingit. *G6*

Ibitoupa: Perhaps a Choctaw subgroup. *R13*

Icafui: A Timucua tribe. *R15*

Iglulik: Despite contacts with other Inuit groups, kept traces of Thule culture. *E13, F13*

Ikogmiut: Speakers of a Yupik, or western, Eskimo language. *C5*

Illinois: Algonquian confederacy. *P13*

Ingalik: Athapaskan tribe; culture resembles neighboring Eskimos. *D5*

Inland Tlingit: Language same as coastal Tlingit but culture Subarctic. *G7*

Iowa: One of last woodland groups to adopt Plains culture; speakers of a Siouan language called Chiwere. *P12*

Ipai: Strongly resisted missionizing; with

Tipai, sometimes called Diegueno. *Q6*
Iroquois: League that exerted influence out of proportion to pop., which never topped 20,000. *See* Cayuga; Mohawk; Oneida; Onondaga; Seneca.
Isleta: Pueblo which did not attack Spanish overlords in revolt of 1680. *Q9*
Itivimiut: Name, "dwellers on the other side," given by Davis Strait people. *J14*

Jeaga: Tiny tribe, extinct early. *S15*
Jemez: Towans who absorbed Pecos group. *Q9*
Jicarilla: Apache tribe especially given to raids for plunder. *Q9*
Jumano: Farming tribe related to Suma. *R9*

Kaialigamiut: Speakers of Yupik Eskimo in an area of plentiful fish and game. *D4*
Kaigani: Haida group; migrated from Queen Charlottes, ousted local Tlingit. *H6*
Kake: Branch of Tlingit. *G6*
Kalapuya: Ravaged by 1824 epidemic. *M6*
Kalispel: Called Pend d'Oreille—"ear drops"—by French traders because of their large shell earrings. Speak Salish. *L8*
Kaniag: Powerful Yupik tribe shattered before 1800 by disease, Russian traders. *E4*
Kansa: Also known as Kaw; speakers of a Siouan language called Dhegiha. *P11*
Karankawa: Sketchily known people extinct by mid-1800's. *S11*
Karok: Culture resembles Yurok; language in a large western family called Hokan. *M6*
Kasihta: Muskogee tribe; head "peace" town of Lower Creeks. *R14*
Kaska: Small Athapaskan tribe. *G7*
Kaskaskia: Key Illinois tribe. Murder of Pontiac by a Kaskaskia brought tribal wars that cost Illinois most of their lands. *P13*
Kavelchadom: Yuman tribe. *Q7*
Kaw: *See* Kansa.
Kawaiisu: Language same as Ute. *P6*
Keres: *See* Eastern Keres, Western Keres.
Keyauwee: Presumably Siouan; known only in first half of 18th century. *Q15*
Keys: Small tribes, extinct by 1763. *T15*
Kiatagmiut: Speakers of a Yupik, or western, Eskimo language. *E4*
Kichai: Merged with Wichita; last speaker of the language died in 1930's. *R11*
Kickapoo: Algonquian kin to Sauk and Fox; large group moved to Mexico in 1852. *N13*
Kigiktagmiut: Means "island people." *J14*
Kiliwa: Small Yuman tribe. *R7*
Kiowa: noted for pictographic "winter counts," resistance to whites; language in Aztec-Tanoan family. *Q11*
Kiowa-Apache: Long associated with Kiowa, though language kin to other Apaches. *Q11*
Kitanemuk: Small, poorly known group;

assimilated into mission culture. *P6*
Kitkehaki: Also called Republican Pawnee from Republican R. location. *P10*
Kittitas: Language related to Umatilla. *L7*
Klamath: Through intertribal contacts at The Dalles, adopted traits of Northwest Coast, Great Basin, and Plains cultures. *M6*
Klikitat: Middlemen in trade between coast and inland tribes. *L7*
Koasati: Muskogeans; some moved to become Coushatta of Louisiana and Texas. *Q14*
Konkow: Major group in Maiduan language family. Decimated by 1850's. *N6*
Koroa: *R12*
Kotzebue Eskimo: Netted seals; speakers of Inuit, or eastern, Eskimo. *C6*
Koyukon: Large Athapaskan group; gold seekers overran territory late 1800's. *D6*
Kuiu: Tlingit tribe; considerable intermarriage with Haida. *H6*
Kuskokwagamiut: Largest group among speakers of Yupik, or western, Eskimo. *D4*
Kutchin: Warlike Athapaskan tribe. *E7*
Kutenai: Driven from Canadian plains by the Blackfoot. Language may be remotely related to Algonquian. *L8*
Kwakiutl: With Nootka, gave names to the branches of Wakashan language family. *K6*
Kwalhiokwa: Athapaskan tribe. *L6*

Labrador Eskimo: Met by Europeans in early days; language Inuit—eastern—Eskimo. *H15*
Laguna: New Mexico pueblo resettled in 1699 by rebels fleeing the Spanish. *Q9*
Lake: Also called Senijextee. Spoke same language as the Okanagan. *K8*
Lake Miwok: Penutian speakers; numbered some 500 at time of white contact. *N6*
Lekwiltok: Large Kwakiutl tribe. *K6*
Lillooet: Major Salishan tribe. *K7*
Lipan: Apache tribe driven into Mexico in the mid-1800's. *S10*
Luiseno: Language related to Cahuilla. *Q6*
Lumbee: Post-colonial tribe, now one of the largest on the continent. *Q15*
Lummi: Straits Salish group. *K7*

Mackenzie Eskimo: Got wealth in fur trade; speakers of Inuit, or eastern, Eskimo. *E8*
Magemiut: Name meant "mink people." *C4*
Mahican: Algonquians, also called Mohican (differ from Mohegan). Descendants in Wisconsin now known as Stockbridge. *N16*
Maidu: Large tribe of Penutian stock. *N6*
Makah: Southernmost Nootkan tribe. *K6*
Maliseet: Inland hunters; split by Canada-U. S. border from related Passamaquoddy. *L17*
Manahoac: Poorly known, perhaps Siouan; extinct after 1650's. *P15*
Mandan: Settled Siouan farmers. *M10*

Maricopa: Yuman tribe. *Q8*
Mascouten: Algonquians; lost identity through merger with neighbor tribes by 1800. *N13*
Maskegon: Cree band in swampy habitat. *K12*
Massachuset: 1600's pop. of 3,000 cut to less than 500 by disease before 1640. *N17*
Mdewkanton: Santee Sioux band. *M12*
Meherrin: Small, poorly known tribe. *Q15*
Menominee: Social ways resembled southern neighbors, economy like northern. *M13*
Mescalero: Apache group. *R9*
Methow: Language same as Okanagan. *L7*
Miami: Algonquians allied with Mascouten, Kickapoo, and Potawatomi. *P13*
Michigamea: In Illinois confederacy. *P13*
Micmac: Algonquians known since 1500. *L17*
Miniconjou: Teton Sioux band. *N10*
Mishongnovi: Pueblo begun in 1680. *P8*
Missisauga: Ojibwa band. *M14*
Missouri: Merged with Oto in early 1800's; spoke Siouan language called Chiwere. *P12*
Miwok: Populous Penutian group; military skills thwarted Spanish advance. *N6*
Mobile: Large tribe. Fought de Soto. Fused with Choctaw about 1770. *R13*
Mococo: Poorly known band. *S15*
Modoc: Closely linked to Klamath; after Modoc War, some removed to Oklahoma. *M6*
Mohave: Populous, warlike Yuman tribe. *Q7*
Mohawk: Iroquois warriors feared by Algonquian neighbors and New England colonists. *M16*
Mohegan: Related to Pequots. Uncas a famous leader in 1600's. Tribe fought with colonists against British. *N16*
Mohican: *See* Mahican.
Moingwena: Linked to Peoria. No mention of tribe after 1700. *P12*
Molala: Poorly recorded tribe. *M6*
Monacan: Lost identity in colonial period; probably Siouan speaking. *P15*
Monache: Some six tribal groups on west slopes of Sierra Nevada; also called Western Mono. Language akin to Utes'. *P6*
Mono: Bands in arid basin on east slope of Sierra Nevada; language related to Utes'. *N6*
Montagnais-Naskapi: Grouping of very similar Algonquian bands. *K16*
Montauk: Last chief died 1875. *N16*
Moose: Band of woodland Cree. *L14*
Mountain: Speakers of the same language as the Dogrib. *F8*
Munsee: Division of the Delaware. *N16*
Muskogee. Family of tribes; dominant element of the Creek confederacy. *R14*

Nabesna: *See* Upper Tanana.
Nahyssan: Small tribe known to Capt. John Smith; later history linked to Saponi. *P15*
Nakipa: Yuman tribe. *R6*

Nambe: Founded in 1300's; now one of the smaller pueblos. *Q10*
Nanaimo: Subdivision of the Cowichan. *K7*
Naniaba: Tribe linked to the Mobile. *R13*
Nansemond: Algonquians resembling the Powhatan. *P16*
Nanticoke: Algonquians; major part of group migrated to join Iroquois after 1722. *P16*
Napochi: Lived near ancient mound site; later perhaps joined Chickasaw. *R13*
Narragansett: Powerful Algonquian tribe shattered in King Philip's War. *N17*
Naskapi: *See* Montagnais-Naskapi.
Natchez: Language distantly related to Muskogean. Survivors of 1731 French attack joined Cherokee and Upper Creek. *R12*
Natchitoches: Spoke divergent dialect of Caddo language. *R12*
Navajo: Culturally distinct from the Apache, but language very close. *Q9*
Nespelem: Language same as Okanagan. *L7*
Netsilik Eskimo: Branch of Central Eskimo. Got wood by trade from west. *F12*
Neusiok: Little known, probably united with Tuscarora around 1712. *Q16*
Neutral: Iroquoians neutral in war between Huron and Iroquois; in turn were destroyed by the latter. *N14*
Nez Perce: Noted horsemen; developed Appaloosa breed. Named by French traders for a group which pierced their noses. Language related to Sahaptin. *L8*
Niantic: Algonquian tribe of two divisions; western shattered in Pequot war, eastern merged with Narragansett in 1670's. *N17*
Nicola: Small northern Athapaskan band. *K7*
Nipissing: Culture like Ojibwa; now called an Algonquin group but original affiliation is uncertain. *M14*
Nipmuck: Little known Algonquians. *N16*
Nisenan: Southernmost branch of Maidu. *N6*
Niska: Tsimshian subgroup. Nass Inlet on which they lived drew tribes from wide area during eulachon season. *H6*
Nisqually: Coast Salishan subgroup. *L7*
Nitinat: Nootkan tribe with a number of Salishan culture-traits. *K6*
Nomlaki: Figured in development of one cult of Ghost Dance religion; kin to Wintu. *N6*
Nooksak: Spoke a Salishan language; called "mountain men" by neighbors. *K7*
Nootka: Important in early fur trade; major branch of the Wakashan language family. *K6*
Noquet: Little known Algonquians; lost to history at an early period. *M14*
Norridgewock: Abenaki group shattered by war with English colonists in 1724. *M16*
North Alaskan Eskimo: Inuit speakers; traveled widely in summer to trade. *C7*
Northern Interior Eskimo: Diet mainly

caribou; extensive trade, some intermarriage with North Alaskan Eskimo. *C7*
Northern Paiute: Also called Paviotso. Language related to that of the Ute. *N7*
Northern Tiwa: Pueblos influenced by Plains culture; speak a Tanoan language. *Q9*
Northern Tonto: Apache hunter-gatherers. *See also* Southern Tonto. *Q8*
Nottoway: Iroquoians; extinct in early 1800's, but kept identity long after neighboring tribes disappeared. *P15*
Nunivak: Dependent on fish; speakers of a Yupik, or western, Eskimo language. *D4*

Ocale: Little known Timucua group. *S15*
Ocaneechi: Chief traders of area; closely associated with Saponi and Tutelo. *Q15*
Ocita: Little known tribe met by de Soto at Tampa Bay; also called Pohoy. *S15*
Oconee: Hitchiti-speaking tribe; ancestors of Miccosukee Seminole. *R14*
Ofo: Siouan language; related to Biloxi and Tutelo. *R13*
Oglala: Important band of Teton Sioux. *N10*
Ojibwa: Major group of Algonquian family. Also called Chippewa. *L12*
Okanagan: Large tribe; spoke a language of the Interior Salishan group. *L7*
Okmulgee: Hitchiti townsmen. *R14*
Omaha: Met by Lewis and Clark; frequently at war with the Sioux. Spoke a Siouan language called Dhegiha. *N11*
Onatheaqua: Timucua group. *S14*
Oneida: Split after Revolution into New York, Wisconsin, and Ontario groups. *N16*
Onondaga: In Iroquois league councils, their chiefs had a judgelike role. *N15*
Opata: Lived in rugged country; harassed by warlike neighbors. Language related to that of the Tarahumara. *R8*
Opelousa: Small tribe; probably joined Atakapa in early 1800's. *R12*
Oraibi: Largest of Hopi pueblos; occupied since 1150. *P8*
Osage: Farmers who spoke a Siouan language called Dhegiha; often at war with plains and woodland neighbors. *Q12*
Oto: Small tribe; moved frequently. Spoke a Siouan language called Chiwere. *P11*
Ottawa: Algonquians; formed "Three Fires" confederacy with Ojibwa, Potawatomi. *M14*
Owens Valley: Large Paiute group. Fertile lands permitted stable band organization. *P6*

Paipai: Yumans; also called Akwa'ala. *Q6*
Paiute: Lifeways disrupted by mining boom, introduction of livestock which destroyed plant foods. Language related to Ute. *P7*
Palus: Spelled also Palouse; spoke a language called Sahaptin. *L7*

Pamlico: Algonquian tribe wiped out before 1715 by disease, war, enslavement. *Q16*
Pamunkey: Tribe of the Powhatan group; still in existence. *P16*
Panamint: Western Shoshone band; ranged a particularly inhospitable region. *P7*
Papago: Farmers, traders. Speak same language as the Pima. *Q7*
Parklands: Plains Cree band; descendants of a Scotch trader and his Cree wife. *K10*
Pascagoula: Small, poorly known tribe. *R13*
Passamaquoddy: Sea hunters; speak same Algonquian language as the Maliseet. *M17*
Patwin: Language related to Wintu. *N6*
Paviotso: *See* Northern Paiute.
Pawnee: One of principal Caddoan tribes; valley farmers with complex rituals. *P11*
Pecos: Pueblo abandoned 1838 on move to Jemez; spoke Towa, a Tanoan language. *Q9*
Pedee: Probably Siouan; majority united with Catawba about 1750. *Q15*
Pend d'Oreille: *See* Kalispel.
Pennacook: Group of Algonquian tribes. *M16*
Penobscot: With Passamaquoddy, only large Indian groups left in New England. *M17*
Pensacola: Similar to Choctaw. *R13*
Pentlatch: Small Salishan group; absorbed by Comox and Nanaimo. *K6*
Penutian: *See* Coast Miwok.
Peoria: Important tribe of Illinois confederacy. *P13*
Pequot: Destroyed as a tribe in Pequot War (1637); survivors' descendants now live in Connecticut. *N17*
Petun: Iroquoians who grew much tobacco. Also called Tobacco Indians, Tionontati. After Iroquois attacks, fled west, fusing with refugee Hurons. *N15*
Piankashaw: Subtribe of the Miami. *P13*
Picuris: Pueblo occupied since 1200. *Q9*
Piegan: Subtribe of the Blackfoot. *L8*
Pima Alto: The Pima gave their name to a branch of Aztec-Tanoan language family. *R8*
Pima Bajo: Like the Pima Alto, farmers of irrigated fields since earliest times. *S8*
Piro: Extinct Tanoan-speaking pueblo. *Q9*
Piscataway: *See* Conoy.
Pitahauerat: Pawnee band. *P11*
Plains Cree: Wanderers like their woodland relatives, these trappers and keen traders reached plains, adapted to that culture. *K10*
Plains Ojibwa: Branch of woodland dwellers who adapted to horse culture. *L11*
Pocutuck: Algonquian tribe. *N16*
Pohoy: *See* Ocita.
Pojoaque: Abandoned for a time after Pueblo revolt; never regained pop. *Q10*
Polar Eskimo: Extremely isolated. Thought selves world's only people until met by John Ross, 1818. Lacked boats, sledges. *C14*

Pomo: Noted makers of baskets, shell disk money; had seven distinct languages. N6
Ponca: Noted today as singers and dancers; speak a Siouan language called Dhegiha. N11
Potano: Powerful Timucua tribe. S15
Potawatomi: Language akin to Ojibwa. N14
Potomac: Tribe of Powhatan state. P15
Powhatan: Conquest state's pop. about 9,000 in 1600; some tribes still exist. P16
Puyallup: Important Salishan tribe. L7

Quapaw: Speakers of Dhegiha Siouan. Q12
Quatsino: Kwakiutl group. K6
Quechan: Large farming tribe whose popular name, Yuma, gave designation to a major branch of the Hokan language family. Q7
Quileute: Daring whalers; with Chemakum formed a small language family. L6
Quinault: Small Coast Salishan tribe. L6

Rabbit Skins: Plains Cree band. L10
River: Major subdivision of the Crow. K9
Roanoke: Little known Algonquians. Q16

Sagdlirmiut: Thule-type culture; extinct by early 1900's. G13
St. Lawrence Iroquoians: Met Cartier; vanished by 1603, victims of intertribal wars to control trade with French. M16
St. Lawrence Island Eskimo: Struck in 1878 by famine that cost 1,500 lives. B5
Salinan: Close cultural relations with Yokuts; language in Hokan family. P6
Salish: See Flathead.
San Carlos: Band of western Apache. Q8
Sandia: Tiwa pueblo whose Spanish-given name means "watermelon." Q9
San Felipe: Conservative pueblo. R9
San Ildefonso: Played important role in Pueblo resistance of 1694-96. Q10
San Juan: Largest Tewa pueblo; home of Popé, a leader in 1680 Pueblo revolt. Q10
Sanpoil: Interior Salishan group. L7
Sans Arc: Teton Sioux band dubbed "without bows" by French, translating Dakota name of one division. M10
Santa Ana: Pueblo founded about 1700. R9
Santa Clara: One of six Tewa pueblos built on the Rio Grande in 1300's. Q10
Santee: Eastern Siouan group; most sold as slaves after defeat in 1716 uprising. Q15
Santee: The Dakota proper; kept farming traits when migrated to the plains. M12
Santo Domingo: Large conservative Keresan pueblo of far-traveled traders. R9
Sanya: Small Tlingit tribe. H6
Saponi: Siouans; moved with Tutelo to Pennsylvania and New York. P15
Sarcee: Small Athapaskan group which allied with the Blackfoot, adopted their ways. K8

Saturiwa: Timucuans; aided French. R15
Sauk: Made successive moves from Michigan into Wisconsin, Iowa, Kansas, and Oklahoma; closely related to the Fox. M13
Sawokli: A Hitchiti tribe. R14
Sechelt: Coastal Salishan group. K7
Secotan: Algonquians met by Raleigh colonists; later extinct. Q16
Sekani: Loosely organized Athapaskan bands that roamed west slopes of Rockies. H8
Seminole: Name applied to migrants from north about 1770. Two bands—Miccosukee (Hitchiti) and Muskogee—left in Florida after 1830's removal to Oklahoma. S15
Seneca: Most populous Iroquois tribe, due partly to absorption of Erie and other conquered peoples. N15
Senijextee: See Lake.
Seri: Fishermen whose language belongs to widespread Hokan family of southwest, California, and Middle America. R7
Serrano: Spanish name meant "highlanders"; language related to that of the Cahuilla. Q6
Sewee: Smallpox, attempt to reach England in canoes all but wiped out tribe. R15
Shakori: Closely associated with Eno. Q15
Shasta: Language in Hokan family; economy simpler than western neighbors. M6
Shawnee: Algonquian; several subdivisions. Perhaps no other tribe divided so often or moved so much; figured in histories of many of the states in the Midwest and South. Q14
Shinnecock: 19th-century whalers; still on Long Island. N16
Shipaulovi: Hopi name, "mosquitoes," derived from fact former site abandoned because of the insects. P8
Shongopovi: Pueblo built about 1680. P9
Shoshone-Bannock: Groups with few sharp boundaries between dialects and cultures; language related to that of the Ute. M8
Shuswap: Important Salishan tribe. K7
Siberian Eskimo: Also called Yuit; cultural roots deep in Asia. B5
Sichomovi: Pueblo built about 1750. P8
Siksika: Means "black feet" (perhaps from their discolored or painted moccasins); subtribe of the Algonquian Blackfoot. K9
Siletz: Extinct; spoke Tillamook dialect. L6
Sioux: Gave name to larger Siouan language family. See Dakota.
Sisseton: Band of Santee Sioux. M12
Sissipahaw: Apparently fused with Catawba after fighting colonists in Yamasee War. Q15
Sitka: Tlingit tribe. G6
Siuslaw: Small, little known tribe. M6
Skagit: Group of Salishan bands. L7
Skidi: Pawnee band. N11
Skitswish: See Coeur d'Alene.
Slave: Athapaskans uprooted by Cree, who

enslaved many, hence their name. H9
Snoqualmi: Coastal Salishan group. L7
Sokoki: Related to Abenaki. M16
Southampton Eskimo: See Sagdlirmiut.
Southern Tiwa: Like northern group, in Aztec-Tanoan language family. Q9
Southern Tonto: Apaches, although term "Tonto" sometimes includes unrelated Yuman peoples. Q8
Southern Tutchone: Athapaskan bands. F6
Spokane: Salish speakers whose territory became focus for early fur trade. L7
Squamish: Coastal Salishan tribe. K7
Stikine: Tlingit tribe which carried on longtime feud with neighboring Sitka. H6
Stoney: See Assiniboin.
Sugeree: Sketchily known. Q15
Sukinninmiut: Subgroup of Labrador Eskimo. H17
Suma: Seminomads exterminated in 1700's by smallpox and war with neighbors. R9
Sumdum: Small Tlingit tribe. G6
Surruque: Little known tribe. S15
Susquehannock: Once populous Iroquoian tribe; dwindled after conquest by Iroquois in 1676. Also called Conestoga. N15
Swampy Cree: See Maskegon.

Tacatacuru: Cumberland I. Timucuans. R15
Taensa: Small, little known tribe. R13
Tagish: Athapaskans; language similar to Kaska and once spoken by Inland Tlingit. G7
Tahagmiut: Labrador Eskimo subgroup. H15
Tahltan: Athapaskan tribe with social customs adopted from Tlingit neighbors. H7
Takelma: Culturally similar to Shasta. M6
Taku: Tlingit tribe. G6
Tali: Creek townsmen encountered by de Soto expedition. Q14
Tamaroa: Tribe in Illinois confederacy; disappeared before 1800. P12
Tamathli: Hitchiti group; remnants after 1704 slavery raids joined the Seminole. R14
Tanaina: Athapaskans; lands important in Russian fur trade based on Kodiak I. E5
Tanana: Small Athapaskan tribe. E6
Tano: Ten pueblos in 1540; dispersed after Pueblo revolt, now extinct. Gave name to Tanoan group in great Aztec-Tanoan language family of Mexico and the west. Q9
Taos: Played key role in 1680 Pueblo revolt against Spanish. Q9
Taposa: Little known Muskogean group. R13
Tarahumara: Populous tribe, Aztec-Tanoan language; noted for running ability. S8
Tataviam: Small group; unique language. Lived near Mission San Fernando. P6
Tawakoni: Wichita tribe hostile to Comanche and Osage. R11
Tawehash: Wichita subtribe; farmers who

traded food to the Comanche for horses. *Q11*
Tekesta: Tied closely to the Calusa. *T15*
Temagami: Ojibwa band. *M14*
Temiskaming: Algonquin band. *M15*
Tenino: Spoke a dialect of Sahaptin. *L6*
Tesuque: Southernmost Tewa pueblo. *Q10*
Tete de Boule Cree: Algonquians called "round heads" by the French. *L15*
Teton: Western Sioux; Lakota speaking, with several well-known bands. *M10*
Tewa: Pueblo groups speaking a Tanoan language. *Q9*
Texas: *See Hasinai.*
Thompson: Interior Salishan tribe. *K7*
Tillamook: Salishan tribe. *L6*
Timucua: Extinct group whose language is not known to be related to any other. *S15*
Tionontati: *See Petun.*
Tiou: Small tribe; joined Natchez. *R13*
Tipai: Yuman farmers who occupied the Imperial Valley. *Q7*
Tiwa: *See Northern Tiwa, Southern Tiwa.*
Tlingit: Many independent tribes speaking a single language remotely related to Athapaskan family. *G6*
Tobacco: *See Petun.*
Tocobaga: Small tribe; warred with the Calusa. Not known after 1612. *S15*
Togiagamiut: Nomadic Yupik speakers; women wore feathered skins of wildfowl. *D4*
Tohome: Early allies of French. Probably merged with Choctaw in late 1700's. *R13*
Tolowa: Athapaskan group; traded dentalium from north with California tribes. *M6*
Tongass: Tlingit tribe. *H6*
Tonkawa: In 19th century, allies of Apache and enemies of Comanche—each a reversal of earlier relationships. *R11*
Tonto: *See Northern Tonto, Southern Tonto.*
Tsetsaut: Spoke Athapaskan language; nearly exterminated by neighbors. *H7*
Tsimshian: Language probably belongs to Penutian family; fine wood-carvers. *H6*
Tubatulabal: Highlanders speaking an Aztec-Tanoan language. *P6*
Tula: Caddo band met by de Soto. *Q12*
Tunica: Allies of French; language remotely related to Muskogean family. *R12*
Tuscarora: Iroquoian tribe; defeat in war with whites and their Indian allies in 1711-13 triggered migration to Iroquois lands in New York. *Q15*
Tuskegee: Small Upper Creek group. *Q14*
Tutchone: Athapaskan bands. *F7*
Tutelo: Siouan group. Tribal wars caused relocations; adopted into Iroquois league. *P15*
Tututni: Small Athapaskan group. *M6*
Twana: Coast Salishan group. *L6*
Two Kettle: Band of Teton Sioux. *N10*

Umatilla: Columbia R. tribe; spoke a language called Sahaptin. *L7*
Unalaska Aleut: Open sea culture. Disease, enslavement cut population 90 per cent after arrival of Russian traders. *D2*
Unami: Division of the Delaware. *N16*
Upper Tanana: Athapaskan group. *F6*
Upper Umpqua: Small Athapaskan tribe. *M6*
Ute: Great Basin people who got horses early, adapted to Plains culture. Language in Aztec-Tanoan family. *P9*
Utina: Major Timucua group. *R15*

Waccamaw: Extinct by 1755. *Q15*
Waco: Wichita group, perhaps originally a Tawakoni village. *R11*
Wahpekute: Band of Santee Sioux. Closely allied with Mdewkanton. *N12*
Wahpeton: Band of Santee Sioux. *N12*
Walapai: Yuman hunters and gatherers. *Q7*
Walla Walla: Spoke the Sahaptin language; closely related to Nez Perce. *L7*
Walpi: Pueblo begun about 1680. *P9*
Wampanoag: Algonquian tribe remembered for chiefs Massasoit and King Philip. *N17*
Wappo: From Spanish *guapo*, "handsome, brave"; language related to Yuki. *N6*
Washo: Small group; little contact with whites until very late. *N6*
Watereee: Once strong tribe; fused with Catawba around 1750. *Q15*
Waxhaw: Probably Siouan tribe; virtually eliminated following Yamasee War. *Q15*
Wea: Subtribe of the Miami. *P13*
Weapemeoc: Algonquian group encountered by Raleigh colonists. *Q16*
Wenatchi: Salishan band linked to Chelan. *L7*
Wenro: Iroquoian tribe; took refuge among Hurons and Neutrals to escape Iroquois. *N15*
Weskarini: Algonquin band. *M15*
West Greenland Eskimo: Christianized early by German and Danish missionaries. *E16*
Western Keres: With E. Keres, formed language group unrelated to any other. *Q9*
Western Mono: *See Monache.*
Western Shoshone: Tribal grouping whose bands often took names meaning "eaters of" whatever regional food they lived on. *N7*
Western Wood Cree: *K10*
White Mountain: Western Apache group. *Q8*
Wichita: Believed inhabitants of "Quivira" sought by Coronado; Caddoan language. *R11*
Wikeno: Bella Bella band. *J6*
Wind River Shoshone: Used dogs in hunting; heavily influenced by Plains culture. *N9*
Winnebago: Siouan language much like that of Oto, Iowa, and Missouri; culture similar to Algonquian neighbors. *N13*
Wintu: Called whites "poison people" for the diseases they brought. *N6*

Winyaw: Small tribe, possibly Siouan; probably joined Catawba in 1700's. *Q15*
Wishram: Upriver tribe of Chinookan language family. *L6*
Wiyot: Language remotely related to Algonquian family. *M6*
Woccon: Small Siouan tribe. *Q15*
Wyandot: *See Huron.*

Yadkin: Little known group, perhaps Siouan; no mention after 1709. *Q15*
Yakima: Culturally similar to Nez Perce; spoke the Sahaptin language. *L7*
Yakutat: Tlingit group noted as sea otter and seal hunters. *F6*
Yamasee: Muskogeans; organized widespread war against whites in 1715; after defeat, fled to Florida, where they lost identity. Called Guale by the Spanish. *R15*
Yana: Hokan stock; had separate speech forms for men and women. *N6*
Yankton: One of the seven major divisions of the Dakota; speakers of the Nakota dialect. *N11*
Yanktonai: Division of the Dakota; speak same dialect as the Yankton. *M11*
Yaqui: Many fled Mexico to settle near Tucson, Arizona, in early 1900's; speak a language in the Aztec-Tanoan family. *S8*
Yaquina: Small tribe; closely associated with the Alsea. *L6*
Yatasi: Caddo band. *R12*
Yavapai: Yuman tribe culturally similar to the Havasupai. *Q7*
Yazoo: Little known group. *R12*
Yellowknife: Also called "Copper Indians"; worked ore into cutting tools for lucrative trade before white contact. Spoke a dialect of Chipewyan. *G10*
Yokuts: Many bands; spoke a single language of the Penutian family, but in some 40 dialects. *P6*
Yuchi: May have met de Soto; became part of Creek confederacy. Language distinct, perhaps remote relative of Siouan. *Q14*
Yui: Timucua tribe. *R15*
Yuit: *See Siberian Eskimo.*
Yuki: Buffer groups between Northwest Coast culture and California types; spoke related Yuki, Coast Yuki, Hutchnom languages. *N6*
Yuma: *See Quechan.*
Yurok: Complex rituals, fine crafts; language remotely related to Algonquian. *M6*
Yustaga: Timucua tribe. *R14*

Zia: Toleration of Spanish by this pueblo after 1692 sparked conflicts with other pueblo groups. *R9*
Zuni: Large pueblo; language unrelated to any others. *Q8*

Index

Text references appear in lightface type, illustrations in **boldface**.

For Indian groups not listed here, consult the Tribal Supplement, page 386.

Composition by National Geographic's Phototypographic Division, Lawrence F. Ludwig, Manager. Color separations by Chanticleer Company, Inc., New York; Colorgraphics, Inc., Beltsville, Md.; Progressive Color Corporation, Rockville, Md.; The J. Wm. Reed Company, Alexandria, Va. Printed and bound by Holladay-Tyler Printing Corporation, Rockville, Md. Paper by Westvaco Corporation, New York

Library of Congress CIP Data

Main entry under title:
The World of the American Indian

(Story of Man Library)
    I. Indians of North America. I. National Geographic Society, Washington, D. C.
E77.w88   970.1   74-16277

ISBN 0-87044-151-5

Acknowledgments

The editors are grateful to many individuals and organizations for assistance in preparation of this volume. For the chapter on man's spread across the New World we benefited from the contributions of Dr. Florence Hawley Ellis, Santa Fe, New Mexico; Dr. Melvin L. Fowler, University of Wisconsin; Dr. Emil W. Haury, University of Arizona; Dr. William N. Irving, University of Toronto; Dr. Robert H. Lister, University of New Mexico; Dr. Richard E. Morlan, National Museum of Man, Ottawa, Ontario; and Dr. Clayton Ray, Dr. Dennis J. Stanford, and Dr. T. Dale Stewart of the Smithsonian Institution.

Details on Eskimos were supplied by Dr. Robert Humphrey, George Washington University; and Dr. Virginia Sidwell, consultant to National Marine Fisheries Service. Valuable cooperation in the chapter on eastern tribes came from Dr. Walter K. Long, Cayuga Museum of History and Art; Phillip Martin, former tribal chairman, Mississippi Band of Choctaw Indians; Wm. Guy Spittal, Iroqrafts, Ohsweken, Ontario; Jacob E. Thomas, Trent University, Peterborough, Ontario; and Dr. James A. Tuck, Memorial University of Newfoundland.

In the language section we turned to Dr. Harvey Pitkin, Columbia University; Dr. Ives Goddard, Smithsonian Institution; and Sandra L. Bayer and Willard N. Mercer of the Georgia Historical Commission. Our southwest chapter had the aid of Dr. Francis Harlow, Los Alamos, New Mexico; Dr. Morris E. Opler, University of Oklahoma; Barton Wright, San Diego Museum of Man; Peter MacDonald, chairman, Navajo Tribal Council; Wendell Chino, president, Mescalero Apache Tribal Council; and Alvin James Makya, Hotevilla, Arizona.

Assistance with the chapter on western tribes was provided by Dr. Wayne Suttles, Portland State University; Dr. Frederick G. Meyer, National Arboretum; Beth Hill, Ganges, British Columbia; and Bill Holm, Washington State Museum. In the book's final chapters we had the advice of Boyce D. Timmons, Oklahoma Indian Rights Assn.; Franklin Hutchinson, Bureau of Indian Affairs; Kirke Kickingbird, Institute for the Development of Indian Law; Ralph Looney, editor, Albuquerque, New Mexico, Tribune; Dr. Wilcomb Washburn, Smithsonian Institution; Mozart Spector, Indian Health Service; and Marshall Tome and Peterson Zah of the Navajo Nation.

In addition we found valuable these works of general scope: Indians of North America by Harold E. Driver, The Native Americans by Robert F. Spencer, Jesse D. Jennings, et al.; The Indian Heritage of America by Alvin M. Josephy; The Indian Tribes of North America by John R. Swanton; Handbook of American Indians by Frederick W. Hodge.

We consulted also Red Man's Religion by Ruth Underhill, American Indian Medicine by Virgil J. Vogel, American Indian Art by Norman Feder, Indian Art in America by Frederick J. Dockstader, In the Trail of the Wind by John Bierhorst, I Have Spoken by Virginia Armstrong, Handbook of American Indian Languages by Franz Boas, Sequoyah by Grant Foreman, Prehistory of North America by Jesse D. Jennings, and An Introduction to American Archaeology by Gordon R. Willey.

The multivolume Report on the Fifth Thule Expedition, published by Gyldendal, Copenhagen, provided definitive Eskimo references, along with The Eskimos by Edward Weyer, The Friendly Arctic and My Life with the Eskimos by Vilhjálmur Stefansson, The Central Eskimo by Franz Boas, and Sculpture of the Eskimo by George Swinton.

Readings on woodland Indians included North American Indians in Historical Perspective edited by Eleanor Leacock and Nancy Lurie, New England Frontier by Alden T. Vaughan, The Woodland Indians by Robert E. and Pat Ritzenthaler, League of the Iroquois by Lewis H. Morgan, The Jesuit Relations edited by Edna Kenton, Indians of the Southeastern United States by John R. Swanton, and Vol. 15 (Bruce G. Trigger, vol. ed.) of the Smithsonian's Handbook of North American Indians.

Insights on southwestern peoples came from New Perspectives on the Pueblos by Alfonso Ortiz, Cycles of Conquest by Edward H. Spicer, The Pueblo Indians of North America by Edward P. Dozier, Pueblo Indian Religion by Elsie Clews Parsons, Hopi Kachinas by Edwin Earle and Edward A. Kennard, The Navajo by Clyde Kluckhohn and Dorothea Leighton, An Apache Life-Way by Morris E. Opler, Southwestern Indian Craft Arts by Clara Tanner.

Helpful works on tribes of the west included California Indians by Robert F. Heizer and M. A. Whipple, Handbook of California Indians by A. L. Kroeber, Under Mount St. Elias by Frederica de Laguna, Cultures of the North Pacific Coast and The Northern and Central Nootkan Tribes by Philip Drucker. Plains Indians references included The Blackfeet and Indian Life on the Upper Missouri by John C. Ewers, Indians of the Plains by Robert H. Lowie, Early Western Travels, edited by Reuben G. Thwaites.

Among references on the clash of cultures and on Indian activities in this century we used A History of the Indians of the United States by Angie Debo, A Short History of the Indians of the United States by Edward H. Spicer, Red Man's Land—White Man's Law by Wilcomb Washburn, Indians and Other Americans by Harold E. Fey and D'Arcy McNickle, Frontiersmen in Blue and Frontier Regulars by Robert M. Utley, Bury My Heart at Wounded Knee by Dee Brown, Custer Died for Your Sins and God Is Red by Vine Deloria, Jr., The New Indians by Stan Steiner.

The editors are grateful for permission to reprint the following: "Summer Camp" by Kalvak, 1967, the Holman Eskimo Cooperative; drawings from petroglyphs (page 24) by Campbell Grant; Winnebago poem from The Road of Life and Death by Paul Radin, © Bollingen Foundation and Princeton University Press 1973; poem from Navajo Myths, Prayers, and Songs by Washington Matthews, University of California Press; "Tomorrow" by Peter blue cloud from Alcatraz Is Not an Island, © 1972 Wingbow Press.